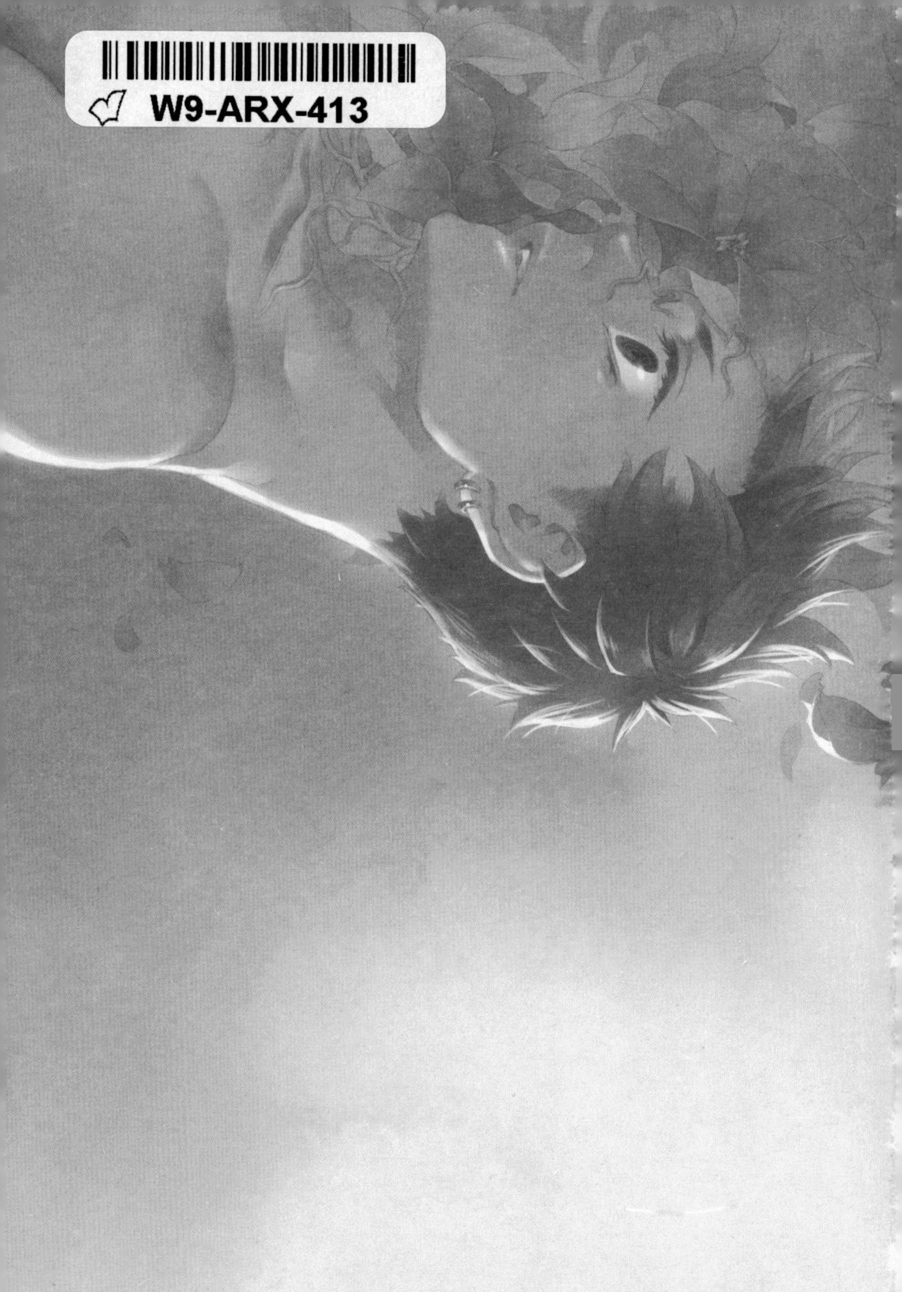

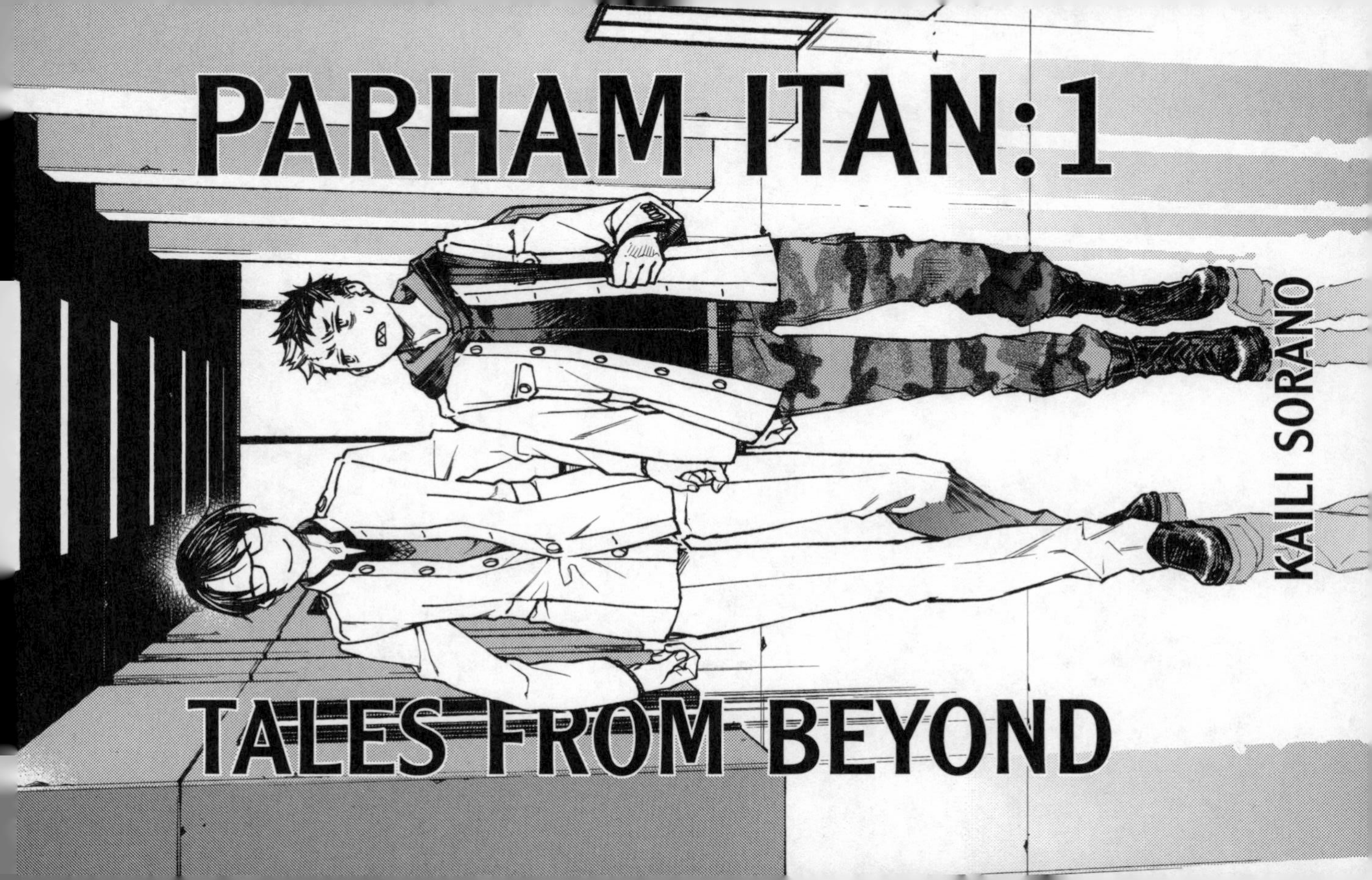
PARHAM ITAN:1
TALES FROM BEYOND
KAILI SORANO

CONTENTS

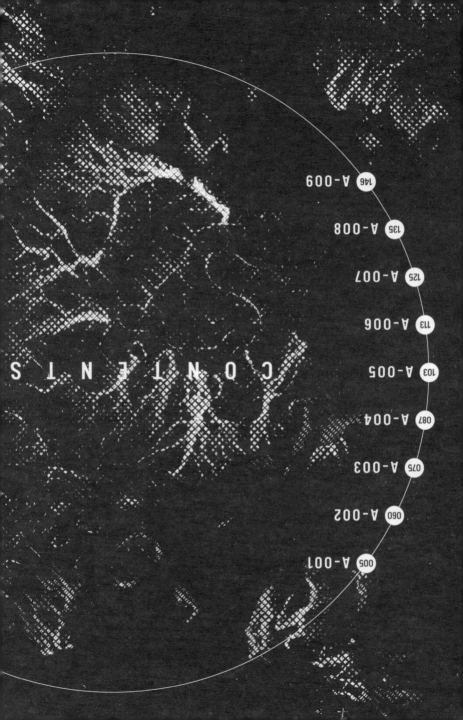

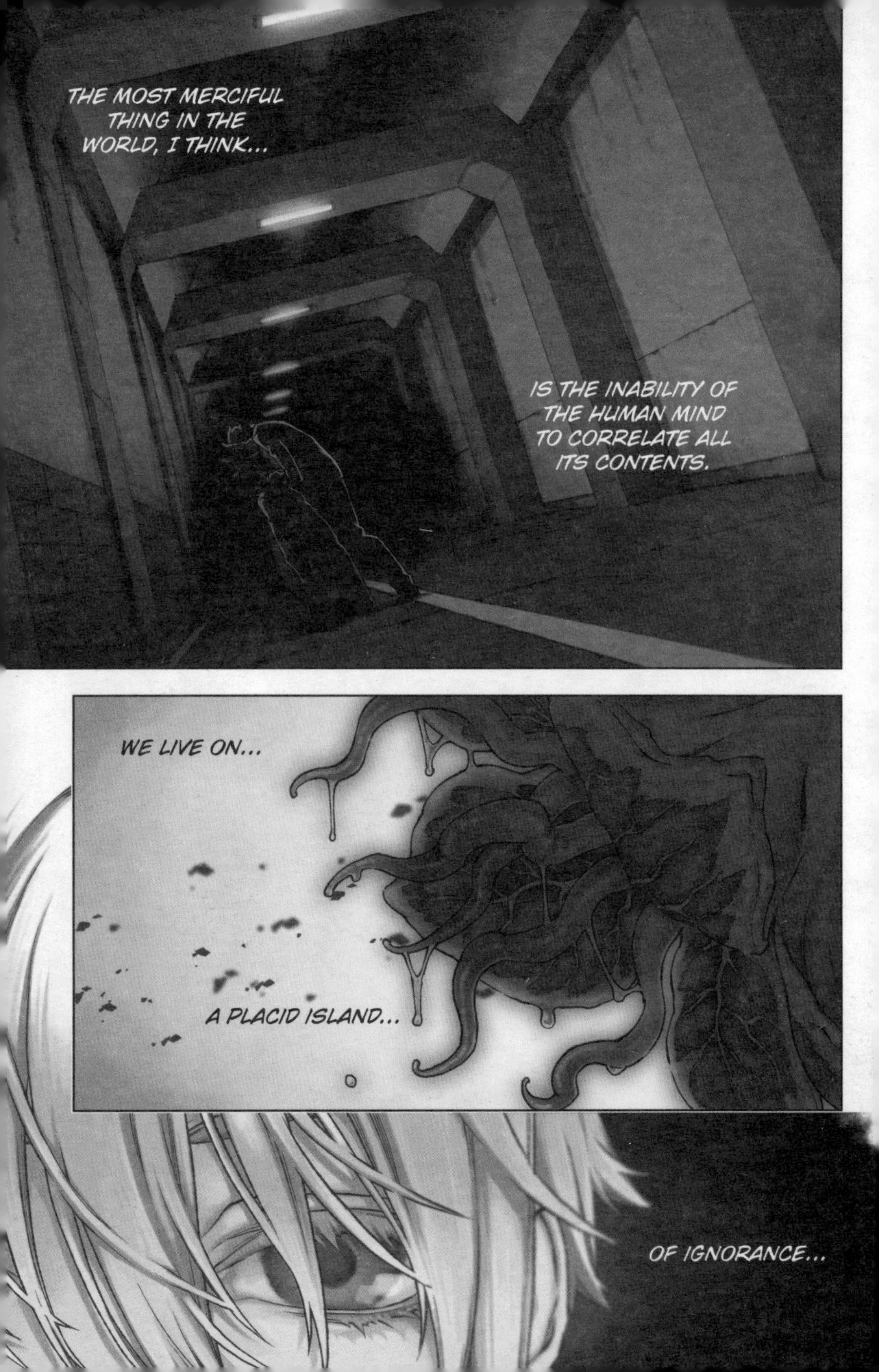
THE MOST MERCIFUL THING IN THE WORLD, I THINK...
IS THE INABILITY OF THE HUMAN MIND TO CORRELATE ALL ITS CONTENTS.
WE LIVE ON...
A PLACID ISLAND...
OF IGNORANCE...

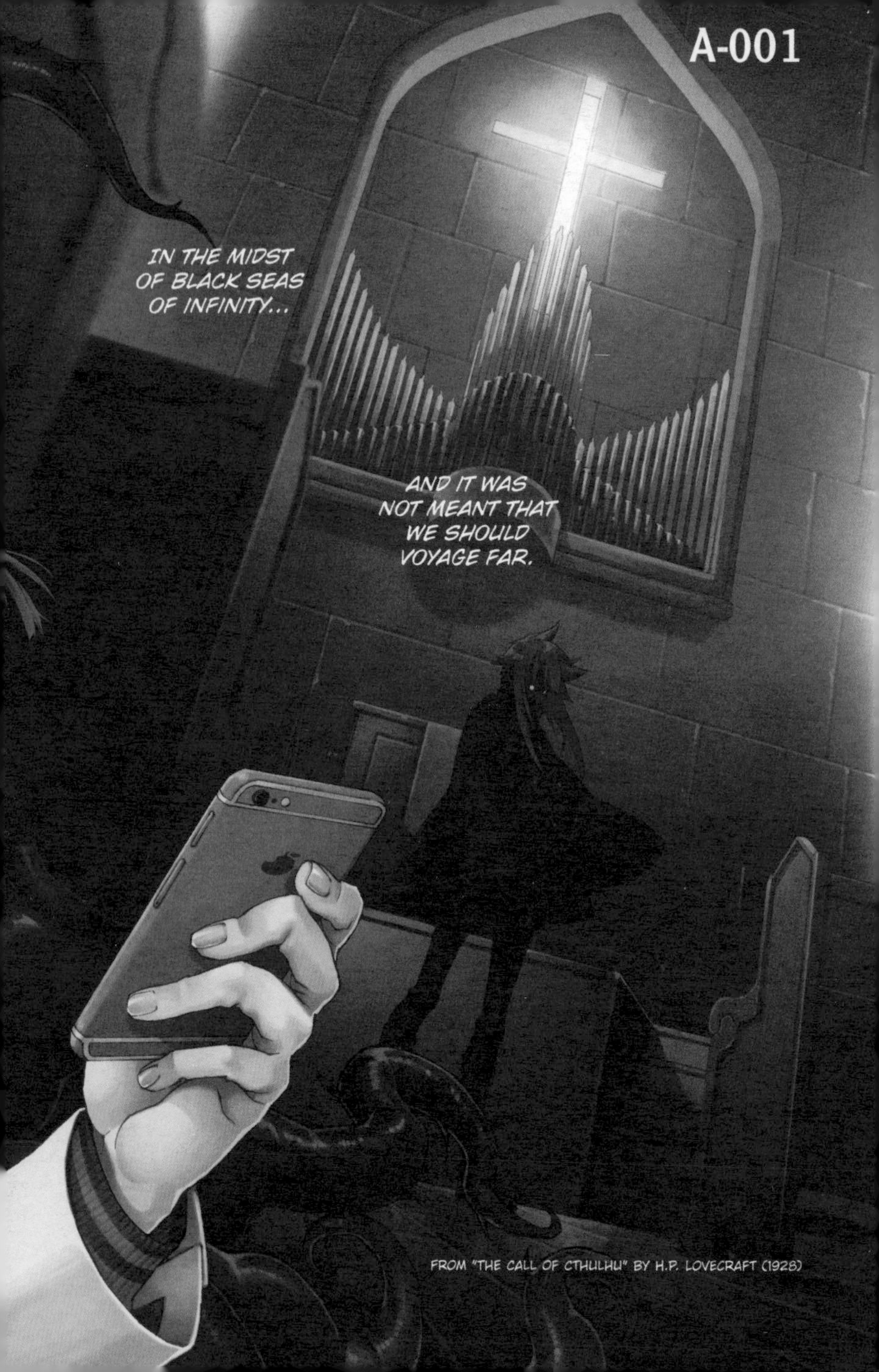
A-001
IN THE MIDST OF BLACK SEAS OF INFINITY...
AND IT WAS NOT MEANT THAT WE SHOULD VOYAGE FAR.
FROM "THE CALL OF CTHULHU" BY H.P. LOVECRAFT (1928)

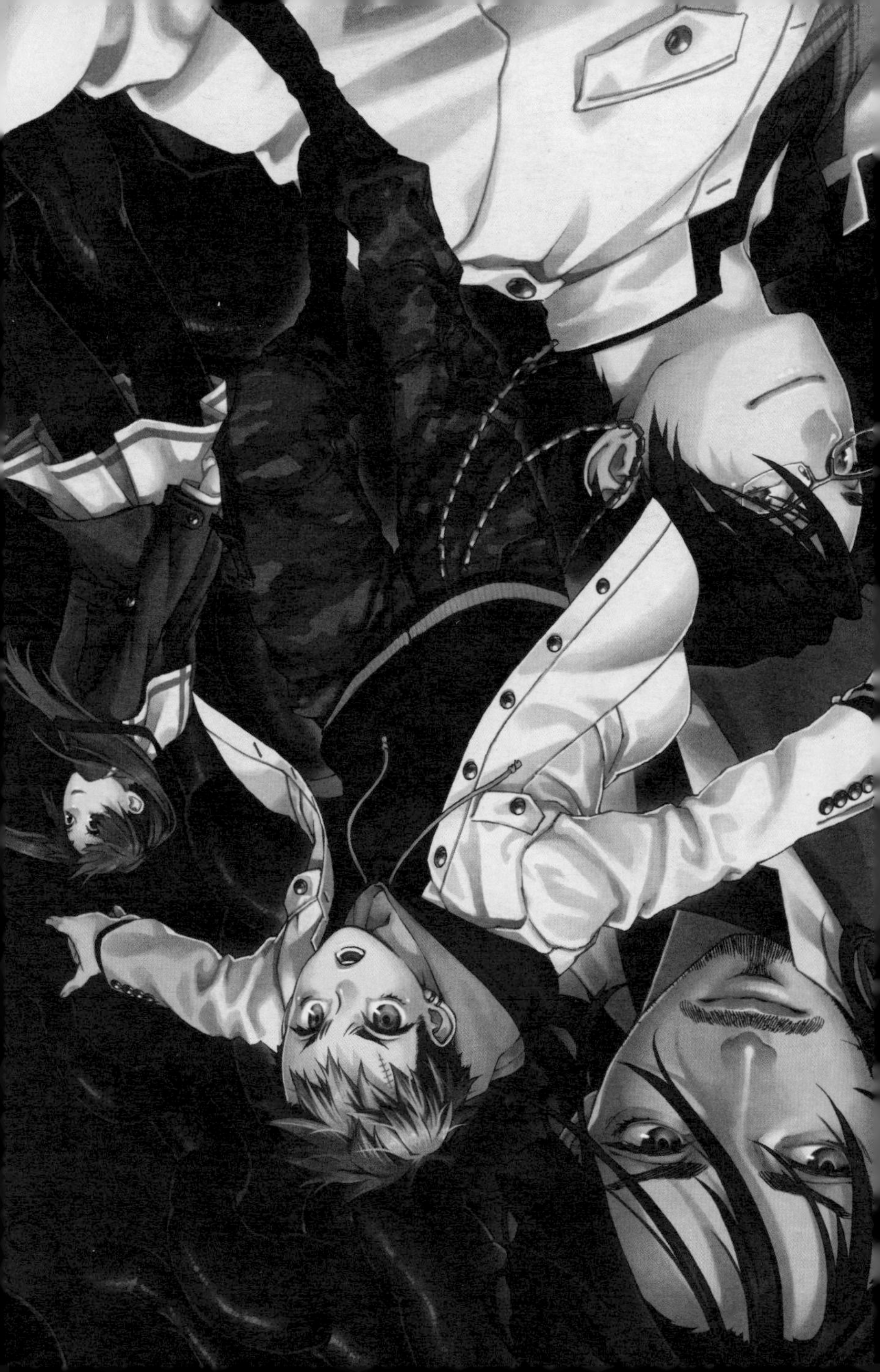

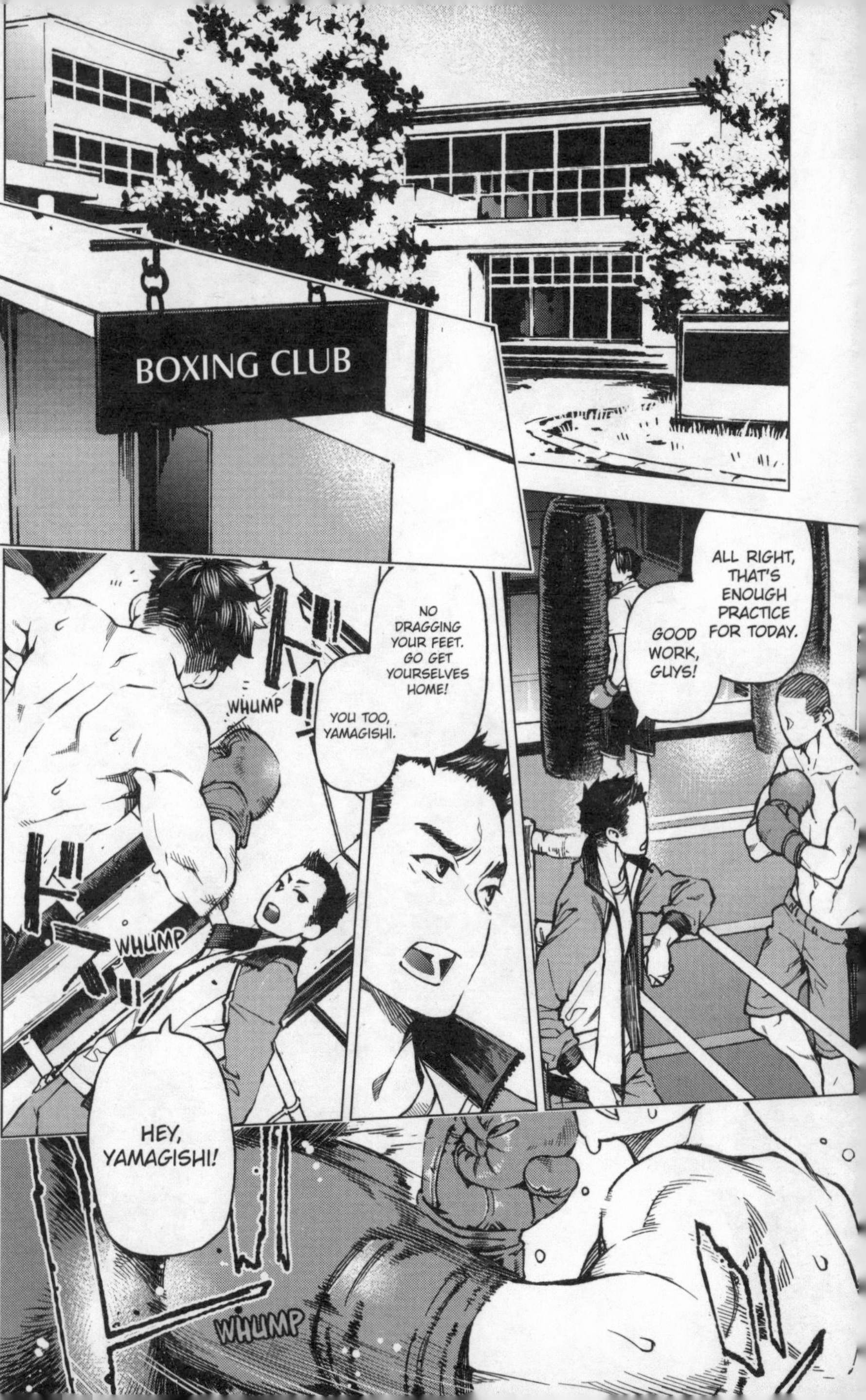
BOXING CLUB
ALL RIGHT, THAT'S ENOUGH PRACTICE FOR TODAY.
GOOD WORK, GUYS!
NO DRAGGING YOUR FEET. GO GET YOURSELVES HOME!
YOU TOO, YAMAGISHI.
WHUMP
WHUMP
HEY, YAMAGISHI!
WHUMP

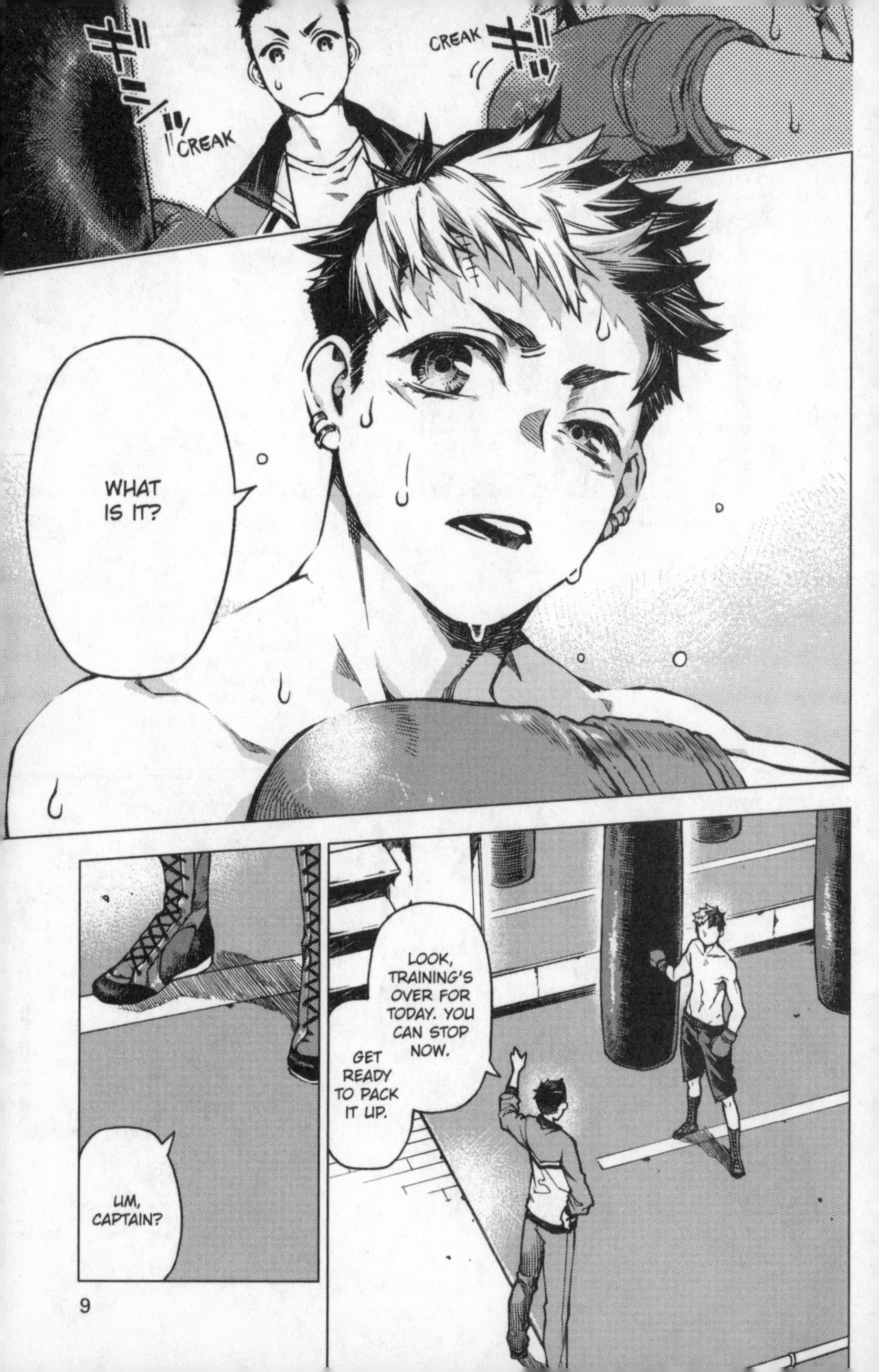
CREAK
CREAK
WHAT IS IT?
LOOK, TRAINING'S OVER FOR TODAY. YOU CAN STOP NOW.
GET READY TO PACK IT UP.
UM, CAPTAIN?

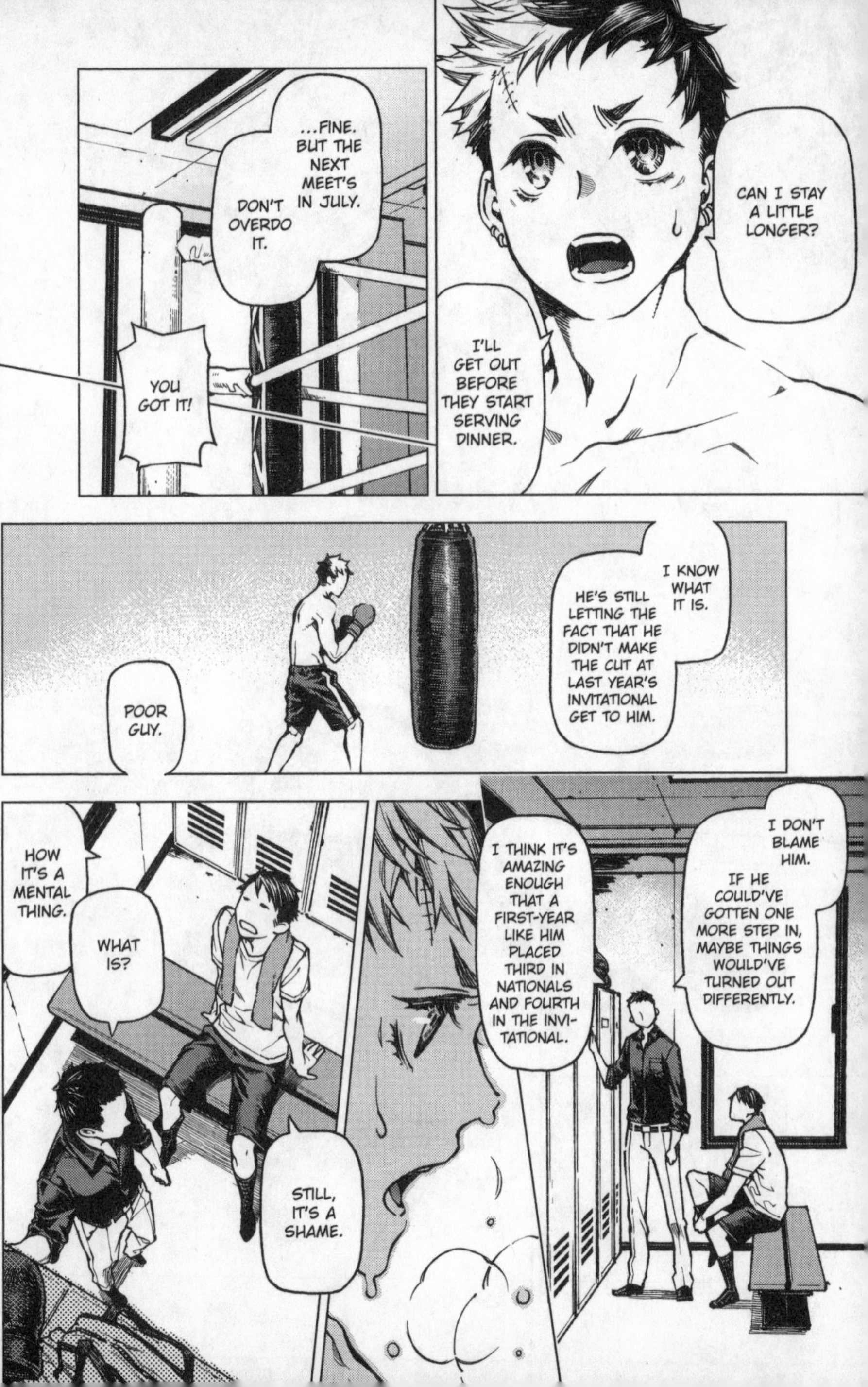
CAN I STAY A LITTLE LONGER?
I'LL GET OUT BEFORE THEY START SERVING DINNER.
...FINE. BUT THE NEXT MEET'S IN JULY.
DON'T OVERDO IT.
YOU GOT IT!
I KNOW WHAT IT IS.
HE'S STILL LETTING THE FACT THAT HE DIDN'T MAKE THE CUT AT LAST YEAR'S INVITATIONAL GET TO HIM.
POOR GUY.
I DON'T BLAME HIM.
IF HE COULD'VE GOTTEN ONE MORE STEP IN, MAYBE THINGS WOULD'VE TURNED OUT DIFFERENTLY.
I THINK IT'S AMAZING ENOUGH THAT A FIRST-YEAR LIKE HIM PLACED THIRD IN NATIONALS AND FOURTH IN THE INVI-TATIONAL.
STILL, IT'S A SHAME.
WHAT IS?
HOW IT'S A MENTAL THING.

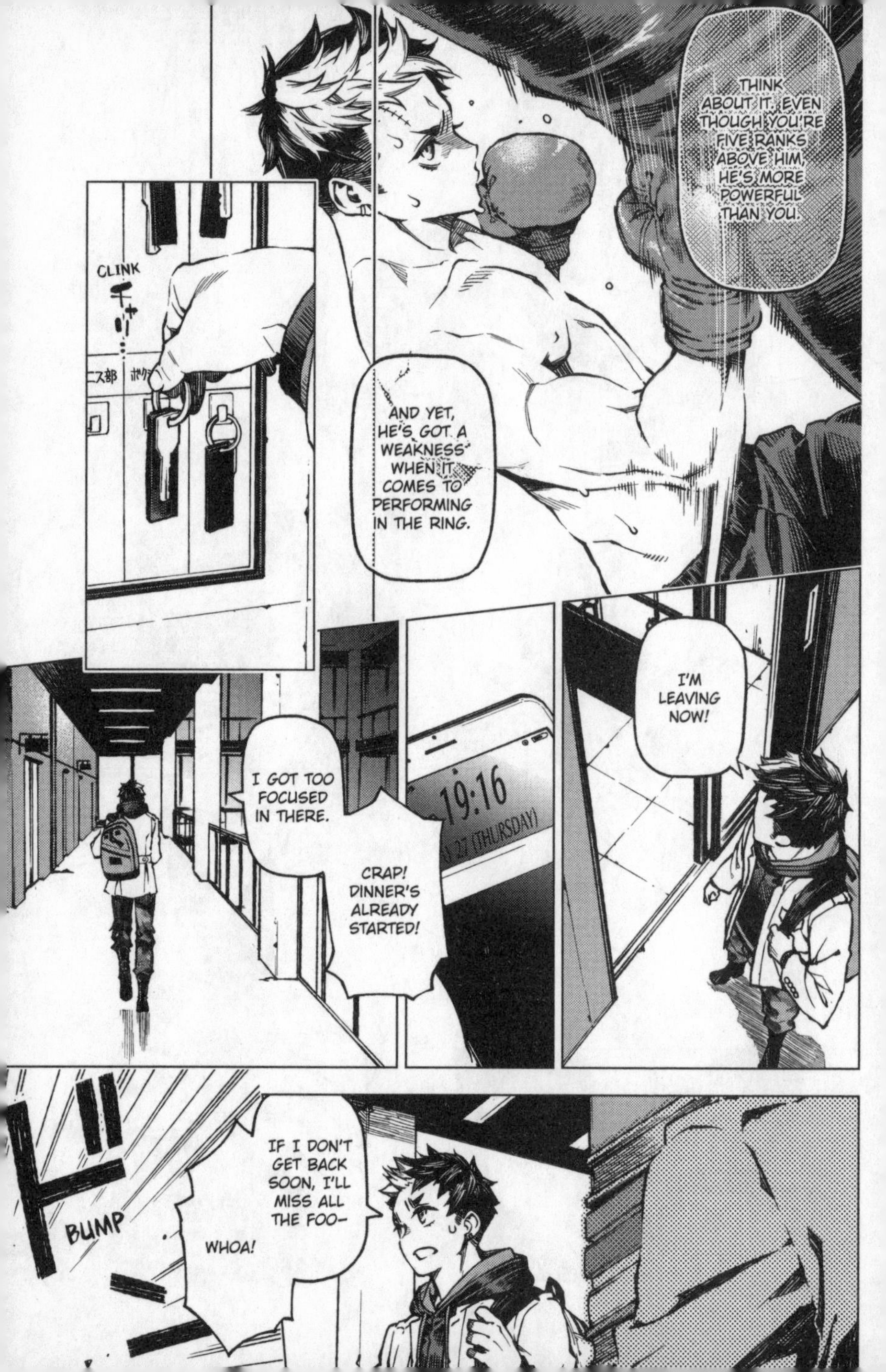
THINK ABOUT IT. EVEN THOUGH YOU'RE FIVE RANKS ABOVE HIM, HE'S MORE POWERFUL THAN YOU.
AND YET, HE'S GOT A WEAKNESS WHEN IT COMES TO PERFORMING IN THE RING.
CLINK
I'M LEAVING NOW!
19:16
CRAP! DINNER'S ALREADY STARTED!
I GOT TOO FOCUSED IN THERE.
IF I DON'T GET BACK SOON, I'LL MISS ALL THE FOO–
WHOA!
BUMP

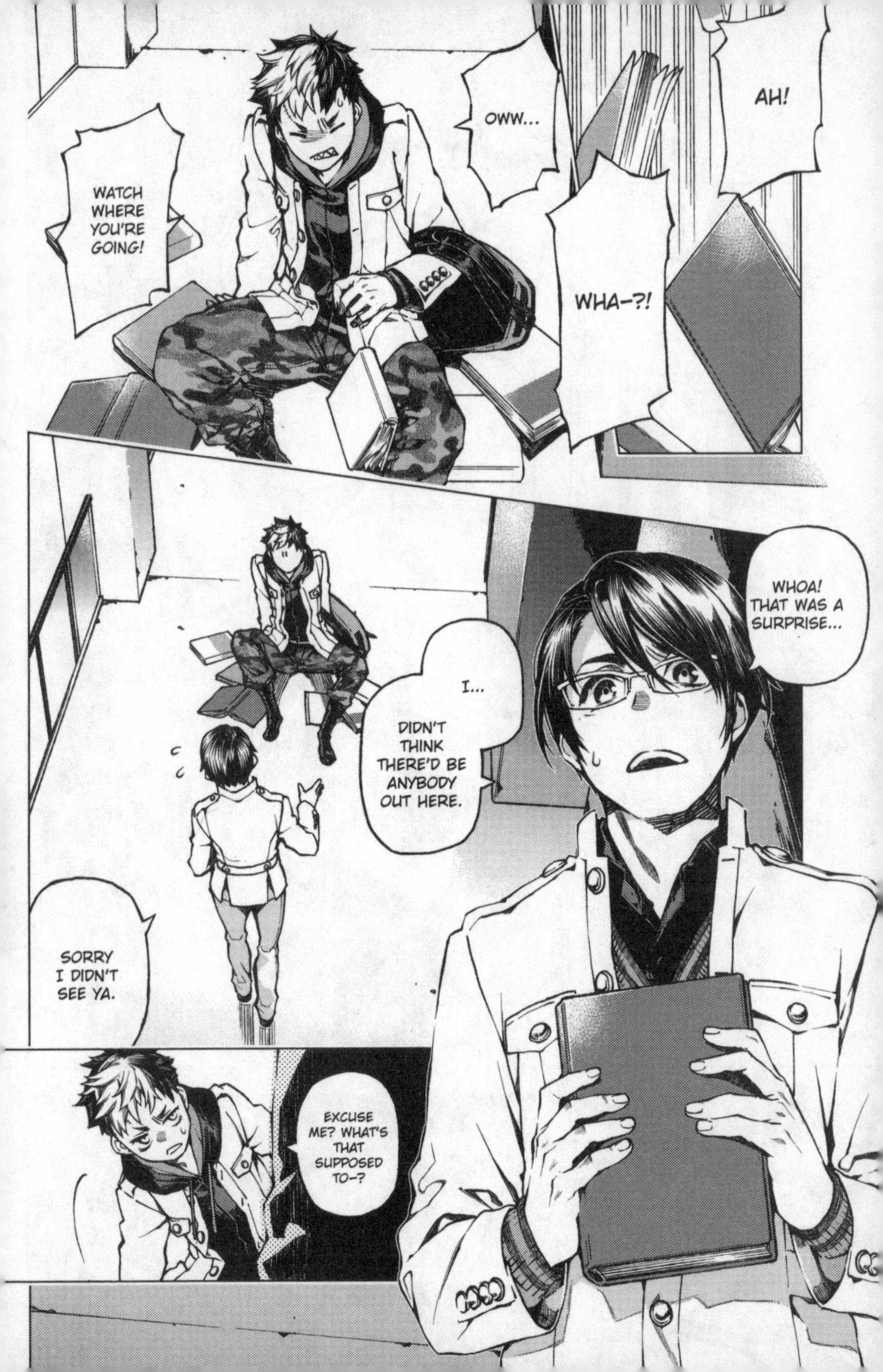
AH!
WHA-?!
OWW...
WATCH WHERE YOU'RE GOING!
WHOA! THAT WAS A SURPRISE...
I...
DIDN'T THINK THERE'D BE ANYBODY OUT HERE.
SORRY I DIDN'T SEE YA.
EXCUSE ME? WHAT'S THAT SUPPOSED TO-?

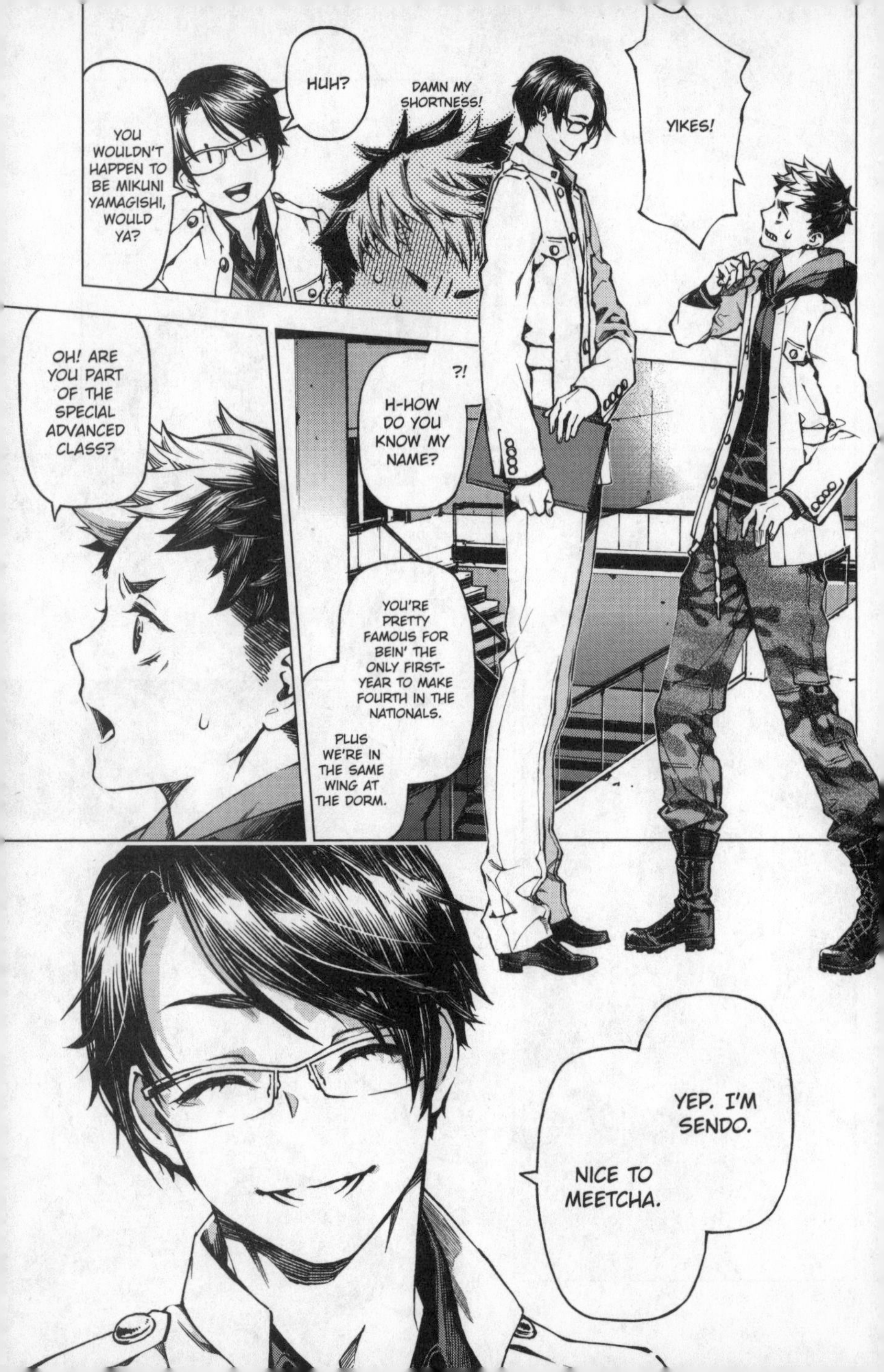
YIKES!
YOU WOULDN'T HAPPEN TO BE MIKUNI YAMAGISHI, WOULD YA?
HUH?
DAMN MY SHORTNESS!
?!
H-HOW DO YOU KNOW MY NAME?
YOU'RE PRETTY FAMOUS FOR BEIN' THE ONLY FIRST-YEAR TO MAKE FOURTH IN THE NATIONALS.
PLUS WE'RE IN THE SAME WING AT THE DORM.
OH! ARE YOU PART OF THE SPECIAL ADVANCED CLASS?
YEP. I'M SENDO.
NICE TO MEETCHA.

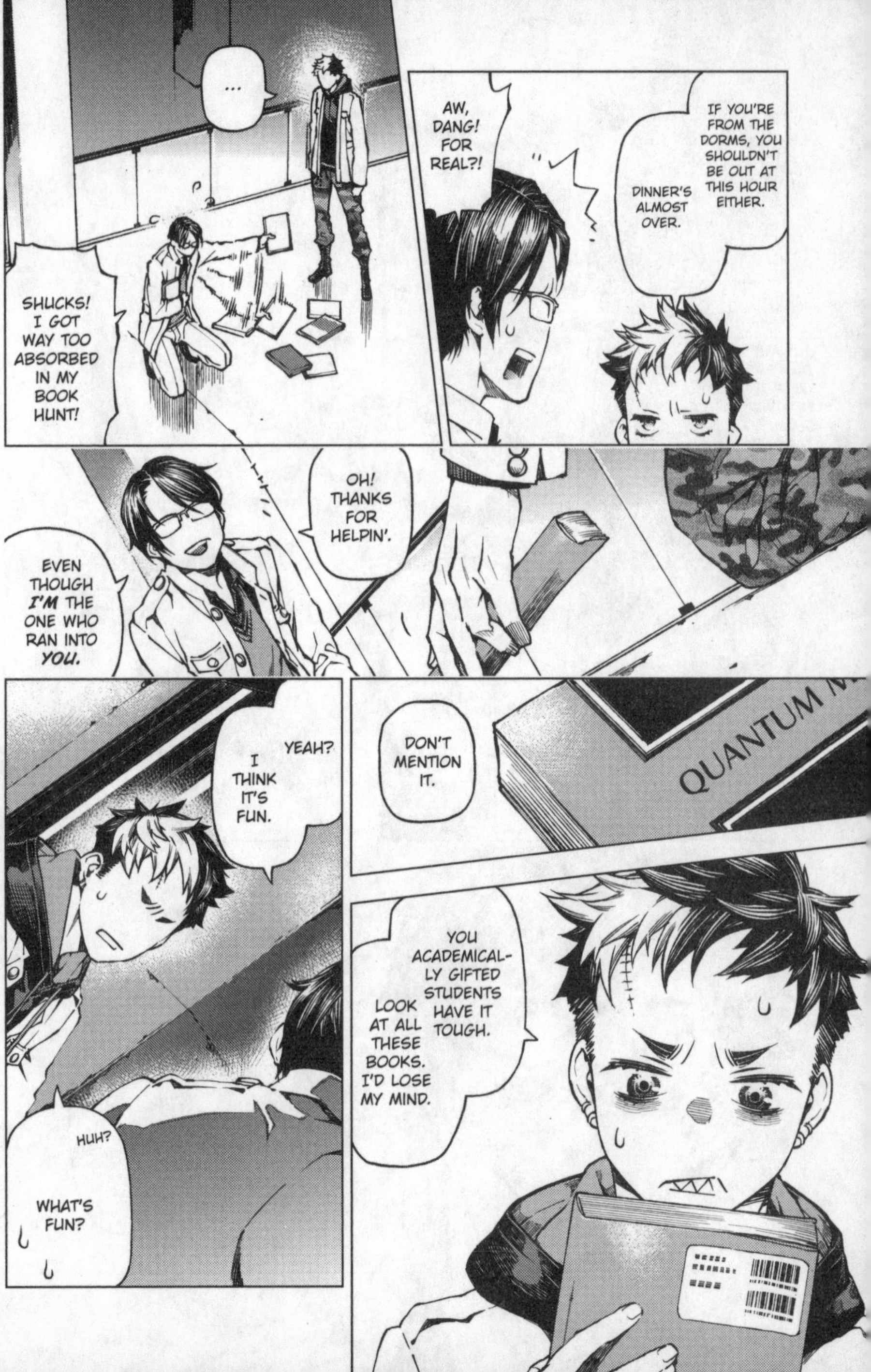
IF YOU'RE FROM THE DORMS, YOU SHOULDN'T BE OUT AT THIS HOUR EITHER.
DINNER'S ALMOST OVER.
AW, DANG! FOR REAL?!
...
SHUCKS! I GOT WAY TOO ABSORBED IN MY BOOK HUNT!
OH! THANKS FOR HELPIN'.
EVEN THOUGH *I'M* THE ONE WHO RAN INTO *YOU*.
DON'T MENTION IT.
YOU ACADEMICALLY GIFTED STUDENTS HAVE IT TOUGH.
LOOK AT ALL THESE BOOKS. I'D LOSE MY MIND.
YEAH?
I THINK IT'S FUN.
HUH?
WHAT'S FUN?
QUANTUM M

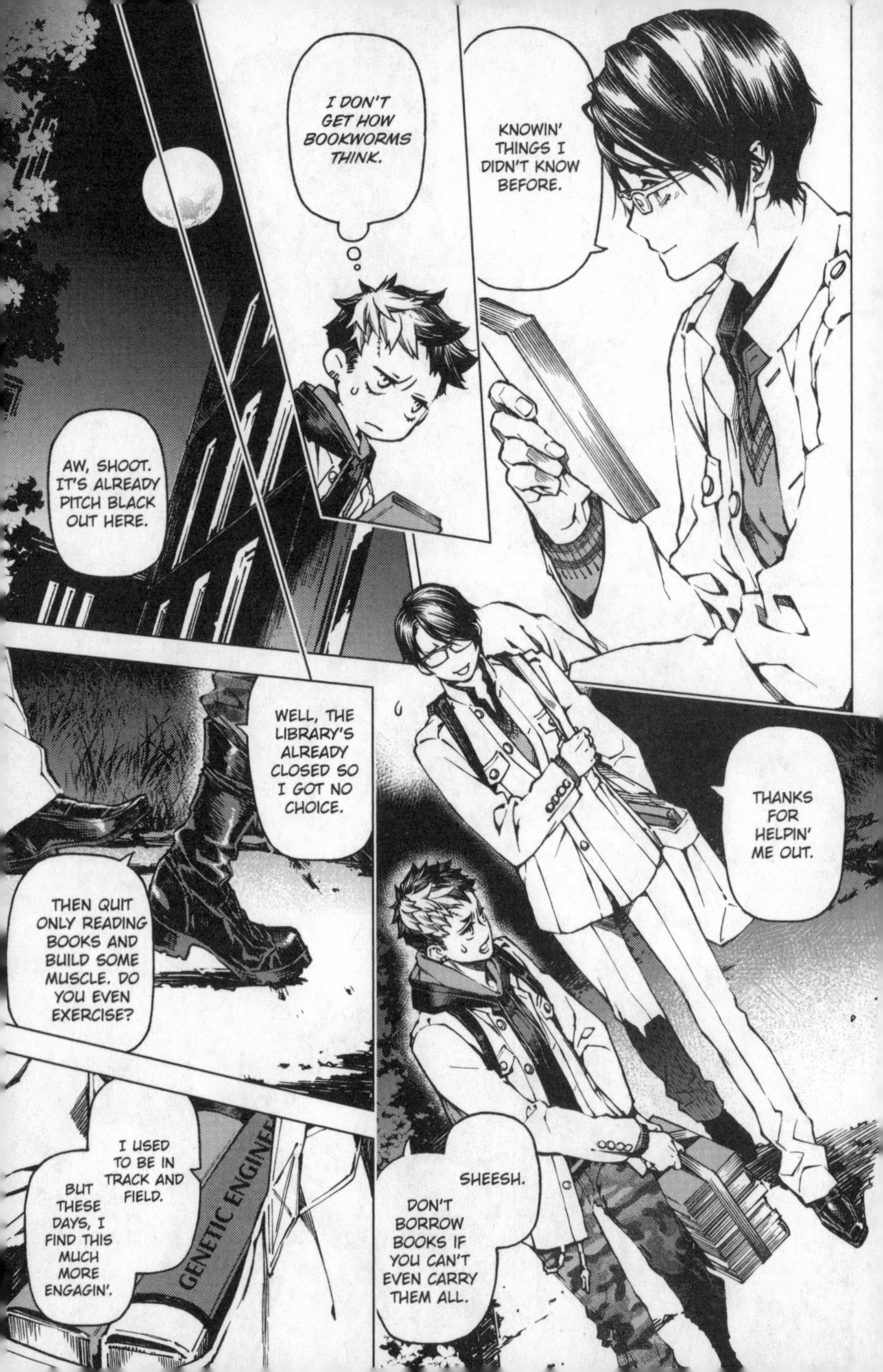
KNOWIN' THINGS I DIDN'T KNOW BEFORE.
I DON'T GET HOW BOOKWORMS THINK.
AW, SHOOT. IT'S ALREADY PITCH BLACK OUT HERE.
THANKS FOR HELPIN' ME OUT.
SHEESH.
DON'T BORROW BOOKS IF YOU CAN'T EVEN CARRY THEM ALL.
WELL, THE LIBRARY'S ALREADY CLOSED SO I GOT NO CHOICE.
THEN QUIT ONLY READING BOOKS AND BUILD SOME MUSCLE. DO YOU EVEN EXERCISE?
I USED TO BE IN TRACK AND FIELD.
BUT THESE DAYS, I FIND THIS MUCH MORE ENGAGIN'.
GENETIC ENGINEE

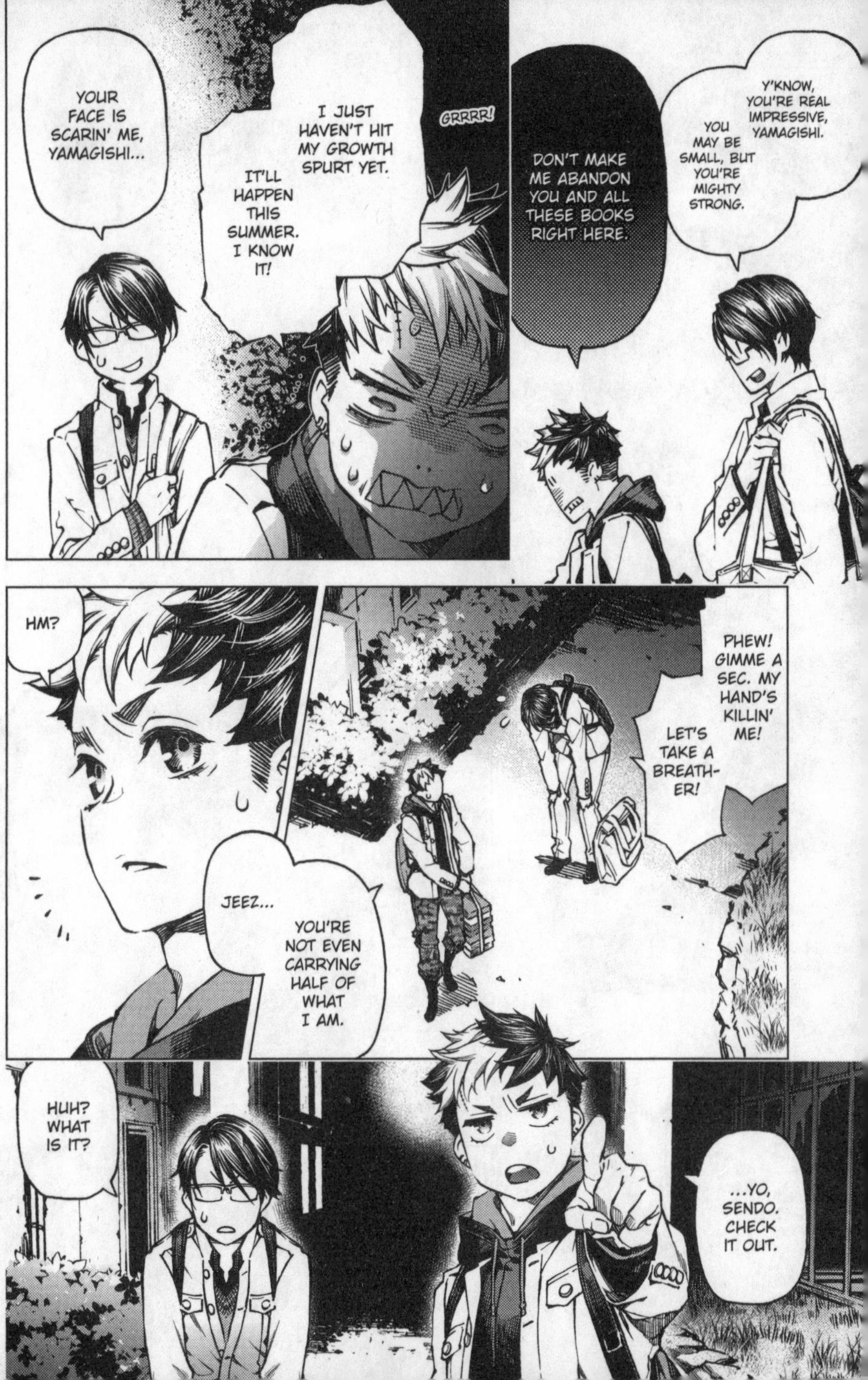
Y'KNOW, YOU'RE REAL IMPRESSIVE, YAMAGISHI.
YOU MAY BE SMALL, BUT YOU'RE MIGHTY STRONG.
DON'T MAKE ME ABANDON YOU AND ALL THESE BOOKS RIGHT HERE.
GRRRR!
I JUST HAVEN'T HIT MY GROWTH SPURT YET.
IT'LL HAPPEN THIS SUMMER. I KNOW IT!
YOUR FACE IS SCARIN' ME, YAMAGISHI...
PHEW! GIMME A SEC. MY HAND'S KILLIN' ME!
LET'S TAKE A BREATHER!
JEEZ...
YOU'RE NOT EVEN CARRYING HALF OF WHAT I AM.
HM?
...YO, SENDO. CHECK IT OUT.
HUH? WHAT IS IT?

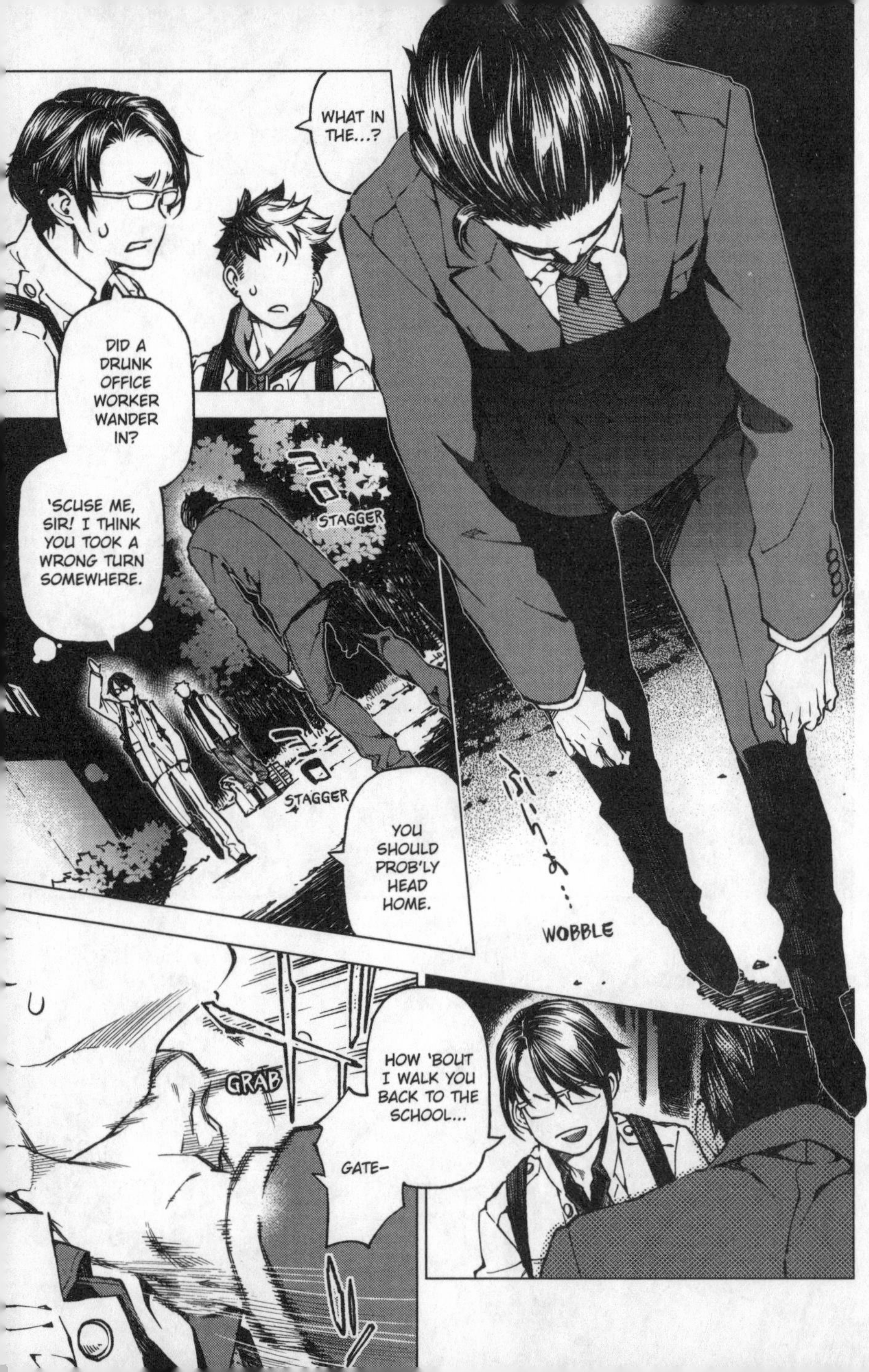
WHAT IN THE...?
DID A DRUNK OFFICE WORKER WANDER IN?
'SCUSE ME, SIR! I THINK YOU TOOK A WRONG TURN SOMEWHERE.
STAGGER
STAGGER
YOU SHOULD PROB'LY HEAD HOME.
WOBBLE
HOW 'BOUT I WALK YOU BACK TO THE SCHOOL...
GATE-
GRAB

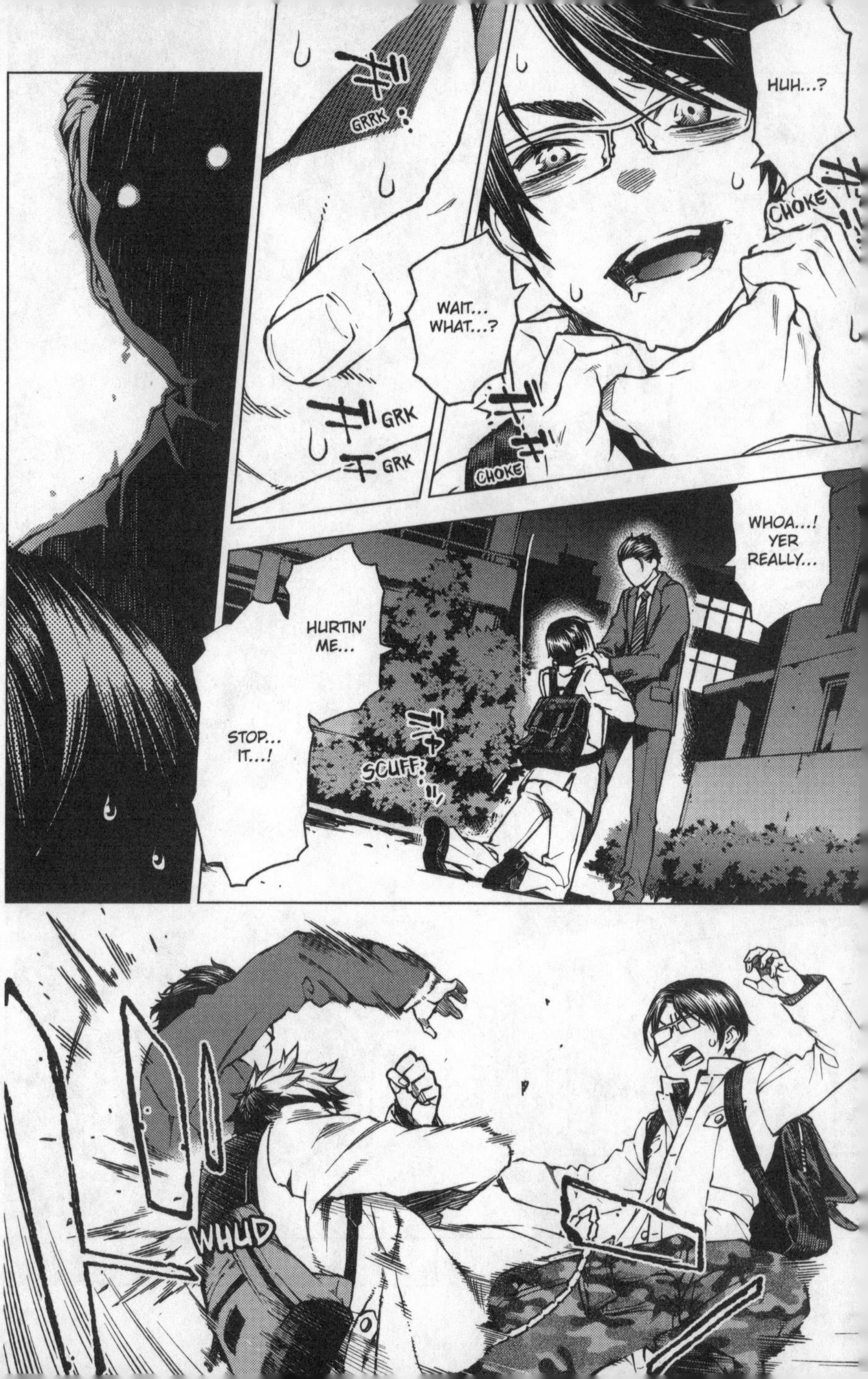
HUH...?
CHOKE
WAIT... WHAT...?
CHOKE
GRRK
GRK
GRK
WHOA...! YER REALLY...
SCUFF
HURTIN' ME...
STOP... IT...!
WHUD

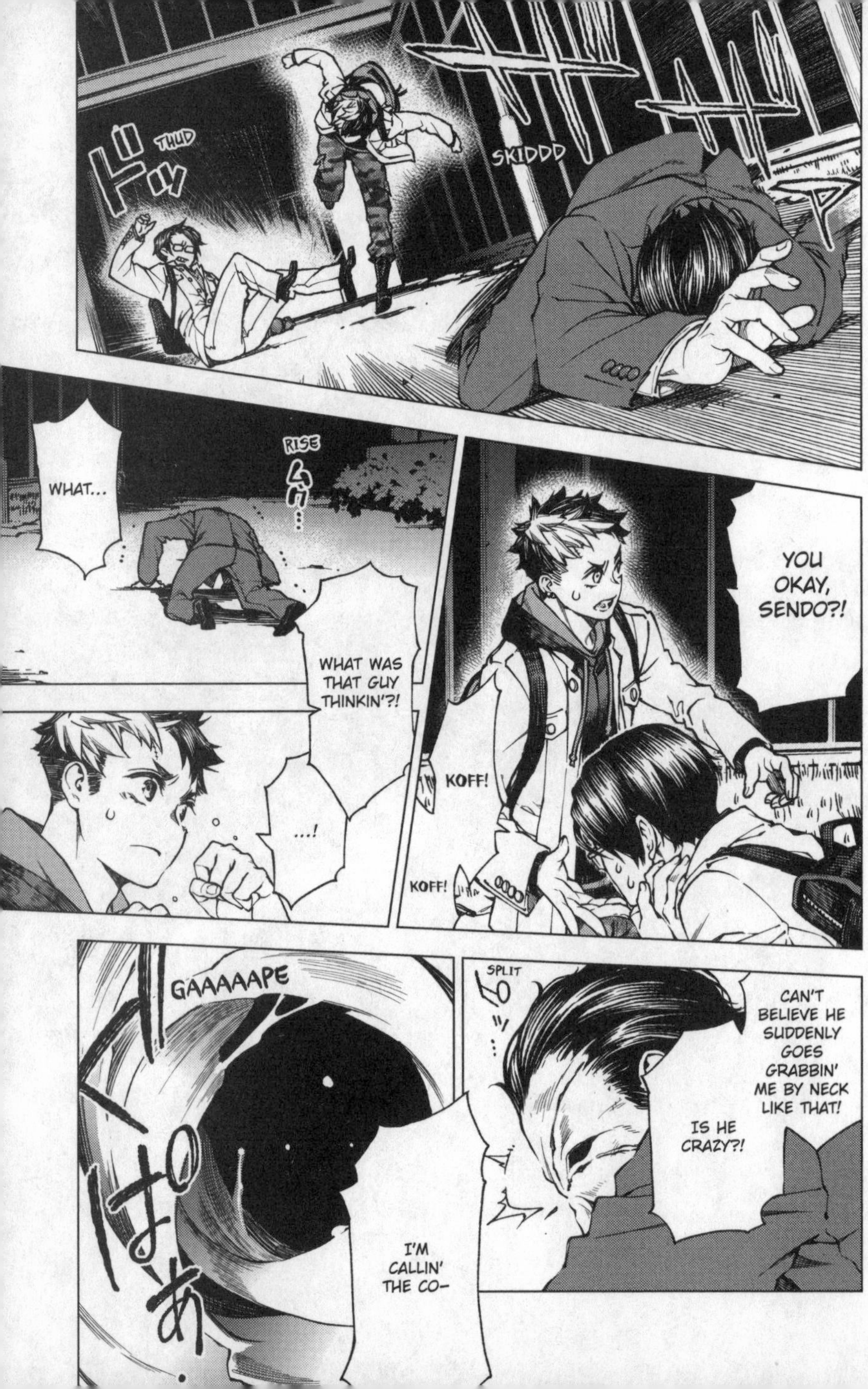
SKIDDD
THUD
YOU OKAY, SENDO?!
KOFF!
KOFF!
WHAT...
RISE
WHAT WAS THAT GUY THINKIN'?!
...!
SPLIT
CAN'T BELIEVE HE SUDDENLY GOES GRABBIN' ME BY NECK LIKE THAT!
IS HE CRAZY?!
GAAAAAPE
I'M CALLIN' THE CO-

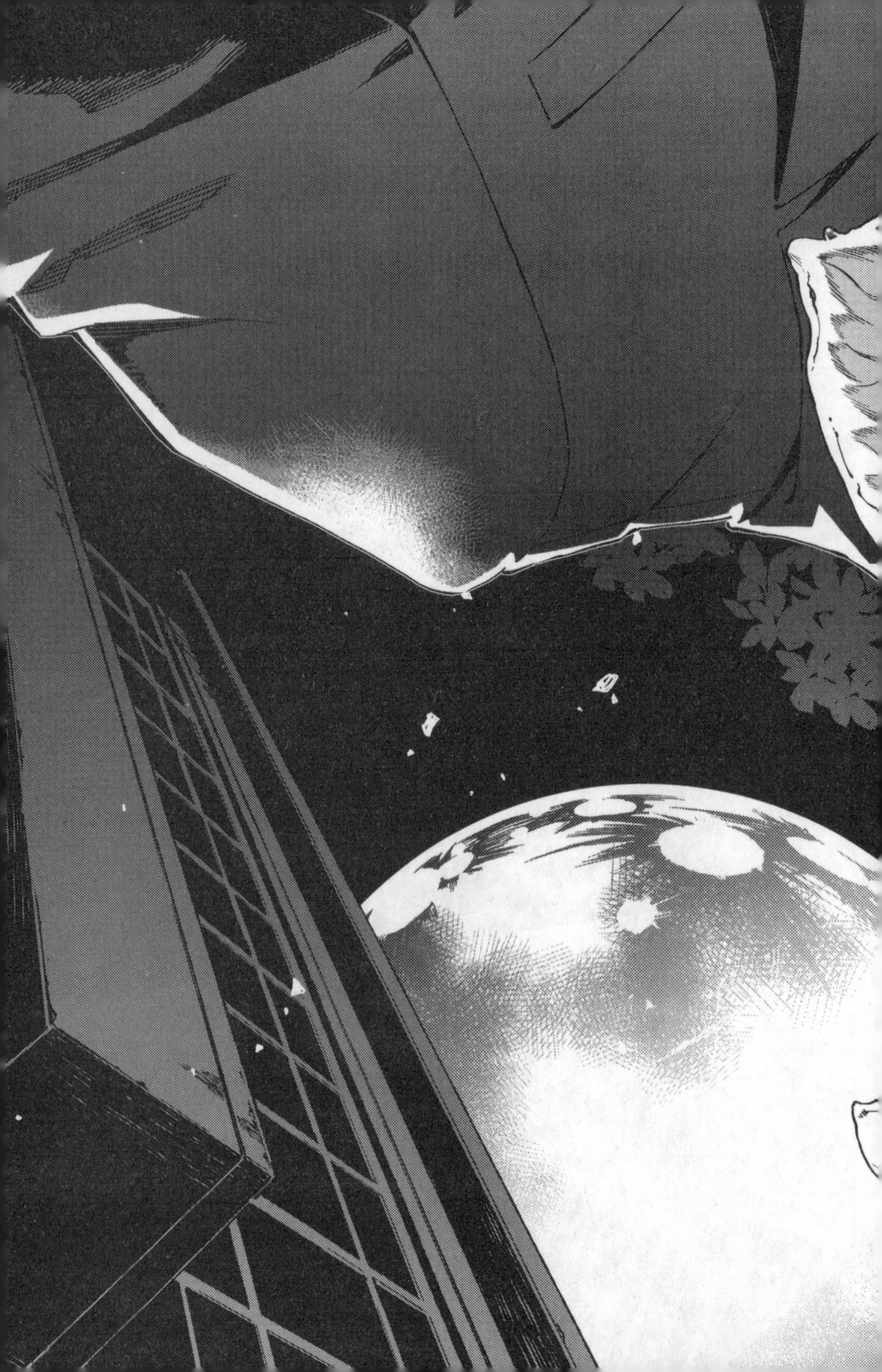

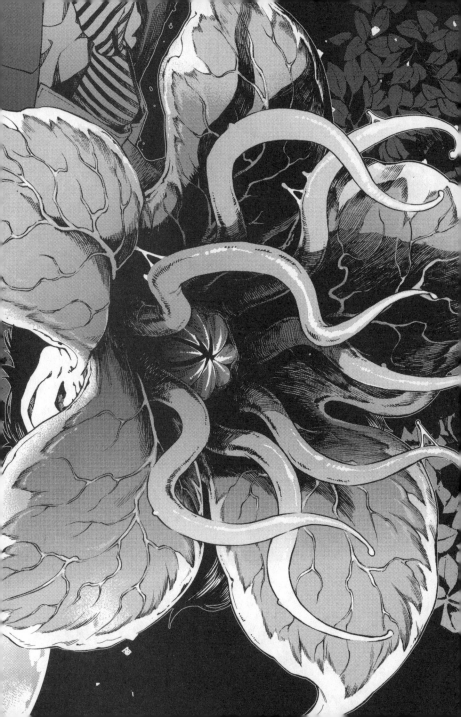

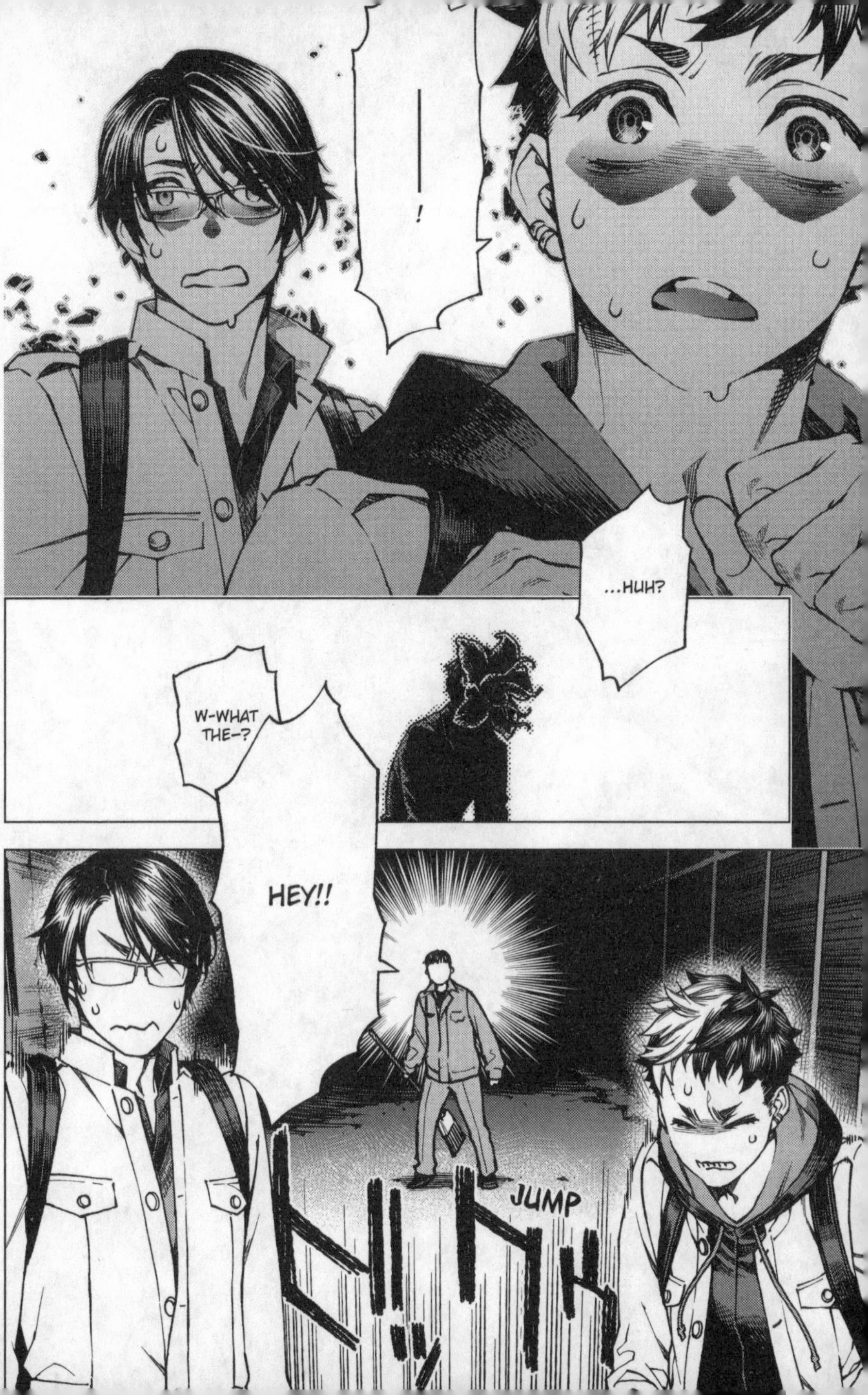

—!
...HUH?
W-WHAT THE-?
HEY!!
JUMP

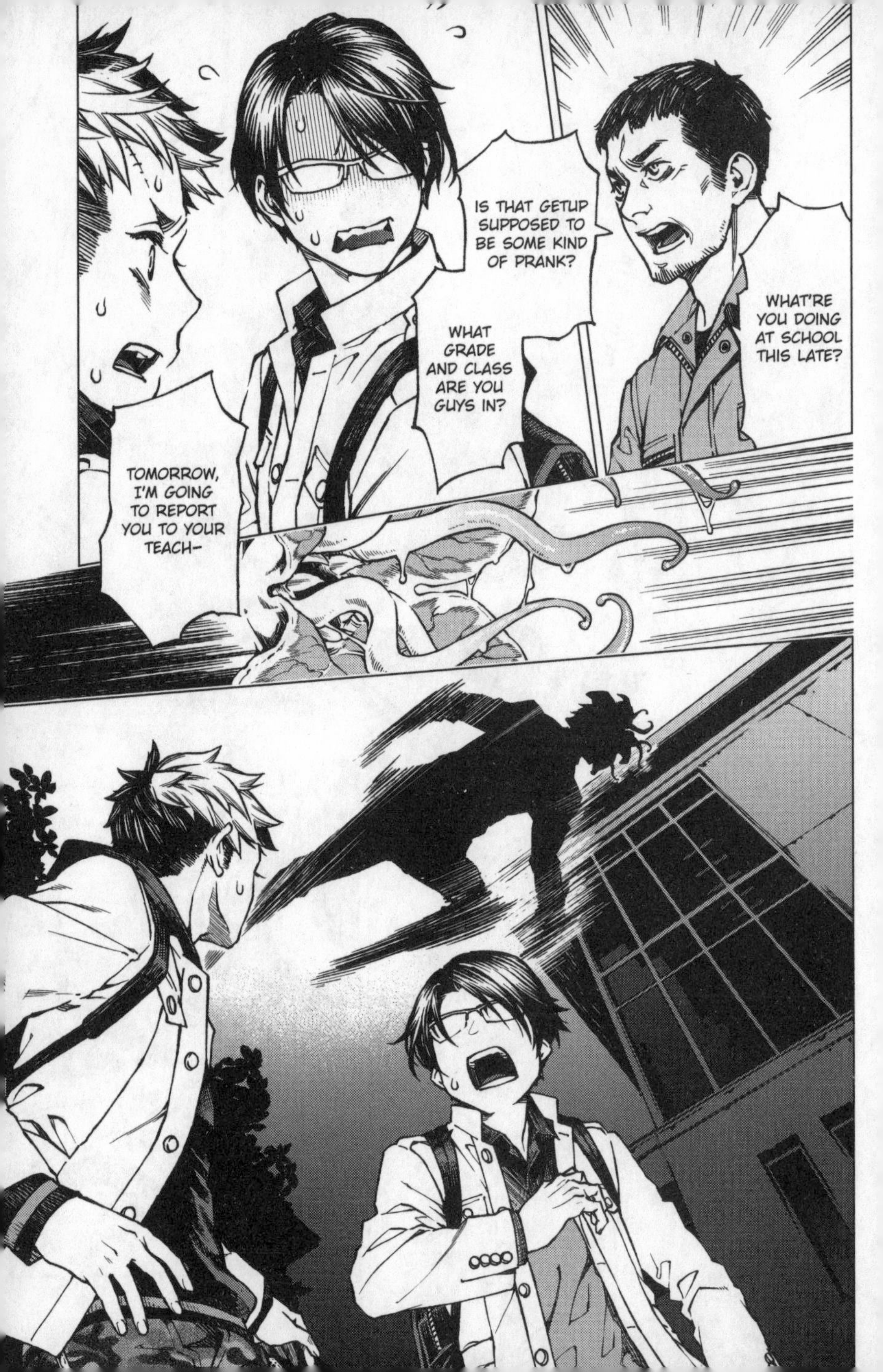
WHAT'RE YOU DOING AT SCHOOL THIS LATE?
IS THAT GETUP SUPPOSED TO BE SOME KIND OF PRANK?
WHAT GRADE AND CLASS ARE YOU GUYS IN?
TOMORROW, I'M GOING TO REPORT YOU TO YOUR TEACH–

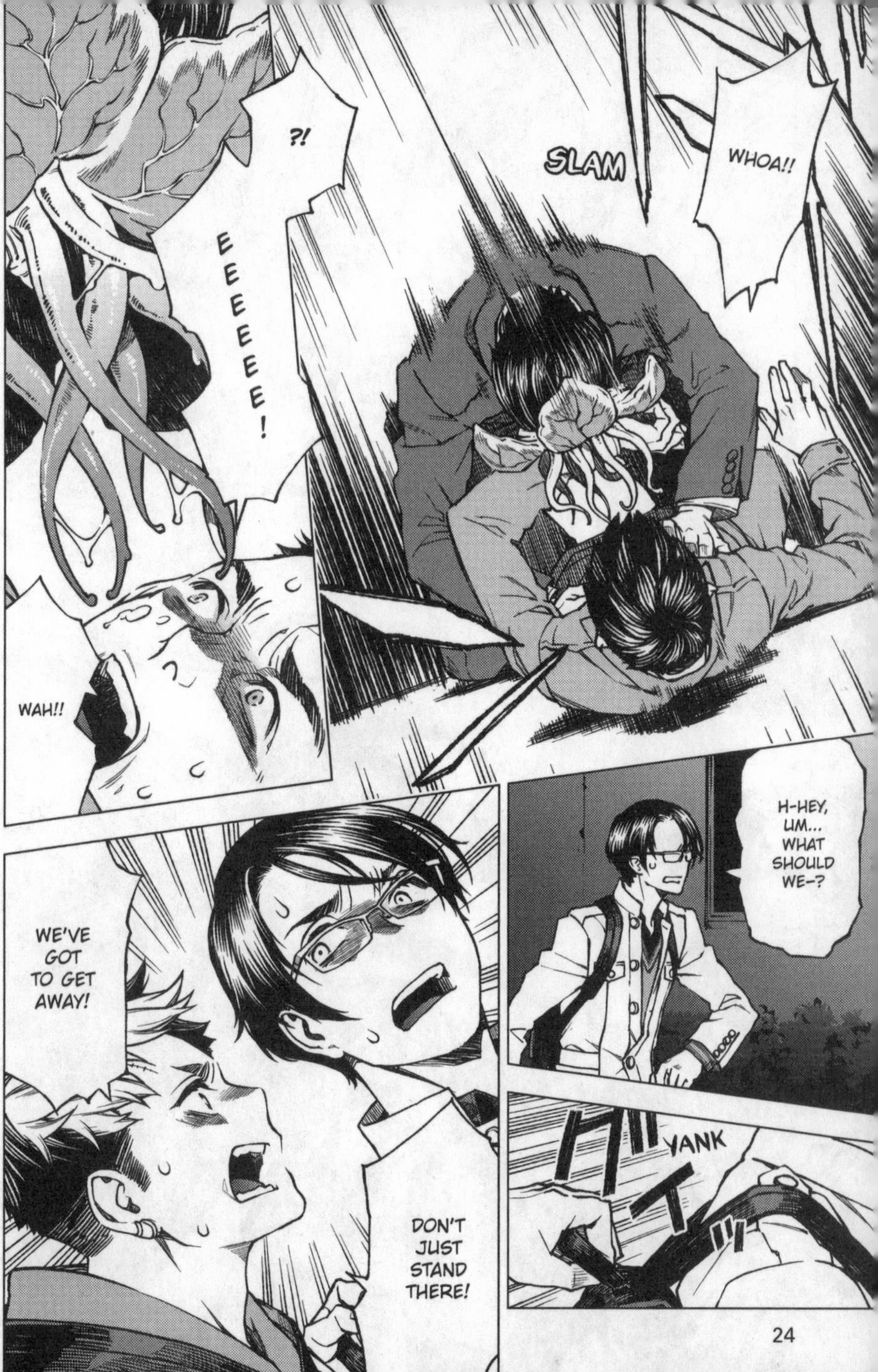
WHOA!!
SLAM
?!
EEEEEEE!
WAH!!
H-HEY, UM... WHAT SHOULD WE-?
YANK
WE'VE GOT TO GET AWAY!
DON'T JUST STAND THERE!

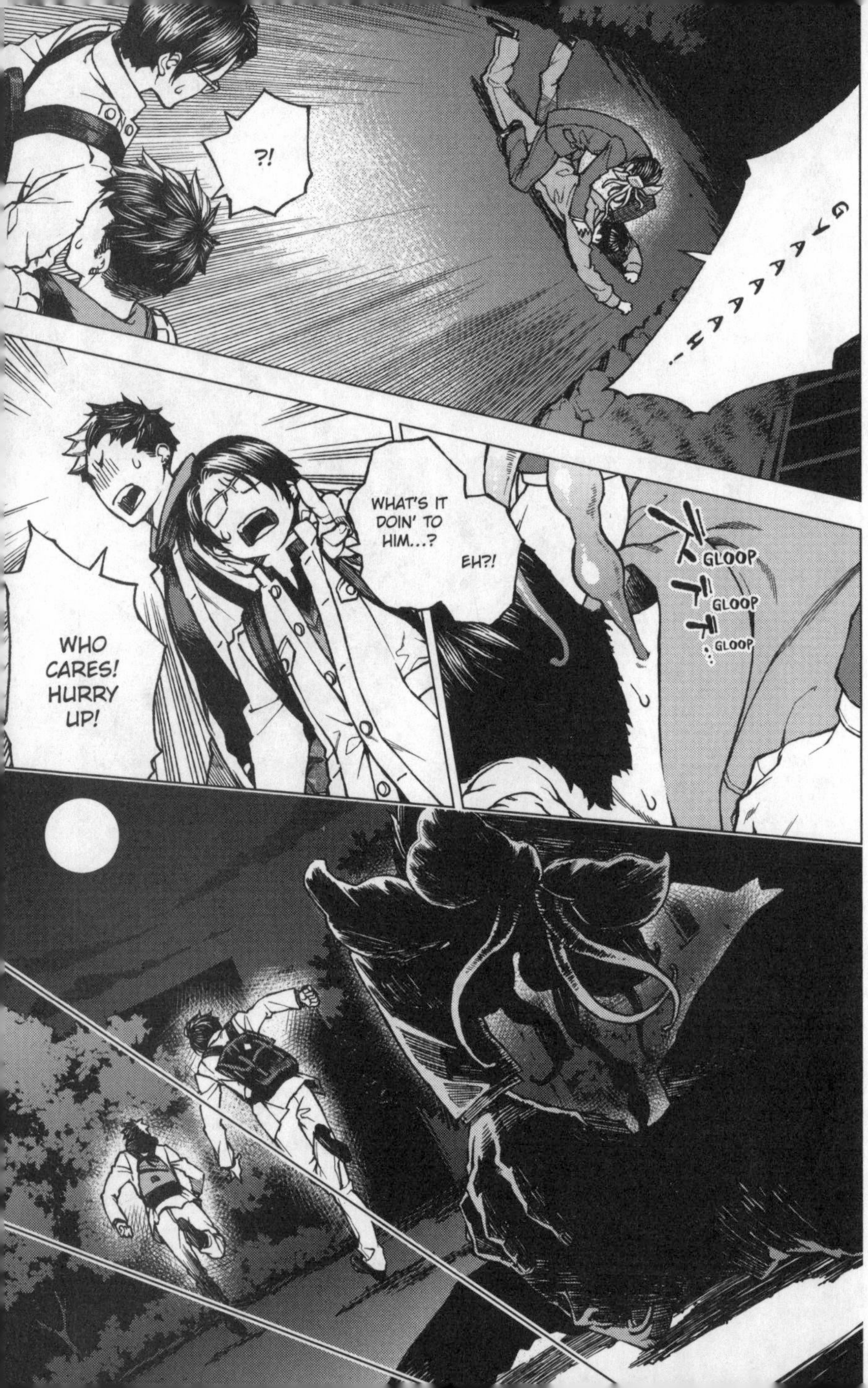
GYAAAAAH--
?!
GLOOP
GLOOP
GLOOP
WHAT'S IT DOIN' TO HIM...?
EH?!
WHO CARES! HURRY UP!

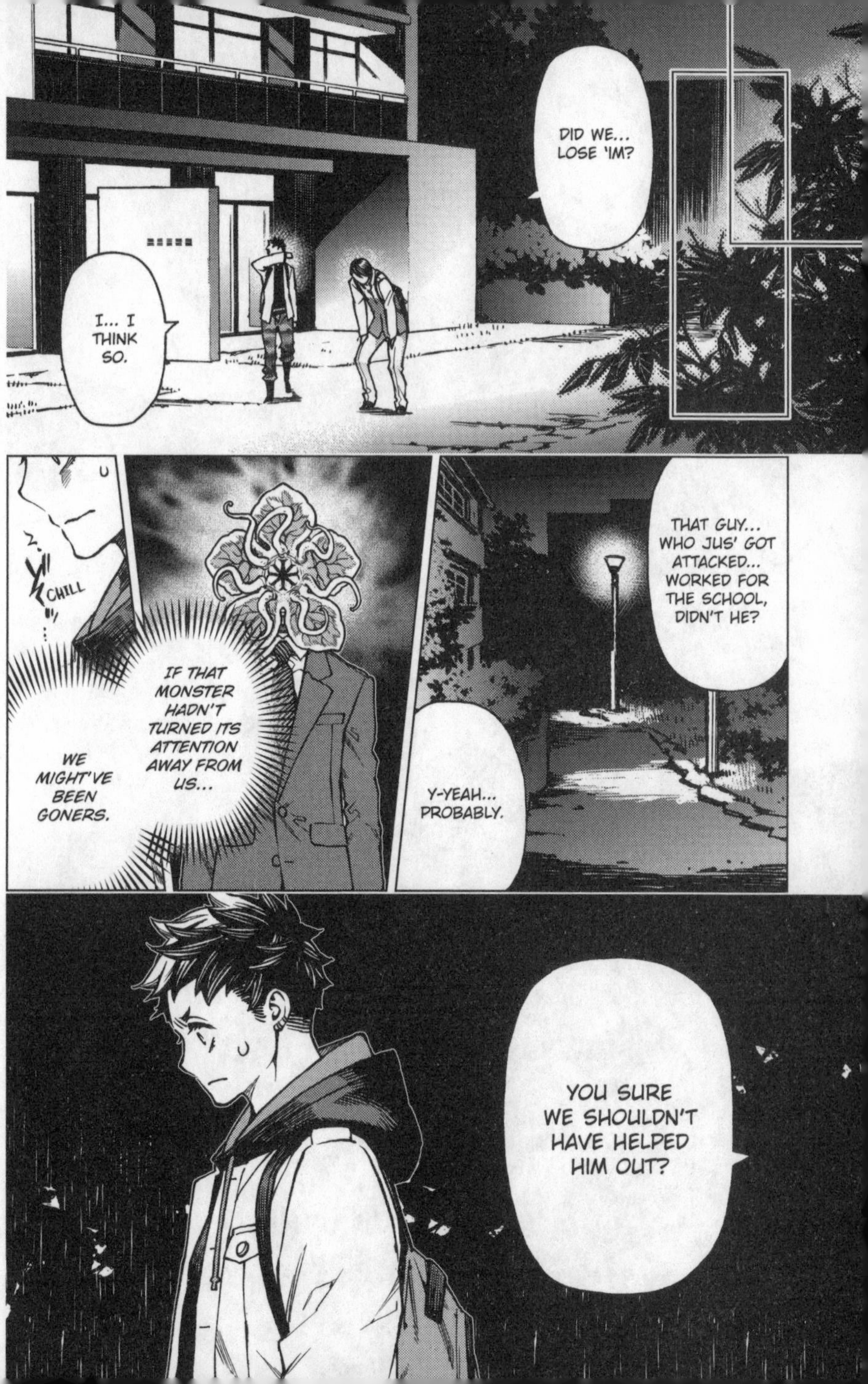
DID WE... LOSE 'IM?
I... I THINK SO.
THAT GUY... WHO JUS' GOT ATTACKED... WORKED FOR THE SCHOOL, DIDN'T HE?
Y-YEAH... PROBABLY.
CHILL
IF THAT MONSTER HADN'T TURNED ITS ATTENTION AWAY FROM US...
WE MIGHT'VE BEEN GONERS.
YOU SURE WE SHOULDN'T HAVE HELPED HIM OUT?

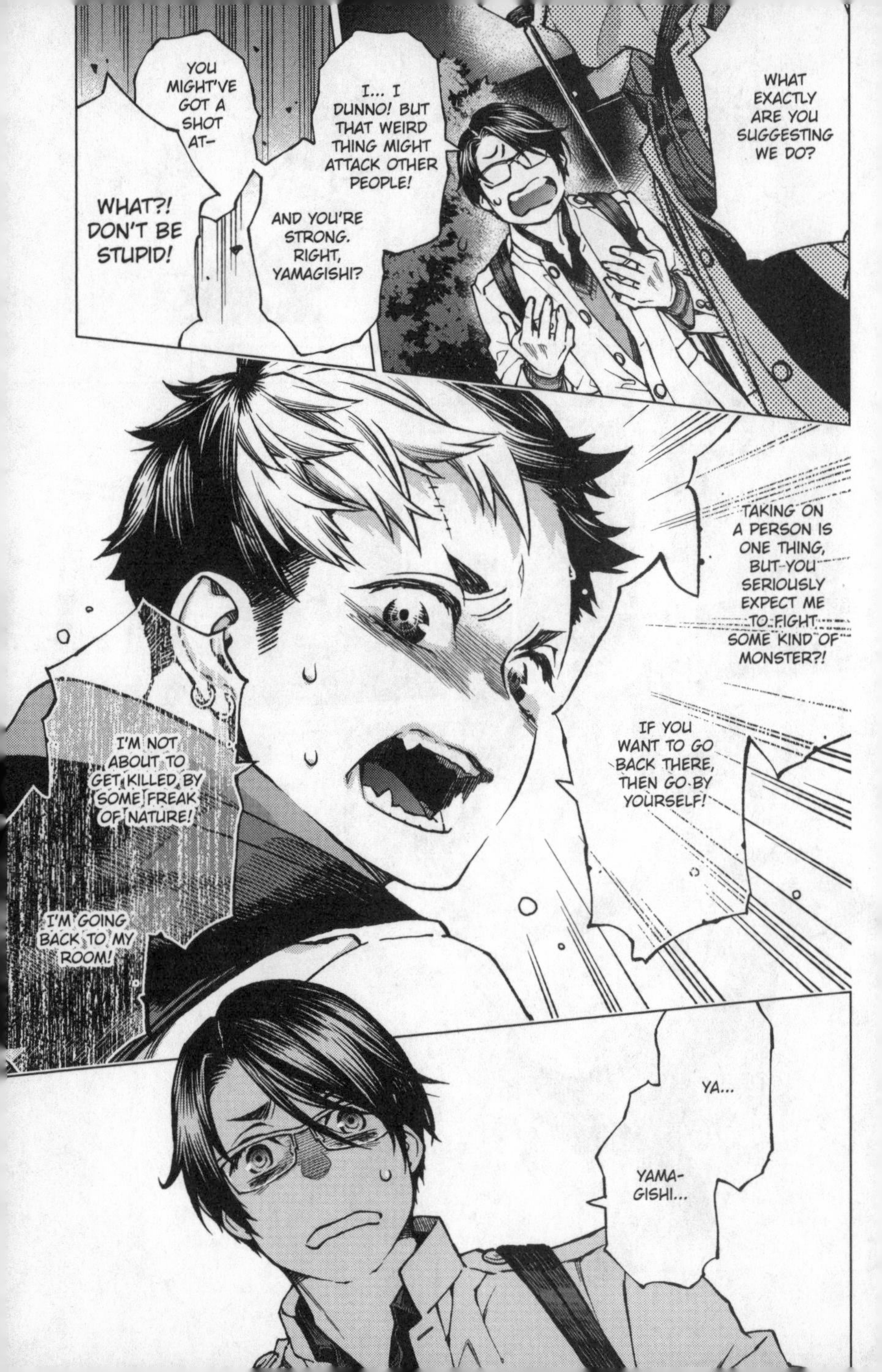
WHAT EXACTLY ARE YOU SUGGESTING WE DO?
I... I DUNNO! BUT THAT WEIRD THING MIGHT ATTACK OTHER PEOPLE!
AND YOU'RE STRONG. RIGHT, YAMAGISHI?
YOU MIGHT'VE GOT A SHOT AT–
WHAT?! DON'T BE STUPID!
TAKING ON A PERSON IS ONE THING, BUT YOU SERIOUSLY EXPECT ME TO FIGHT SOME KIND OF MONSTER?!
IF YOU WANT TO GO BACK THERE, THEN GO BY YOURSELF!
I'M NOT ABOUT TO GET KILLED BY SOME FREAK OF NATURE!
I'M GOING BACK TO MY ROOM!
YA...
YAMA-GISHI...

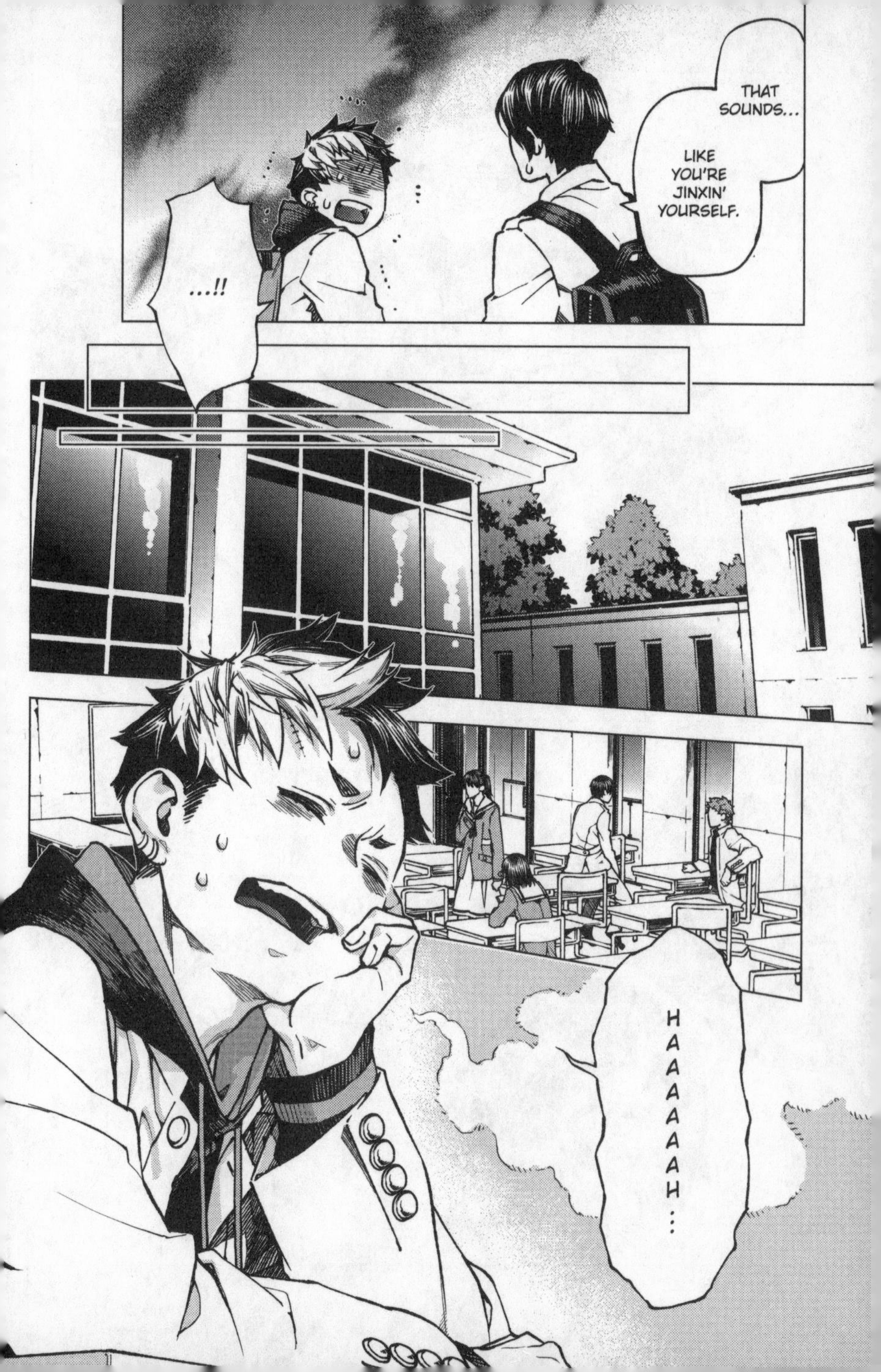
THAT SOUNDS...
LIKE YOU'RE JINXIN' YOURSELF.
...!!
HAAAAAAAH...

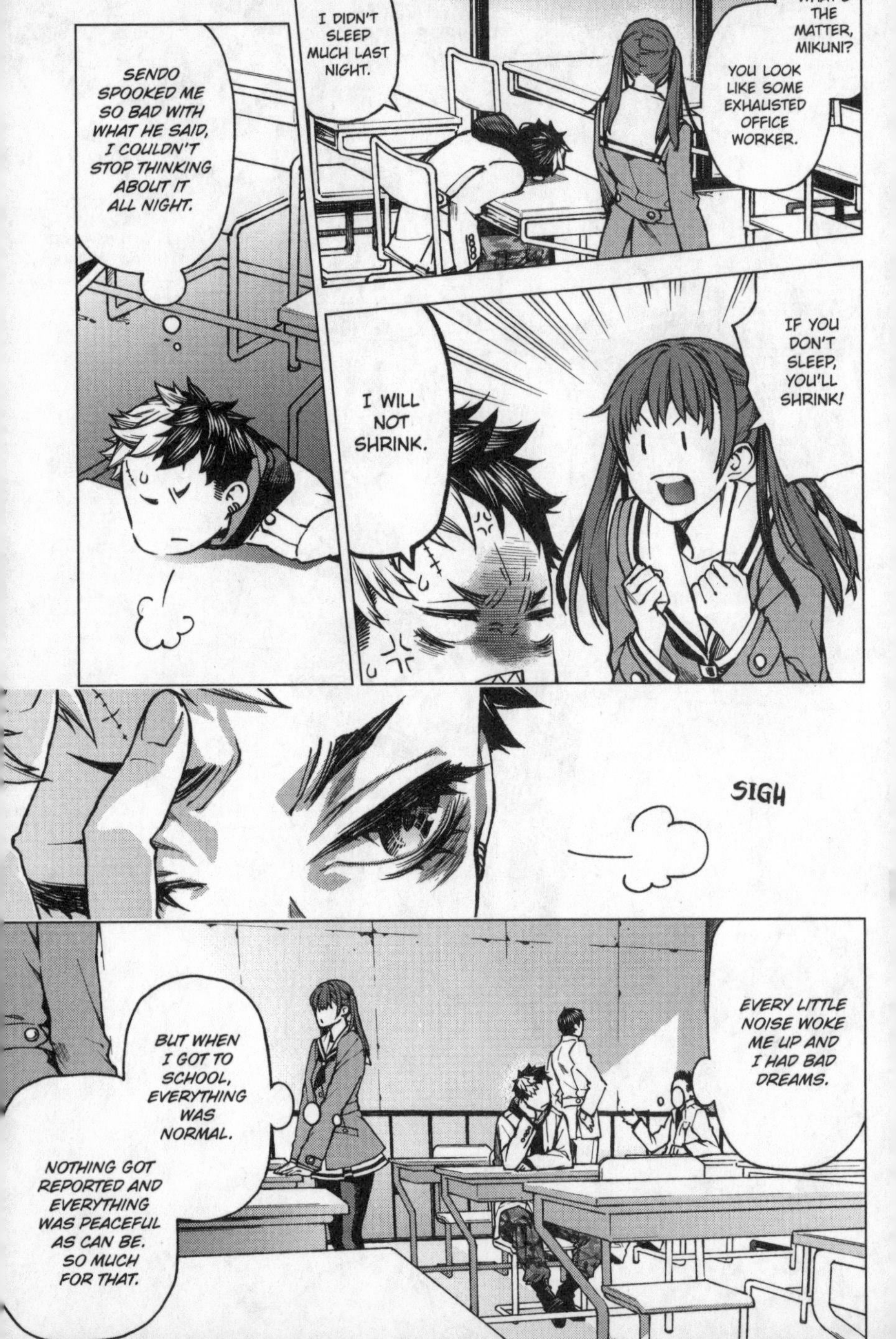
WHAT'S THE MATTER, MIKUNI?
YOU LOOK LIKE SOME EXHAUSTED OFFICE WORKER.
I DIDN'T SLEEP MUCH LAST NIGHT.
SENDO SPOOKED ME SO BAD WITH WHAT HE SAID, I COULDN'T STOP THINKING ABOUT IT ALL NIGHT.
IF YOU DON'T SLEEP, YOU'LL SHRINK!
I WILL NOT SHRINK.
SIGH
EVERY LITTLE NOISE WOKE ME UP AND I HAD BAD DREAMS.
BUT WHEN I GOT TO SCHOOL, EVERYTHING WAS NORMAL.
NOTHING GOT REPORTED AND EVERYTHING WAS PEACEFUL AS CAN BE. SO MUCH FOR THAT.

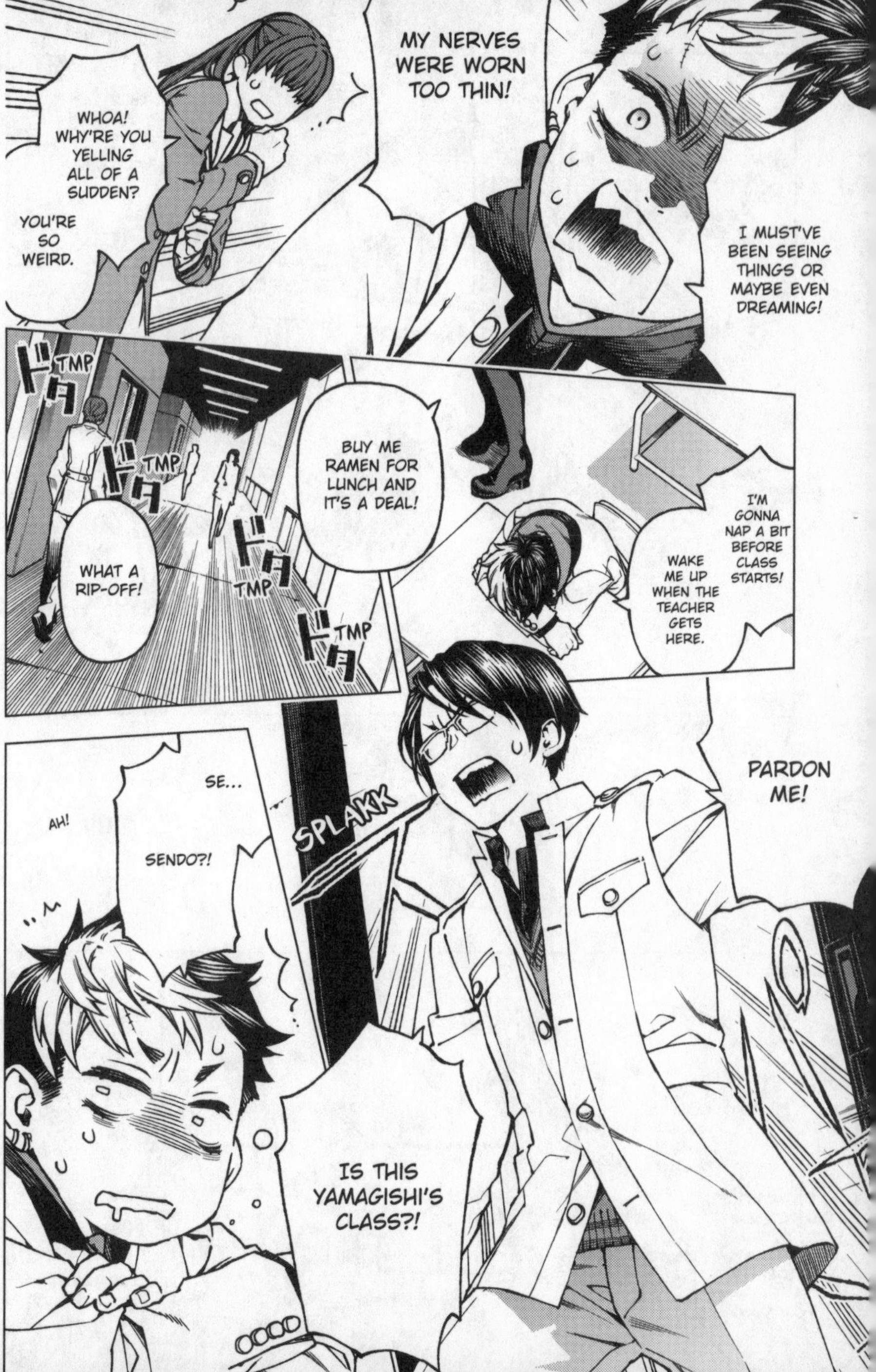
I MUST'VE BEEN SEEING THINGS OR MAYBE EVEN DREAMING!
MY NERVES WERE WORN TOO THIN!
...
WHOA! WHY'RE YOU YELLING ALL OF A SUDDEN?
YOU'RE SO WEIRD.
I'M GONNA NAP A BIT BEFORE CLASS STARTS!
WAKE ME UP WHEN THE TEACHER GETS HERE.
BUY ME RAMEN FOR LUNCH AND IT'S A DEAL!
TMP
TMP
WHAT A RIP-OFF!
TMP
TMP
PARDON ME!
SPLAKK
IS THIS YAMAGISHI'S CLASS?!
...
SE...
AH!
SENDO?!
..ん

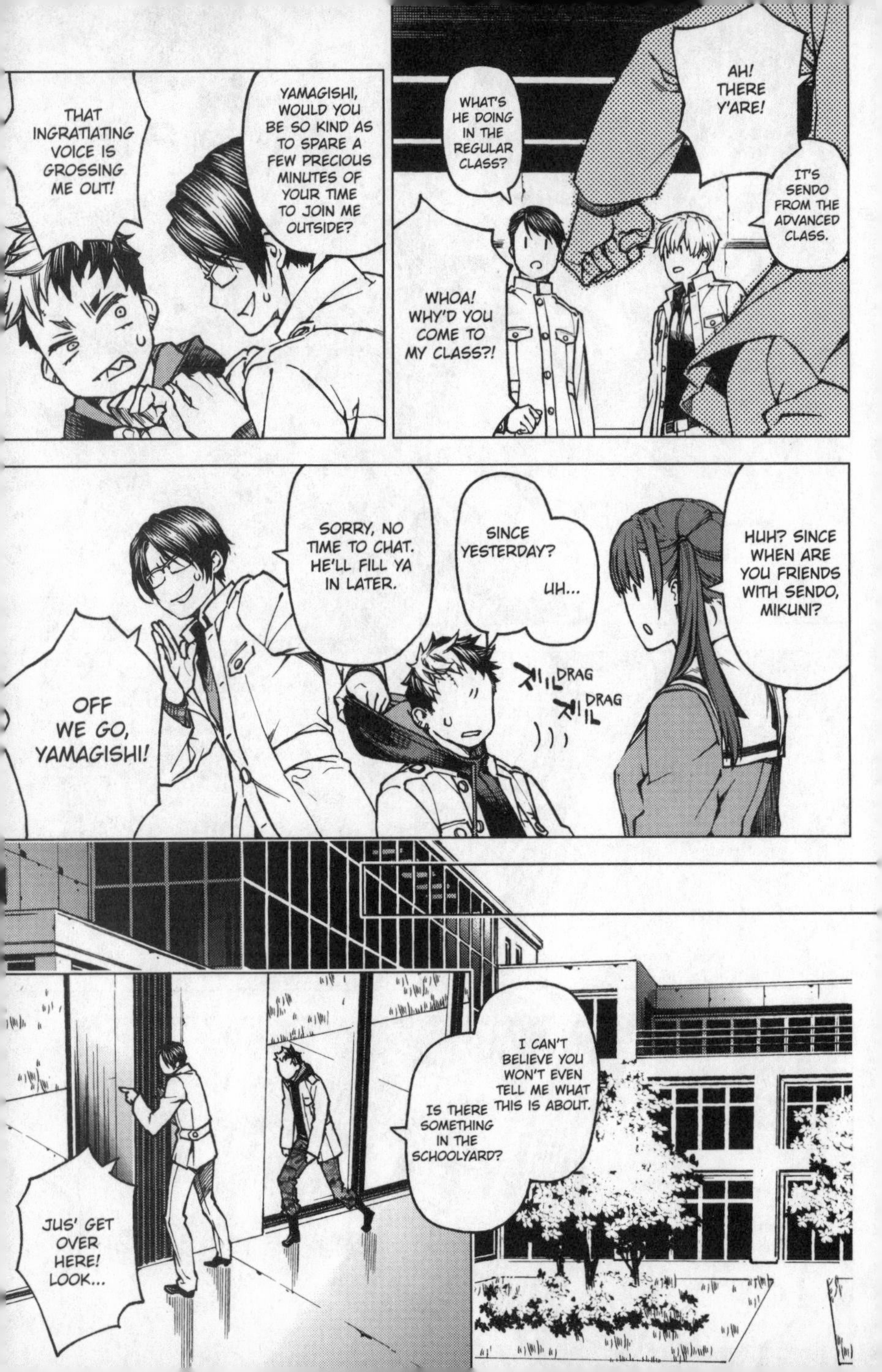
AH! THERE Y'ARE!
IT'S SENDO FROM THE ADVANCED CLASS.
WHAT'S HE DOING IN THE REGULAR CLASS?
WHOA! WHY'D YOU COME TO MY CLASS?!
YAMAGISHI, WOULD YOU BE SO KIND AS TO SPARE A FEW PRECIOUS MINUTES OF YOUR TIME TO JOIN ME OUTSIDE?
THAT INGRATIATING VOICE IS GROSSING ME OUT!
HUH? SINCE WHEN ARE YOU FRIENDS WITH SENDO, MIKUNI?
SINCE YESTERDAY?
UH...
DRAG
DRAG
SORRY, NO TIME TO CHAT. HE'LL FILL YA IN LATER.
OFF WE GO, YAMAGISHI!
I CAN'T BELIEVE YOU WON'T EVEN TELL ME WHAT THIS IS ABOUT.
IS THERE SOMETHING IN THE SCHOOLYARD?
JUS' GET OVER HERE! LOOK...

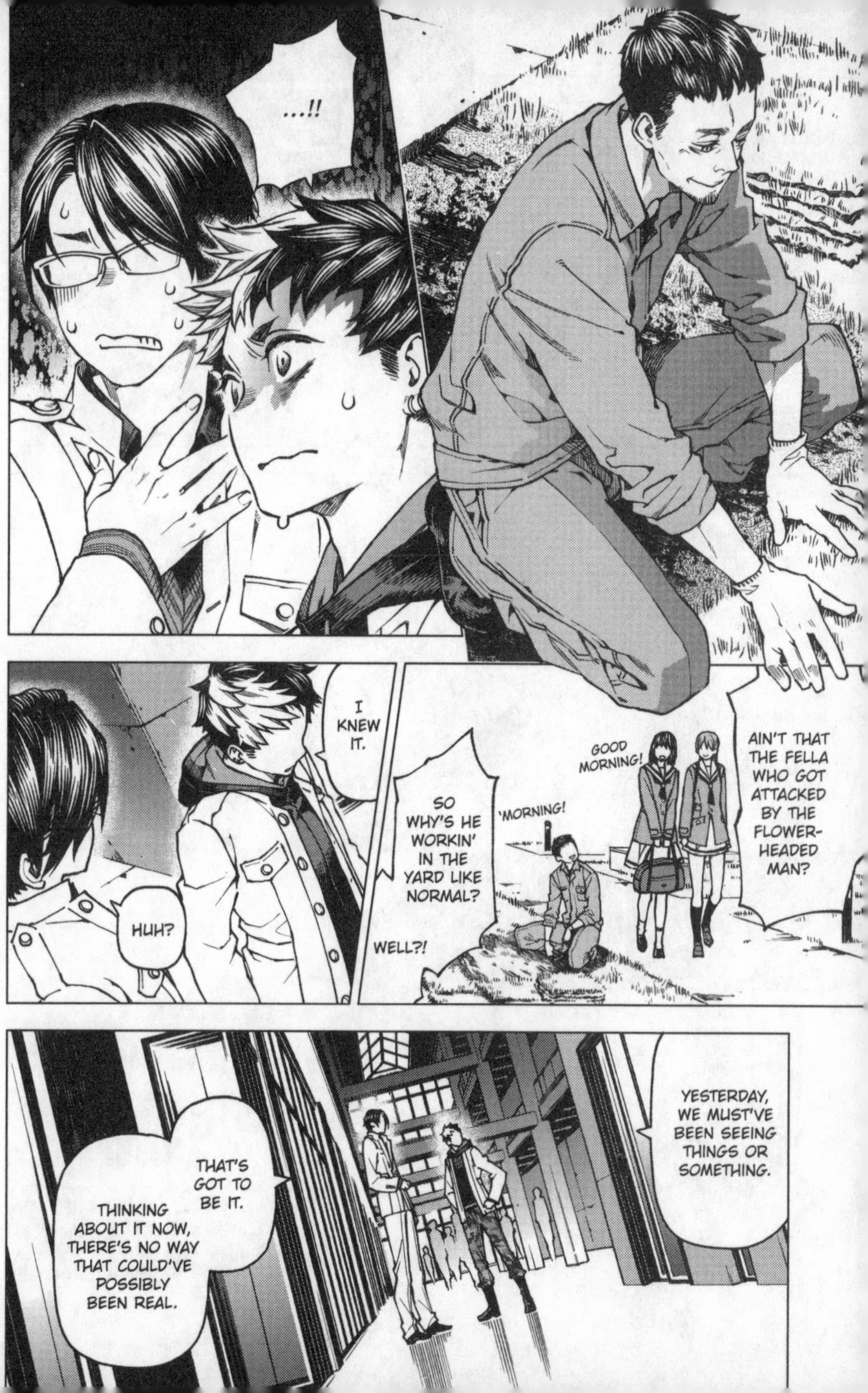
...!!
AIN'T THAT THE FELLA WHO GOT ATTACKED BY THE FLOWER-HEADED MAN?
GOOD MORNING!
'MORNING!
SO WHY'S HE WORKIN' IN THE YARD LIKE NORMAL?
WELL?!
I KNEW IT.
HUH?
YESTERDAY, WE MUST'VE BEEN SEEING THINGS OR SOMETHING.
THAT'S GOT TO BE IT.
THINKING ABOUT IT NOW, THERE'S NO WAY THAT COULD'VE POSSIBLY BEEN REAL.

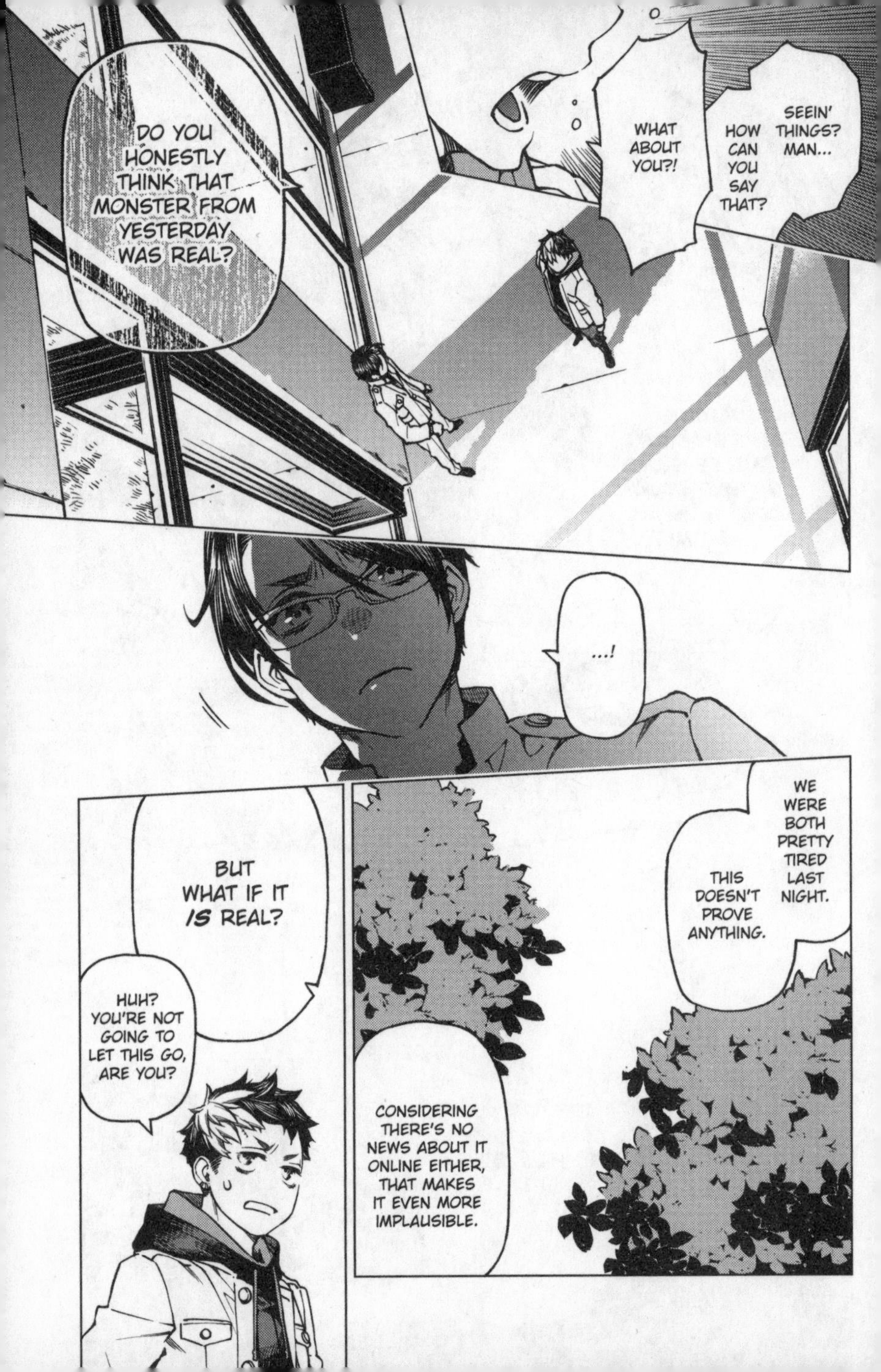
SEEIN' THINGS? MAN...
HOW CAN YOU SAY THAT?
WHAT ABOUT YOU?!
DO YOU HONESTLY THINK THAT MONSTER FROM YESTERDAY WAS REAL?
...!
WE WERE BOTH PRETTY TIRED LAST NIGHT.
THIS DOESN'T PROVE ANYTHING.
CONSIDERING THERE'S NO NEWS ABOUT IT ONLINE EITHER, THAT MAKES IT EVEN MORE IMPLAUSIBLE.
BUT WHAT IF IT *IS* REAL?
HUH? YOU'RE NOT GOING TO LET THIS GO, ARE YOU?

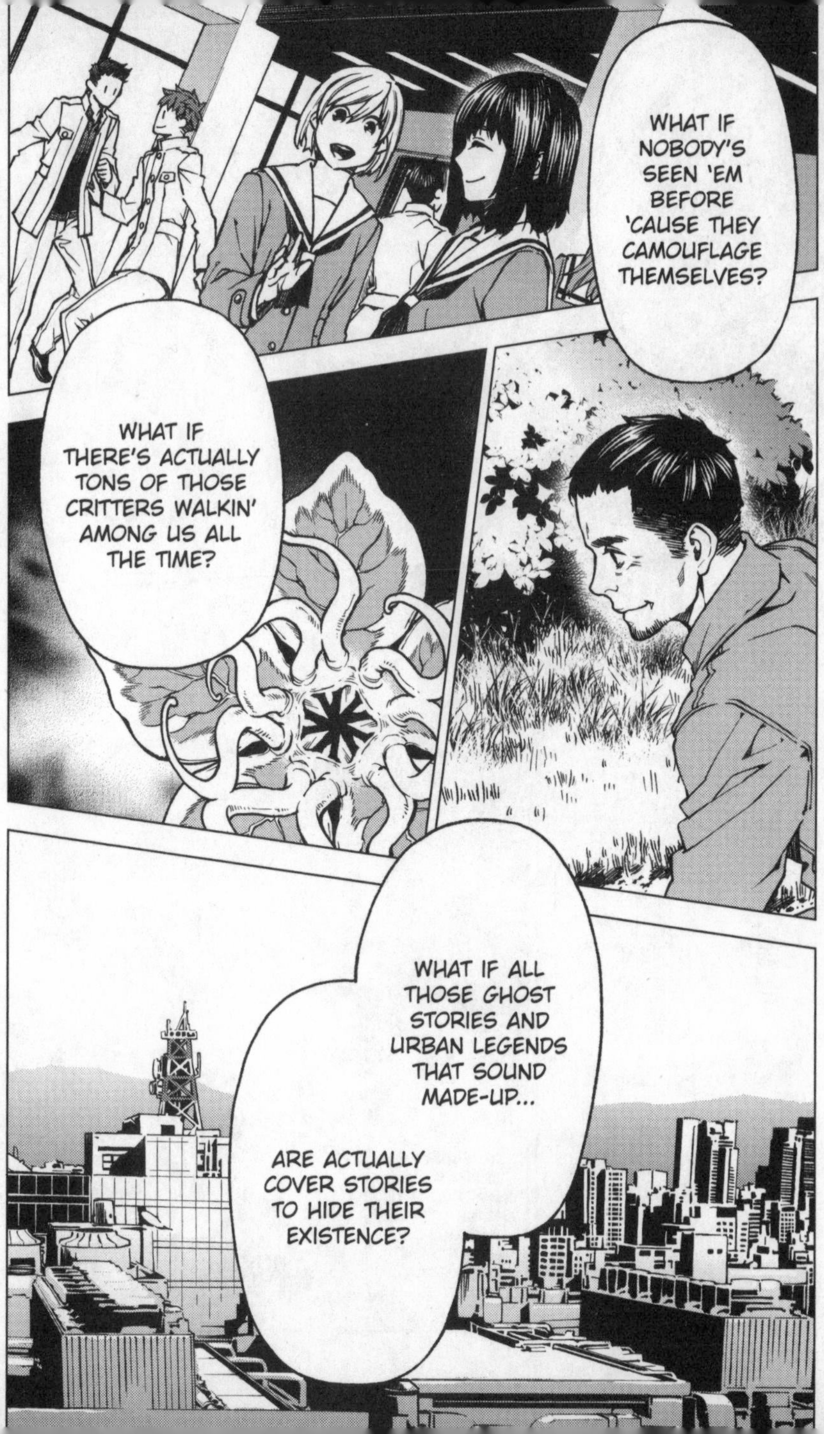
WHAT IF NOBODY'S SEEN 'EM BEFORE 'CAUSE THEY CAMOUFLAGE THEMSELVES?
WHAT IF THERE'S ACTUALLY TONS OF THOSE CRITTERS WALKIN' AMONG US ALL THE TIME?
WHAT IF ALL THOSE GHOST STORIES AND URBAN LEGENDS THAT SOUND MADE-UP...
ARE ACTUALLY COVER STORIES TO HIDE THEIR EXISTENCE?

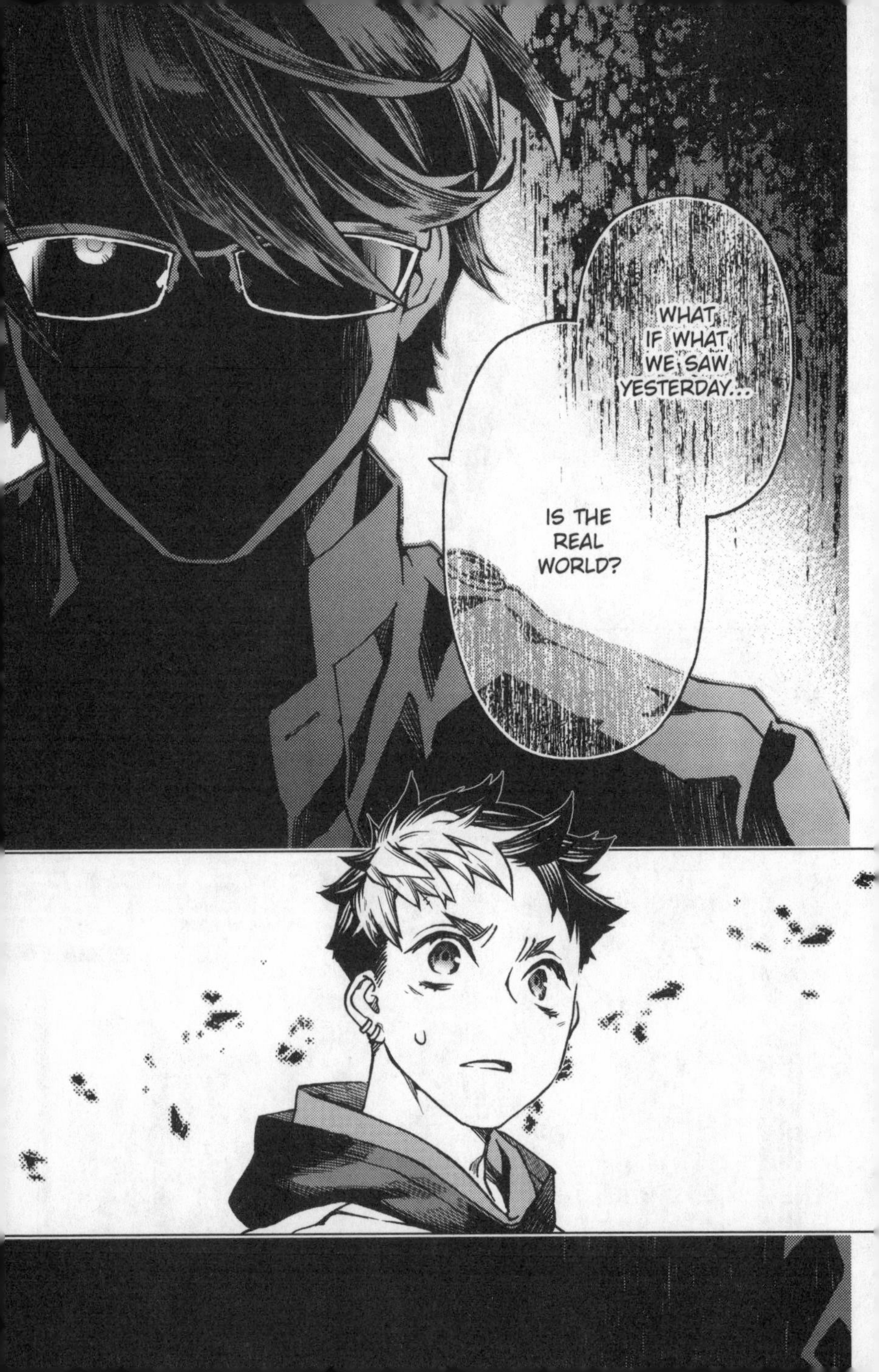
WHAT IF WHAT WE SAW YESTERDAY...
IS THE REAL WORLD?

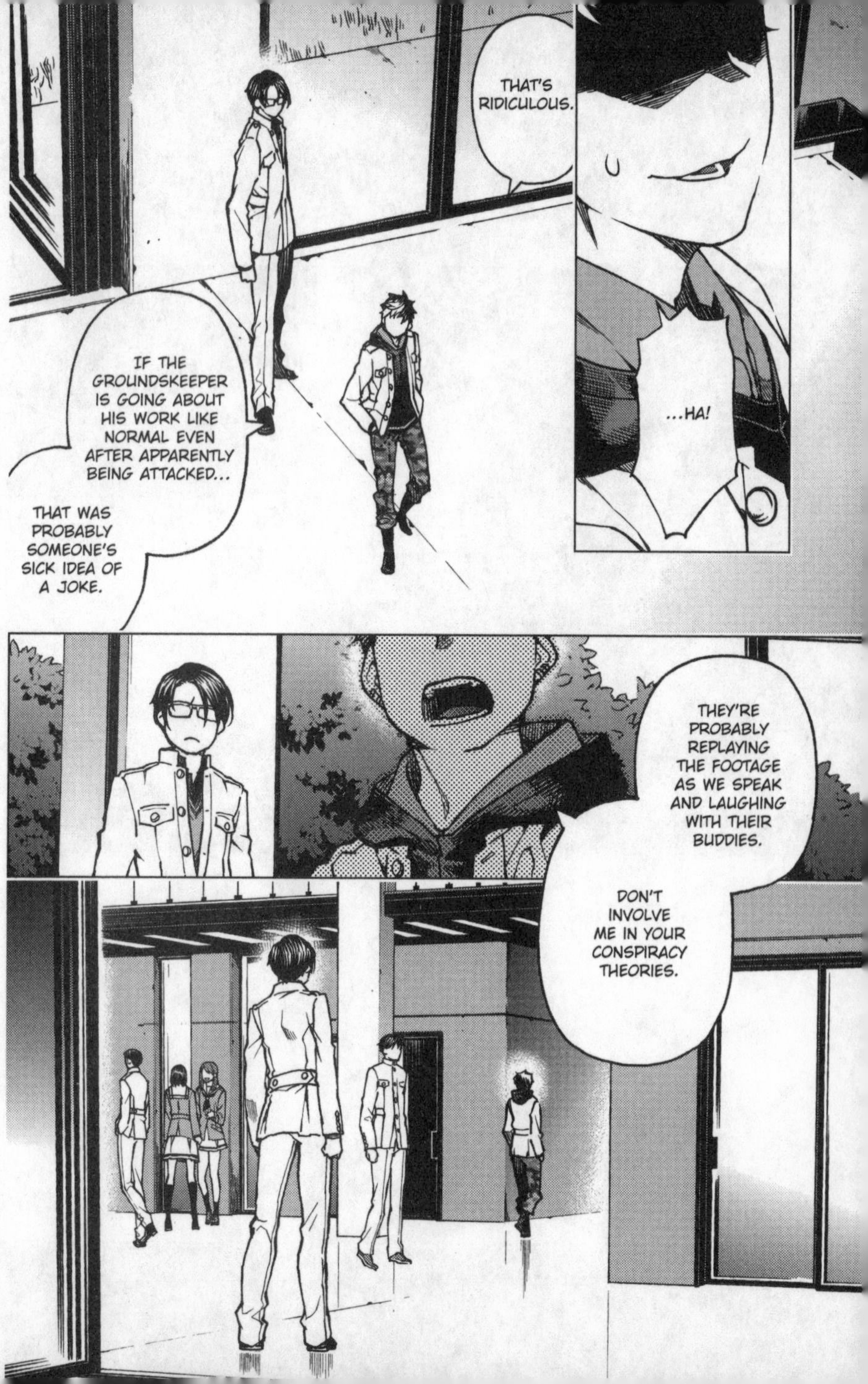
...HA!
THAT'S RIDICULOUS.
IF THE GROUNDSKEEPER IS GOING ABOUT HIS WORK LIKE NORMAL EVEN AFTER APPARENTLY BEING ATTACKED...
THAT WAS PROBABLY SOMEONE'S SICK IDEA OF A JOKE.
THEY'RE PROBABLY REPLAYING THE FOOTAGE AS WE SPEAK AND LAUGHING WITH THEIR BUDDIES.
DON'T INVOLVE ME IN YOUR CONSPIRACY THEORIES.

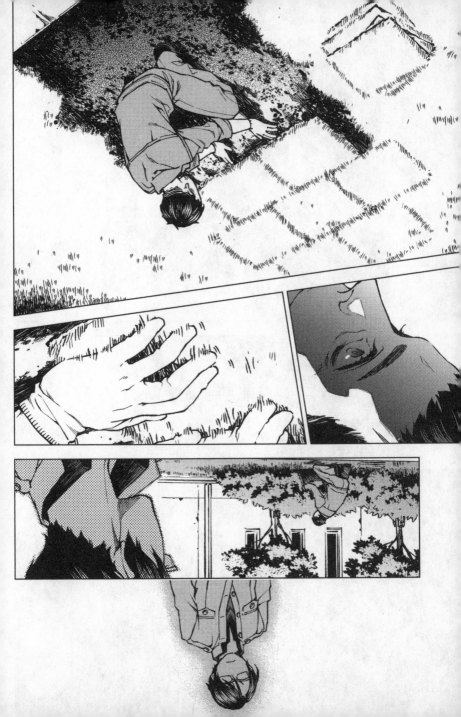

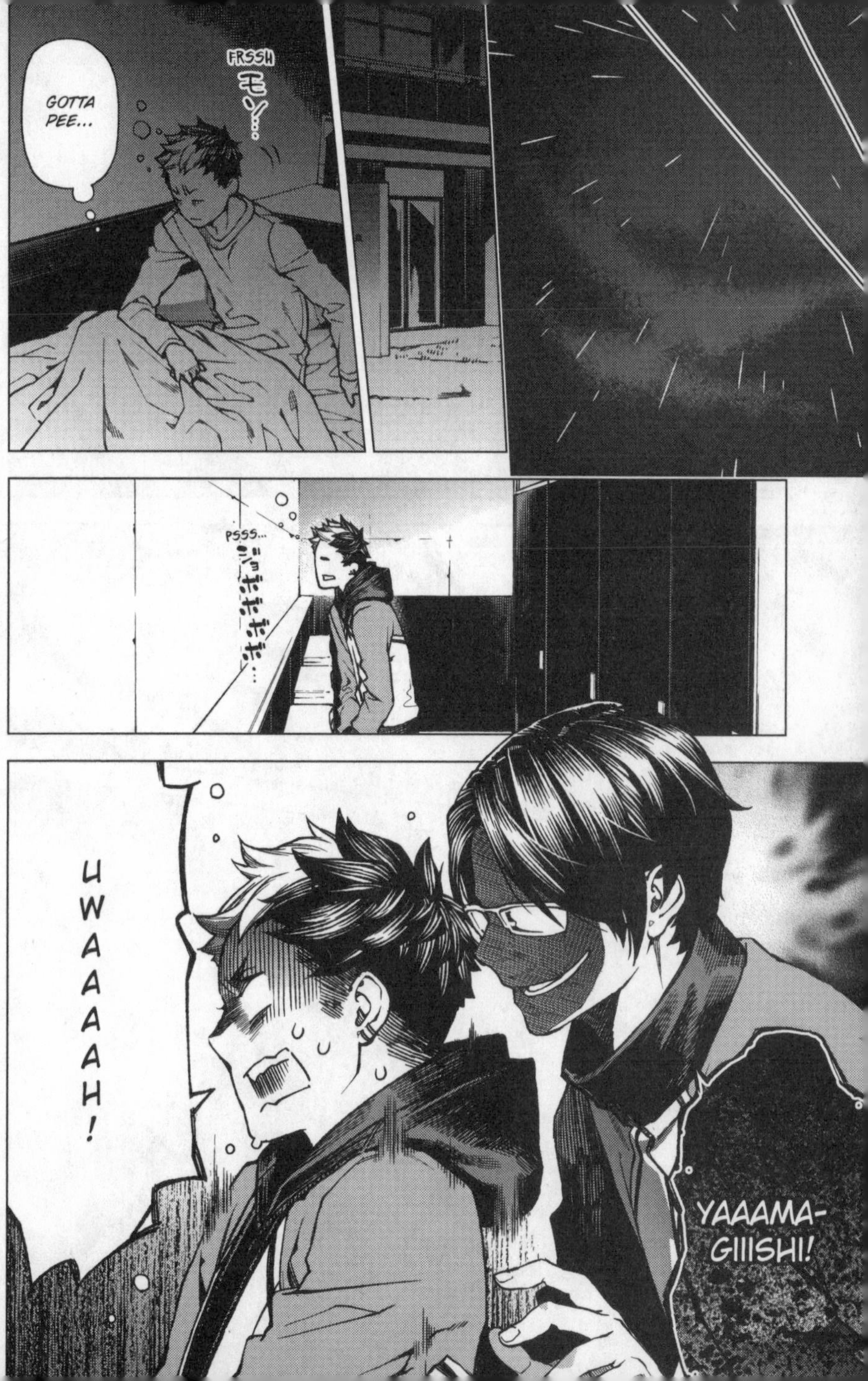
FRSSH
モソ…
GOTTA PEE...
PSSS...
ジョボボボボ…
YAAAMA-GIIISHI!
UWAAAAAH!

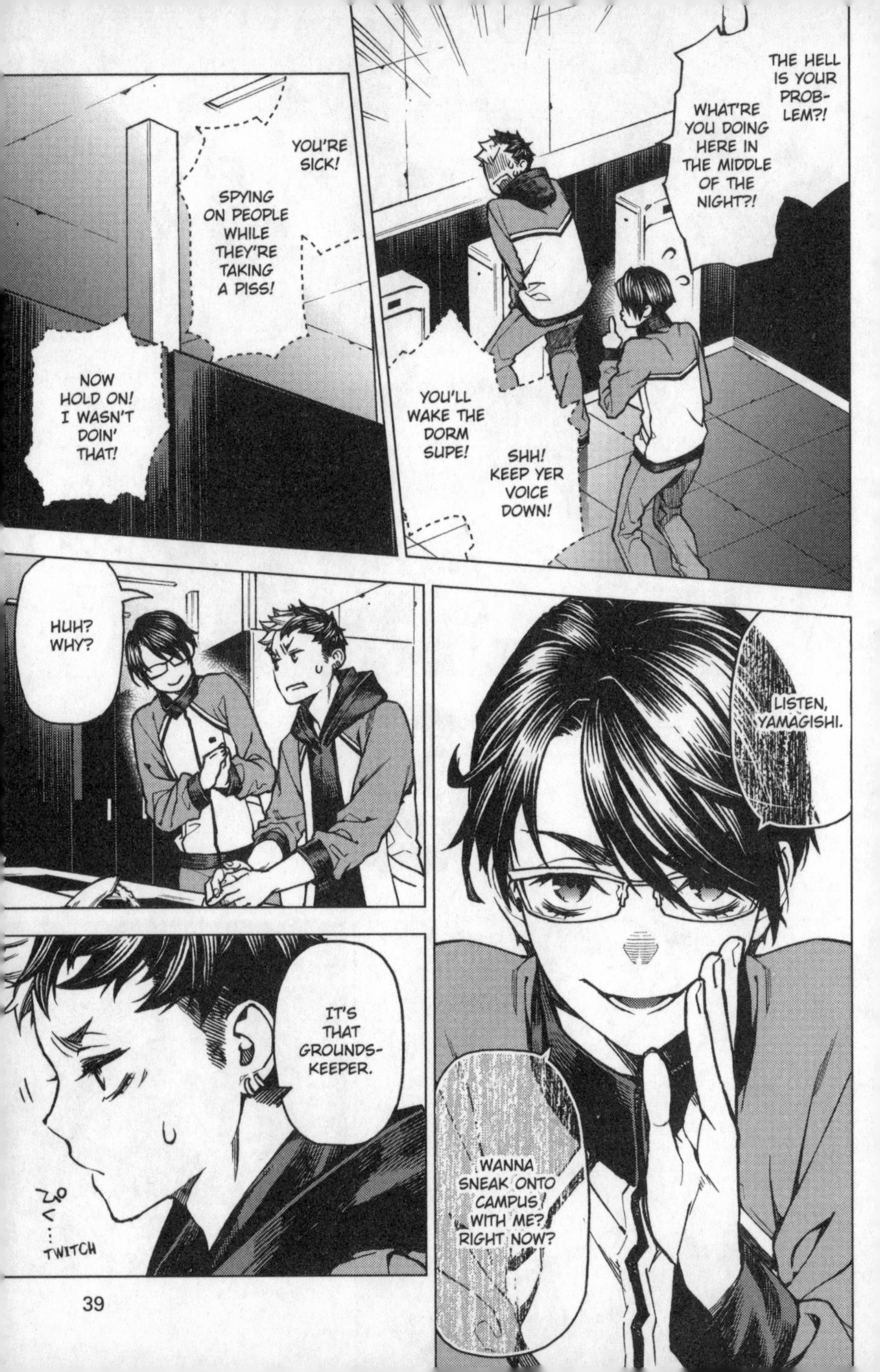
THE HELL IS YOUR PROB- LEM?!
WHAT'RE YOU DOING HERE IN THE MIDDLE OF THE NIGHT?!
YOU'LL WAKE THE DORM SUPE!
SHH! KEEP YER VOICE DOWN!
YOU'RE SICK!
SPYING ON PEOPLE WHILE THEY'RE TAKING A PISS!
NOW HOLD ON! I WASN'T DOIN' THAT!
LISTEN, YAMAGISHI.
WANNA SNEAK ONTO CAMPUS WITH ME? RIGHT NOW?
HUH? WHY?
IT'S THAT GROUNDS- KEEPER.
TWITCH

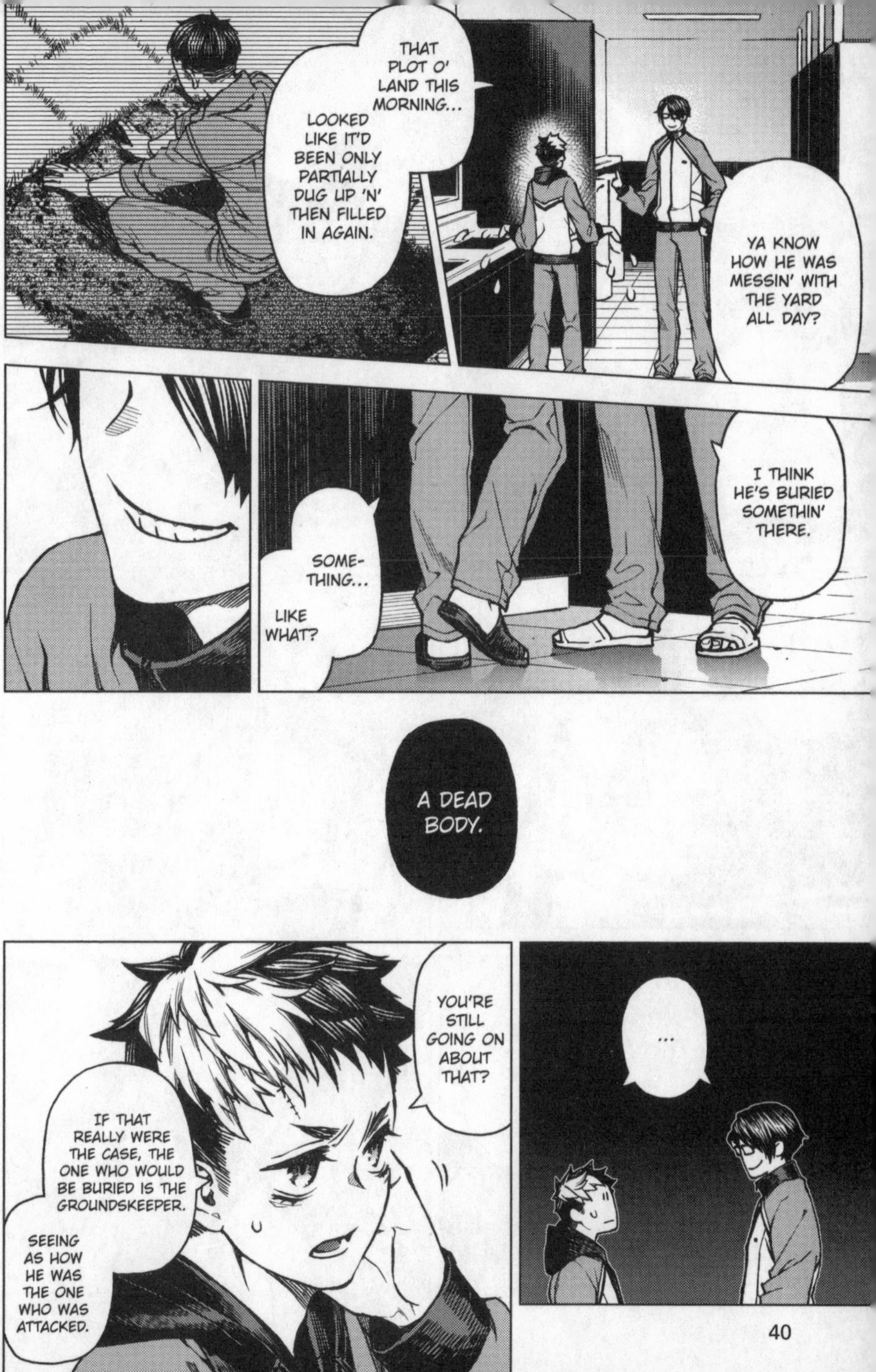
YA KNOW HOW HE WAS MESSIN' WITH THE YARD ALL DAY?
THAT PLOT O' LAND THIS MORNING...
LOOKED LIKE IT'D BEEN ONLY PARTIALLY DUG UP 'N' THEN FILLED IN AGAIN.
I THINK HE'S BURIED SOMETHIN' THERE.
SOME-THING...
LIKE WHAT?
A DEAD BODY.
...
YOU'RE STILL GOING ON ABOUT THAT?
IF THAT REALLY WERE THE CASE, THE ONE WHO WOULD BE BURIED IS THE GROUNDSKEEPER.
SEEING AS HOW HE WAS THE ONE WHO WAS ATTACKED.

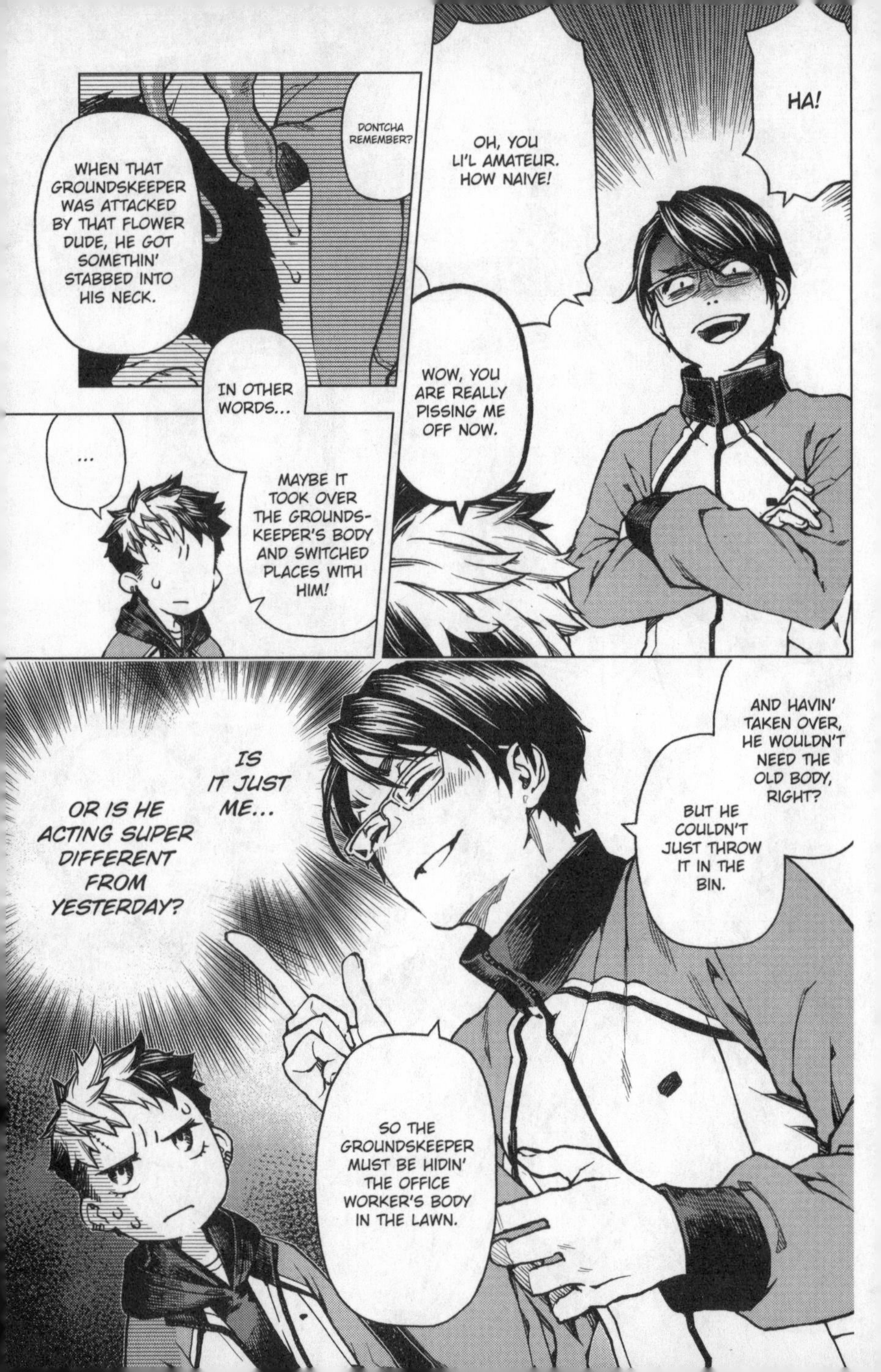
HA!
OH, YOU LI'L AMATEUR. HOW NAIVE!
WOW, YOU ARE REALLY PISSING ME OFF NOW.
DONTCHA REMEMBER?
WHEN THAT GROUNDSKEEPER WAS ATTACKED BY THAT FLOWER DUDE, HE GOT SOMETHIN' STABBED INTO HIS NECK.
IN OTHER WORDS...
MAYBE IT TOOK OVER THE GROUNDS-KEEPER'S BODY AND SWITCHED PLACES WITH HIM!
...
AND HAVIN' TAKEN OVER, HE WOULDN'T NEED THE OLD BODY, RIGHT?
BUT HE COULDN'T JUST THROW IT IN THE BIN.
IS IT JUST ME...
OR IS HE ACTING SUPER DIFFERENT FROM YESTERDAY?
SO THE GROUNDSKEEPER MUST BE HIDIN' THE OFFICE WORKER'S BODY IN THE LAWN.

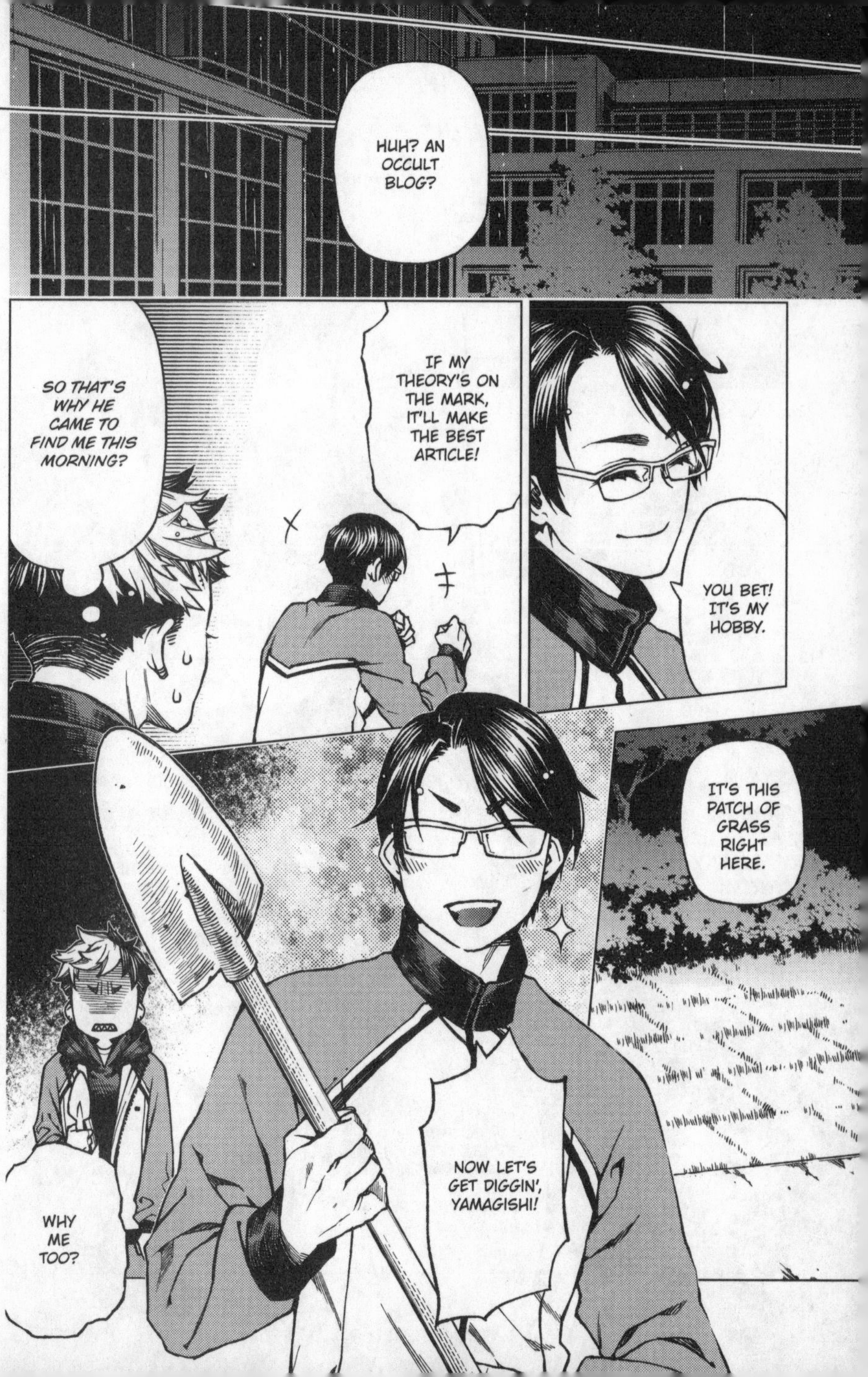
HUH? AN OCCULT BLOG?
YOU BET! IT'S MY HOBBY.
IF MY THEORY'S ON THE MARK, IT'LL MAKE THE BEST ARTICLE!
SO THAT'S WHY HE CAME TO FIND ME THIS MORNING?
IT'S THIS PATCH OF GRASS RIGHT HERE.
NOW LET'S GET DIGGIN', YAMAGISHI!
WHY ME TOO?

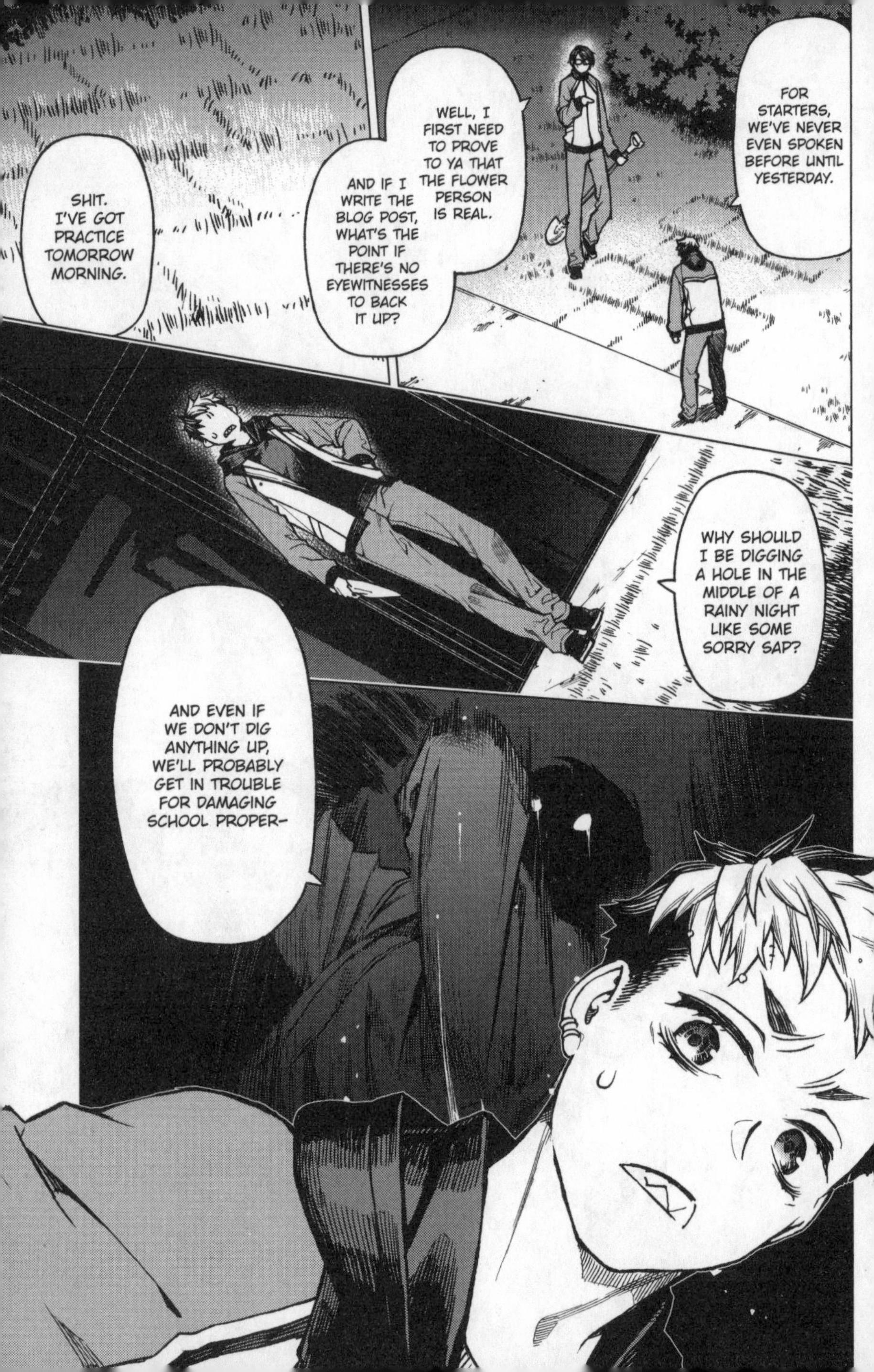
FOR STARTERS, WE'VE NEVER EVEN SPOKEN BEFORE UNTIL YESTERDAY.
WELL, I FIRST NEED TO PROVE TO YA THAT THE FLOWER PERSON IS REAL.
AND IF I WRITE THE BLOG POST, WHAT'S THE POINT IF THERE'S NO EYEWITNESSES TO BACK IT UP?
SHIT. I'VE GOT PRACTICE TOMORROW MORNING.
WHY SHOULD I BE DIGGING A HOLE IN THE MIDDLE OF A RAINY NIGHT LIKE SOME SORRY SAP?
AND EVEN IF WE DON'T DIG ANYTHING UP, WE'LL PROBABLY GET IN TROUBLE FOR DAMAGING SCHOOL PROPER-

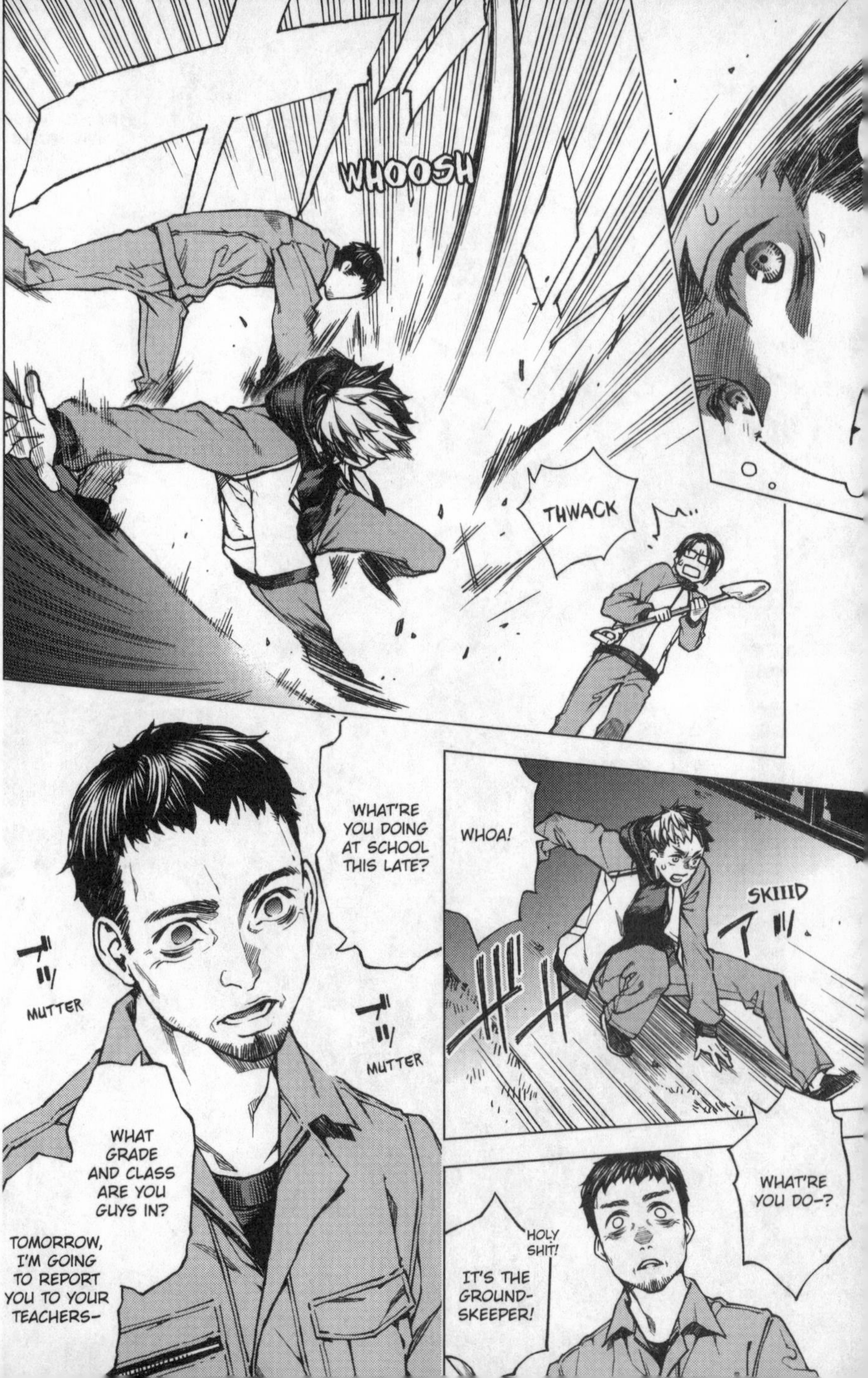
WHOOSH
THWACK
...
WHOA!
SKIIID
WHAT'RE YOU DO-?
HOLY SHIT!
IT'S THE GROUND-SKEEPER!
WHAT'RE YOU DOING AT SCHOOL THIS LATE?
MUTTER
MUTTER
WHAT GRADE AND CLASS ARE YOU GUYS IN?
TOMORROW, I'M GOING TO REPORT YOU TO YOUR TEACHERS-

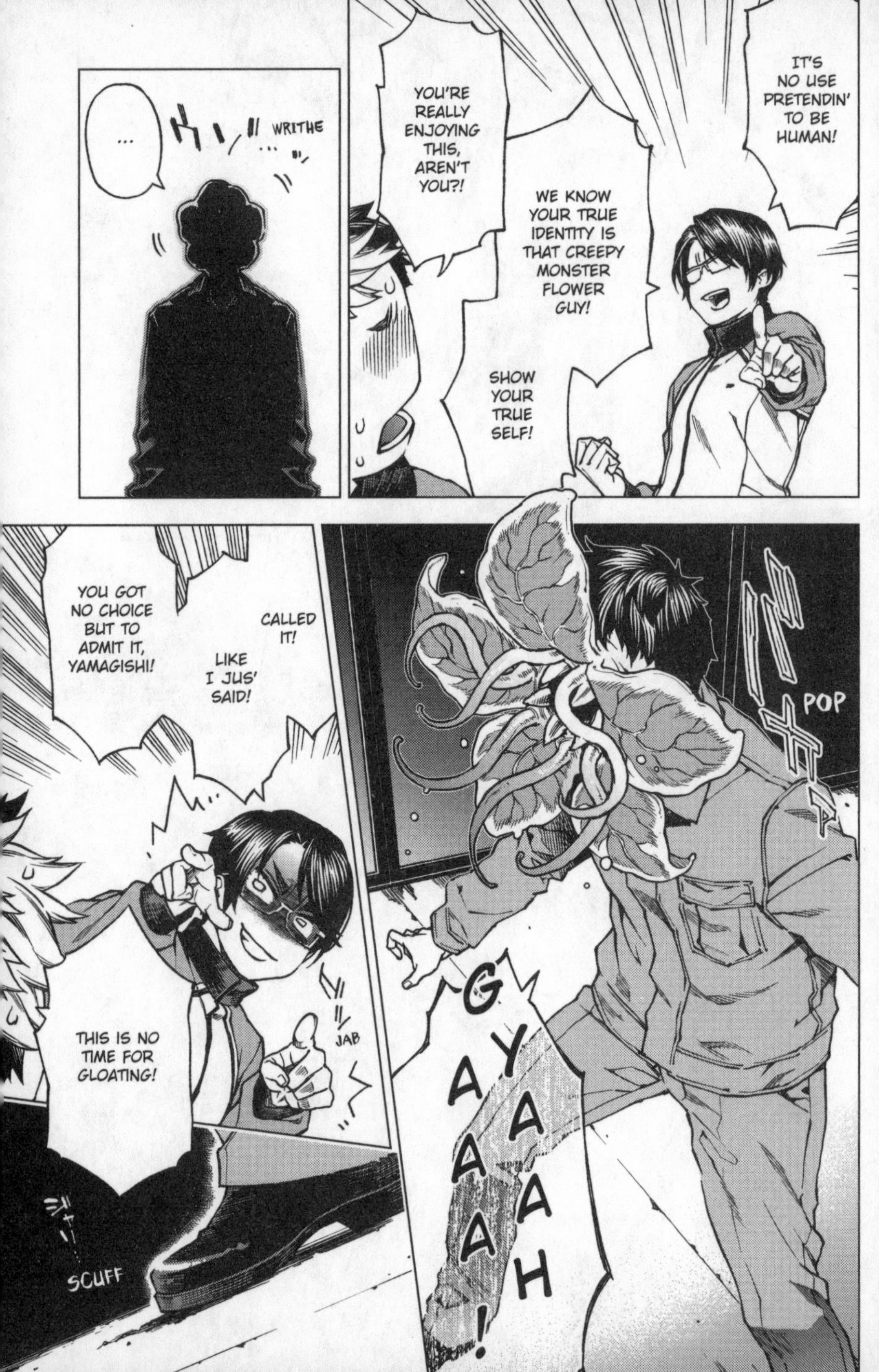
IT'S NO USE PRETENDIN' TO BE HUMAN!
WE KNOW YOUR TRUE IDENTITY IS THAT CREEPY MONSTER FLOWER GUY!
YOU'RE REALLY ENJOYING THIS, AREN'T YOU?!
SHOW YOUR TRUE SELF!
WRITHE
...
POP
GYAAAAAH!
YOU GOT NO CHOICE BUT TO ADMIT IT, YAMAGISHI!
CALLED IT!
LIKE I JUS' SAID!
JAB
THIS IS NO TIME FOR GLOATING!
SCUFF

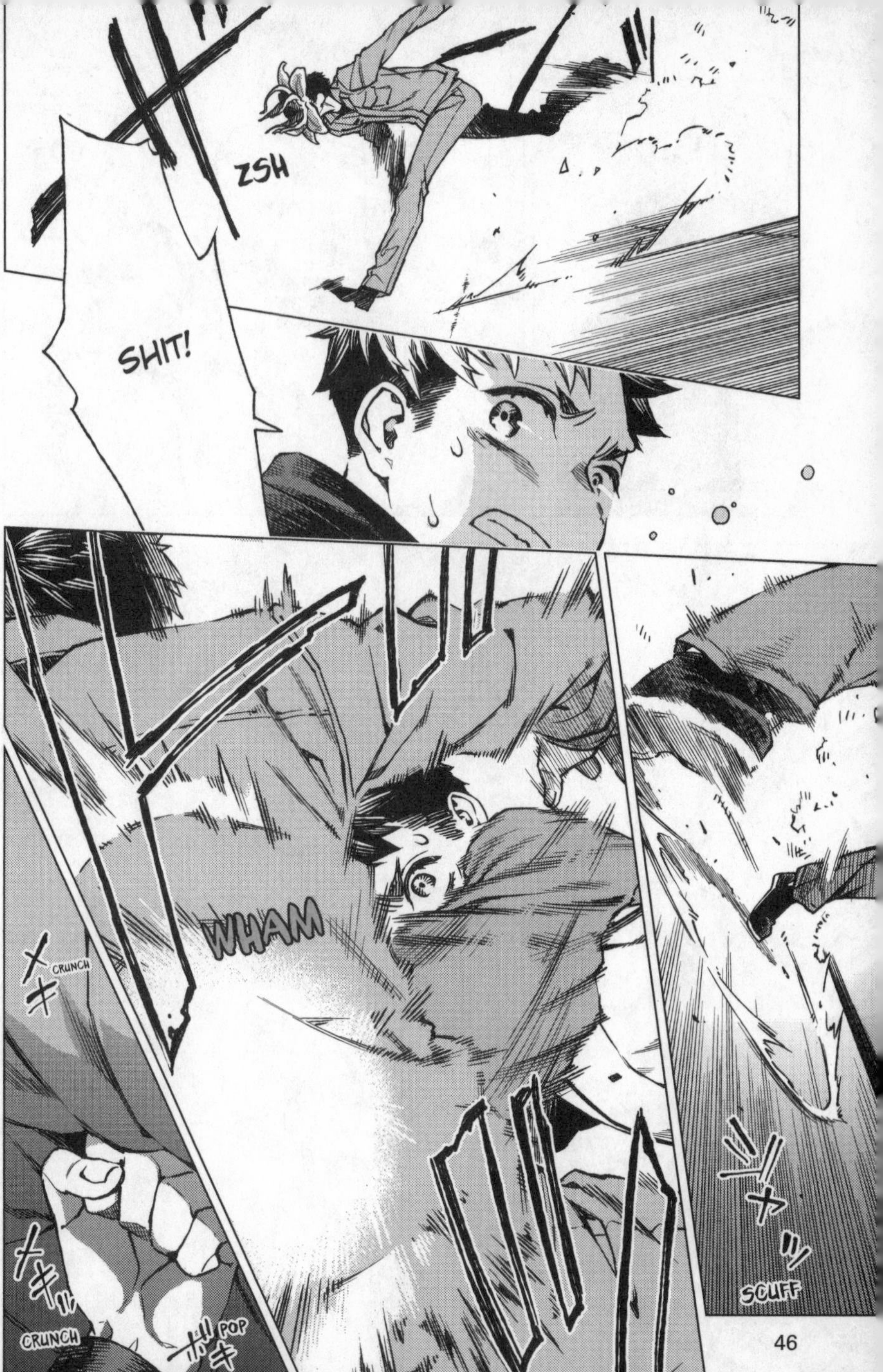
ZSH
SHIT!
SCUFF
WHAM
CRUNCH
CRUNCH
POP

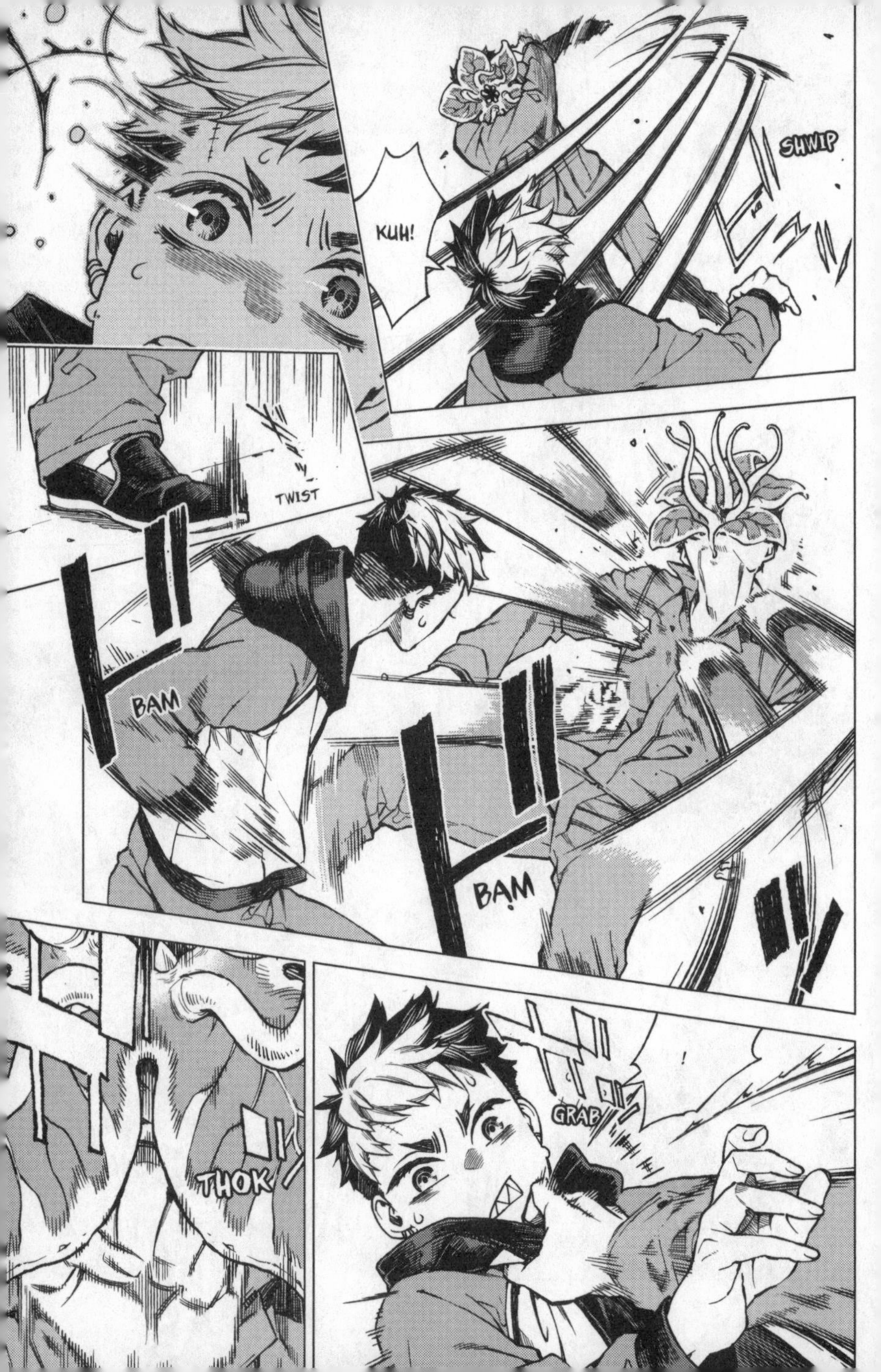
SHWIP
KUH!
BAM
BAM
TWIST
GRAB
THOK

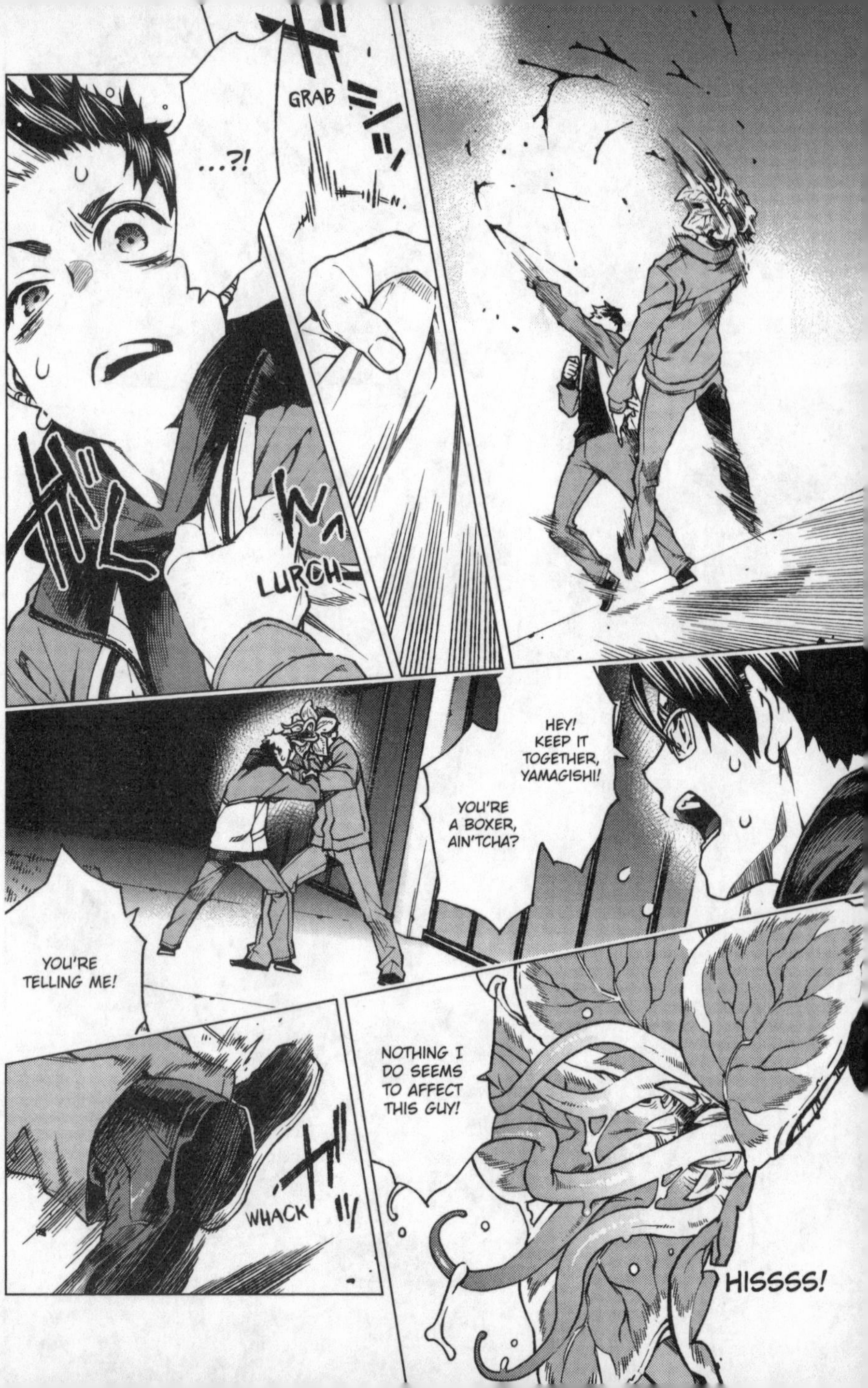
GRAB
...?!
LURCH
HEY! KEEP IT TOGETHER, YAMAGISHI!
YOU'RE A BOXER, AIN'TCHA?
YOU'RE TELLING ME!
NOTHING I DO SEEMS TO AFFECT THIS GUY!
HISSSS!
WHACK

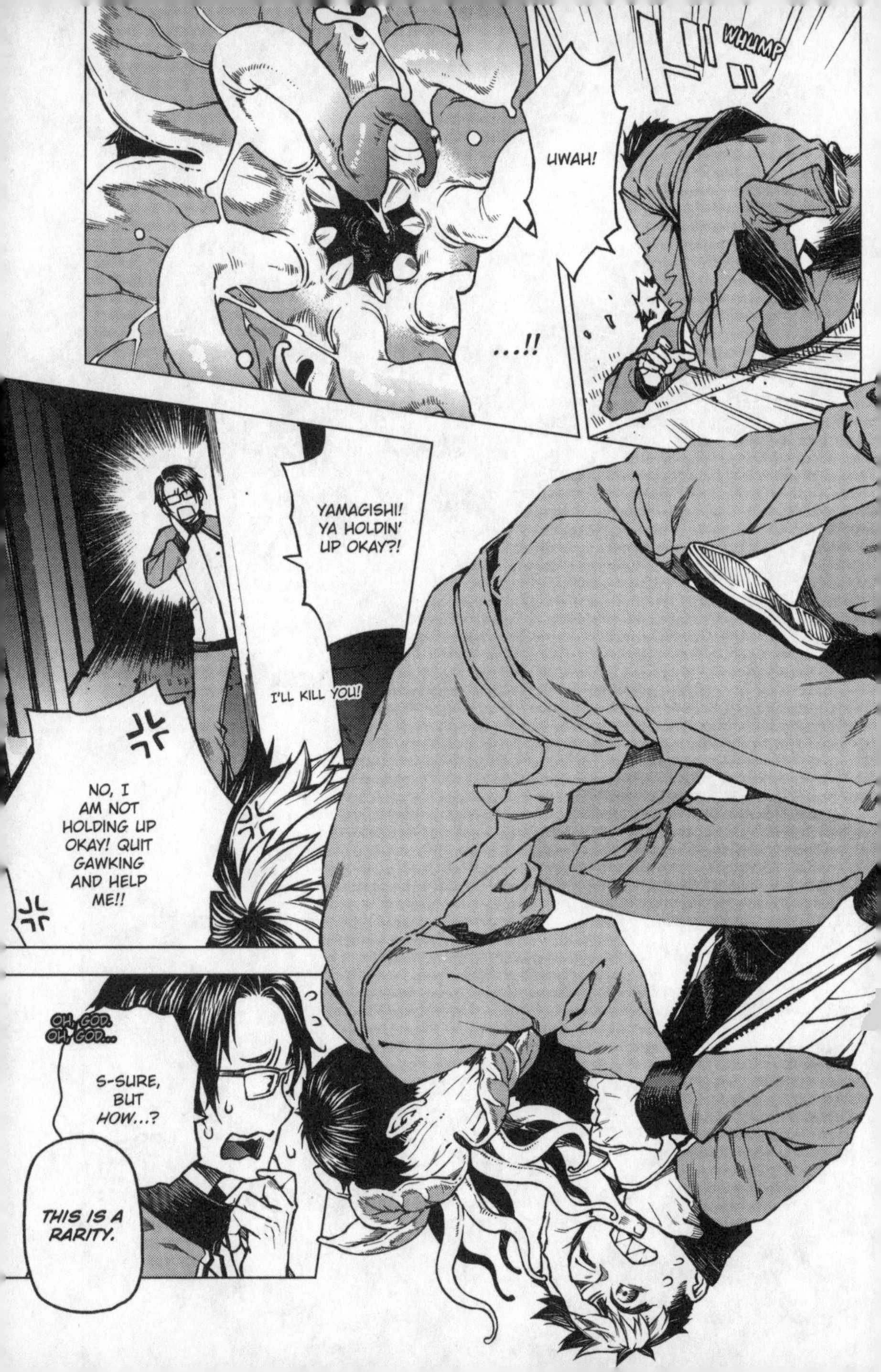
WHUMP
UWAH!
...!!
YAMAGISHI! YA HOLDIN' UP OKAY?!
I'LL KILL YOU!
NO, I AM NOT HOLDING UP OKAY! QUIT GAWKING AND HELP ME!!
OH, GOD. OH, GOD...
S-SURE, BUT HOW...?
THIS IS A RARITY.

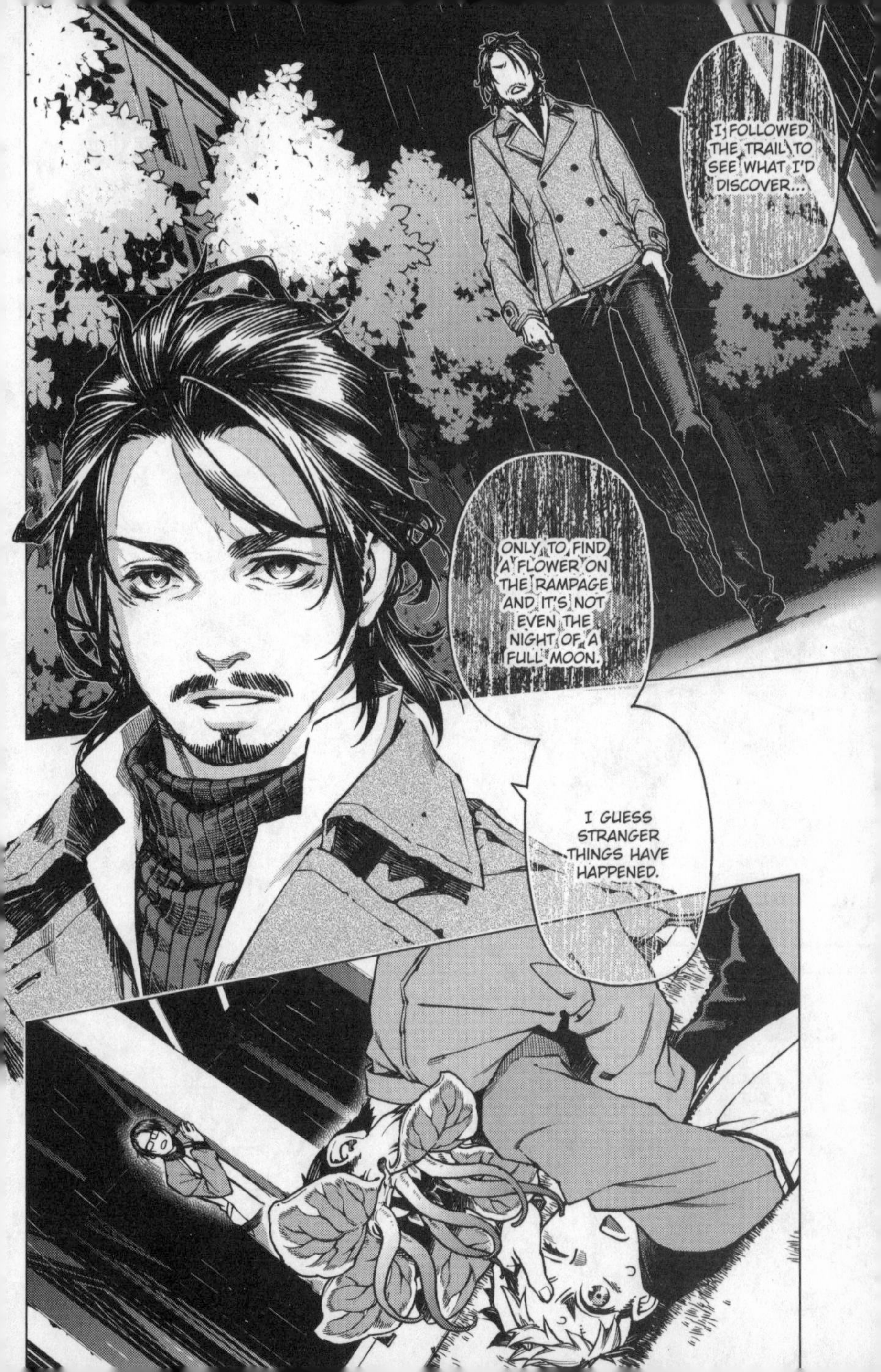
I FOLLOWED THE TRAIL TO SEE WHAT I'D DISCOVER...
ONLY TO FIND A FLOWER ON THE RAMPAGE AND IT'S NOT EVEN THE NIGHT OF A FULL MOON.
I GUESS STRANGER THINGS HAVE HAPPENED.

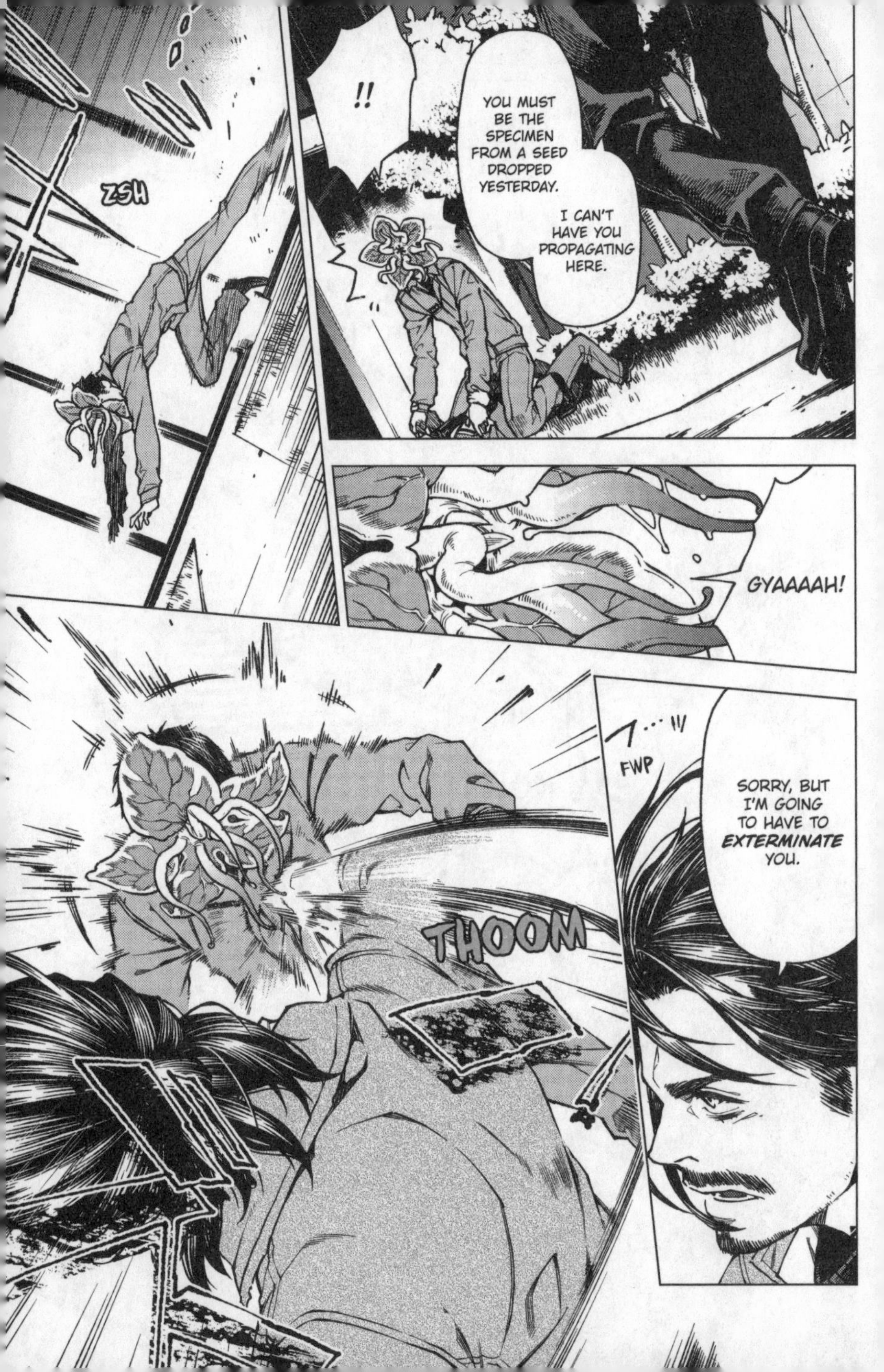
!!
YOU MUST BE THE SPECIMEN FROM A SEED DROPPED YESTERDAY.
I CAN'T HAVE YOU PROPAGATING HERE.
ZSH
GYAAAAH!
FWP
SORRY, BUT I'M GOING TO HAVE TO ***EXTERMINATE*** YOU.
THOOM

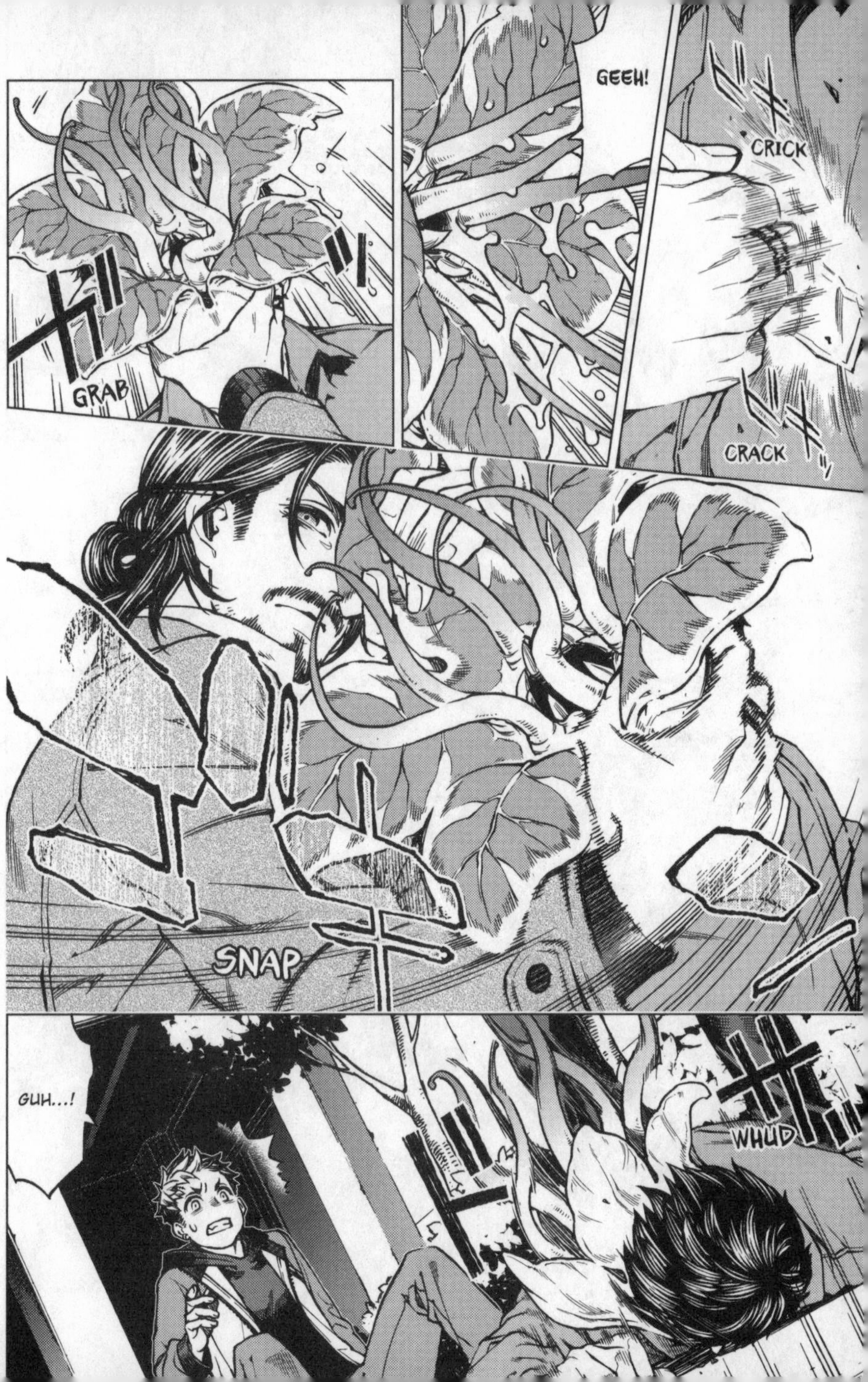
CRICK
CRACK
GEEH!
GRAB
SNAP
WHUD
GUH...!

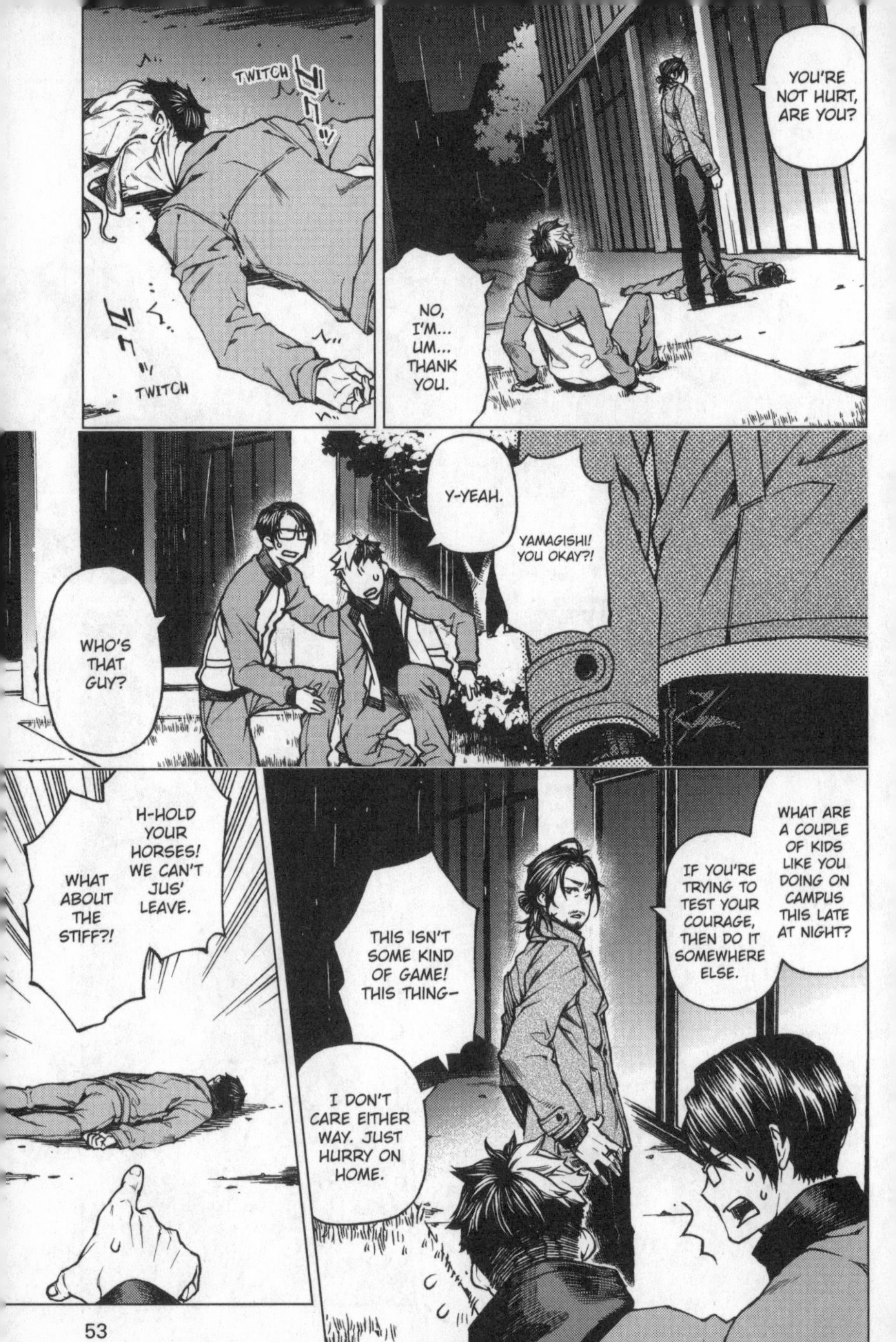
YOU'RE NOT HURT, ARE YOU?
NO, I'M... UM... THANK YOU.
TWITCH
TWITCH
YAMAGISHI! YOU OKAY?!
Y-YEAH.
WHO'S THAT GUY?
WHAT ARE A COUPLE OF KIDS LIKE YOU DOING ON CAMPUS THIS LATE AT NIGHT?
IF YOU'RE TRYING TO TEST YOUR COURAGE, THEN DO IT SOMEWHERE ELSE.
THIS ISN'T SOME KIND OF GAME! THIS THING–
I DON'T CARE EITHER WAY. JUST HURRY ON HOME.
H-HOLD YOUR HORSES! WE CAN'T JUS' LEAVE.
WHAT ABOUT THE STIFF?!

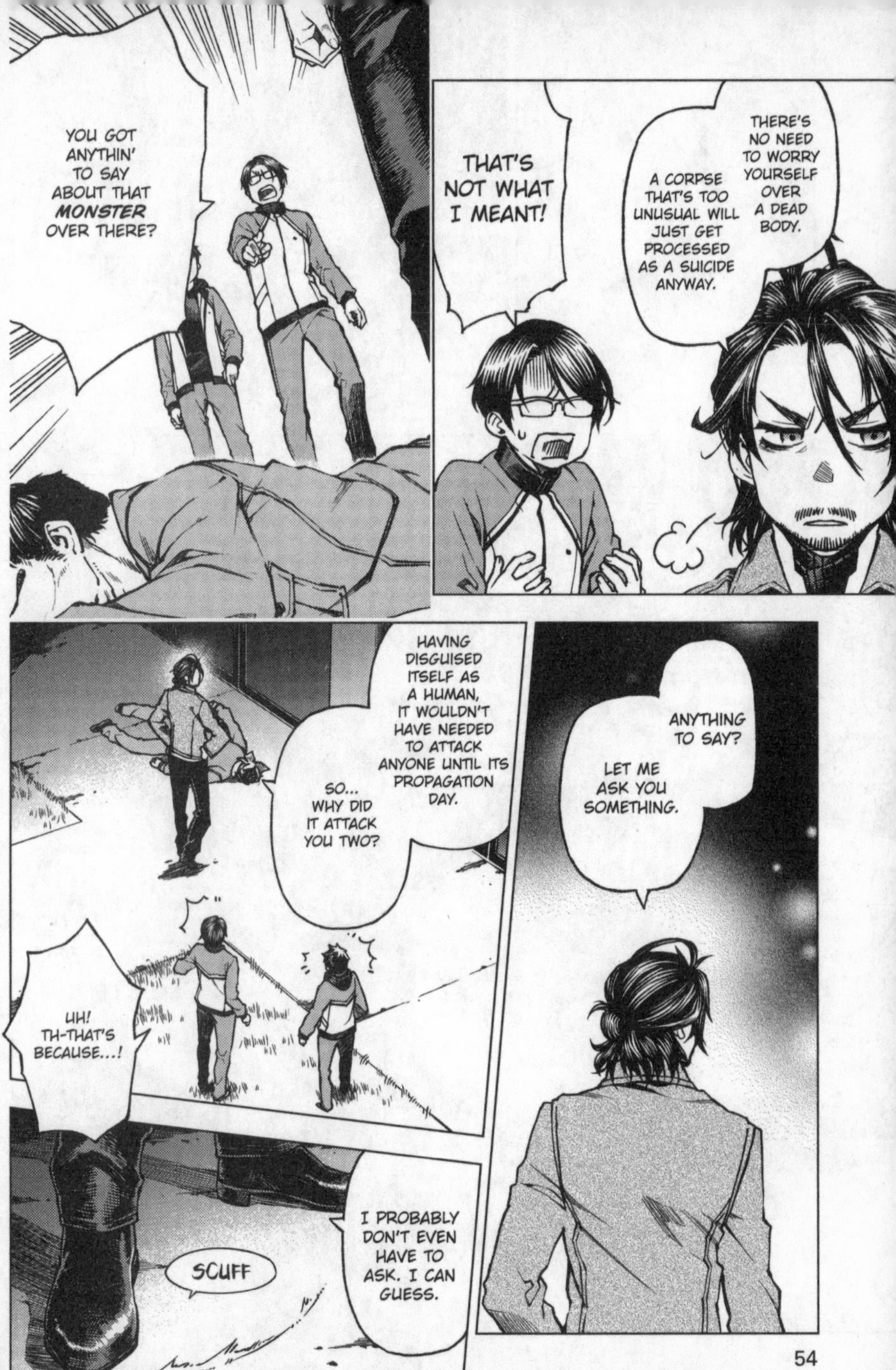
THERE'S NO NEED TO WORRY YOURSELF OVER A DEAD BODY.
A CORPSE THAT'S TOO UNUSUAL WILL JUST GET PROCESSED AS A SUICIDE ANYWAY.
THAT'S NOT WHAT I MEANT!
YOU GOT ANYTHIN' TO SAY ABOUT THAT **MONSTER** OVER THERE?
ANYTHING TO SAY?
LET ME ASK YOU SOMETHING.
HAVING DISGUISED ITSELF AS A HUMAN, IT WOULDN'T HAVE NEEDED TO ATTACK ANYONE UNTIL ITS PROPAGATION DAY.
SO... WHY DID IT ATTACK YOU TWO?
UH! TH-THAT'S BECAUSE...!
I PROBABLY DON'T EVEN HAVE TO ASK. I CAN GUESS.
SCUFF

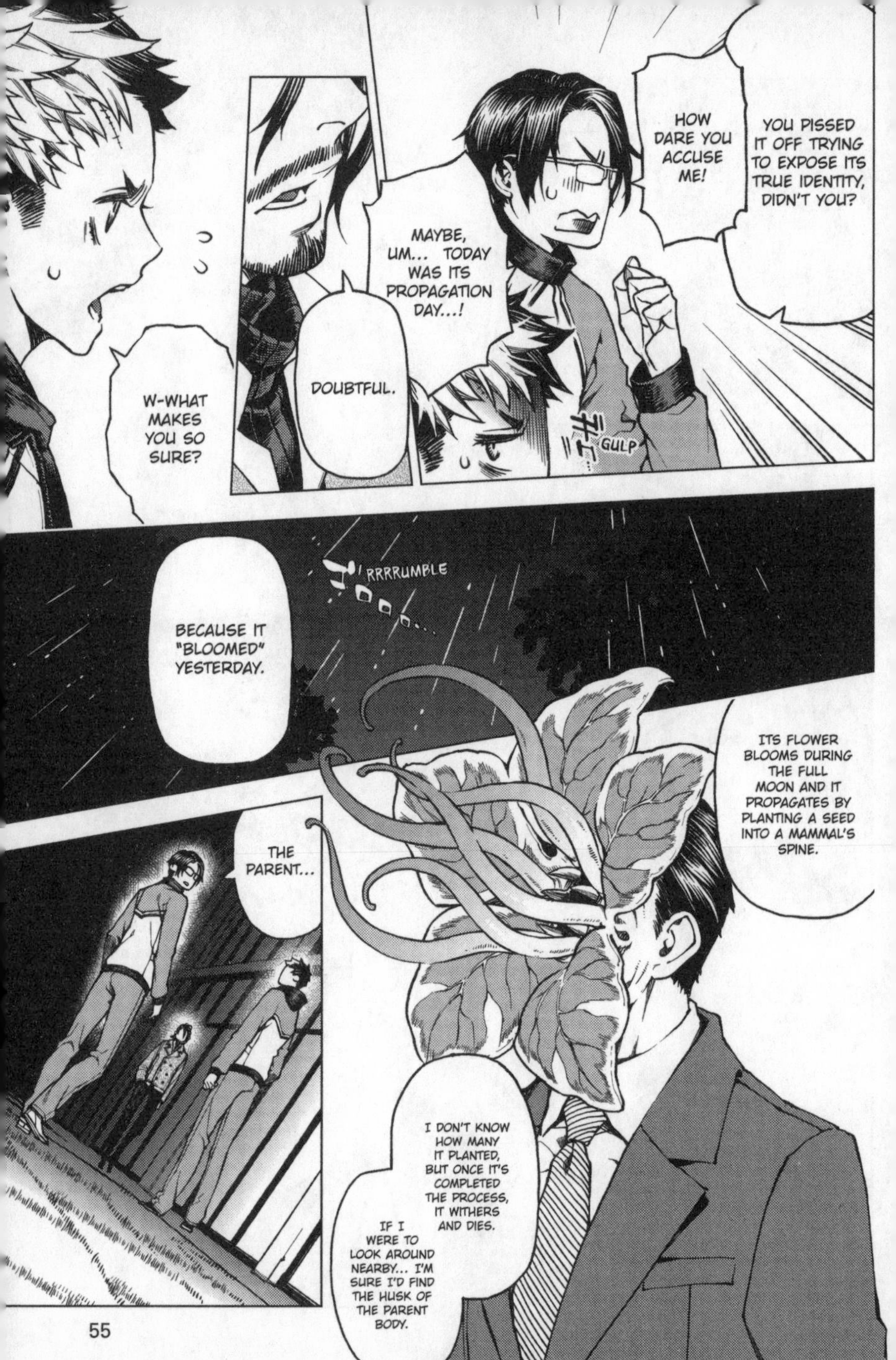
YOU PISSED IT OFF TRYING TO EXPOSE ITS TRUE IDENTITY, DIDN'T YOU?
HOW DARE YOU ACCUSE ME!
GULP
MAYBE, UM... TODAY WAS ITS PROPAGATION DAY...!
DOUBTFUL.
W-WHAT MAKES YOU SO SURE?
RRRRUMBLE
BECAUSE IT "BLOOMED" YESTERDAY.
ITS FLOWER BLOOMS DURING THE FULL MOON AND IT PROPAGATES BY PLANTING A SEED INTO A MAMMAL'S SPINE.
THE PARENT...
I DON'T KNOW HOW MANY IT PLANTED, BUT ONCE IT'S COMPLETED THE PROCESS, IT WITHERS AND DIES.
IF I WERE TO LOOK AROUND NEARBY... I'M SURE I'D FIND THE HUSK OF THE PARENT BODY.

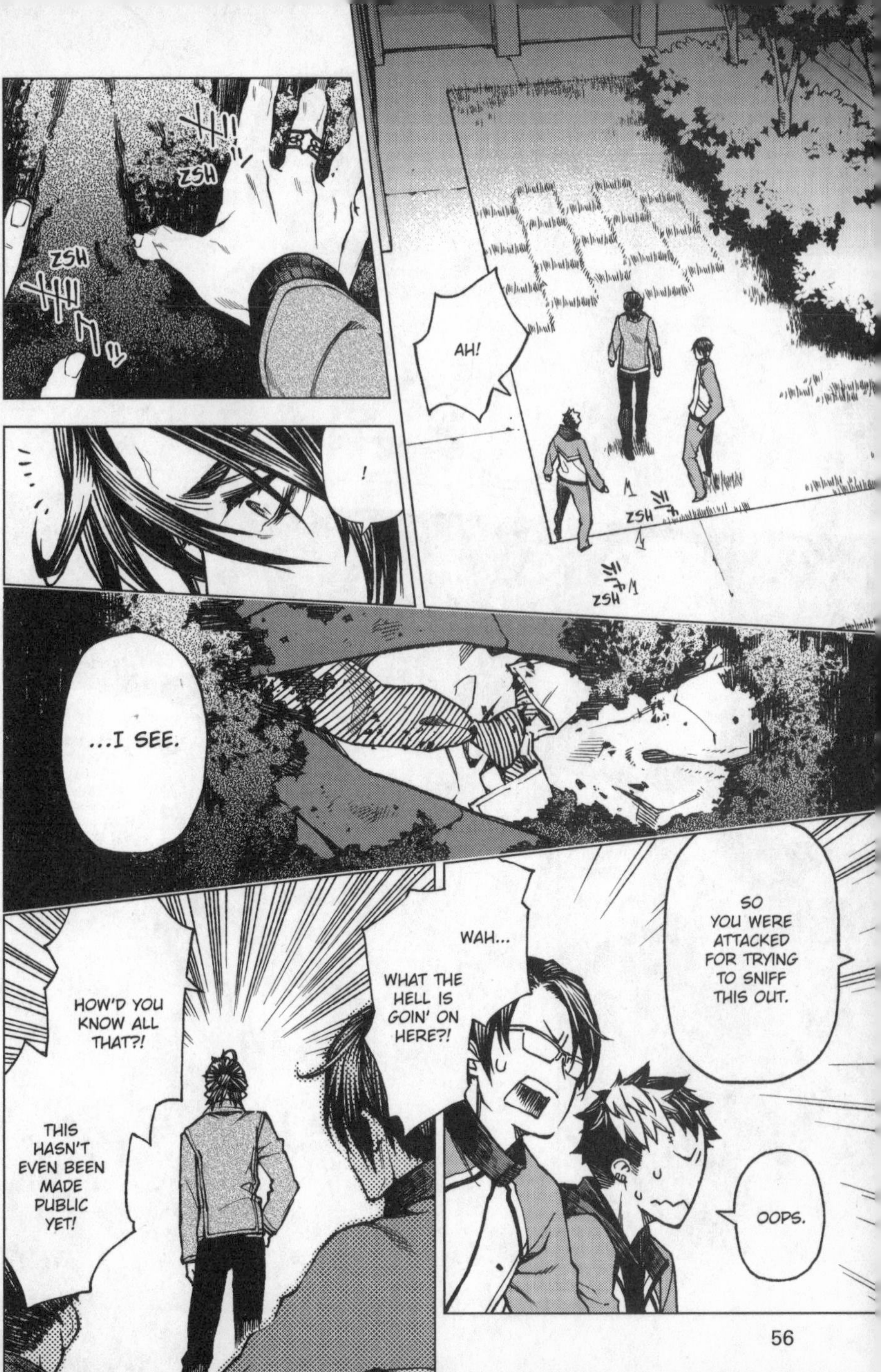
AH!
ZSH
ZSH
ZSH
ZSH
!
...I SEE.
SO YOU WERE ATTACKED FOR TRYING TO SNIFF THIS OUT.
WAH...
WHAT THE HELL IS GOIN' ON HERE?!
OOPS.
HOW'D YOU KNOW ALL THAT?!
THIS HASN'T EVEN BEEN MADE PUBLIC YET!

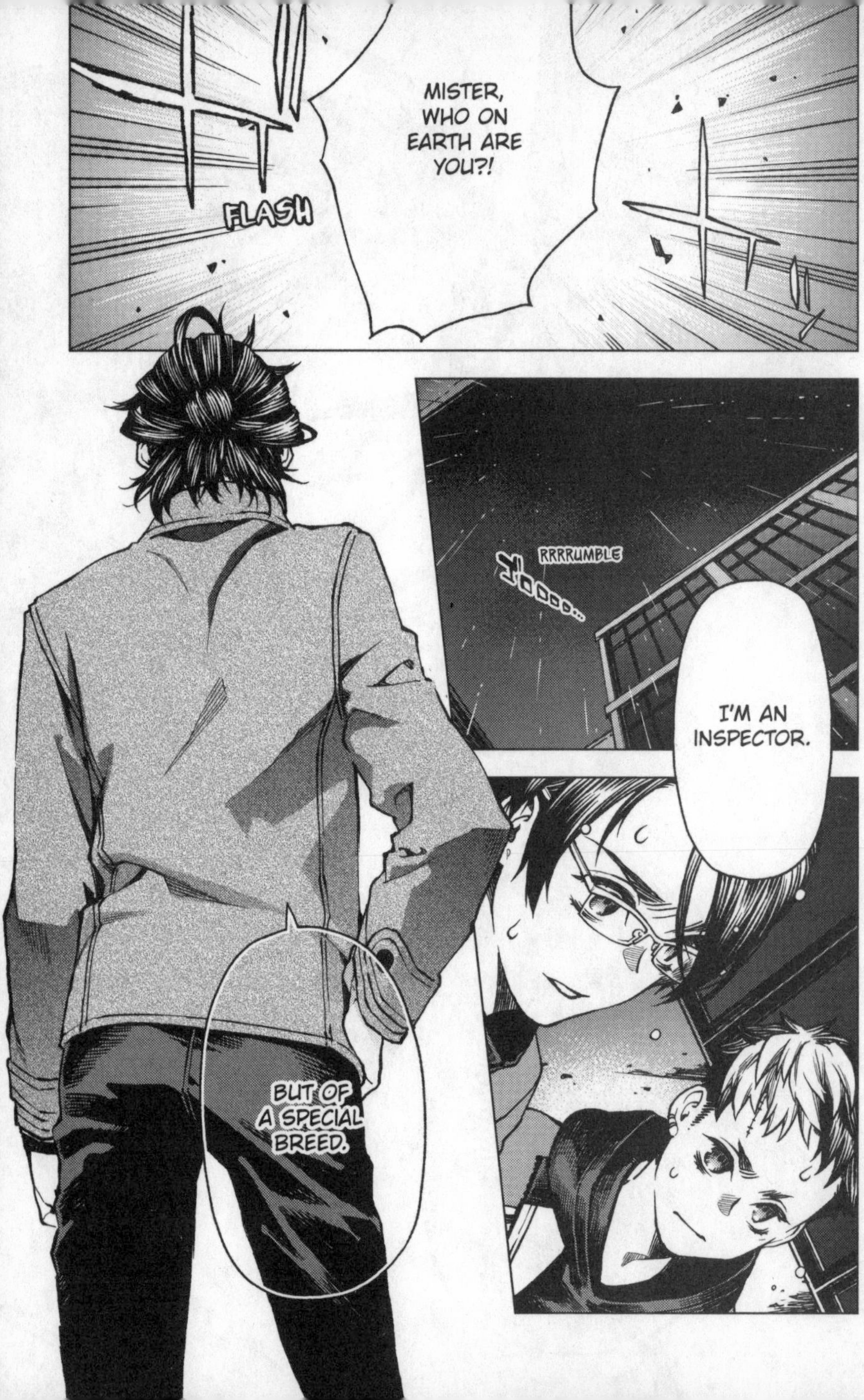
MISTER, WHO ON EARTH ARE YOU?!
FLASH
RRRRUMBLE
I'M AN INSPECTOR.
BUT OF A SPECIAL BREED.

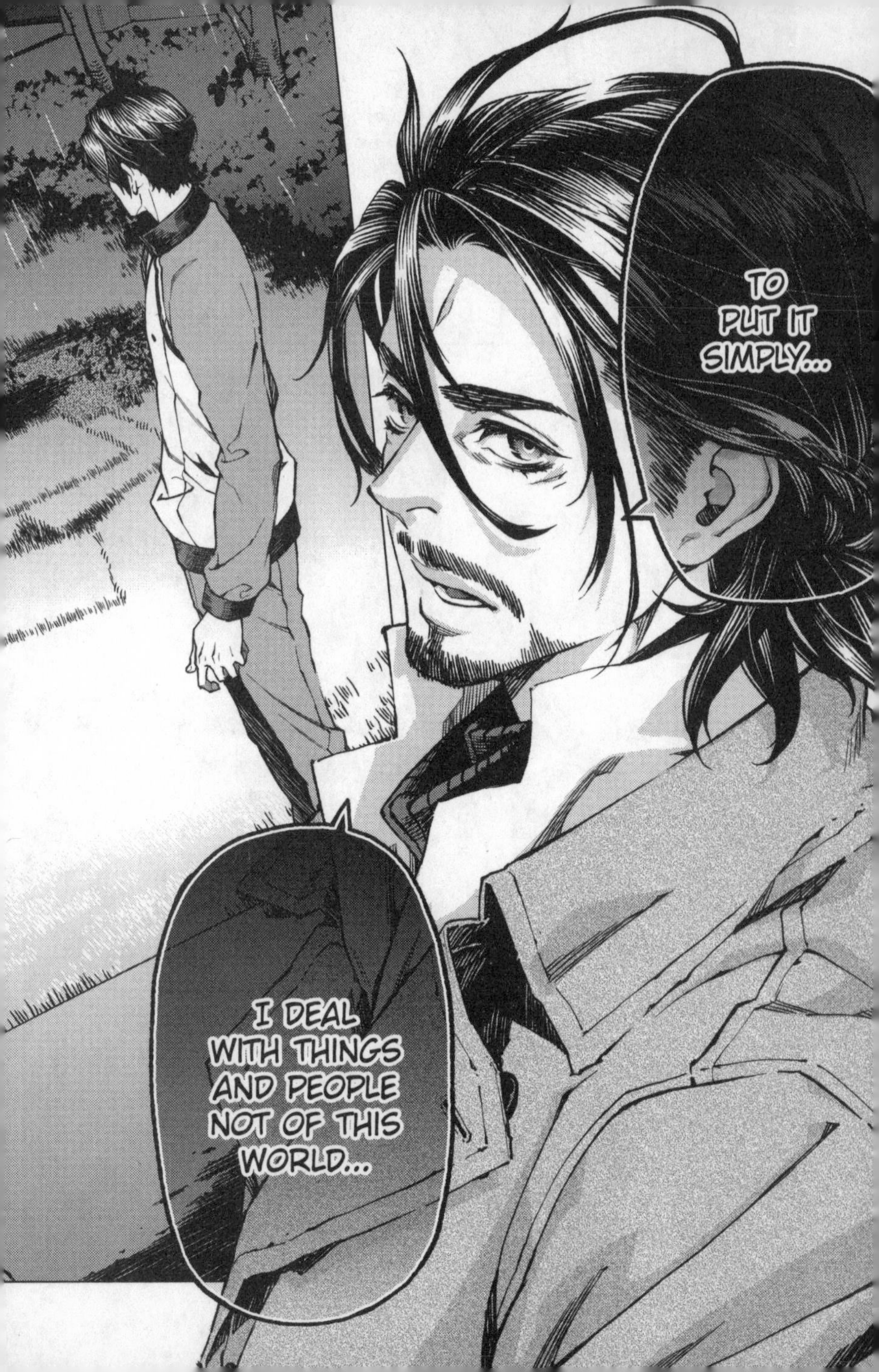
TO PUT IT SIMPLY...
I DEAL WITH THINGS AND PEOPLE NOT OF THIS WORLD...

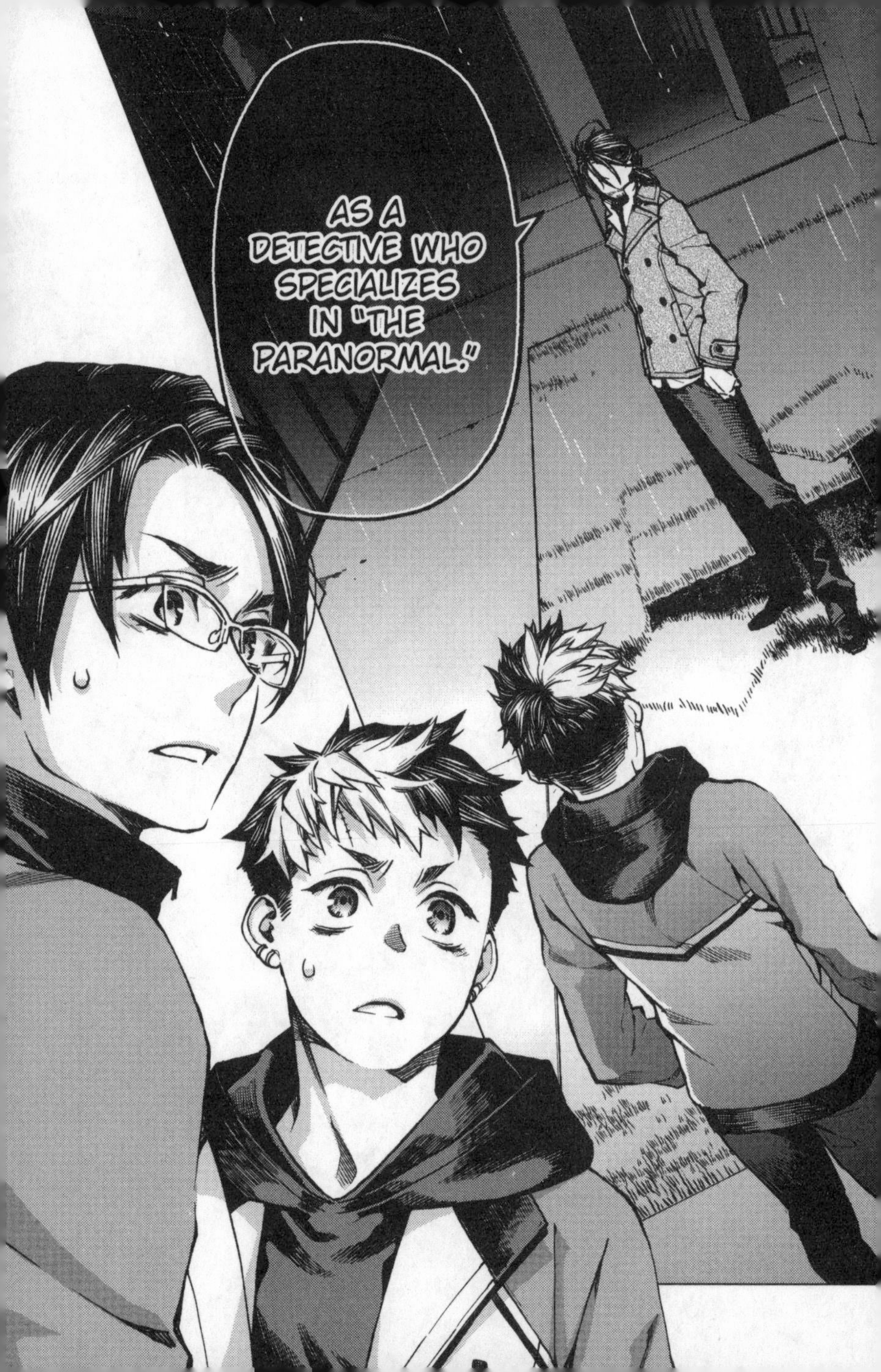
AS A DETECTIVE WHO SPECIALIZES IN "THE PARANORMAL."

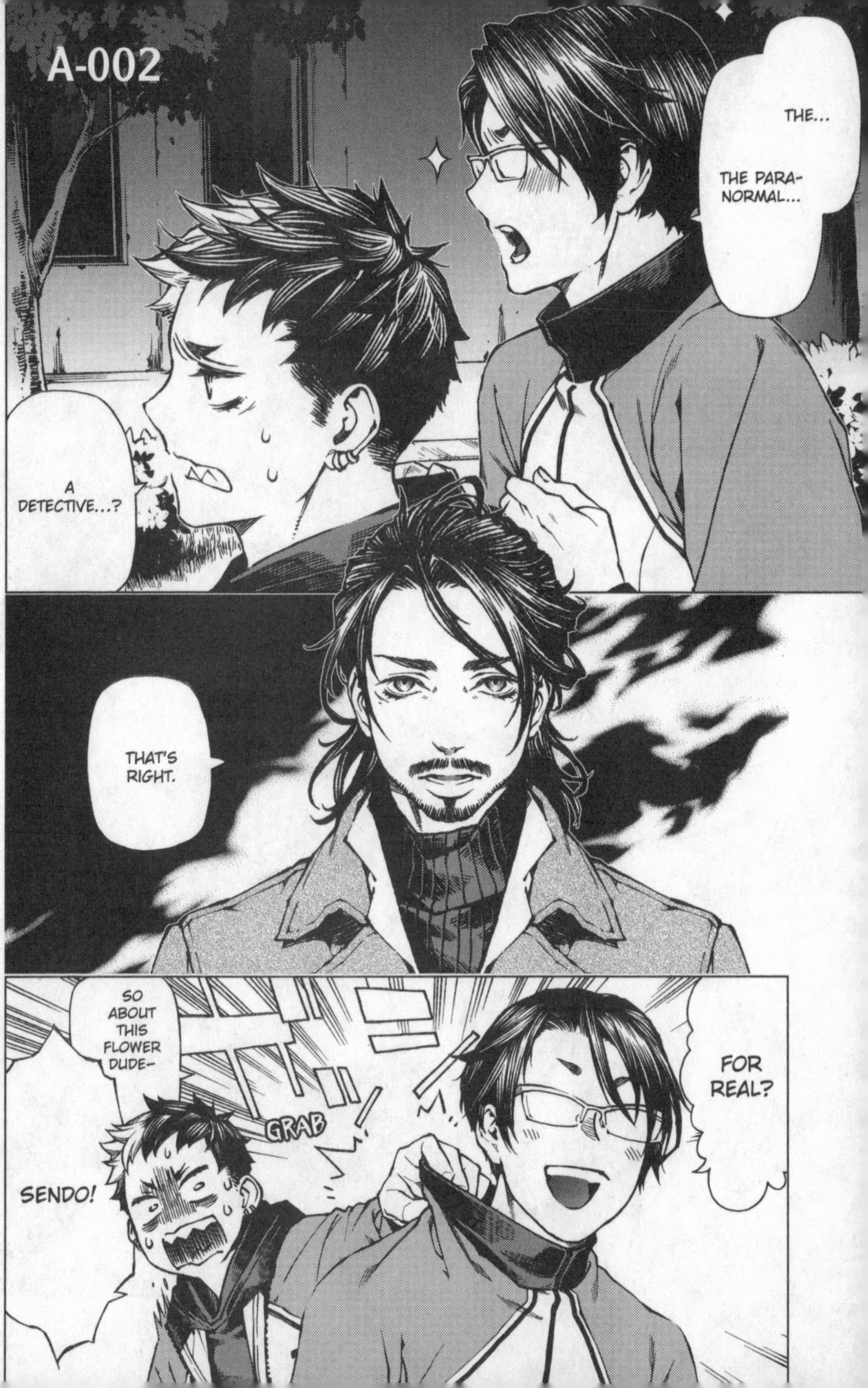
A-002
THE...
THE PARA-NORMAL...
A DETECTIVE...?
THAT'S RIGHT.
FOR REAL?
SO ABOUT THIS FLOWER DUDE-
GRAB
SENDO!

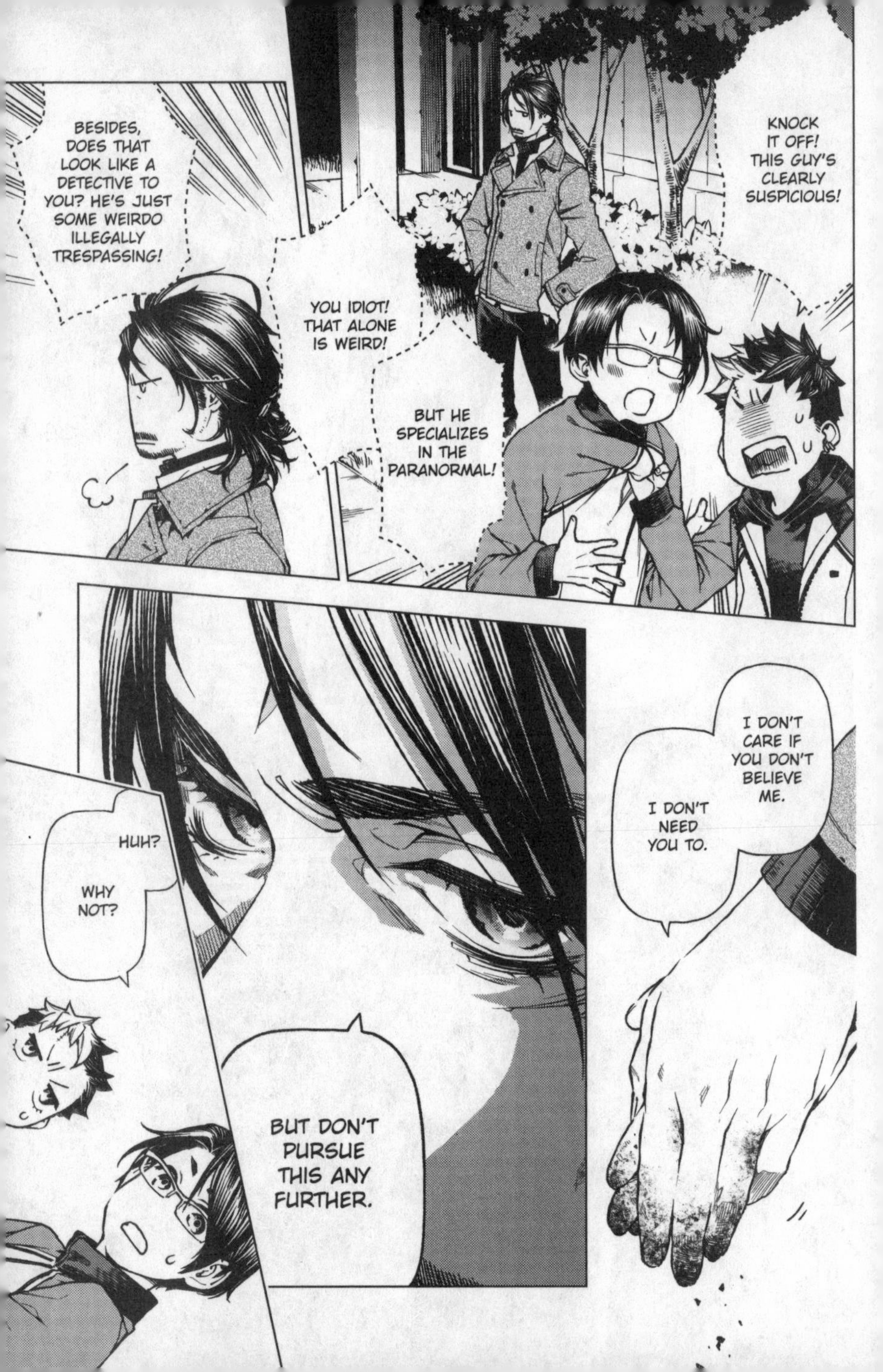
KNOCK IT OFF! THIS GUY'S CLEARLY SUSPICIOUS!
BUT HE SPECIALIZES IN THE PARANORMAL!
YOU IDIOT! THAT ALONE IS WEIRD!
BESIDES, DOES THAT LOOK LIKE A DETECTIVE TO YOU? HE'S JUST SOME WEIRDO ILLEGALLY TRESPASSING!
I DON'T CARE IF YOU DON'T BELIEVE ME.
I DON'T NEED YOU TO.
BUT DON'T PURSUE THIS ANY FURTHER.
HUH?
WHY NOT?

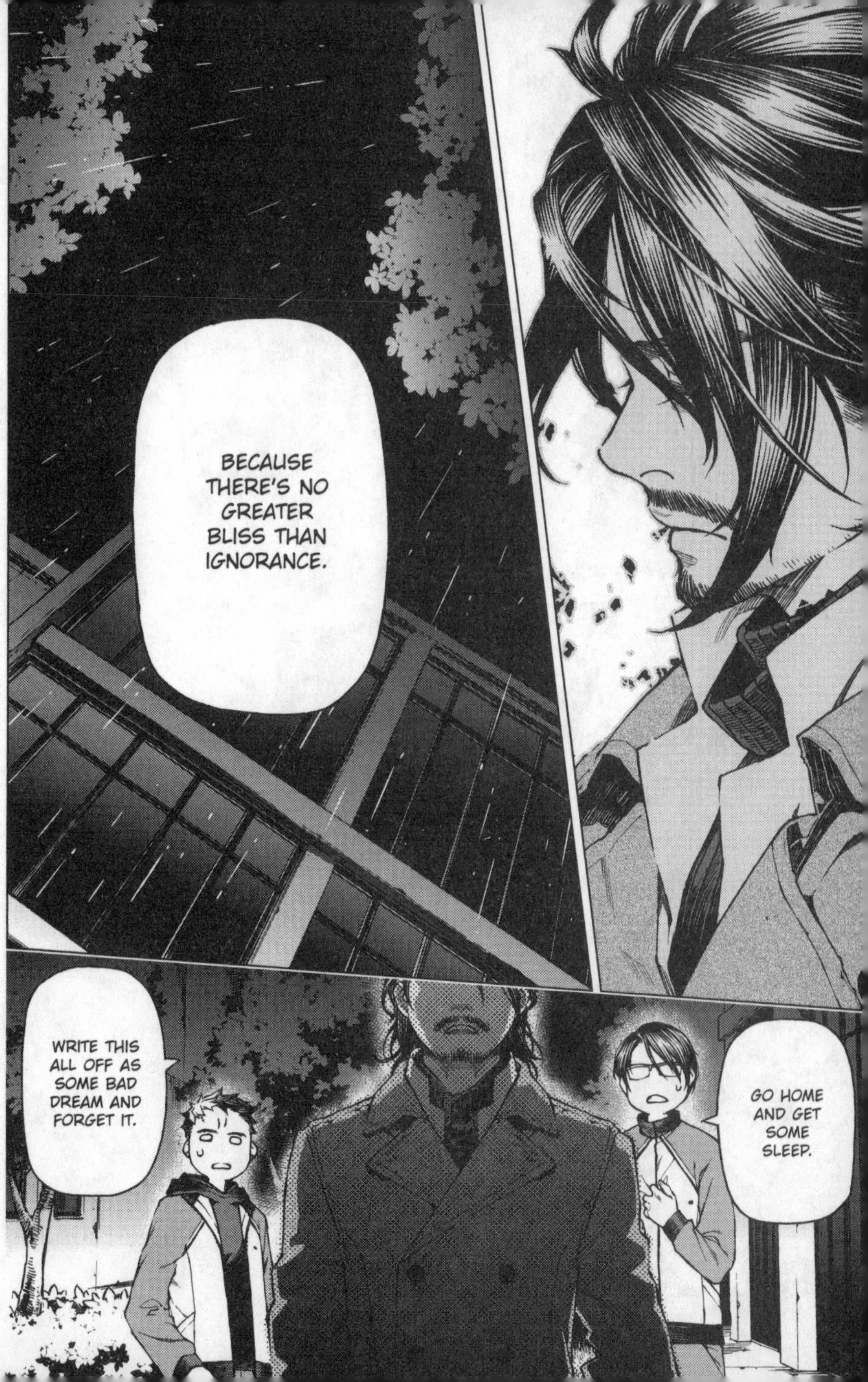
BECAUSE THERE'S NO GREATER BLISS THAN IGNORANCE.
GO HOME AND GET SOME SLEEP.
WRITE THIS ALL OFF AS SOME BAD DREAM AND FORGET IT.

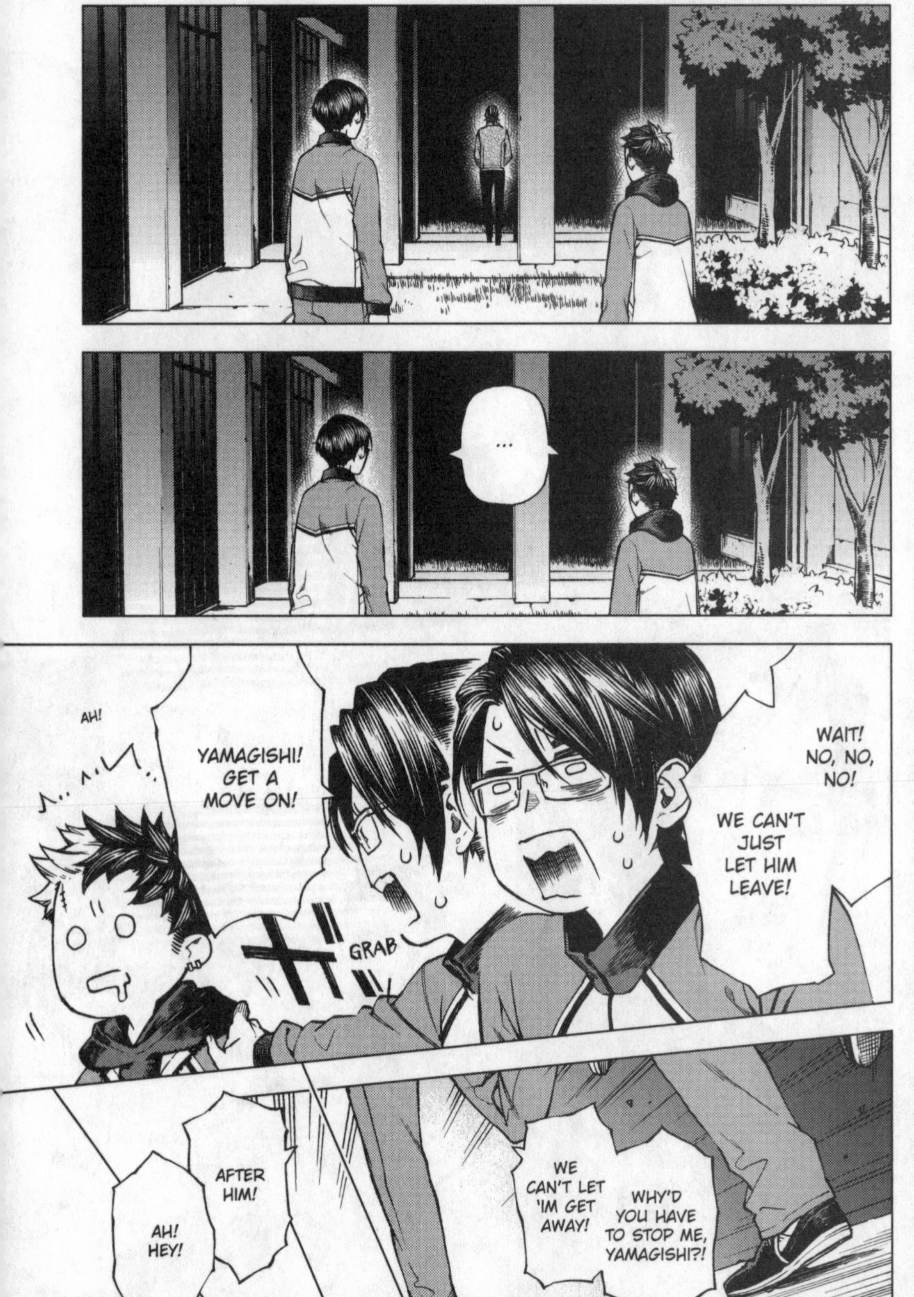
...
WAIT! NO, NO, NO!
WE CAN'T JUST LET HIM LEAVE!
YAMAGISHI! GET A MOVE ON!
AH!
GRAB
WHY'D YOU HAVE TO STOP ME, YAMAGISHI?!
WE CAN'T LET 'IM GET AWAY!
AFTER HIM!
AH! HEY!

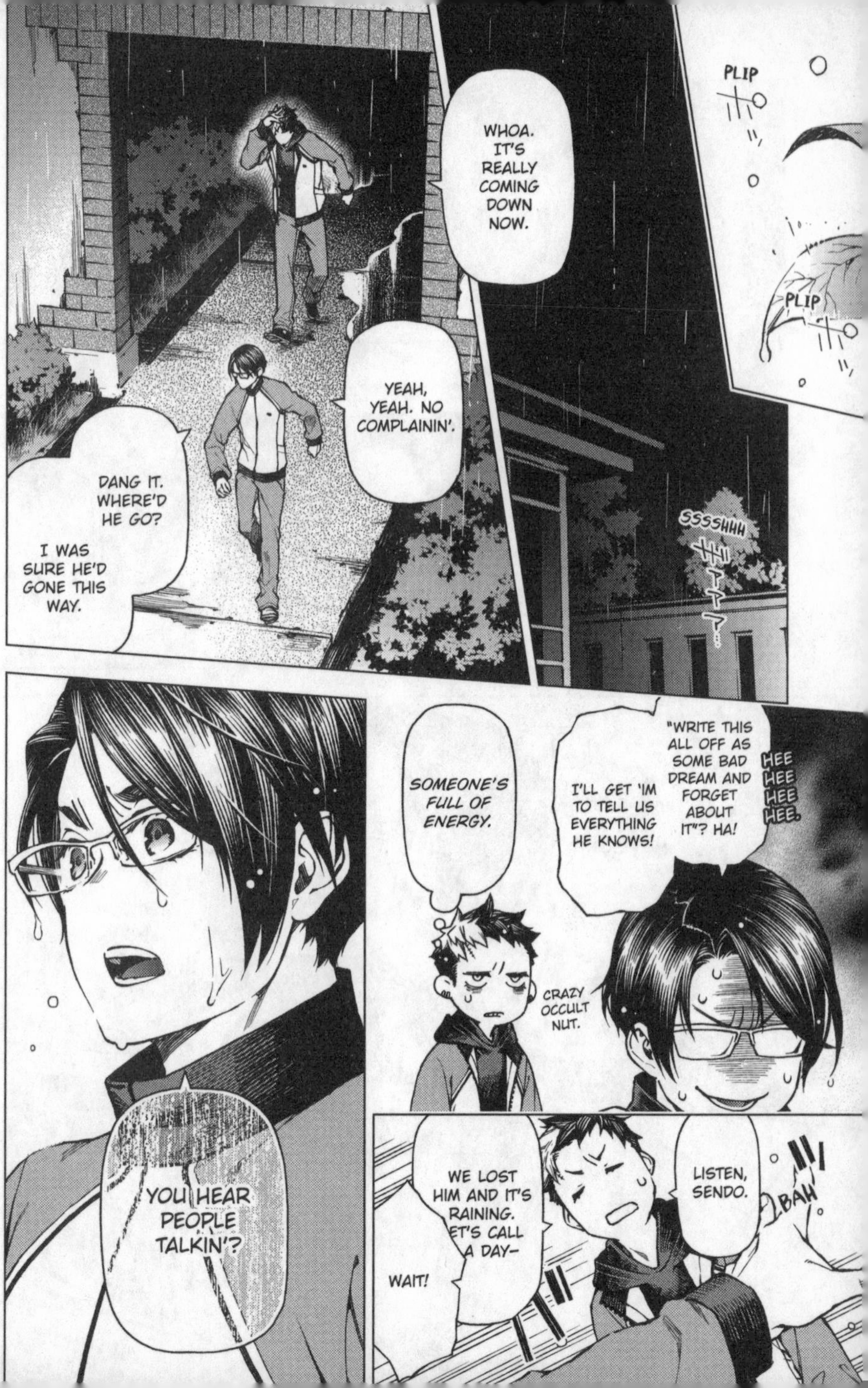
PLIP
PLIP
WHOA. IT'S REALLY COMING DOWN NOW.
SSSSHHH
YEAH, YEAH. NO COMPLAININ'.
DANG IT. WHERE'D HE GO?
I WAS SURE HE'D GONE THIS WAY.
HEE HEE HEE HEE.
"WRITE THIS ALL OFF AS SOME BAD DREAM AND FORGET ABOUT IT"? HA!
I'LL GET 'IM TO TELL US EVERYTHING HE KNOWS!
SOMEONE'S FULL OF ENERGY.
CRAZY OCCULT NUT.
BAH
LISTEN, SENDO.
WE LOST HIM AND IT'S RAINING. ET'S CALL A DAY—
WAIT!
YOU HEAR PEOPLE TALKIN'?

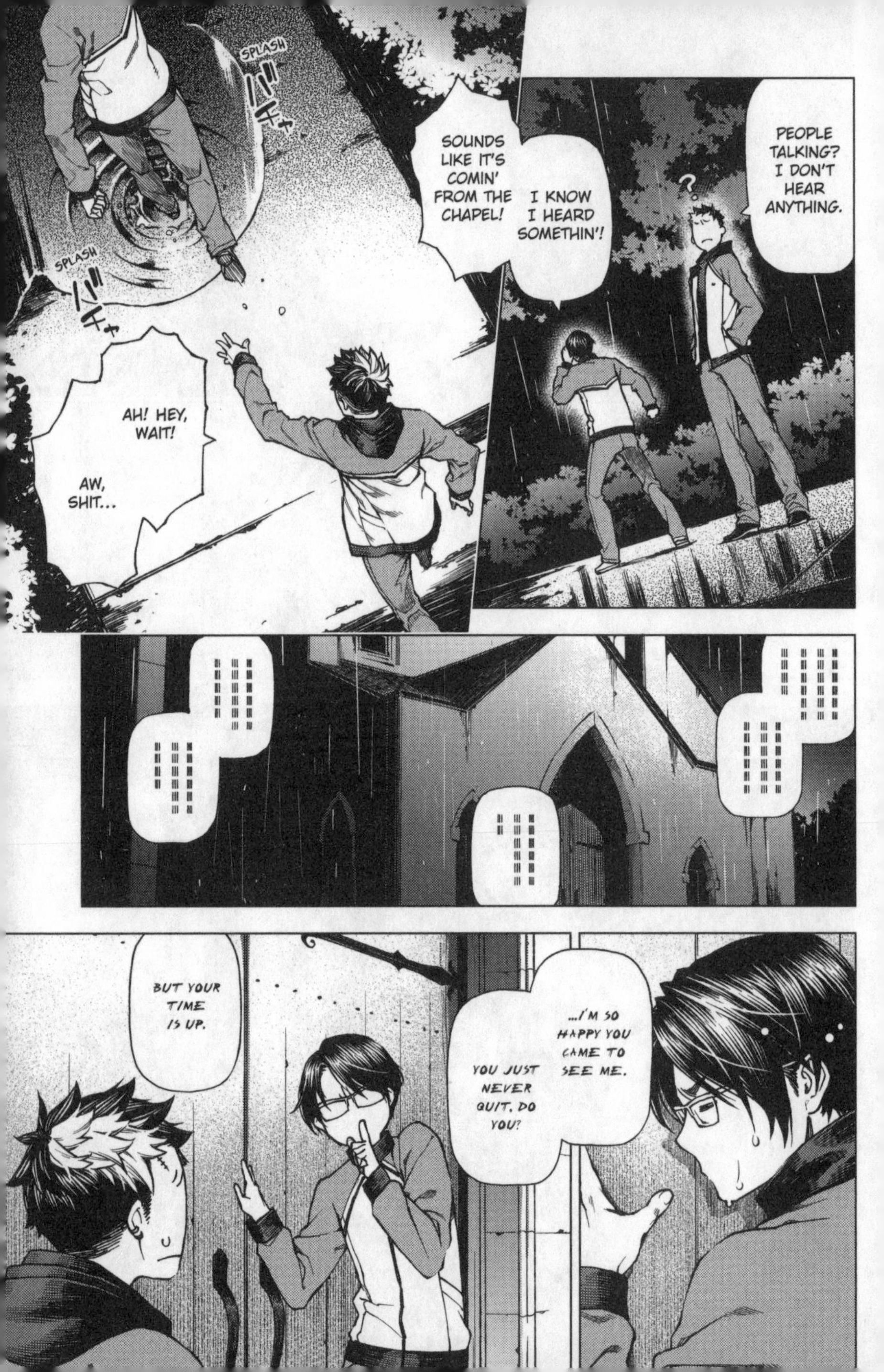
PEOPLE TALKING? I DON'T HEAR ANYTHING.
I KNOW I HEARD SOMETHIN'!
SOUNDS LIKE IT'S COMIN' FROM THE CHAPEL!
SPLASH
SPLASH
AH! HEY, WAIT!
AW, SHIT...
...I'M SO HAPPY YOU CAME TO SEE ME.
YOU JUST NEVER QUIT, DO YOU?
BUT YOUR TIME IS UP.

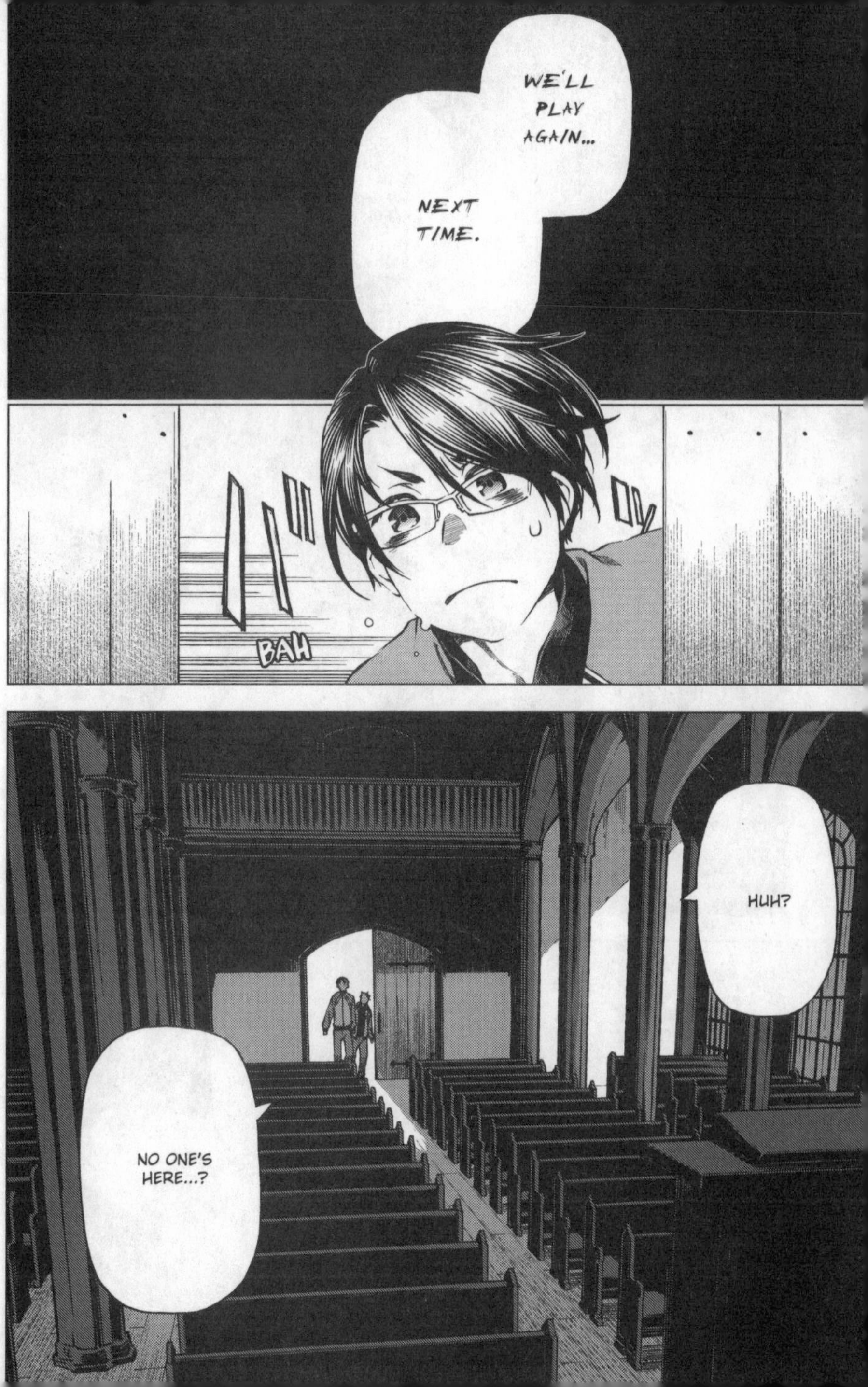
WE'LL PLAY AGAIN...
NEXT TIME.
BAH
HUH?
NO ONE'S HERE...?

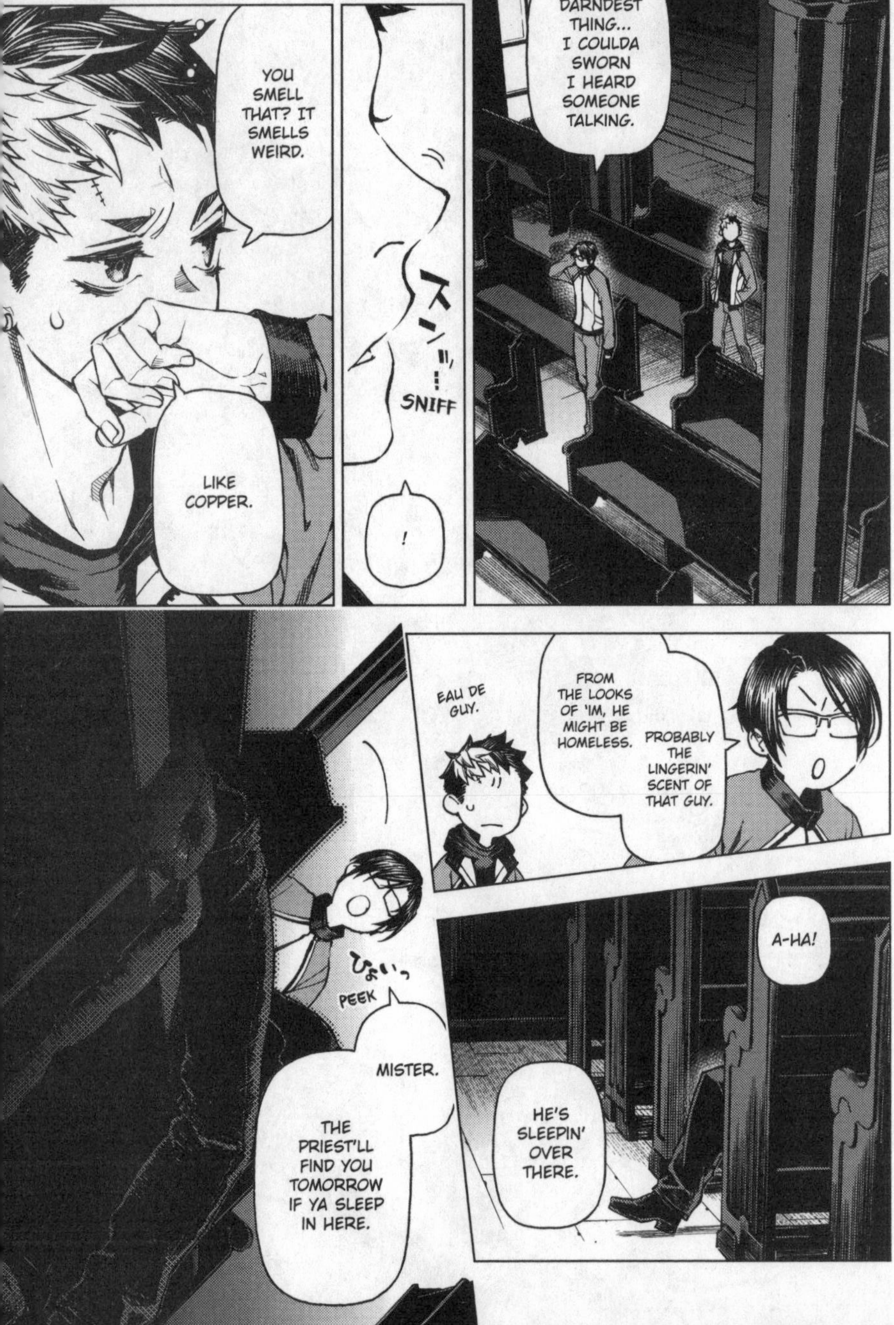
IT'S THE DARNDEST THING... I COULDA SWORN I HEARD SOMEONE TALKING.
!
SNIFF
YOU SMELL THAT? IT SMELLS WEIRD.
LIKE COPPER.
PROBABLY THE LINGERIN' SCENT OF THAT GUY.
FROM THE LOOKS OF 'IM, HE MIGHT BE HOMELESS.
EAU DE GUY.
A-HA!
HE'S SLEEPIN' OVER THERE.
PEEK
MISTER.
THE PRIEST'LL FIND YOU TOMORROW IF YA SLEEP IN HERE.

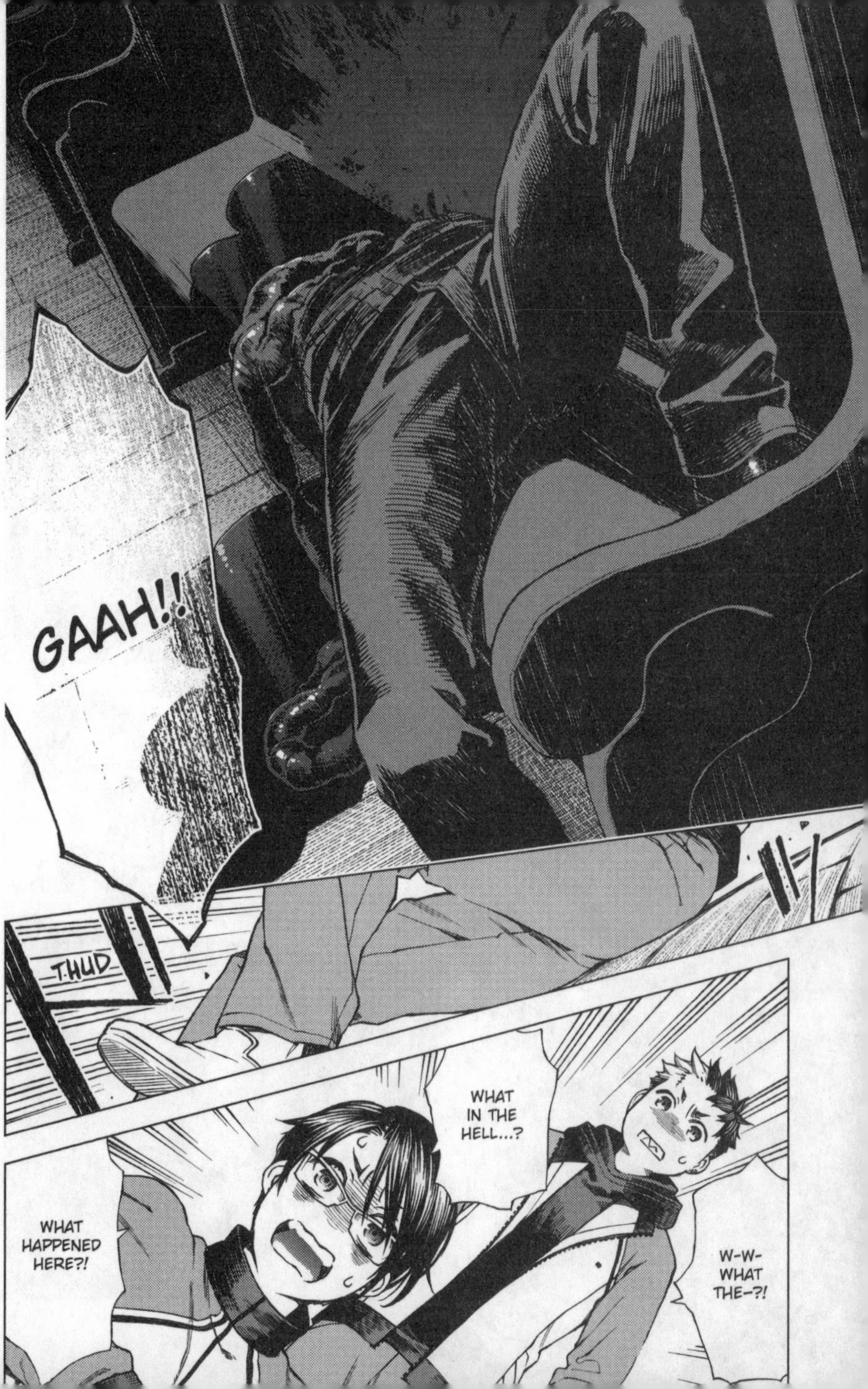
GAAH!!
THUD
WHAT IN THE HELL...?
W-W-WHAT THE-?!
WHAT HAPPENED HERE?!

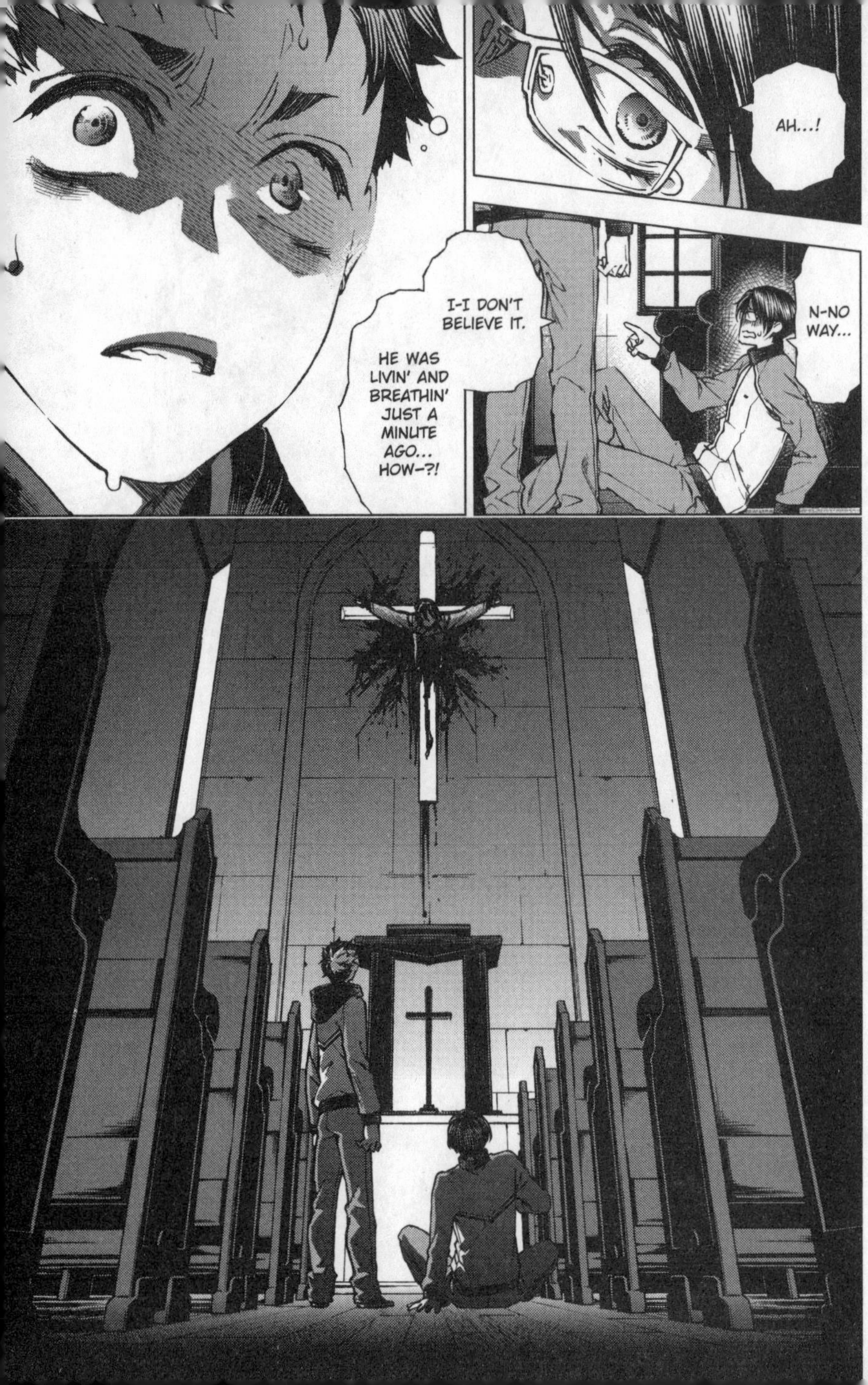
AH...!
N-NO WAY...
I-I DON'T BELIEVE IT.
HE WAS LIVIN' AND BREATHIN' JUST A MINUTE AGO... HOW-?!

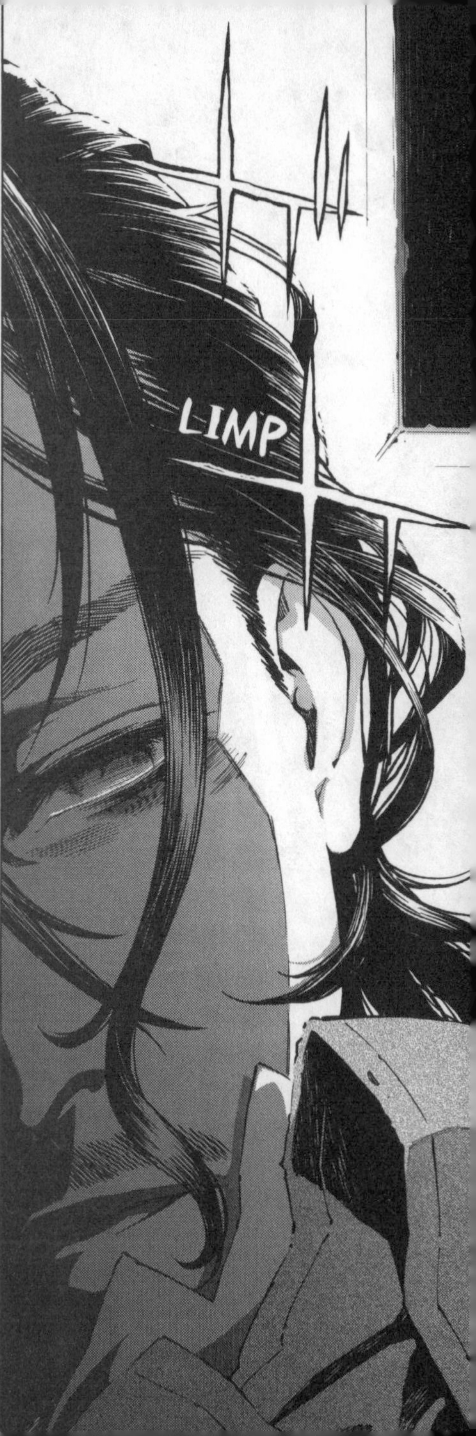
LIMP
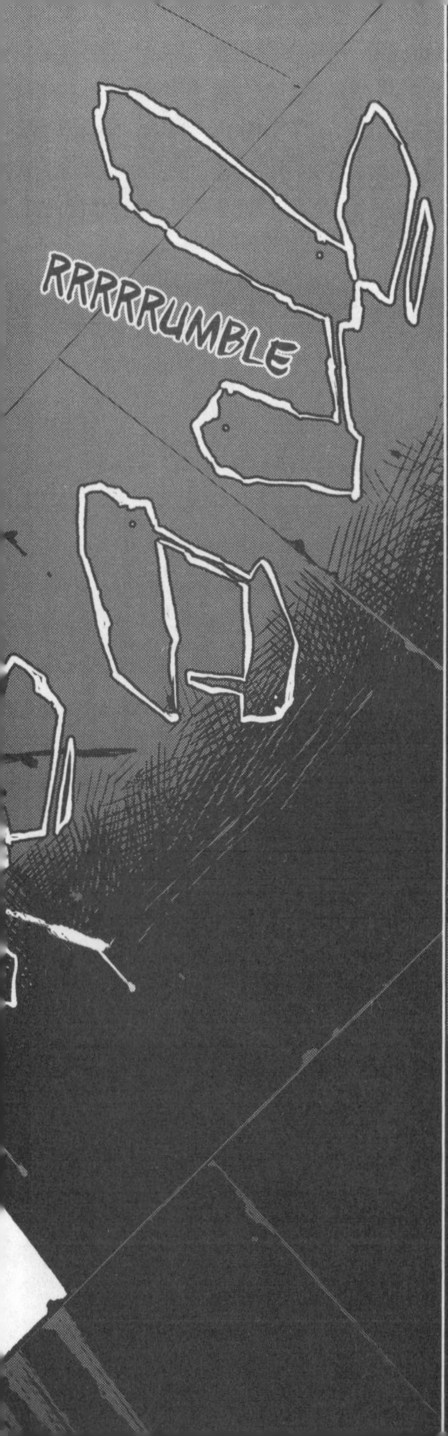
RRRRRUMBLE

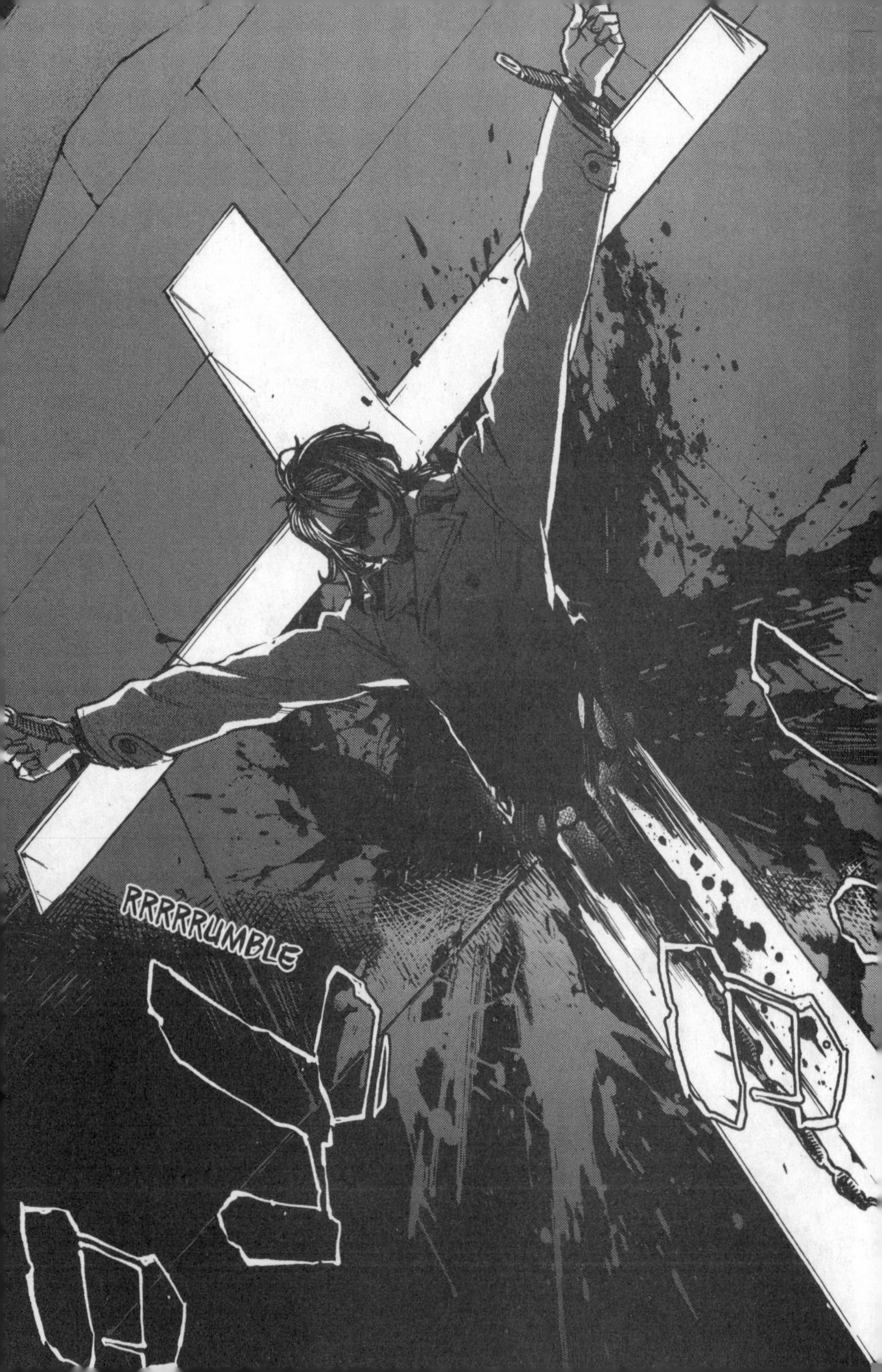
RRRRRUMBLE

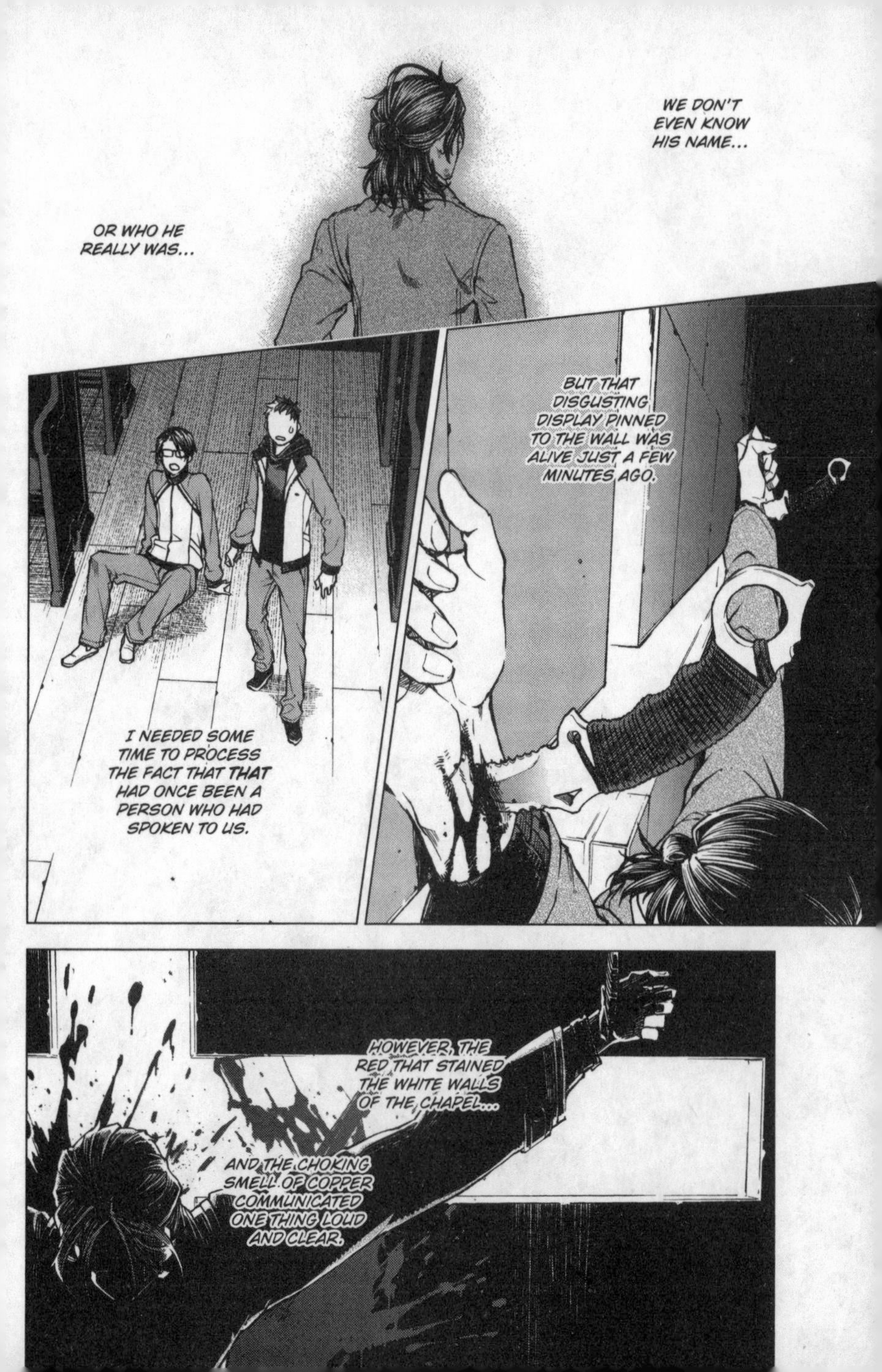
WE DON'T EVEN KNOW HIS NAME...
OR WHO HE REALLY WAS...
BUT THAT DISGUSTING DISPLAY PINNED TO THE WALL WAS ALIVE JUST A FEW MINUTES AGO.
I NEEDED SOME TIME TO PROCESS THE FACT THAT THAT HAD ONCE BEEN A PERSON WHO HAD SPOKEN TO US.
HOWEVER, THE RED THAT STAINED THE WHITE WALLS OF THE CHAPEL...
AND THE CHOKING SMELL OF COPPER COMMUNICATED ONE THING LOUD AND CLEAR.

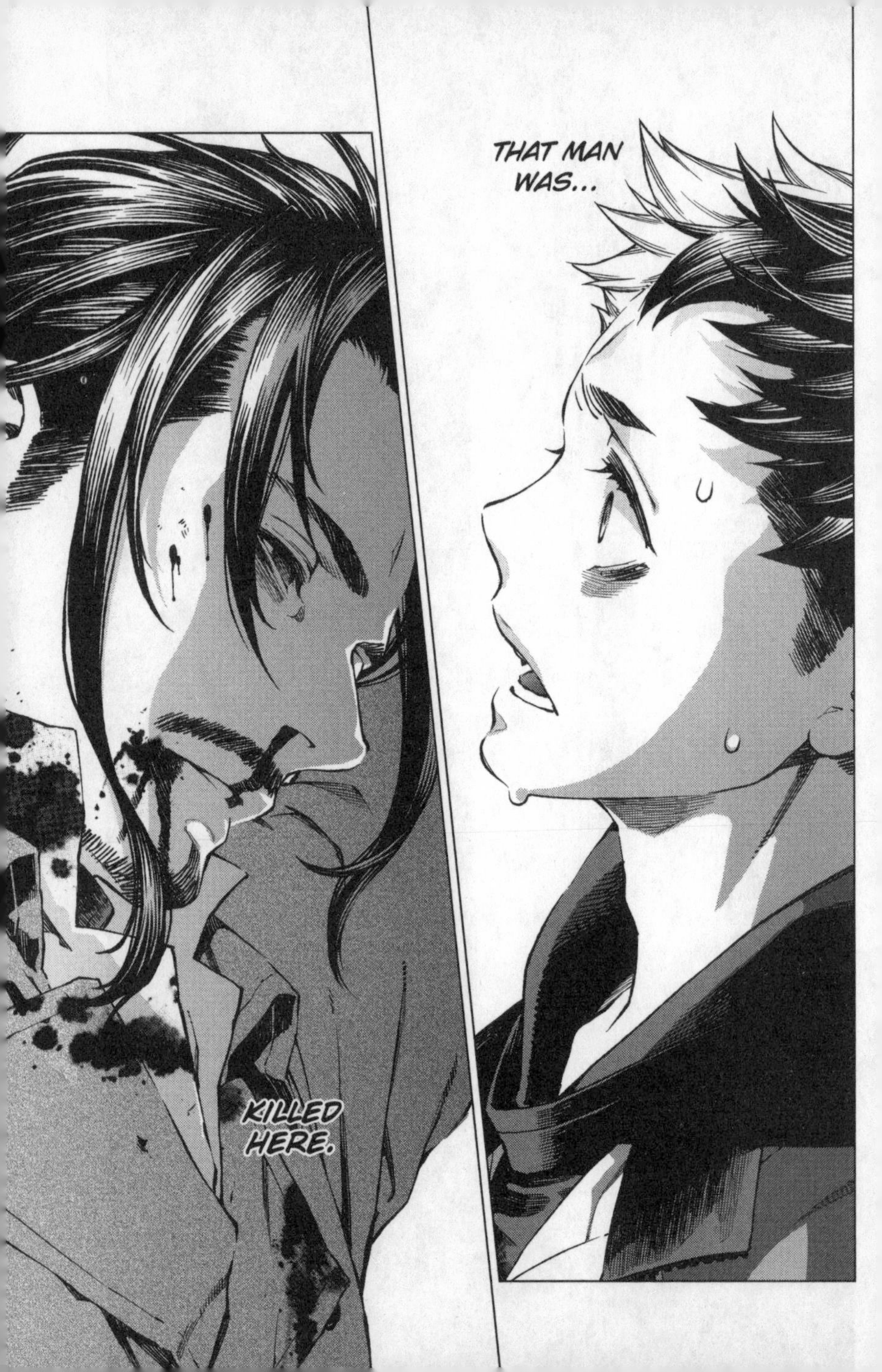
THAT MAN WAS...
KILLED HERE.

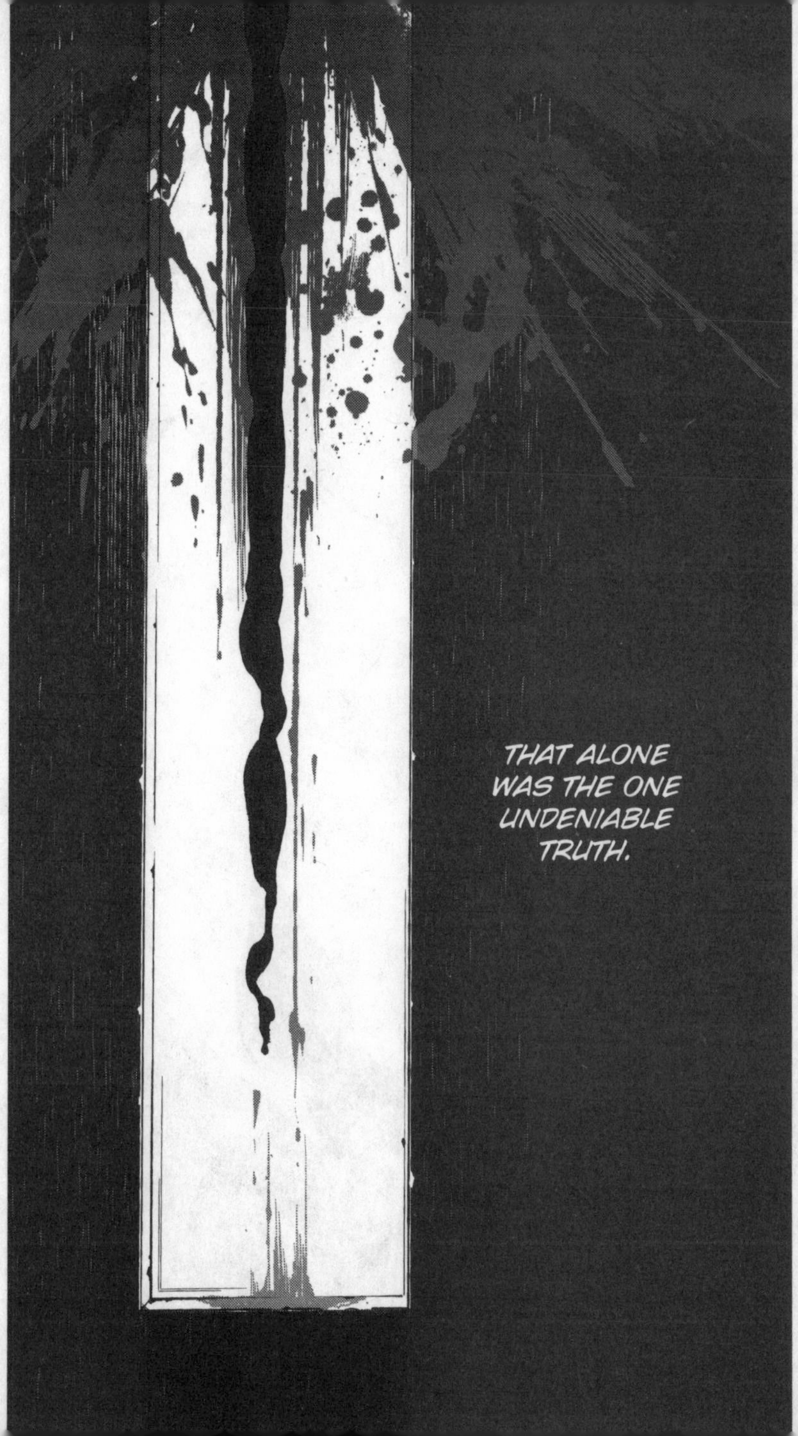
THAT ALONE WAS THE ONE UNDENIABLE TRUTH.

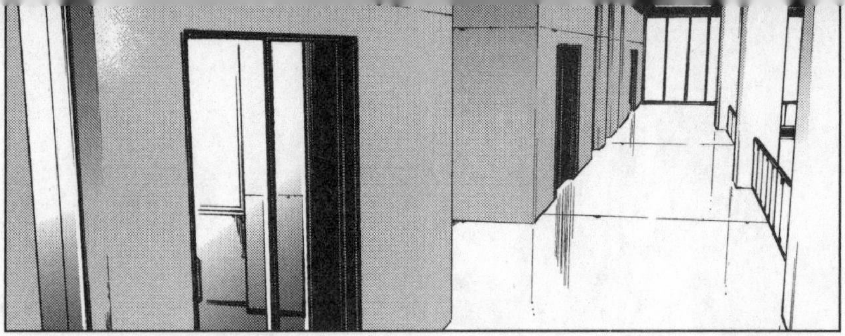

A-003

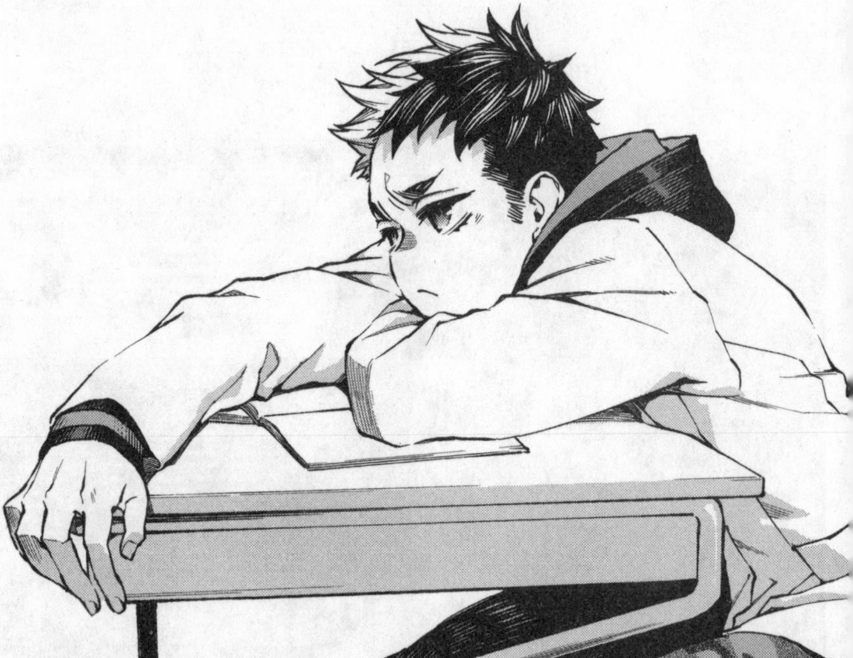

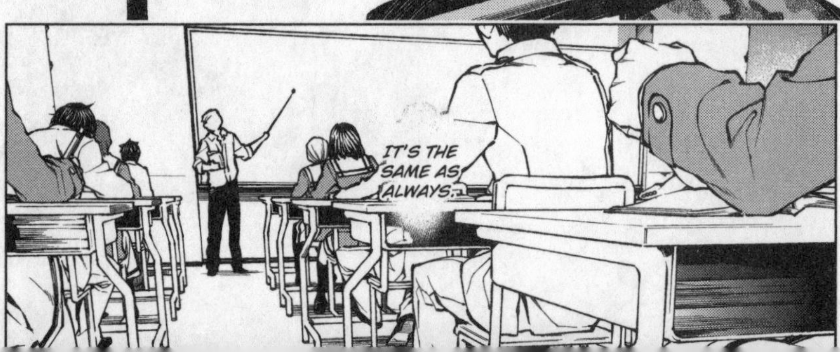
IT'S THE SAME AS ALWAYS.

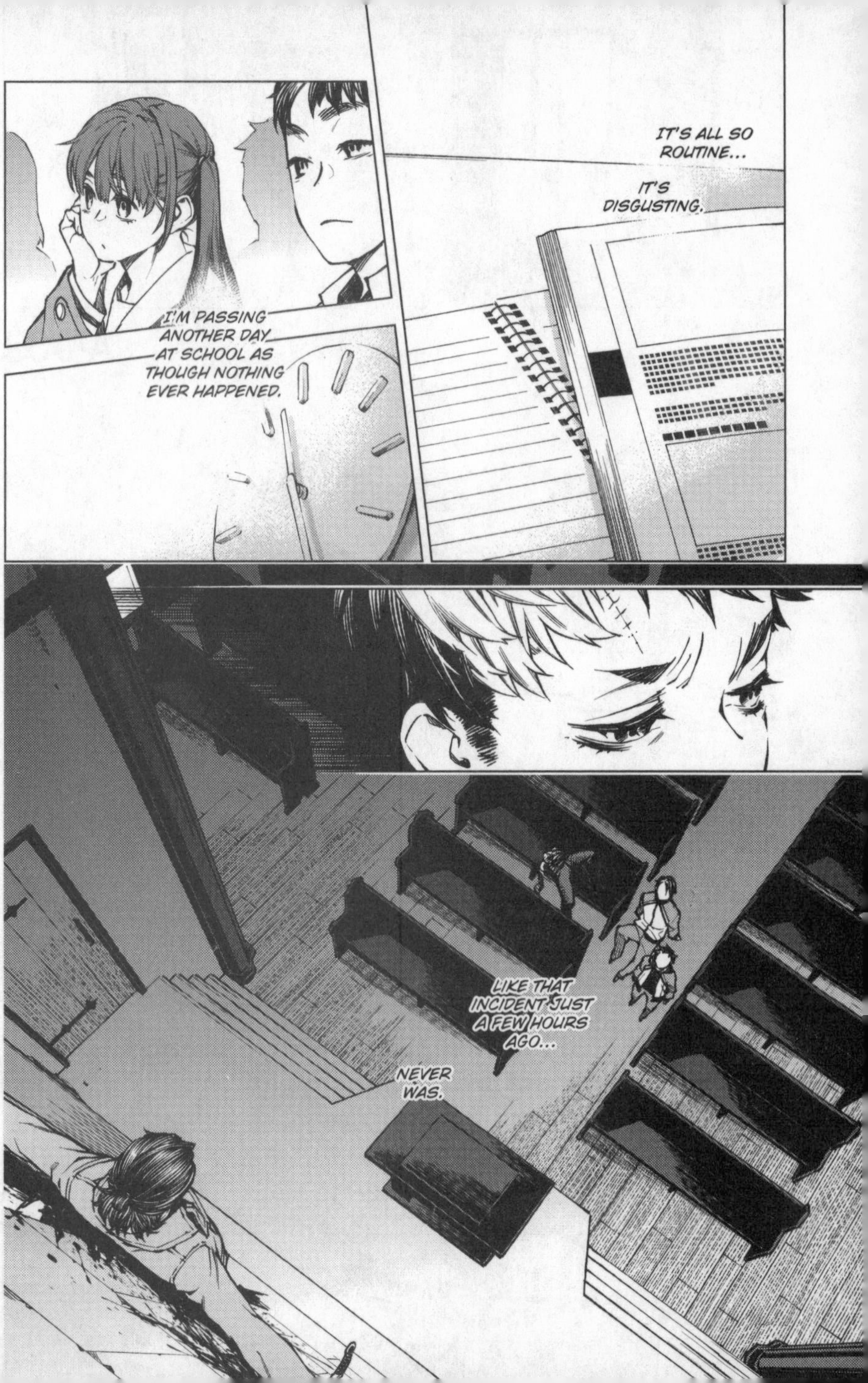
IT'S ALL SO ROUTINE...
IT'S DISGUSTING.
I'M PASSING ANOTHER DAY AT SCHOOL AS THOUGH NOTHING EVER HAPPENED.
LIKE THAT INCIDENT JUST A FEW HOURS AGO...
NEVER WAS.

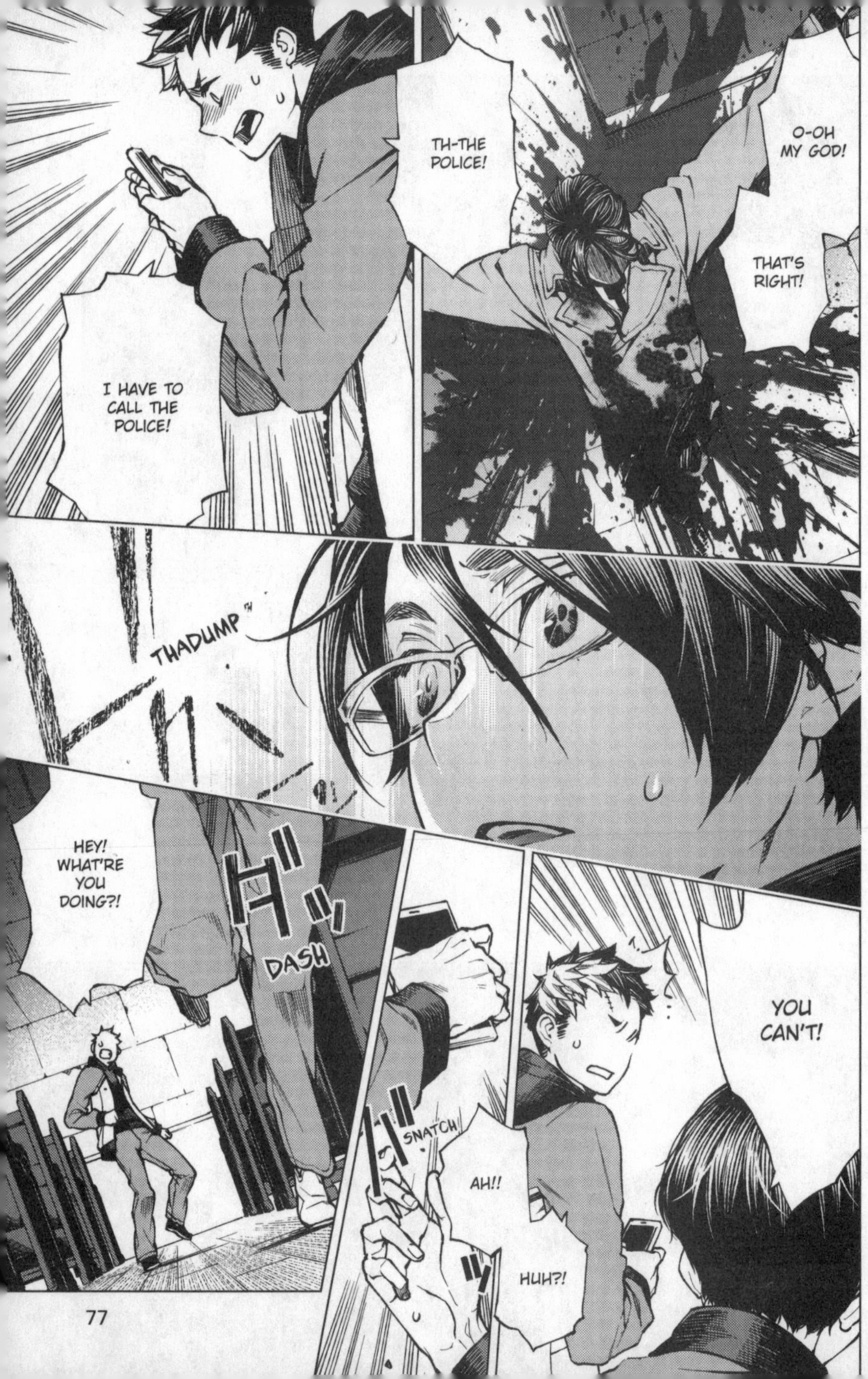
O-OH MY GOD!
THAT'S RIGHT!
TH-THE POLICE!
I HAVE TO CALL THE POLICE!
THADUMP
YOU CAN'T!
HUH?!
SNATCH
AH!!
HEY! WHAT'RE YOU DOING?!
DASH

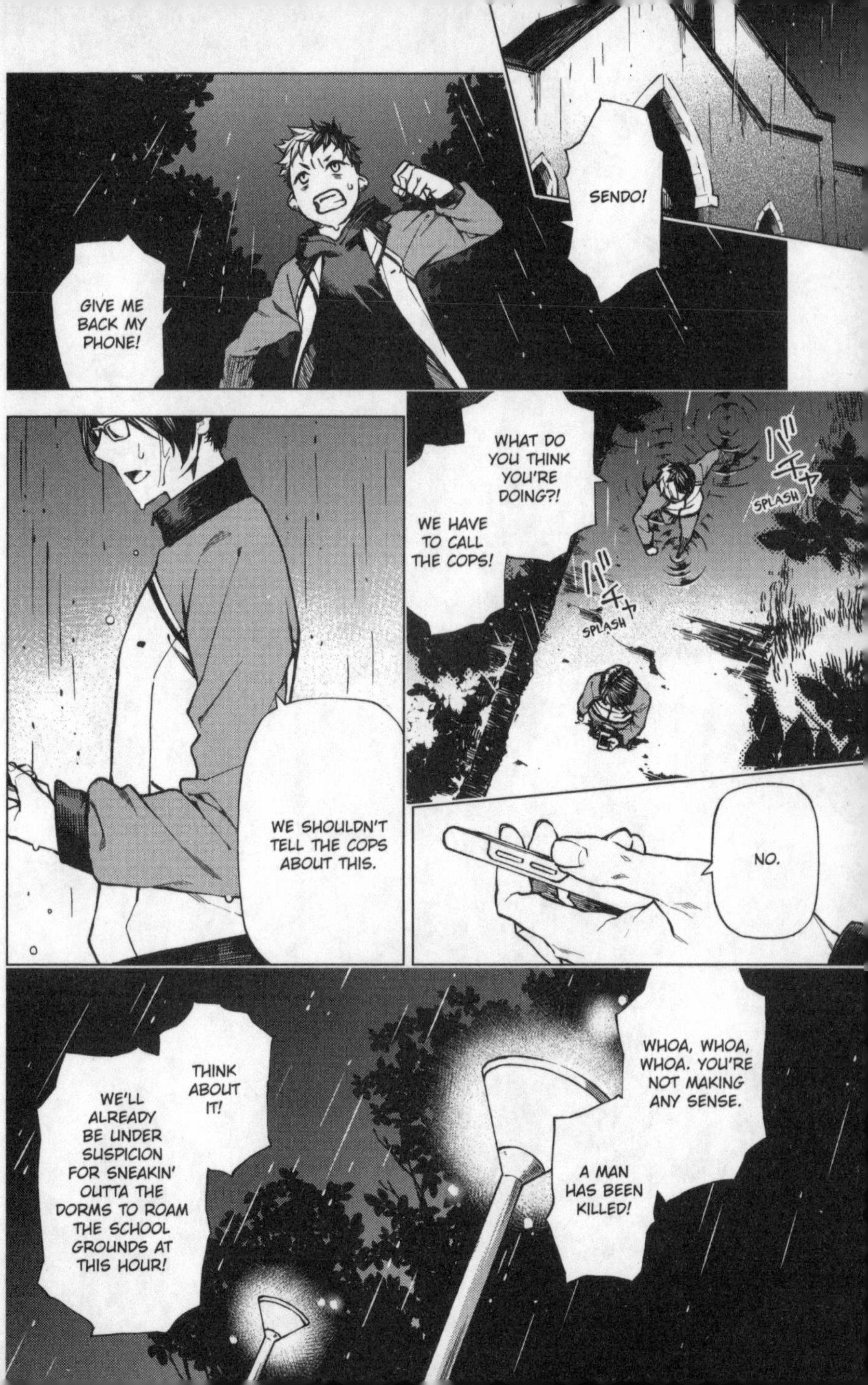
SENDO!
GIVE ME BACK MY PHONE!
WHAT DO YOU THINK YOU'RE DOING?!
WE HAVE TO CALL THE COPS!
SPLASH
SPLASH
NO.
WE SHOULDN'T TELL THE COPS ABOUT THIS.
WHOA, WHOA, WHOA. YOU'RE NOT MAKING ANY SENSE.
A MAN HAS BEEN KILLED!
THINK ABOUT IT!
WE'LL ALREADY BE UNDER SUSPICION FOR SNEAKIN' OUTTA THE DORMS TO ROAM THE SCHOOL GROUNDS AT THIS HOUR!

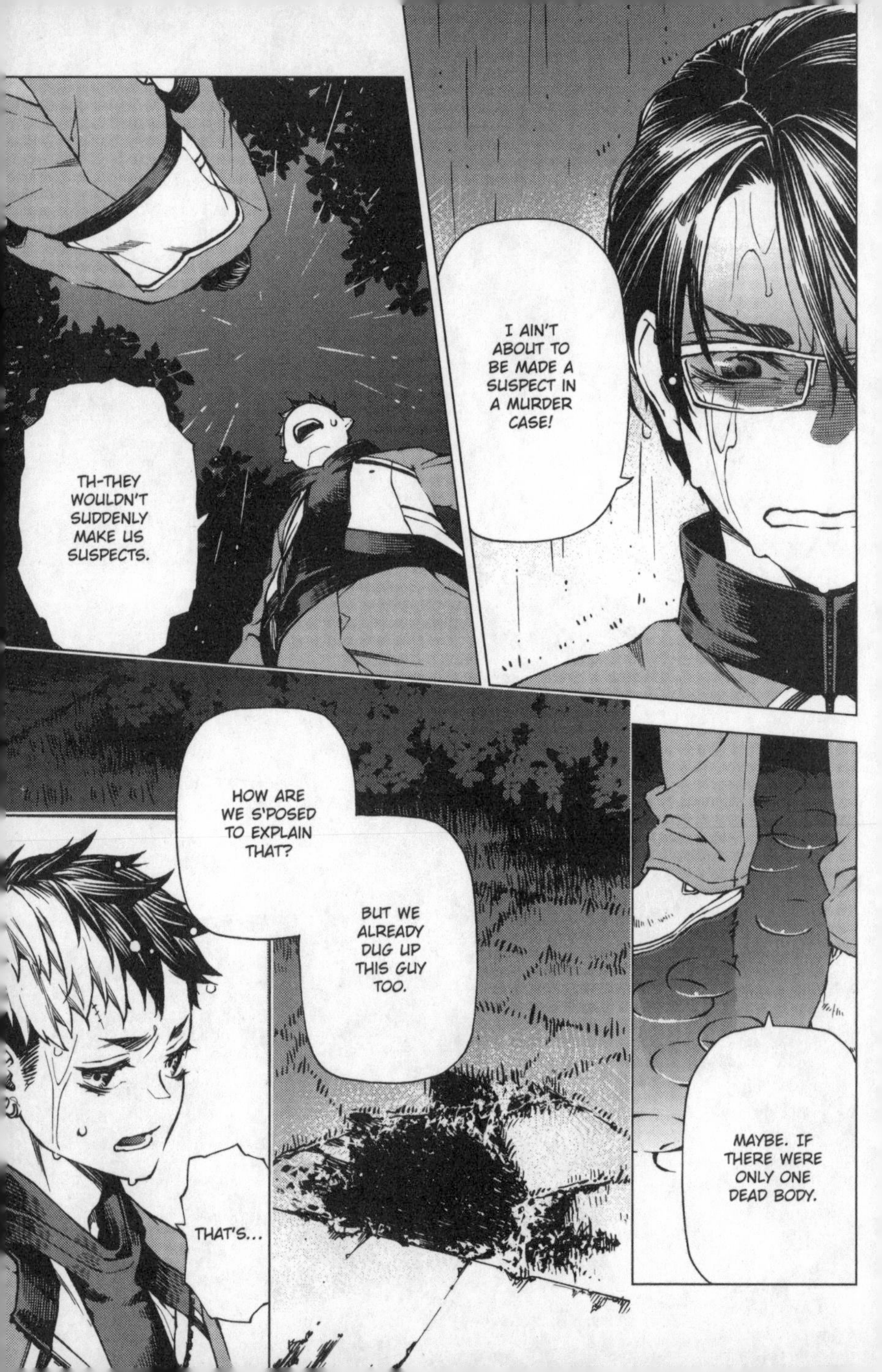
I AIN'T ABOUT TO BE MADE A SUSPECT IN A MURDER CASE!
TH-THEY WOULDN'T SUDDENLY MAKE US SUSPECTS.
MAYBE. IF THERE WERE ONLY ONE DEAD BODY.
HOW ARE WE S'POSED TO EXPLAIN THAT?
BUT WE ALREADY DUG UP THIS GUY TOO.
THAT'S...

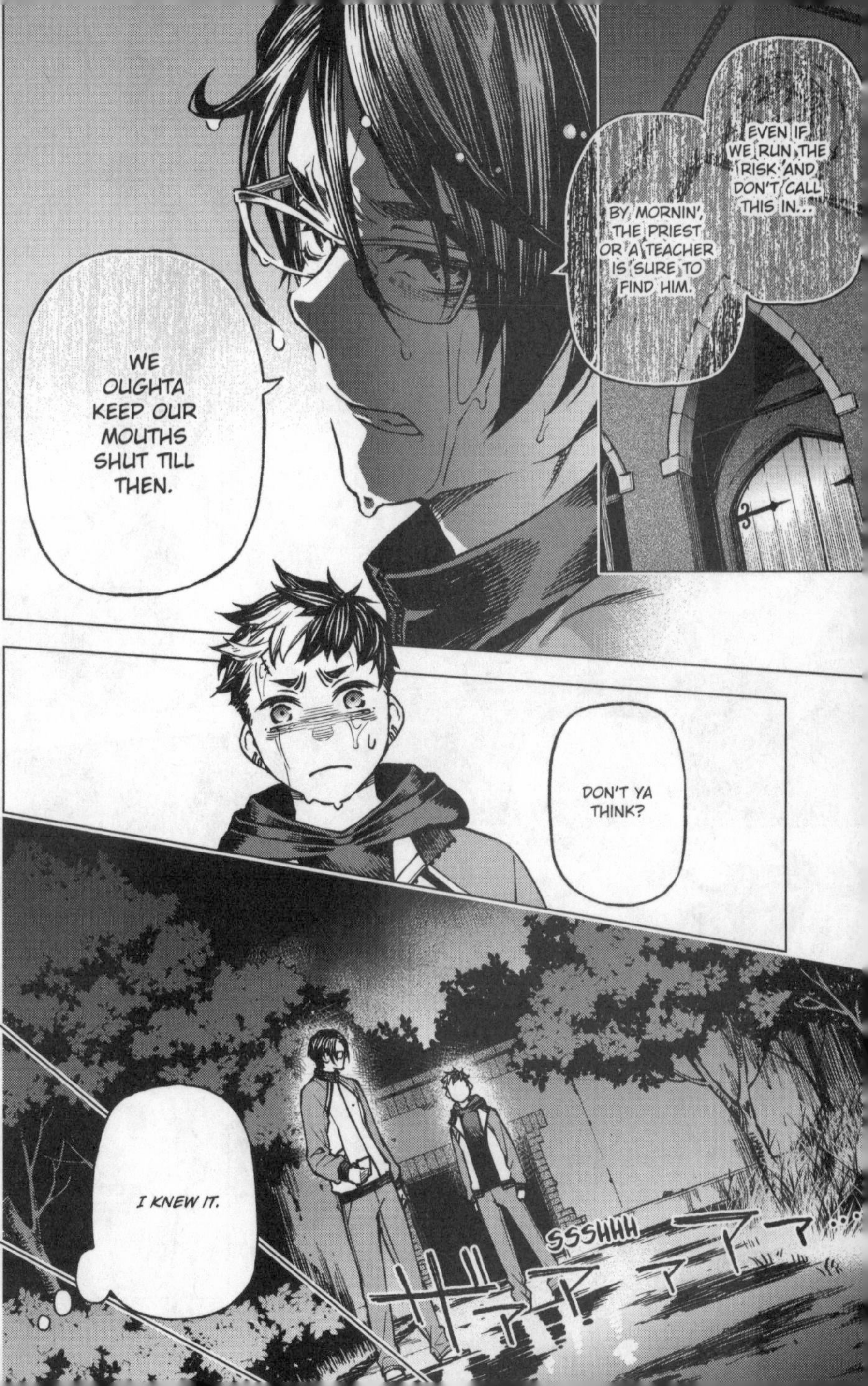
EVEN IF WE RUN THE RISK AND DON'T CALL THIS IN...
BY MORNIN', THE PRIEST OR A TEACHER IS SURE TO FIND HIM.
WE OUGHTA KEEP OUR MOUTHS SHUT TILL THEN.
DON'T YA THINK?
I KNEW IT.
SSSHHH

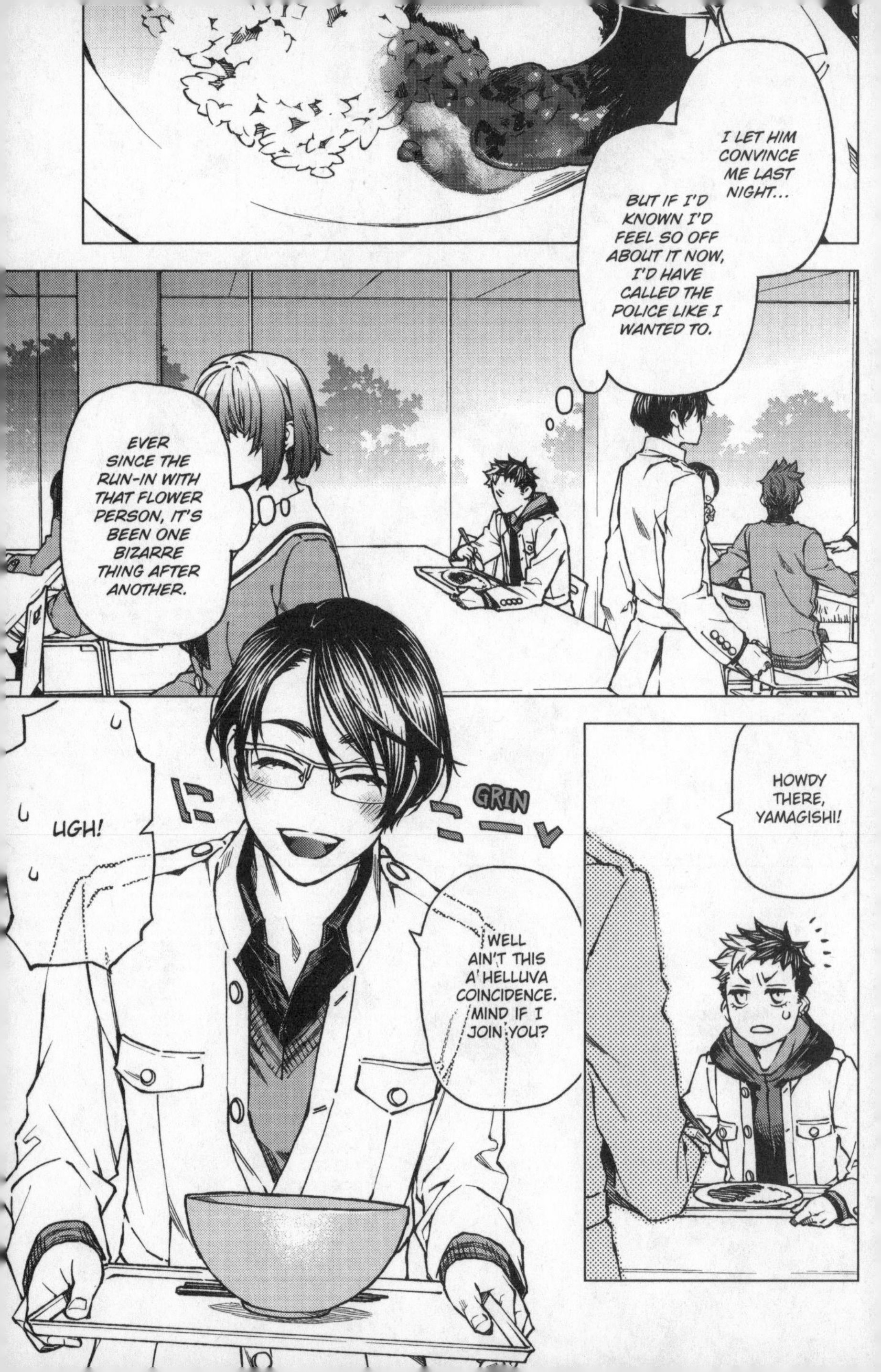
I LET HIM CONVINCE ME LAST NIGHT...
BUT IF I'D KNOWN I'D FEEL SO OFF ABOUT IT NOW, I'D HAVE CALLED THE POLICE LIKE I WANTED TO.
EVER SINCE THE RUN-IN WITH THAT FLOWER PERSON, IT'S BEEN ONE BIZARRE THING AFTER ANOTHER.
HOWDY THERE, YAMAGISHI!
GRIN
WELL AIN'T THIS A' HELLUVA COINCIDENCE. MIND IF I JOIN YOU?
UGH!

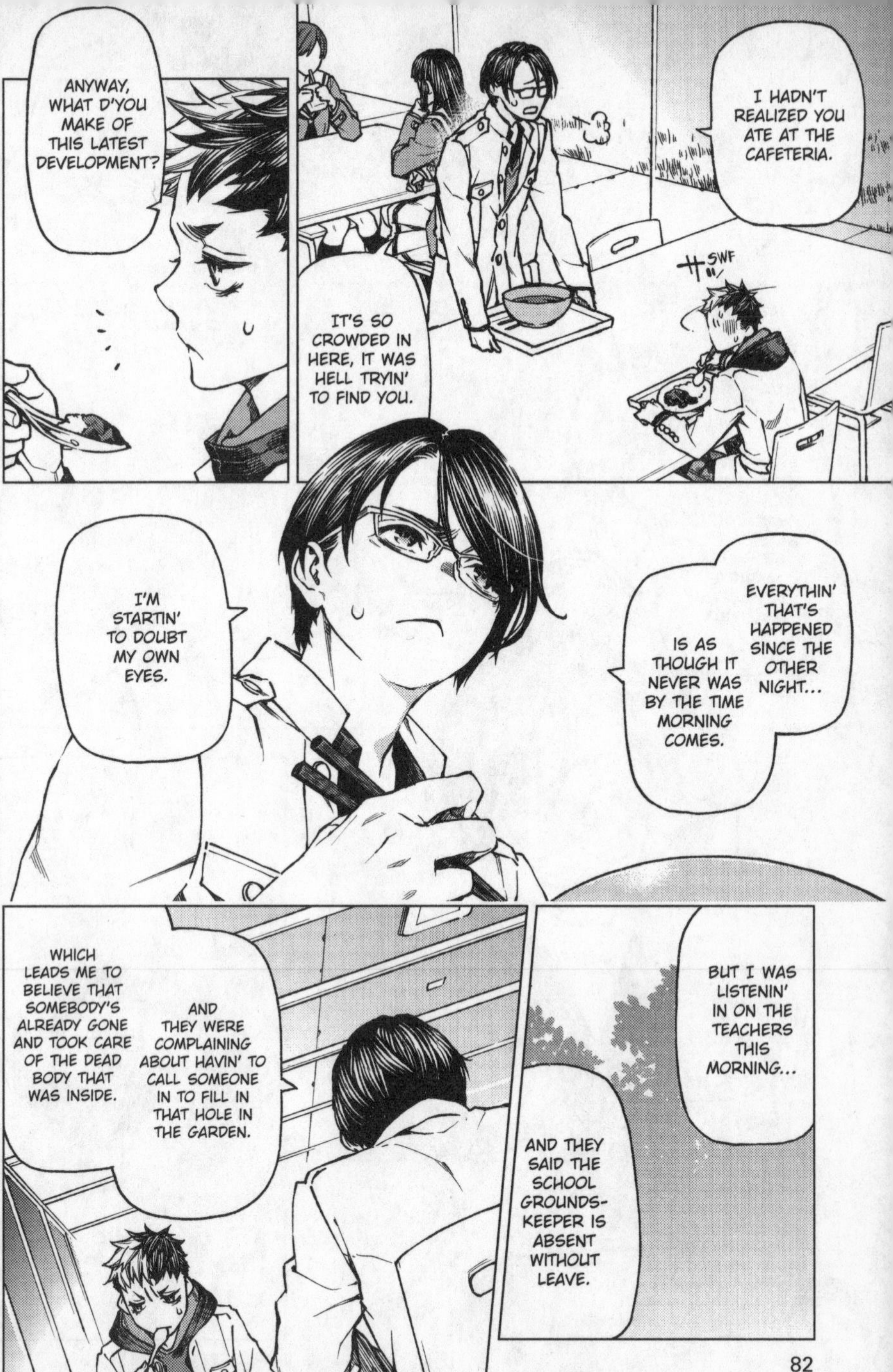
I HADN'T REALIZED YOU ATE AT THE CAFETERIA.
SWF
IT'S SO CROWDED IN HERE, IT WAS HELL TRYIN' TO FIND YOU.
ANYWAY, WHAT D'YOU MAKE OF THIS LATEST DEVELOPMENT?
EVERYTHIN' THAT'S HAPPENED SINCE THE OTHER NIGHT...
IS AS THOUGH IT NEVER WAS BY THE TIME MORNING COMES.
I'M STARTIN' TO DOUBT MY OWN EYES.
BUT I WAS LISTENIN' IN ON THE TEACHERS THIS MORNING...
AND THEY SAID THE SCHOOL GROUNDS-KEEPER IS ABSENT WITHOUT LEAVE.
AND THEY WERE COMPLAINING ABOUT HAVIN' TO CALL SOMEONE IN TO FILL IN THAT HOLE IN THE GARDEN.
WHICH LEADS ME TO BELIEVE THAT SOMEBODY'S ALREADY GONE AND TOOK CARE OF THE DEAD BODY THAT WAS INSIDE.

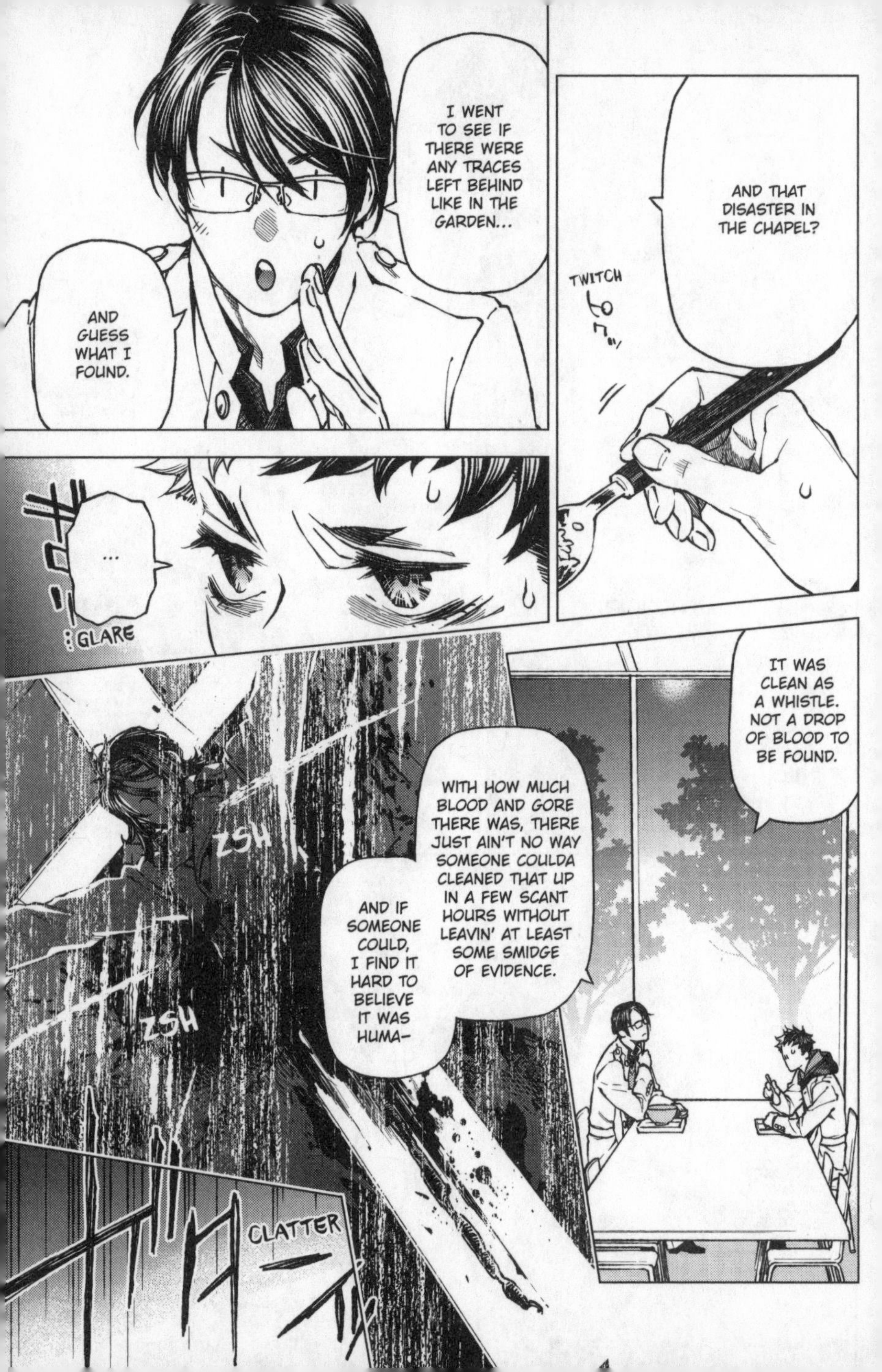
AND THAT DISASTER IN THE CHAPEL?
TWITCH
I WENT TO SEE IF THERE WERE ANY TRACES LEFT BEHIND LIKE IN THE GARDEN...
AND GUESS WHAT I FOUND.
...
GLARE
IT WAS CLEAN AS A WHISTLE. NOT A DROP OF BLOOD TO BE FOUND.
WITH HOW MUCH BLOOD AND GORE THERE WAS, THERE JUST AIN'T NO WAY SOMEONE COULDA CLEANED THAT UP IN A FEW SCANT HOURS WITHOUT LEAVIN' AT LEAST SOME SMIDGE OF EVIDENCE.
AND IF SOMEONE COULD, I FIND IT HARD TO BELIEVE IT WAS HUMA-
ZSH
ZSH
CLATTER

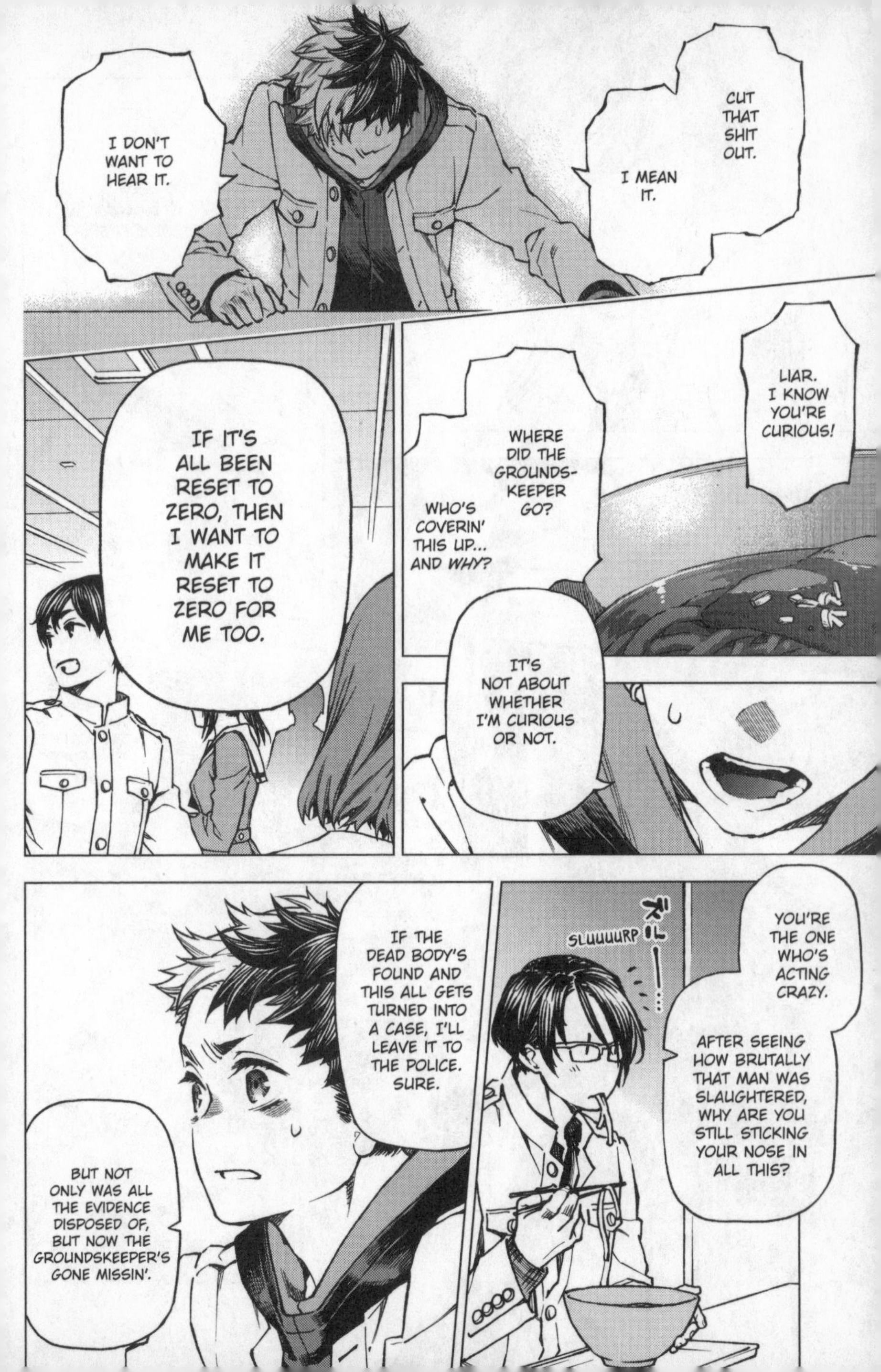
CUT THAT SHIT OUT.
I MEAN IT.
I DON'T WANT TO HEAR IT.
LIAR. I KNOW YOU'RE CURIOUS!
WHERE DID THE GROUNDS-KEEPER GO?
WHO'S COVERIN' THIS UP... AND WHY?
IT'S NOT ABOUT WHETHER I'M CURIOUS OR NOT.
IF IT'S ALL BEEN RESET TO ZERO, THEN I WANT TO MAKE IT RESET TO ZERO FOR ME TOO.
YOU'RE THE ONE WHO'S ACTING CRAZY.
SLUUUURP
AFTER SEEING HOW BRUTALLY THAT MAN WAS SLAUGHTERED, WHY ARE YOU STILL STICKING YOUR NOSE IN ALL THIS?
IF THE DEAD BODY'S FOUND AND THIS ALL GETS TURNED INTO A CASE, I'LL LEAVE IT TO THE POLICE. SURE.
BUT NOT ONLY WAS ALL THE EVIDENCE DISPOSED OF, BUT NOW THE GROUNDSKEEPER'S GONE MISSIN'.

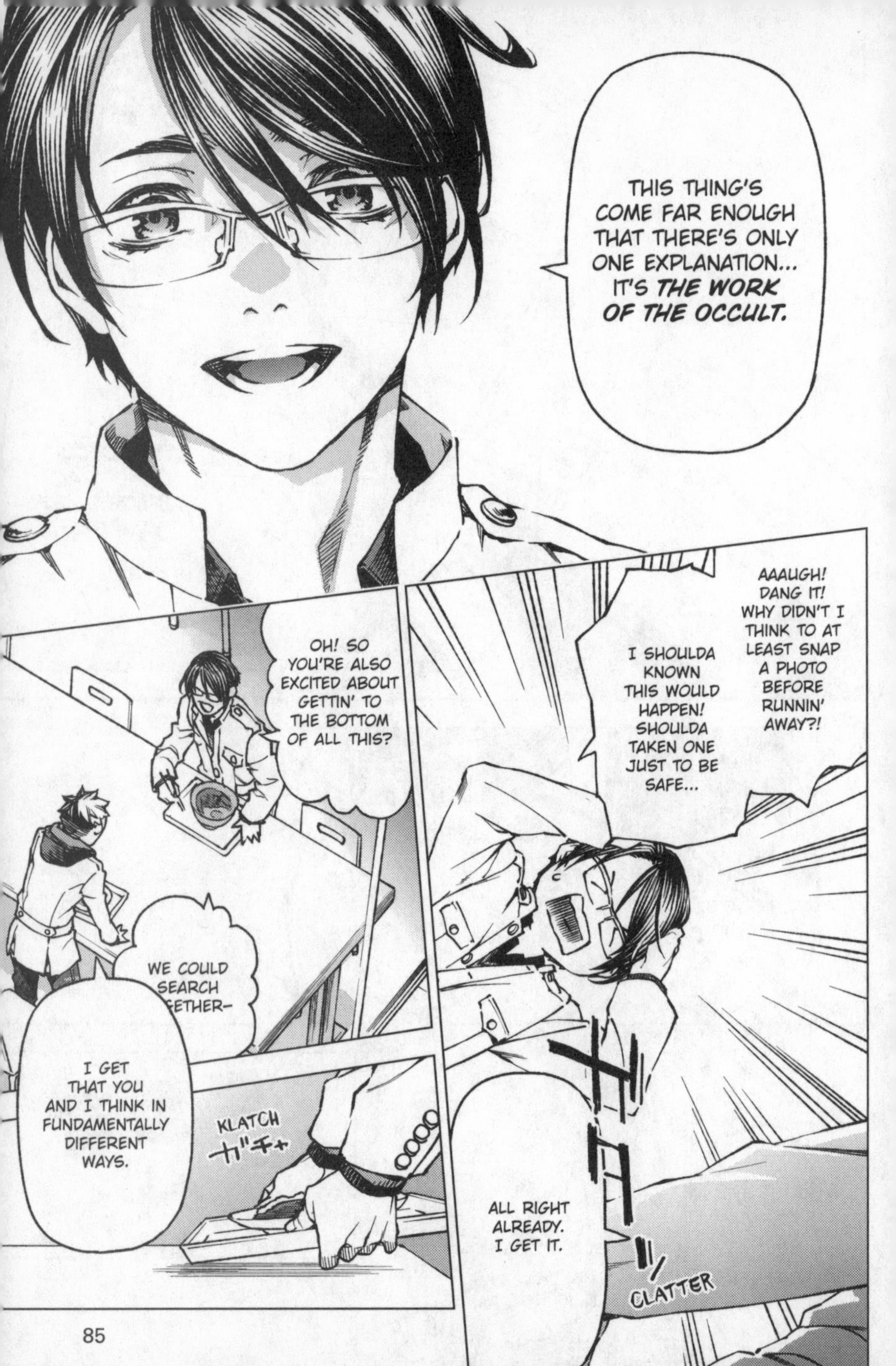
THIS THING'S COME FAR ENOUGH THAT THERE'S ONLY ONE EXPLANATION... IT'S ***THE WORK OF THE OCCULT.***
AAAUGH! DANG IT! WHY DIDN'T I THINK TO AT LEAST SNAP A PHOTO BEFORE RUNNIN' AWAY?!
I SHOULDA KNOWN THIS WOULD HAPPEN! SHOULDA TAKEN ONE JUST TO BE SAFE...
ALL RIGHT ALREADY. I GET IT.
CLATTER
OH! SO YOU'RE ALSO EXCITED ABOUT GETTIN' TO THE BOTTOM OF ALL THIS?
WE COULD SEARCH GETHER-
I GET THAT YOU AND I THINK IN FUNDAMENTALLY DIFFERENT WAYS.
KLATCH

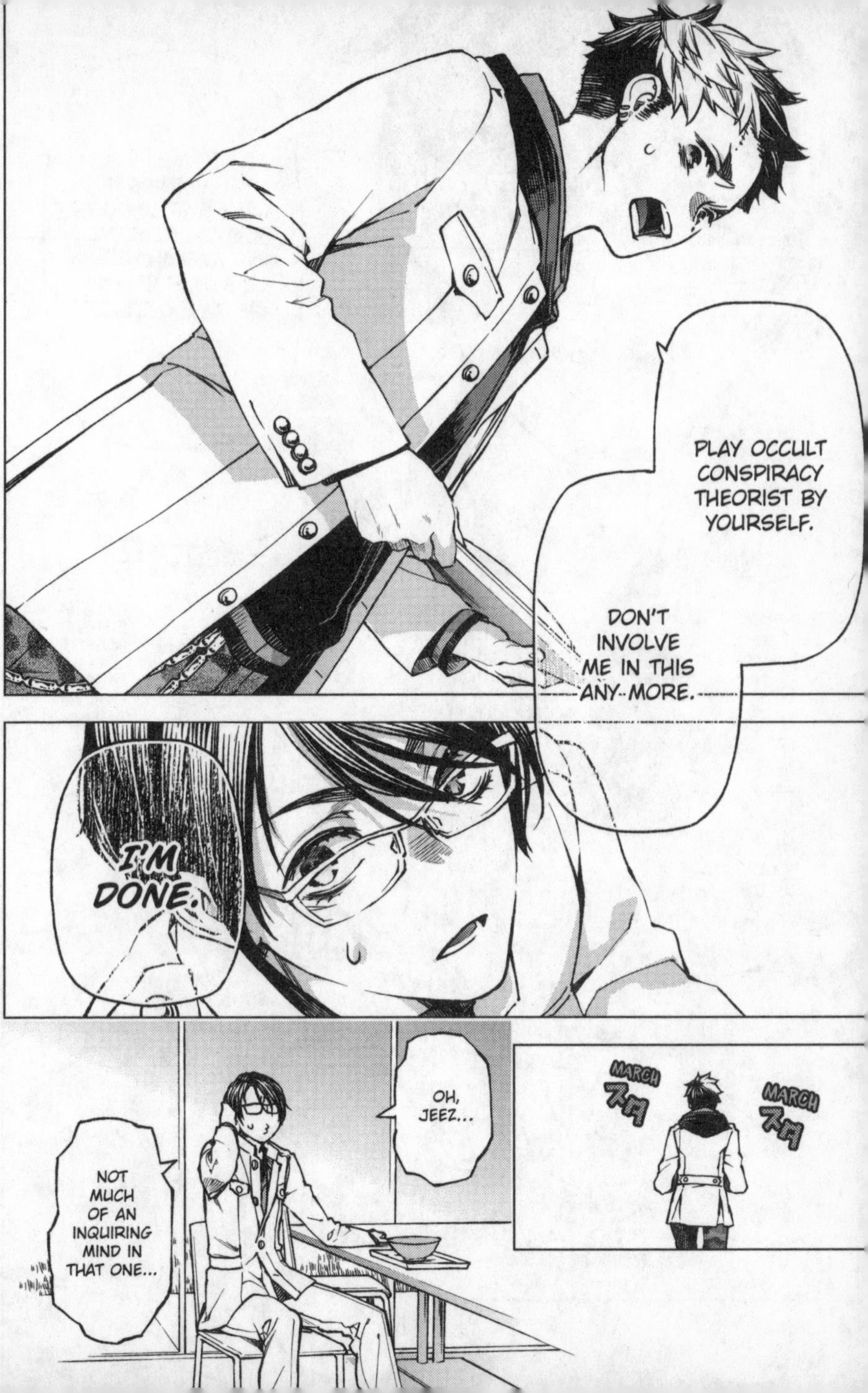
PLAY OCCULT CONSPIRACY THEORIST BY YOURSELF.
DON'T INVOLVE ME IN THIS ANY-MORE.
I'M DONE.
MARCH
スタ
MARCH
スタ
OH, JEEZ...
NOT MUCH OF AN INQUIRING MIND IN THAT ONE...

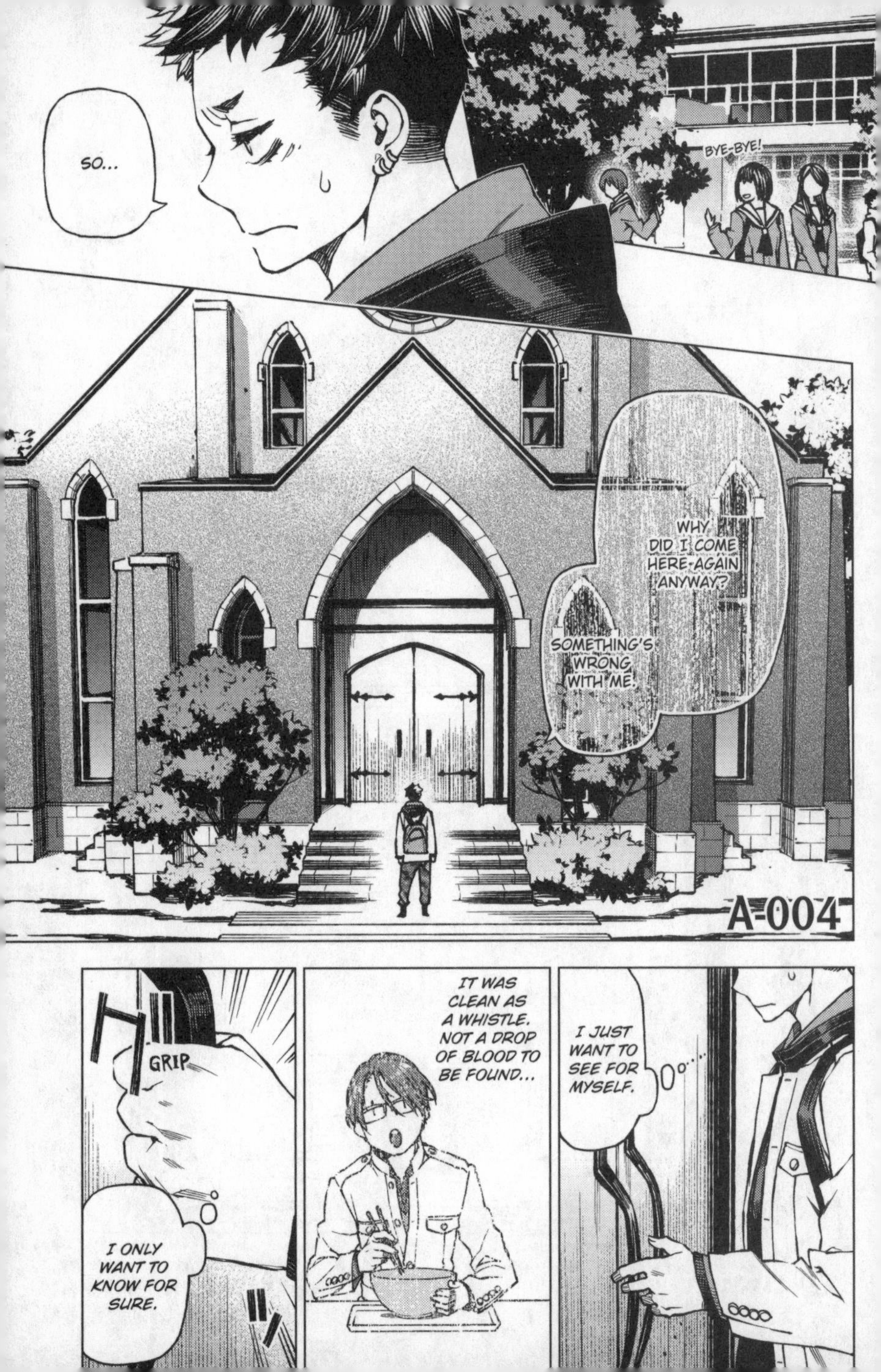
BYE-BYE!
SO...
WHY DID I COME HERE AGAIN ANYWAY?
SOMETHING'S WRONG WITH ME.
A-004
I JUST WANT TO SEE FOR MYSELF.
IT WAS CLEAN AS A WHISTLE. NOT A DROP OF BLOOD TO BE FOUND...
GRIP
I ONLY WANT TO KNOW FOR SURE.

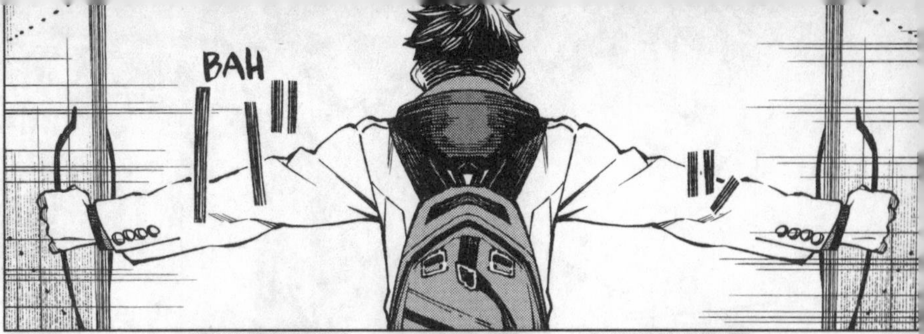
BAH
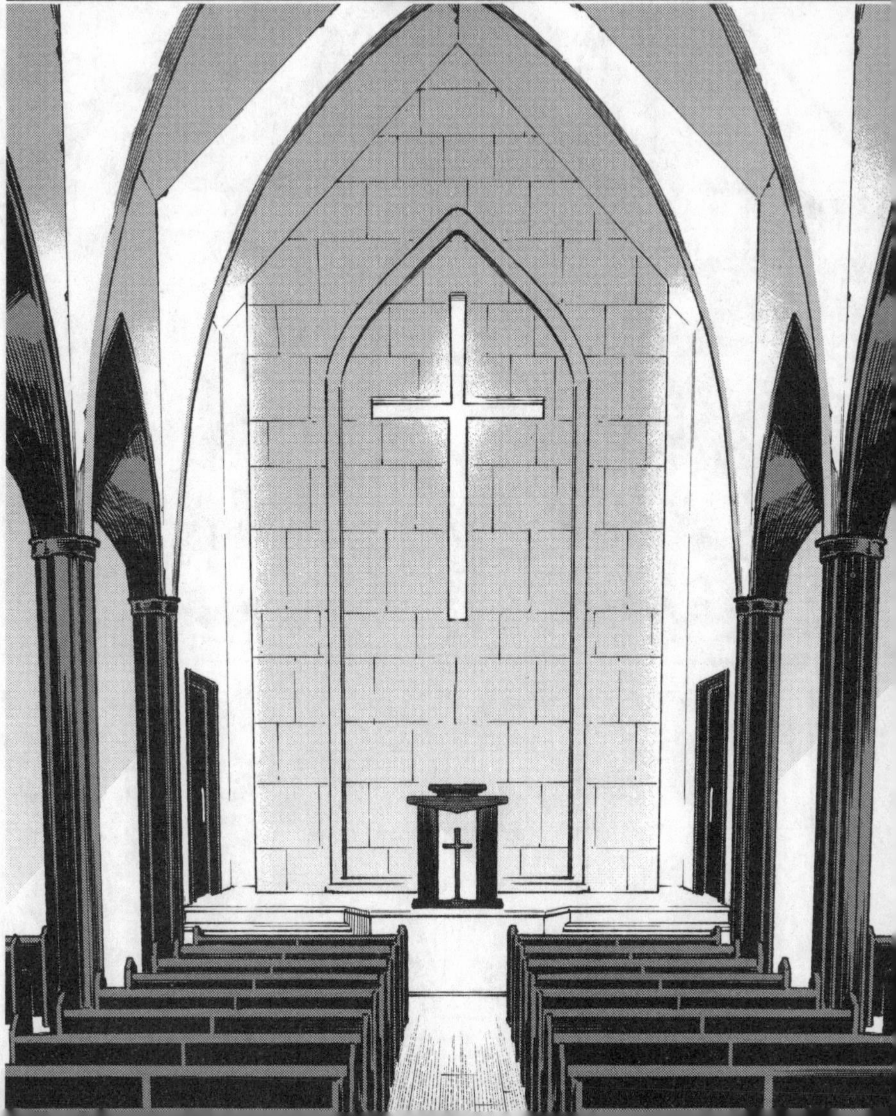

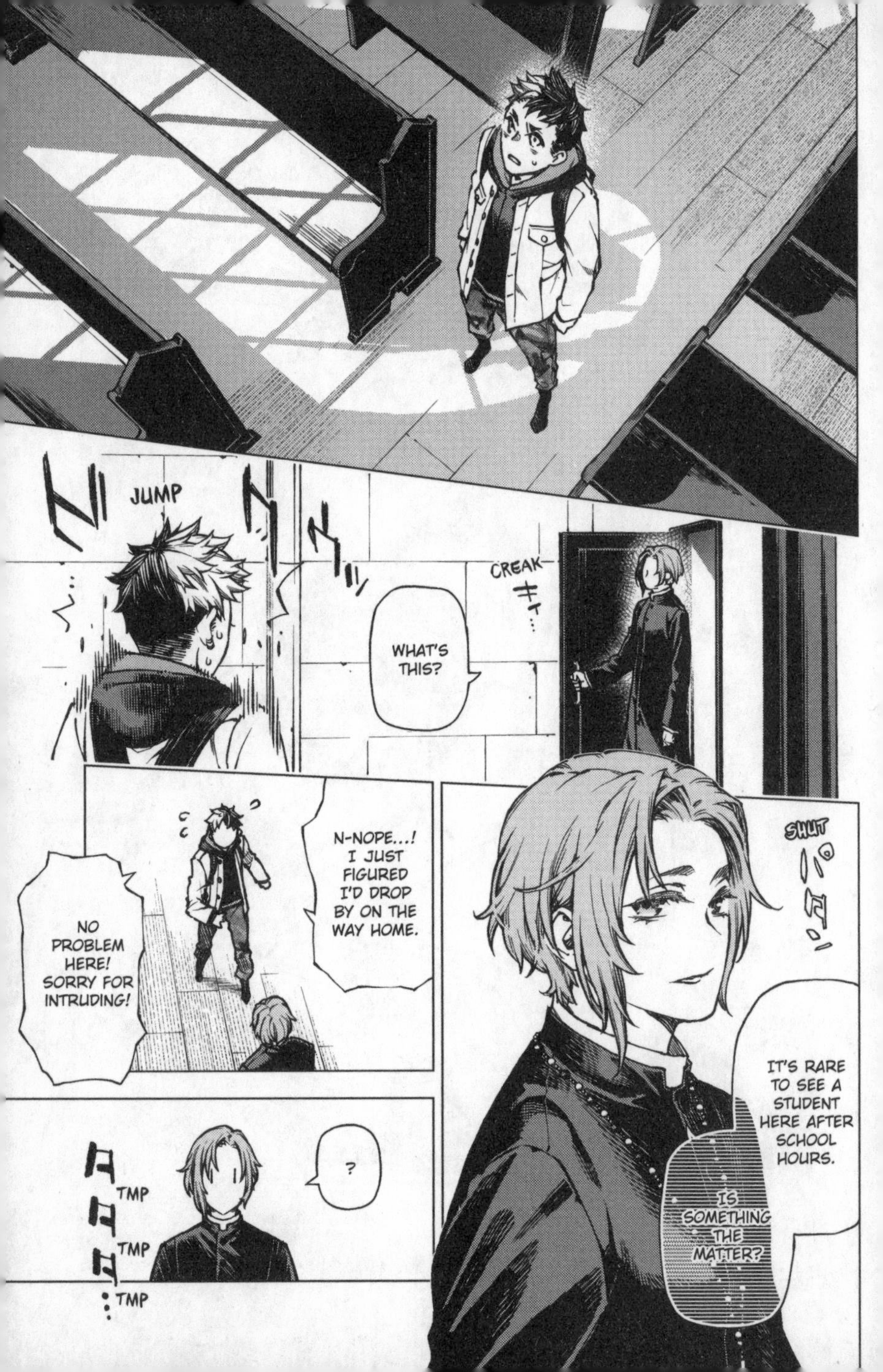
CREAK
WHAT'S THIS?
JUMP
SHUT
IT'S RARE TO SEE A STUDENT HERE AFTER SCHOOL HOURS.
IS SOMETHING THE MATTER?
N-NOPE...! I JUST FIGURED I'D DROP BY ON THE WAY HOME.
NO PROBLEM HERE! SORRY FOR INTRUDING!
?
TMP
TMP
TMP

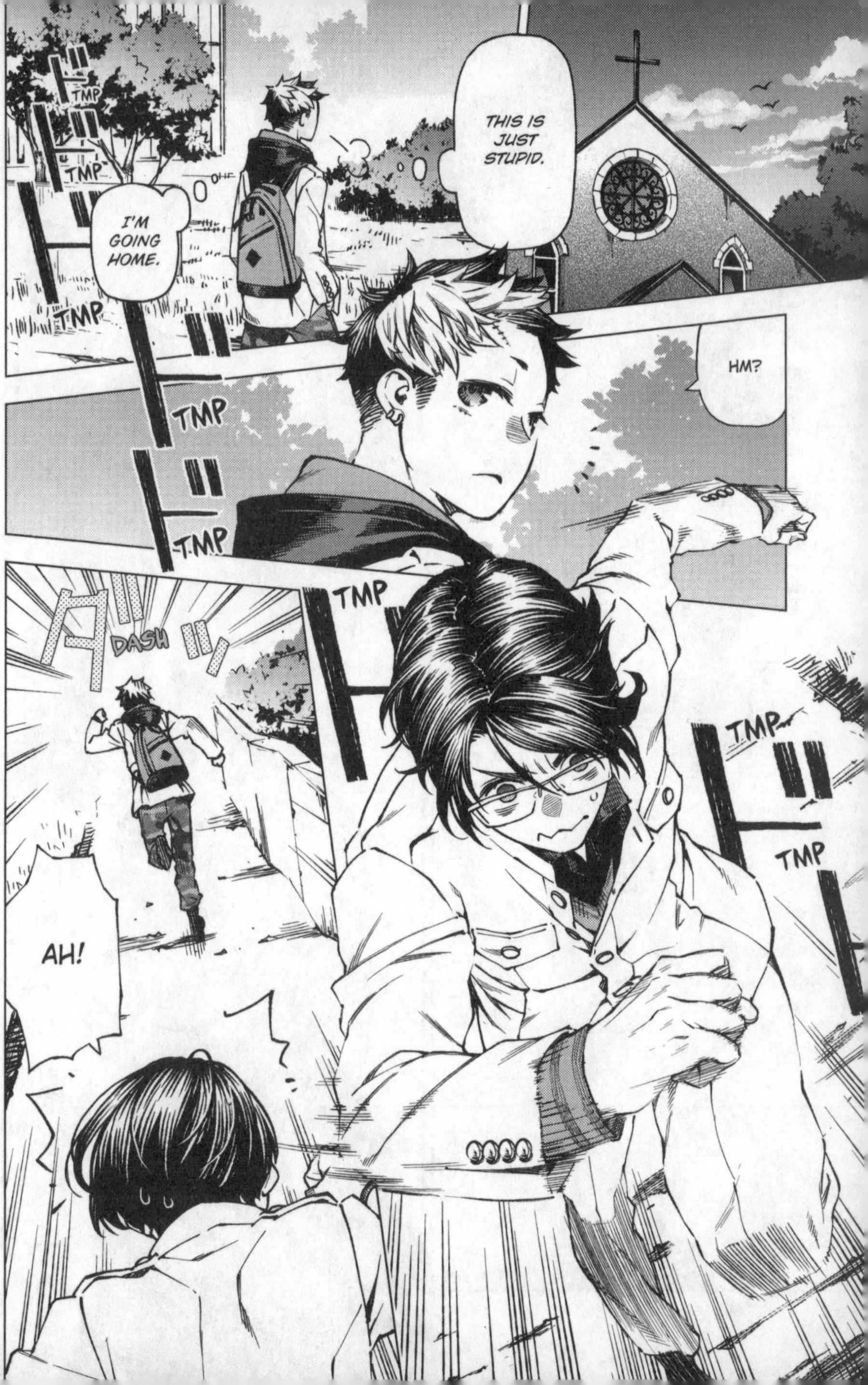
THIS IS JUST STUPID.
I'M GOING HOME.
TMP
TMP
TMP
HM?
TMP
TMP
TMP
TMP
TMP
DASH
AH!

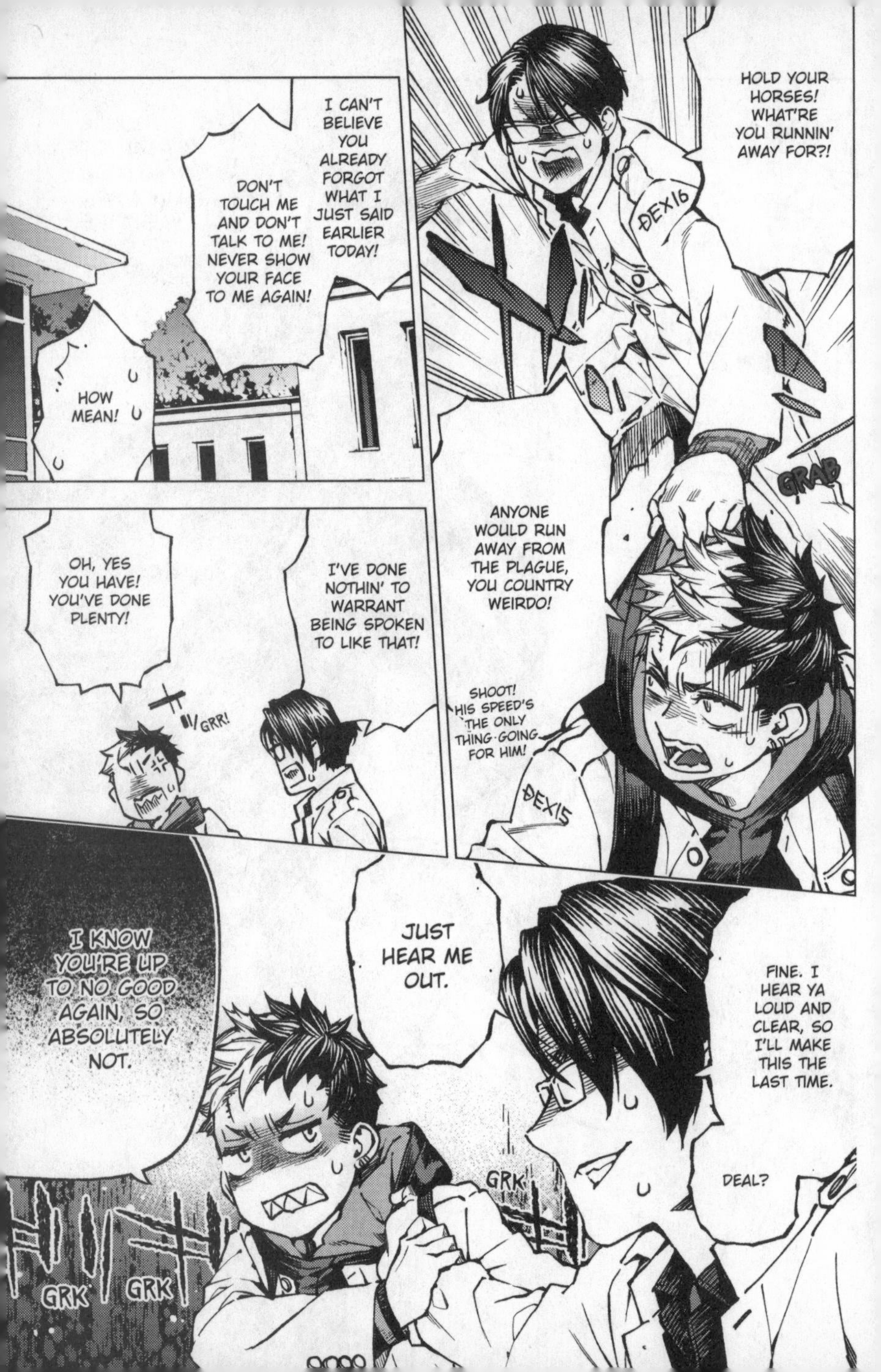

HOLD YOUR HORSES! WHAT'RE YOU RUNNIN' AWAY FOR?!
ĐEX16
GRAB
ANYONE WOULD RUN AWAY FROM THE PLAGUE, YOU COUNTRY WEIRDO!
SHOOT! HIS SPEED'S THE ONLY THING GOING FOR HIM!
ĐEX15
I CAN'T BELIEVE YOU ALREADY FORGOT WHAT I JUST SAID EARLIER TODAY!
DON'T TOUCH ME AND DON'T TALK TO ME! NEVER SHOW YOUR FACE TO ME AGAIN!
HOW MEAN!
I'VE DONE NOTHIN' TO WARRANT BEING SPOKEN TO LIKE THAT!
OH, YES YOU HAVE! YOU'VE DONE PLENTY!
GRR!
FINE. I HEAR YA LOUD AND CLEAR, SO I'LL MAKE THIS THE LAST TIME.
JUST HEAR ME OUT.
I KNOW YOU'RE UP TO NO GOOD AGAIN, SO ABSOLUTELY NOT.
DEAL?
GRK
GRK
GRK

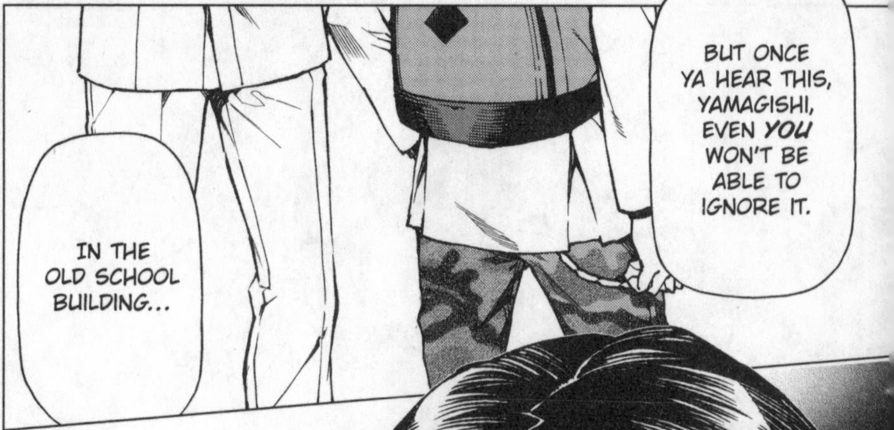
BUT ONCE YA HEAR THIS, YAMAGISHI, EVEN *YOU* WON'T BE ABLE TO IGNORE IT.
IN THE OLD SCHOOL BUILDING...
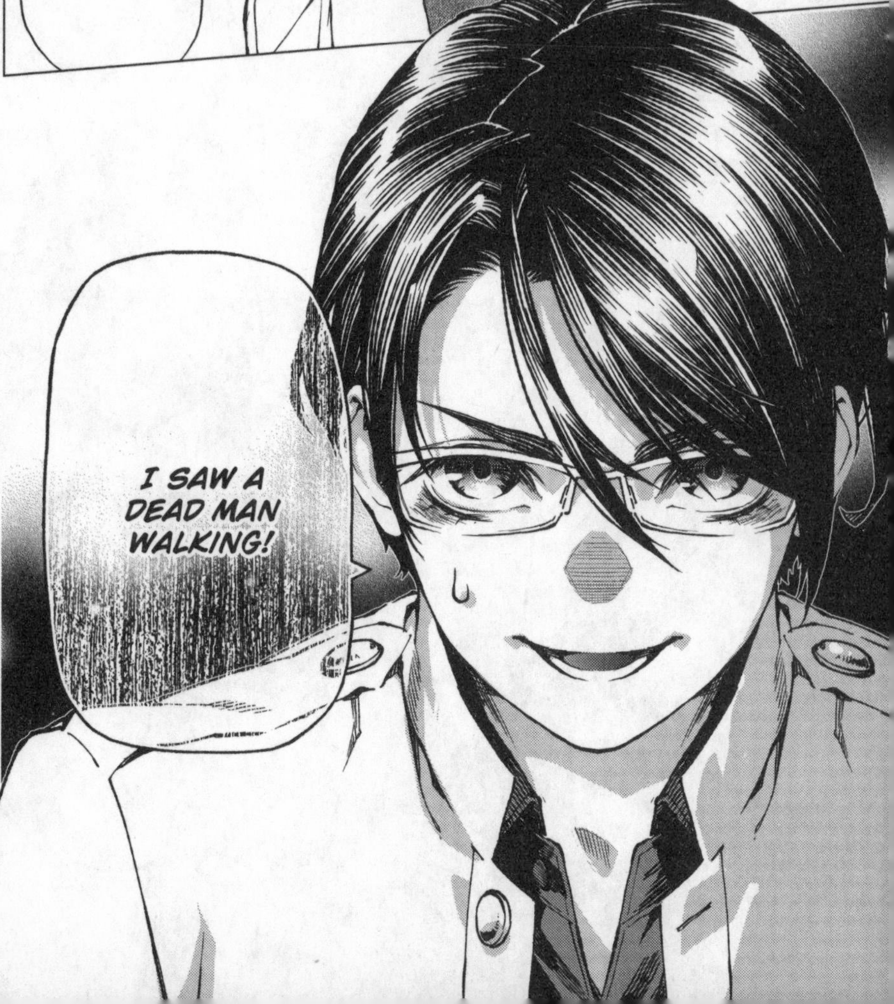
I SAW A DEAD MAN WALKING!

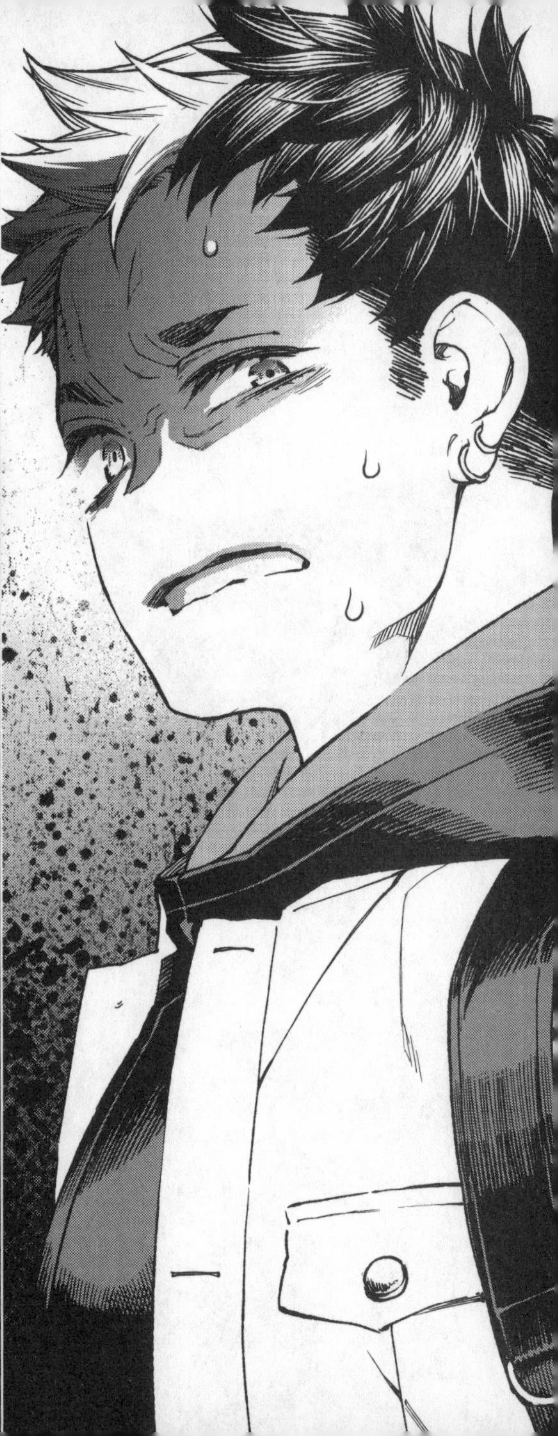

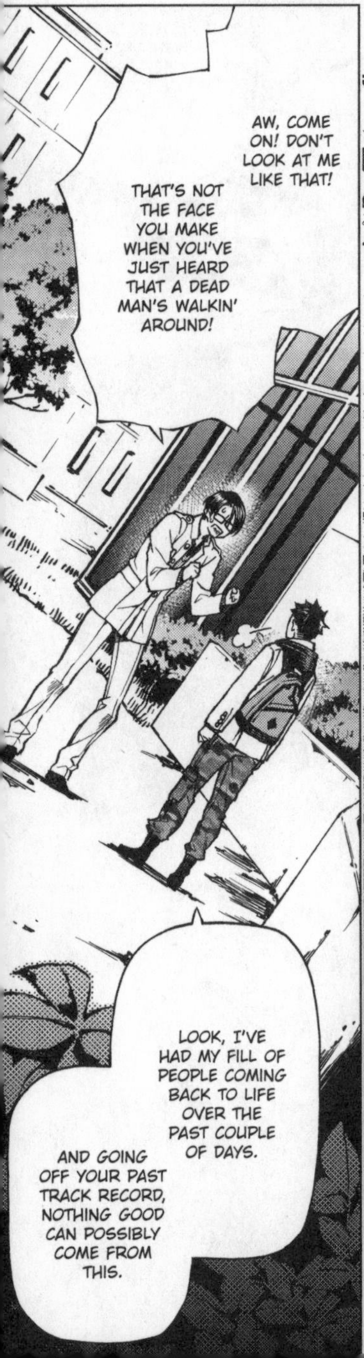
AW, COME ON! DON'T LOOK AT ME LIKE THAT!
THAT'S NOT THE FACE YOU MAKE WHEN YOU'VE JUST HEARD THAT A DEAD MAN'S WALKIN' AROUND!
LOOK, I'VE HAD MY FILL OF PEOPLE COMING BACK TO LIFE OVER THE PAST COUPLE OF DAYS.
AND GOING OFF YOUR PAST TRACK RECORD, NOTHING GOOD CAN POSSIBLY COME FROM THIS.

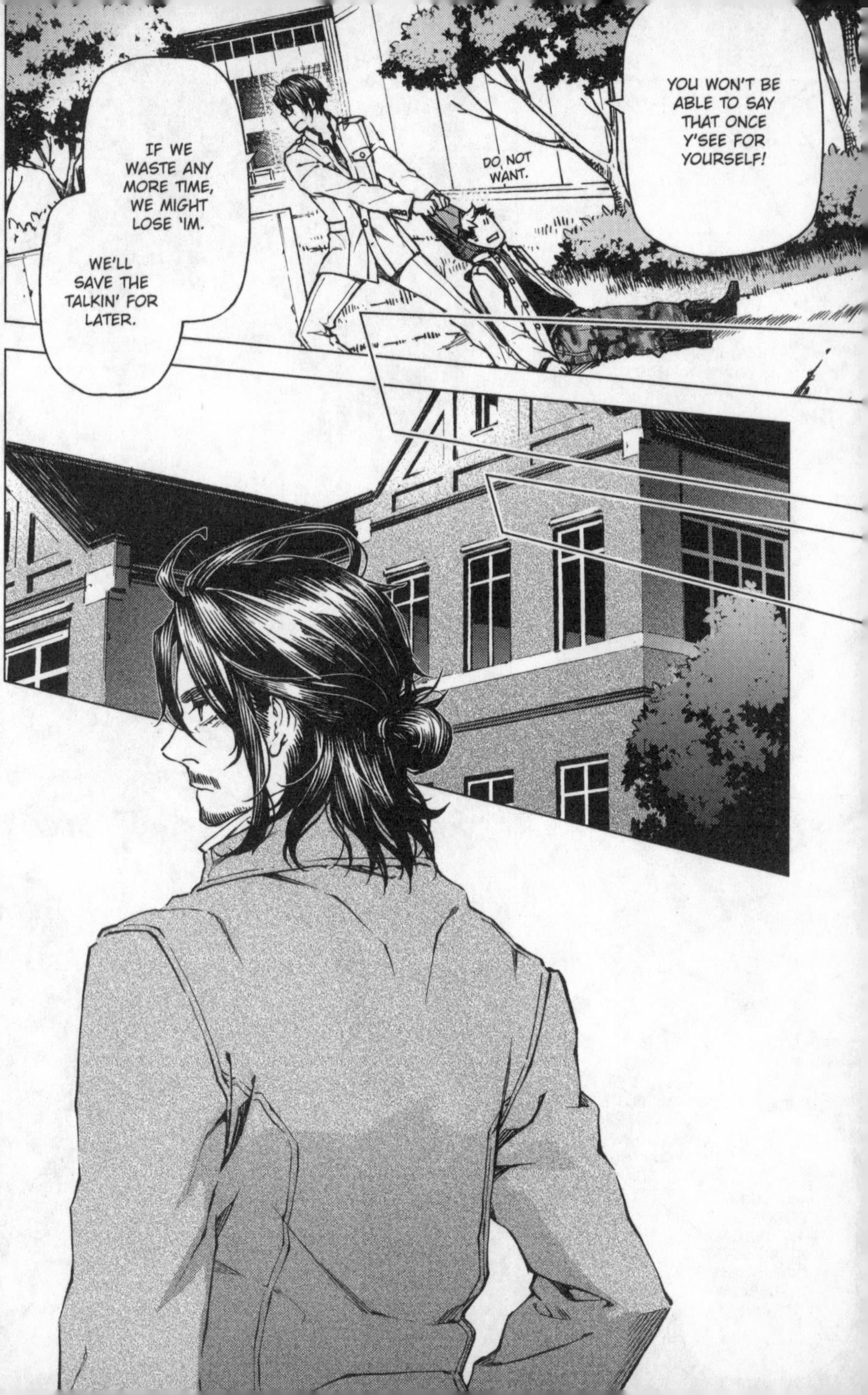
YOU WON'T BE ABLE TO SAY THAT ONCE Y'SEE FOR YOURSELF!
DO NOT WANT.
IF WE WASTE ANY MORE TIME, WE MIGHT LOSE 'IM.
WE'LL SAVE THE TALKIN' FOR LATER.

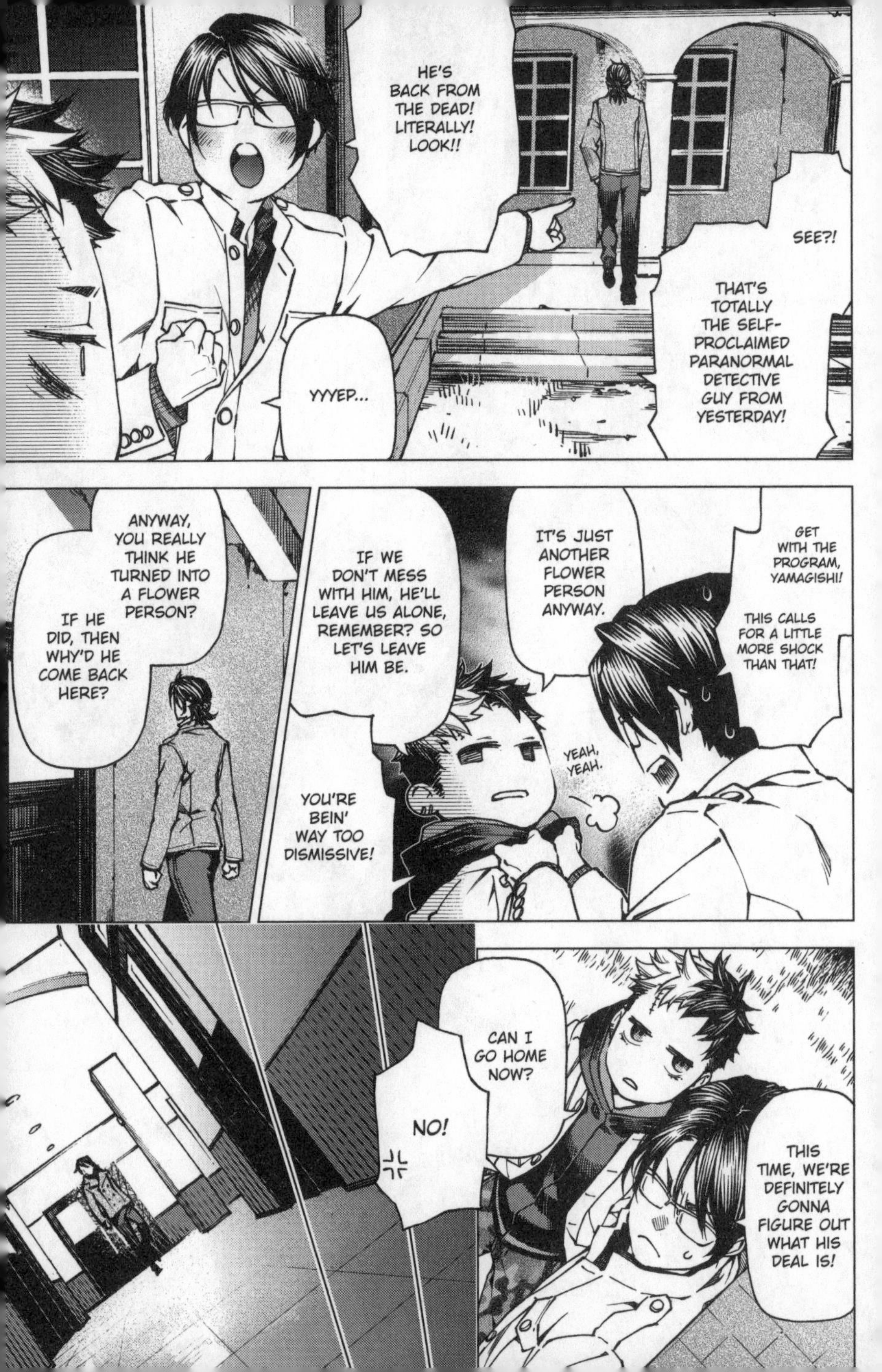
HE'S BACK FROM THE DEAD! LITERALLY! LOOK!!
SEE?!
THAT'S TOTALLY THE SELF-PROCLAIMED PARANORMAL DETECTIVE GUY FROM YESTERDAY!
YYYEP...
GET WITH THE PROGRAM, YAMAGISHI!
THIS CALLS FOR A LITTLE MORE SHOCK THAN THAT!
IT'S JUST ANOTHER FLOWER PERSON ANYWAY.
YEAH, YEAH.
IF WE DON'T MESS WITH HIM, HE'LL LEAVE US ALONE, REMEMBER? SO LET'S LEAVE HIM BE.
YOU'RE BEIN' WAY TOO DISMISSIVE!
ANYWAY, YOU REALLY THINK HE TURNED INTO A FLOWER PERSON?
IF HE DID, THEN WHY'D HE COME BACK HERE?
THIS TIME, WE'RE DEFINITELY GONNA FIGURE OUT WHAT HIS DEAL IS!
CAN I GO HOME NOW?
NO!

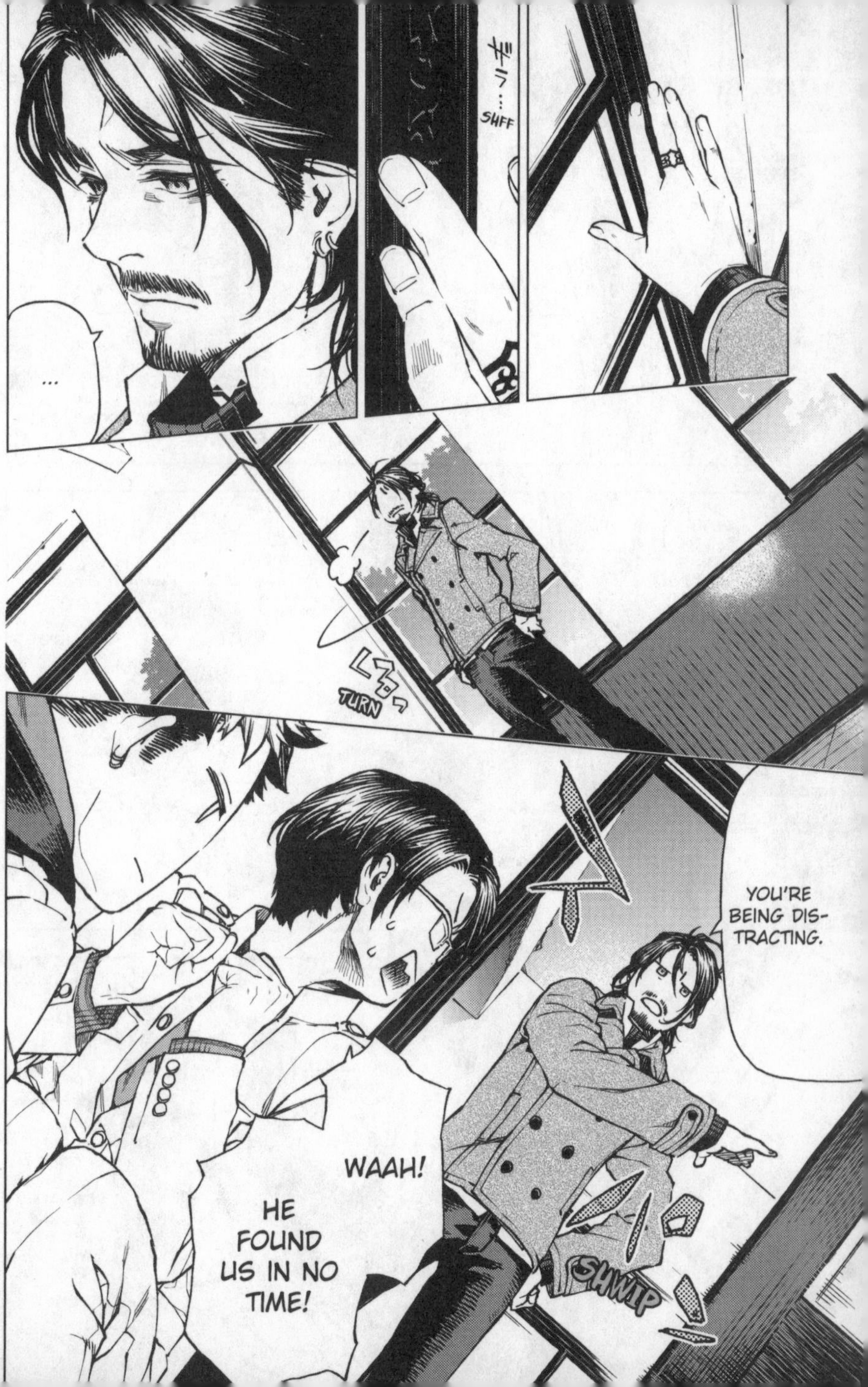
SHUFF
...
TURN
YOU'RE BEING DIS-TRACTING.
SHWIP
WAAH!
HE FOUND US IN NO TIME!

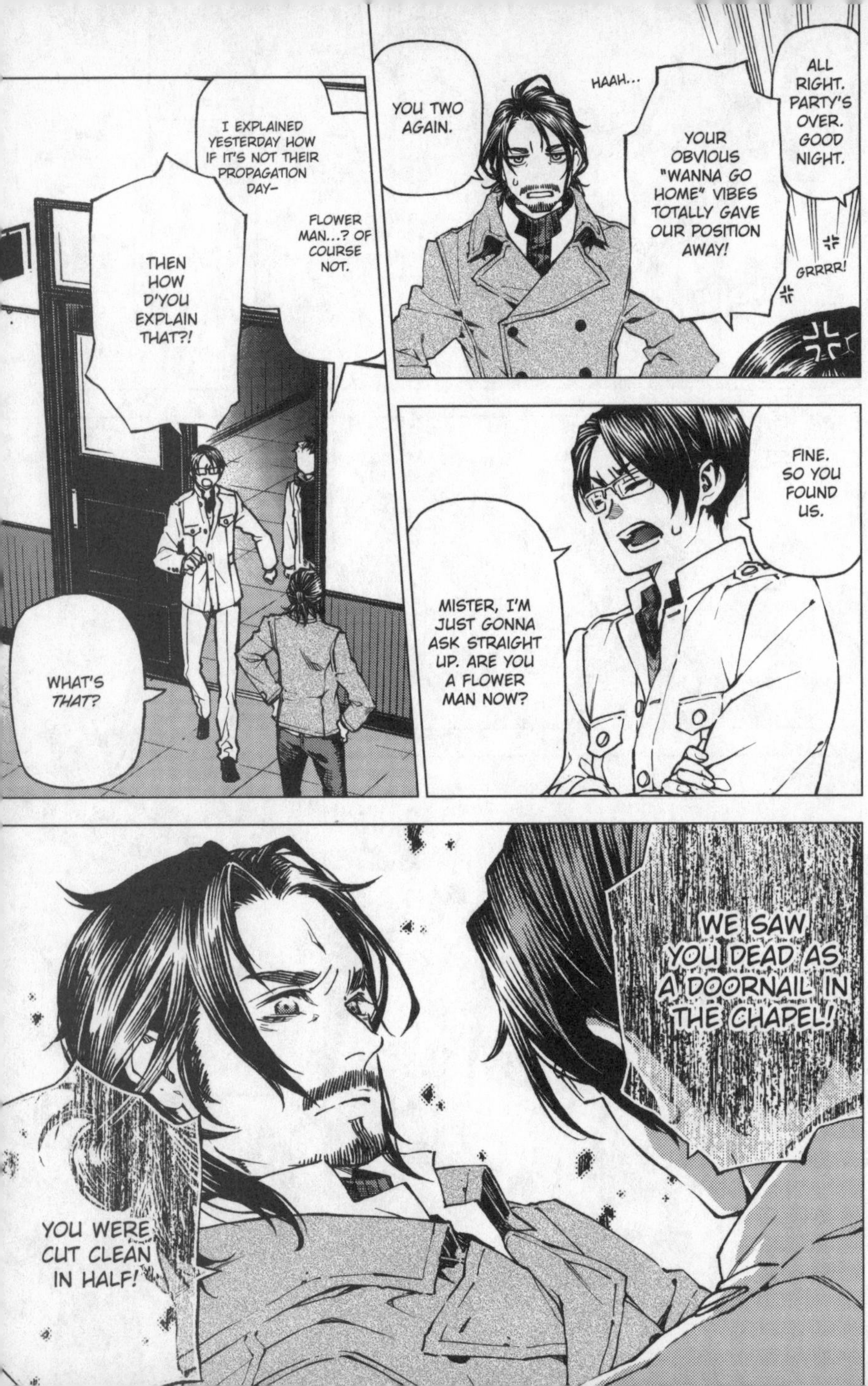
ALL RIGHT. PARTY'S OVER. GOOD NIGHT.
GRRRR!
YOUR OBVIOUS "WANNA GO HOME" VIBES TOTALLY GAVE OUR POSITION AWAY!
HAAH...
YOU TWO AGAIN.
FINE. SO YOU FOUND US.
MISTER, I'M JUST GONNA ASK STRAIGHT UP. ARE YOU A FLOWER MAN NOW?
I EXPLAINED YESTERDAY HOW IF IT'S NOT THEIR PROPAGATION DAY–
FLOWER MAN...? OF COURSE NOT.
THEN HOW D'YOU EXPLAIN THAT?!
WHAT'S THAT?
WE SAW YOU DEAD AS A DOORNAIL IN THE CHAPEL!
YOU WERE CUT CLEAN IN HALF!

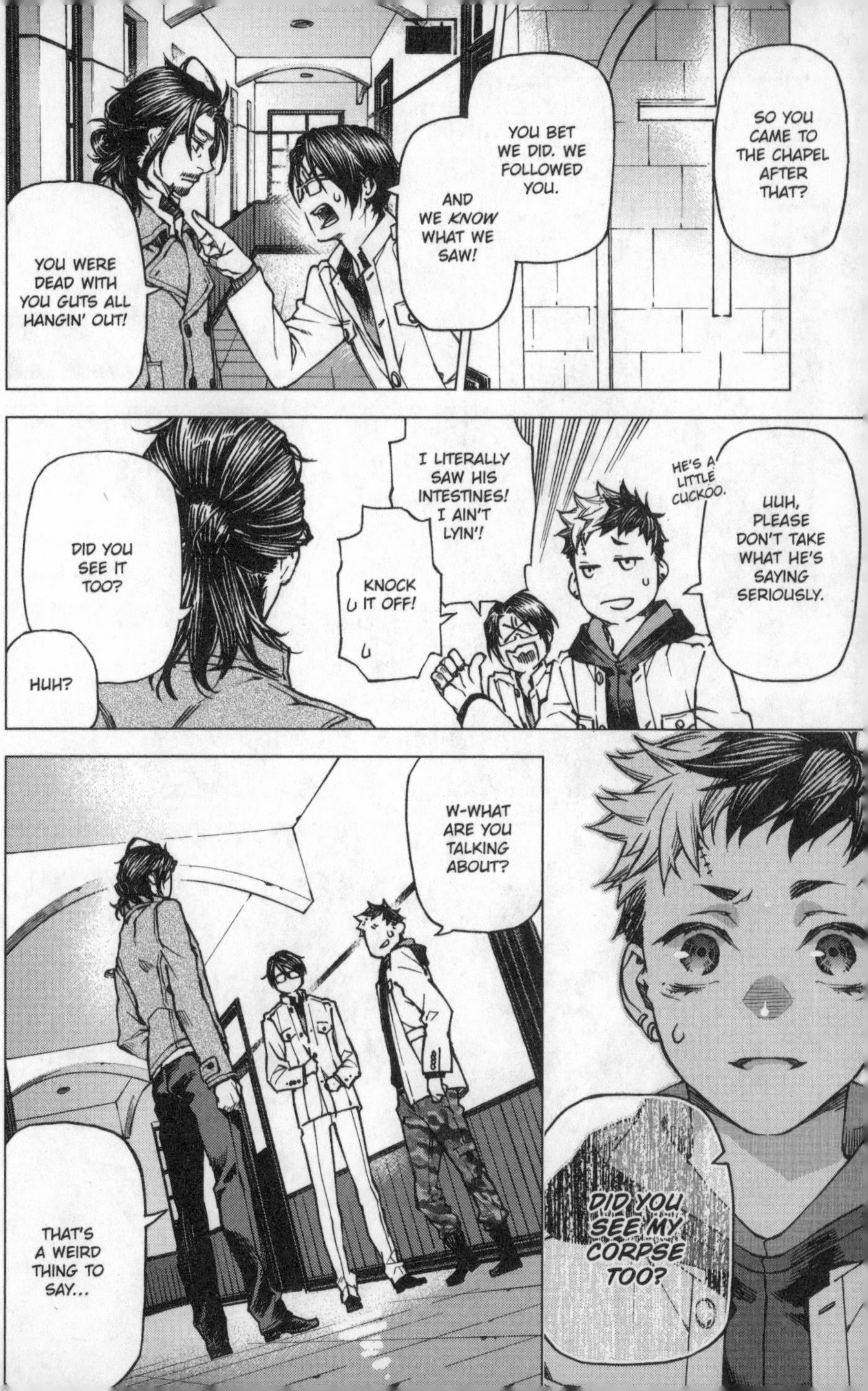
SO YOU CAME TO THE CHAPEL AFTER THAT?
YOU BET WE DID. WE FOLLOWED YOU.
AND WE KNOW WHAT WE SAW!
YOU WERE DEAD WITH YOU GUTS ALL HANGIN' OUT!
HE'S A LITTLE CUCKOO.
UUH, PLEASE DON'T TAKE WHAT HE'S SAYING SERIOUSLY.
I LITERALLY SAW HIS INTESTINES! I AIN'T LYIN'!
KNOCK IT OFF!
DID YOU SEE IT TOO?
HUH?
DID YOU SEE MY CORPSE TOO?
W-WHAT ARE YOU TALKING ABOUT?
THAT'S A WEIRD THING TO SAY...

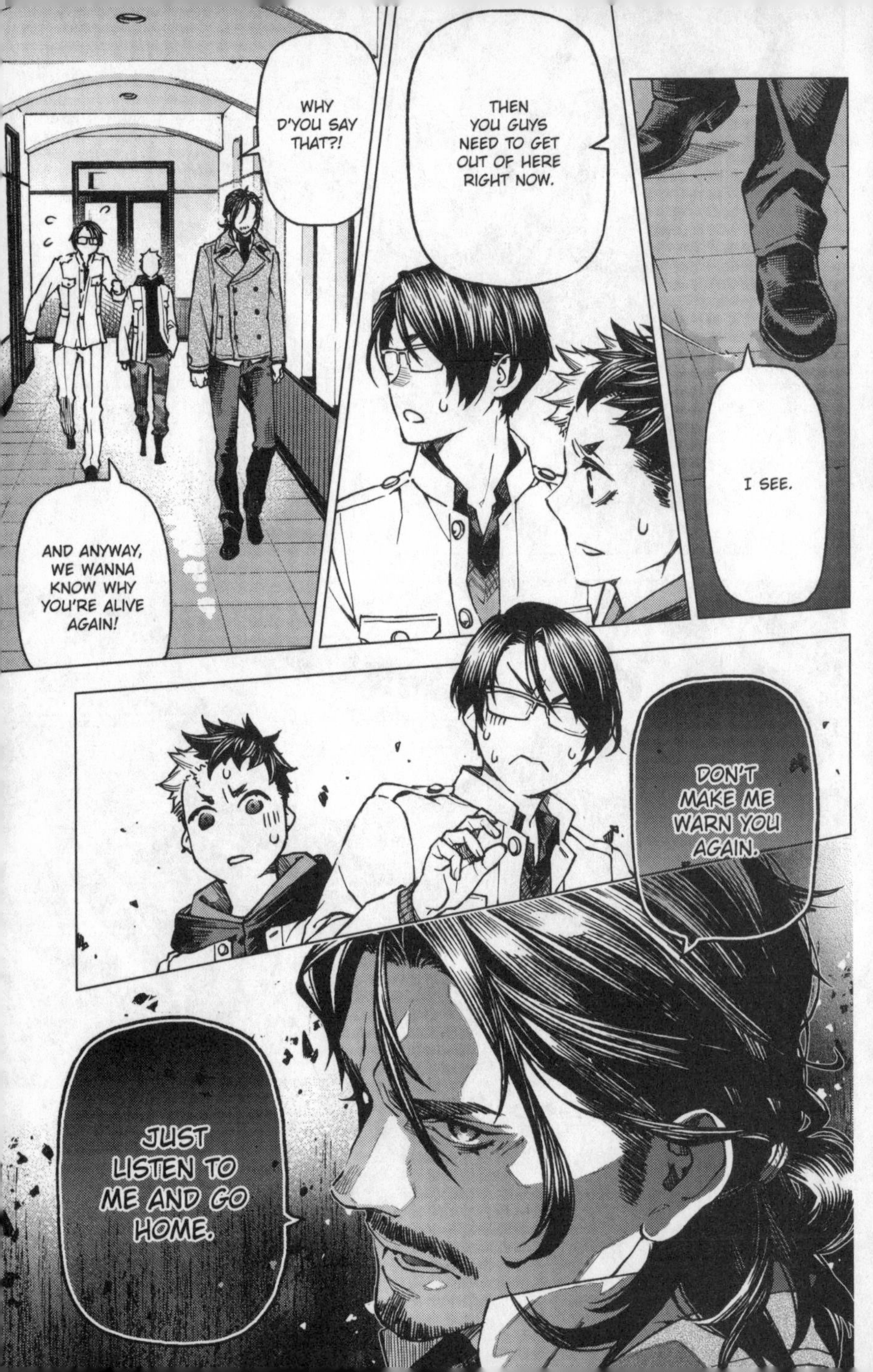
I SEE.
THEN YOU GUYS NEED TO GET OUT OF HERE RIGHT NOW.
WHY D'YOU SAY THAT?!
AND ANYWAY, WE WANNA KNOW WHY YOU'RE ALIVE AGAIN!
DON'T MAKE ME WARN YOU AGAIN.
JUST LISTEN TO ME AND GO HOME.

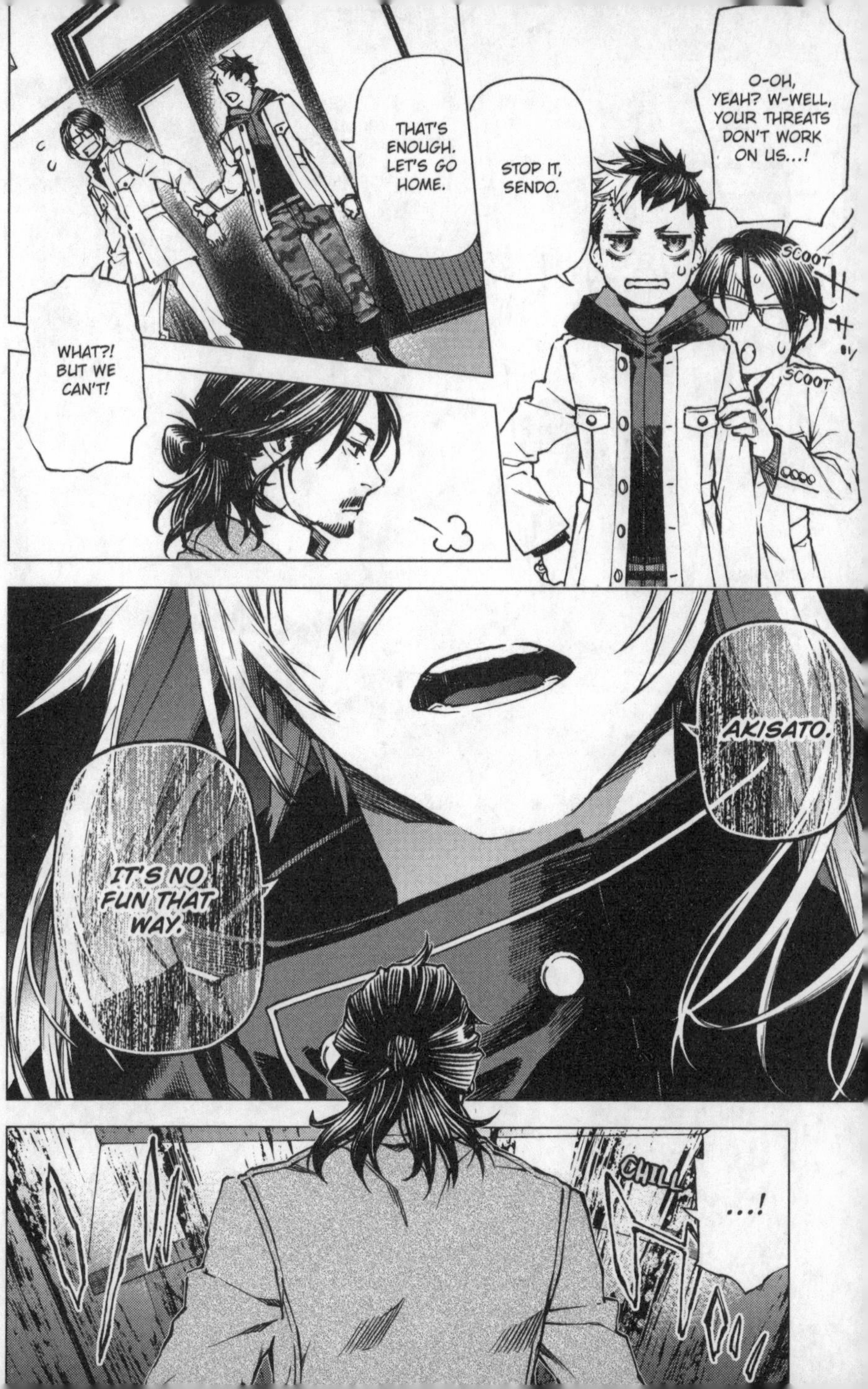
O-OH, YEAH? W-WELL, YOUR THREATS DON'T WORK ON US...!
SCOOT
SCOOT
STOP IT, SENDO.
THAT'S ENOUGH. LET'S GO HOME.
WHAT?! BUT WE CAN'T!
AKISATO.
IT'S NO FUN THAT WAY.
CHILL
...!

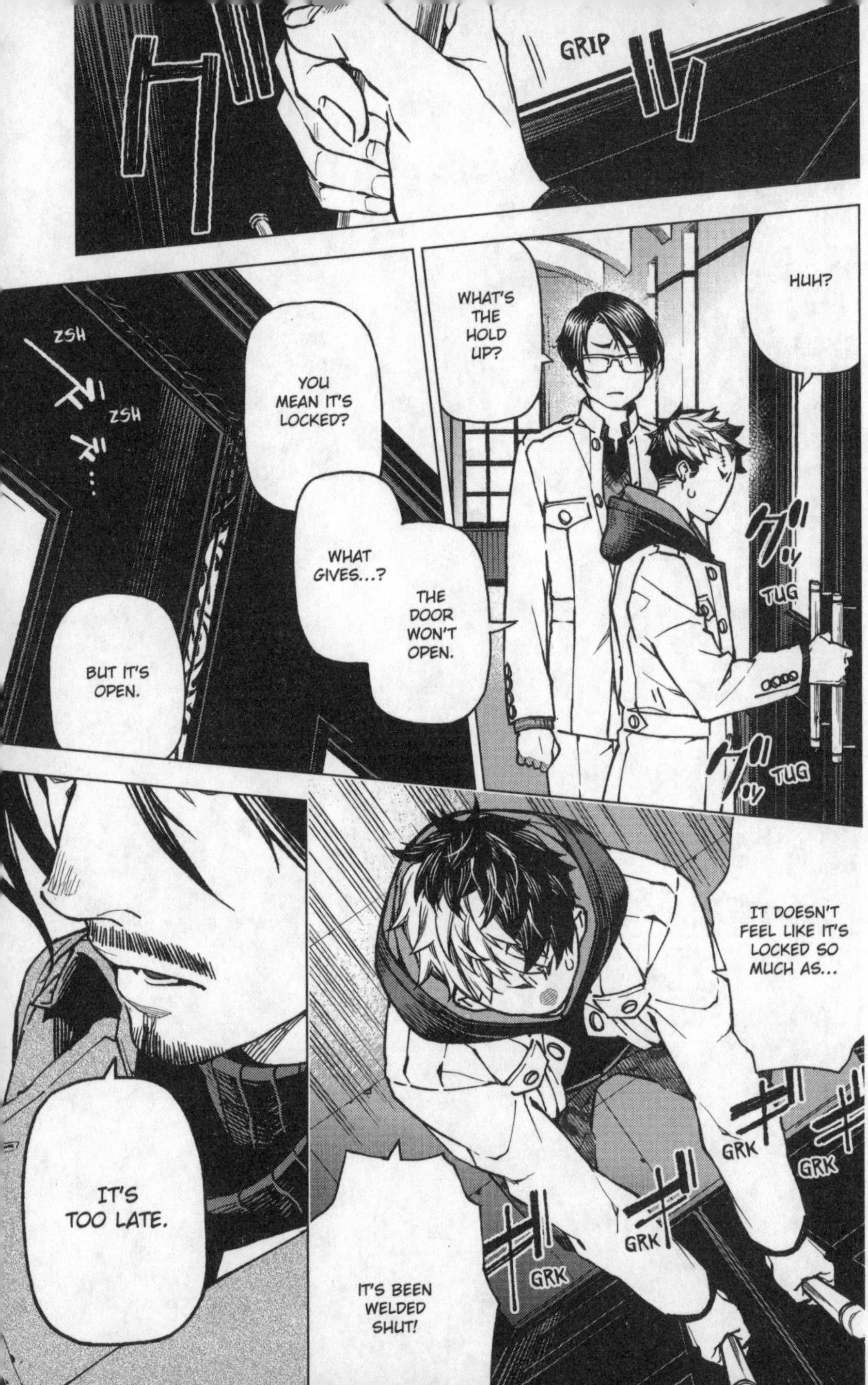
GRIP
HUH?
TUG
TUG
WHAT'S THE HOLD UP?
YOU MEAN IT'S LOCKED?
THE DOOR WON'T OPEN.
WHAT GIVES...?
ZSH
ZSH
BUT IT'S OPEN.
IT DOESN'T FEEL LIKE IT'S LOCKED SO MUCH AS...
GRK
GRK
GRK
GRK
IT'S BEEN WELDED SHUT!
IT'S TOO LATE.

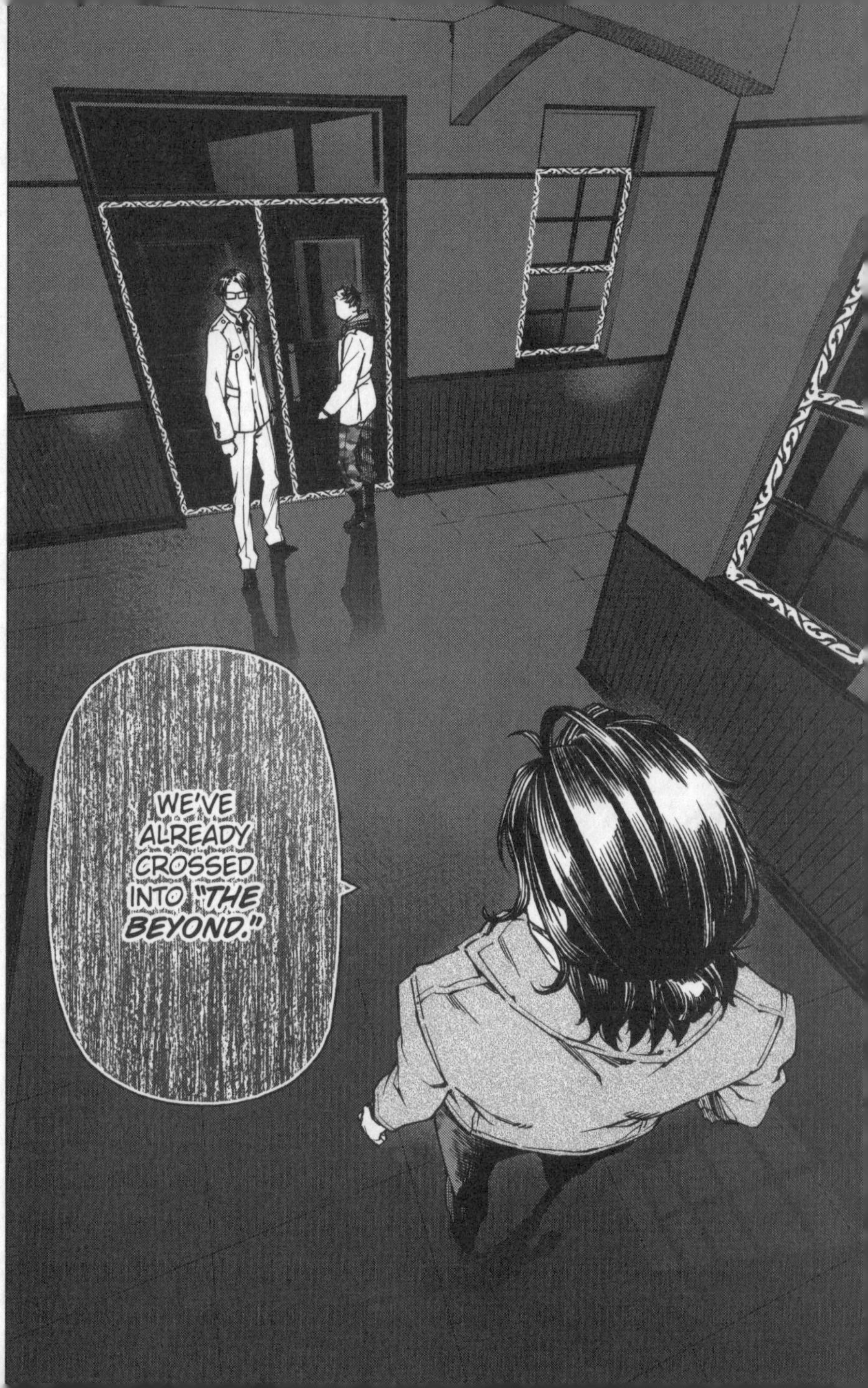
WE'VE ALREADY CROSSED INTO "THE BEYOND."

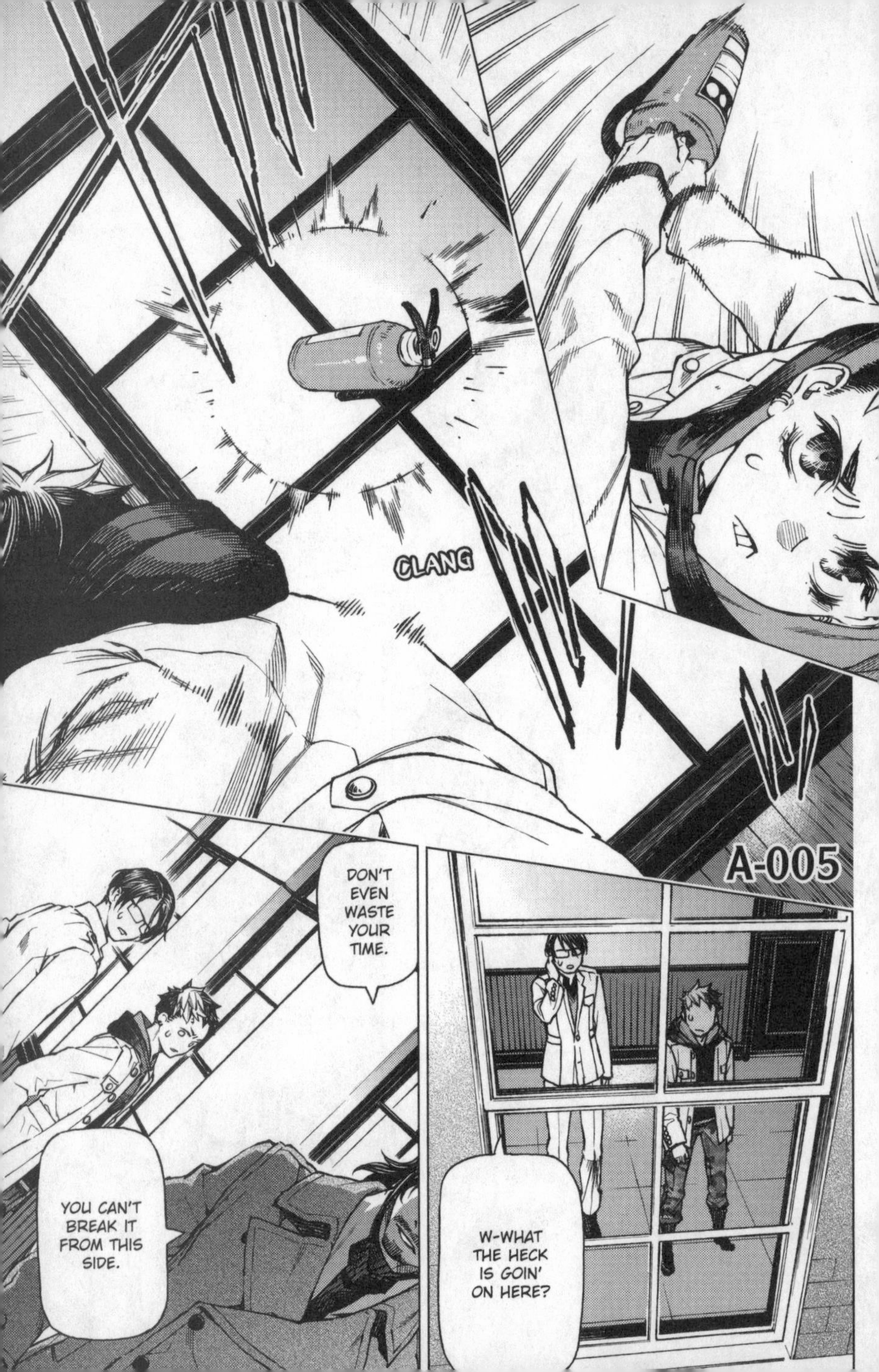
CLANG
A-005
W-WHAT THE HECK IS GOIN' ON HERE?
DON'T EVEN WASTE YOUR TIME.
YOU CAN'T BREAK IT FROM THIS SIDE.

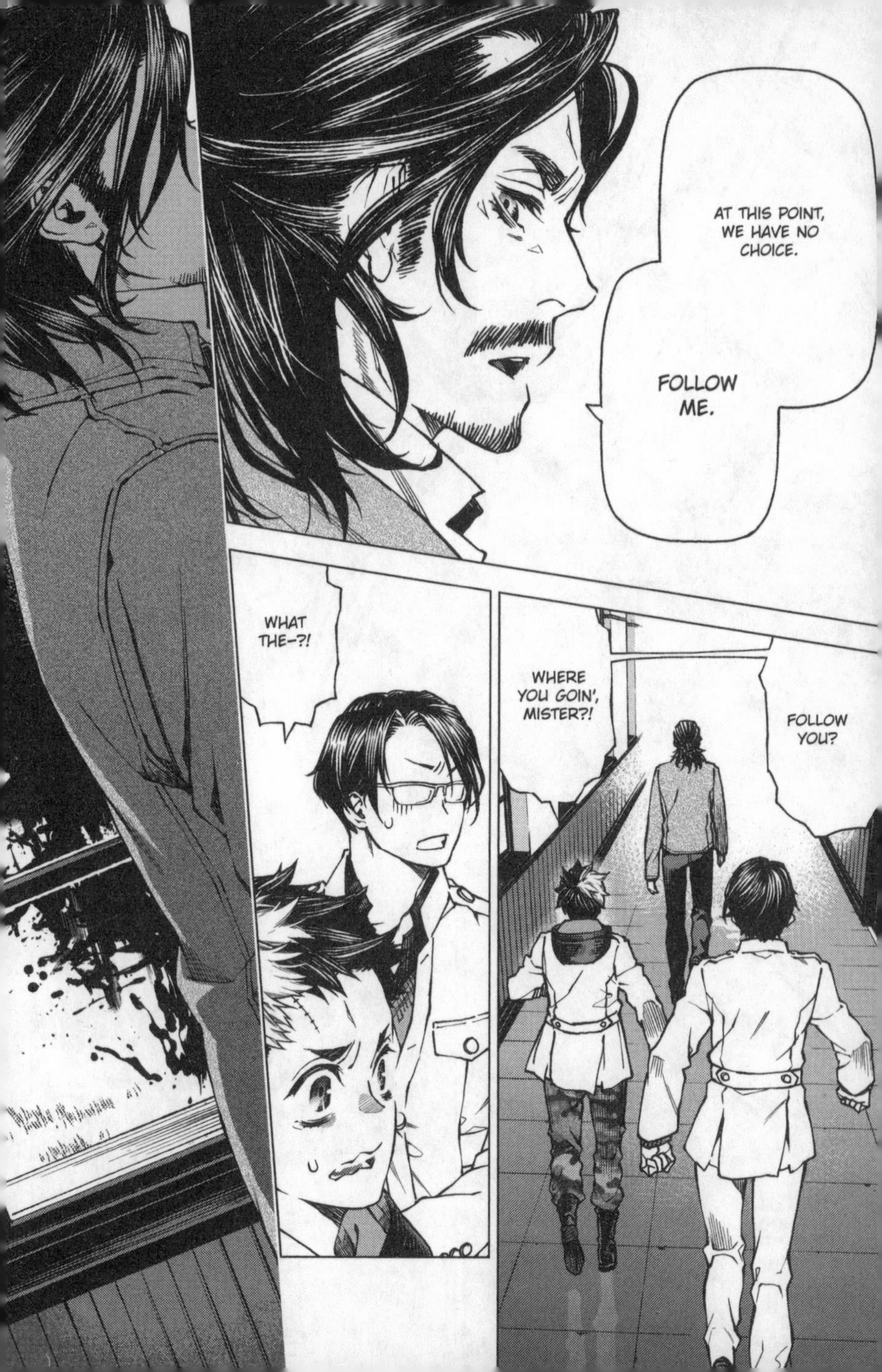
AT THIS POINT, WE HAVE NO CHOICE.
FOLLOW ME.
FOLLOW YOU?
WHERE YOU GOIN', MISTER?!
WHAT THE-?!

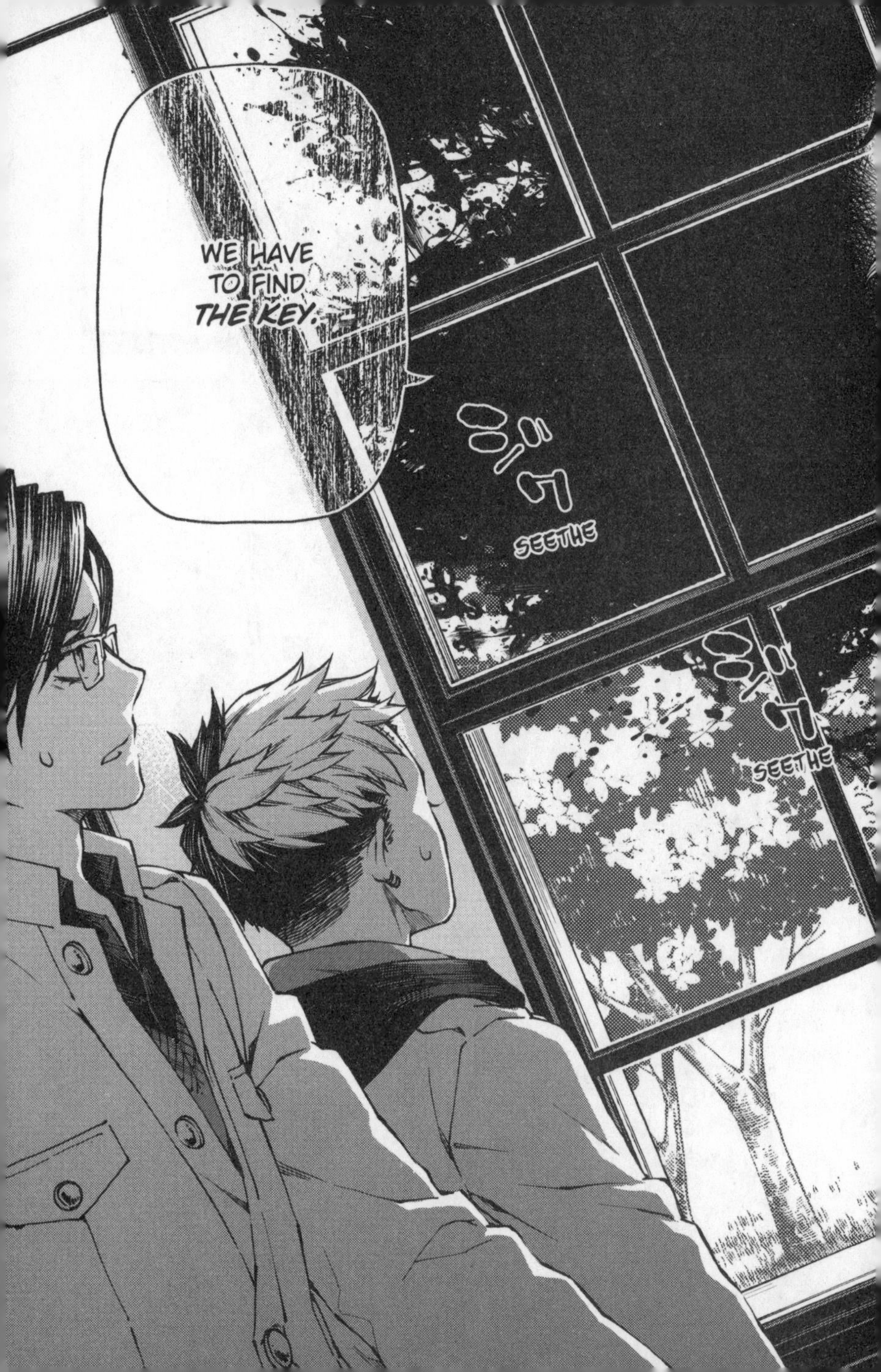
WE HAVE TO FIND THE KEY.
SEETHE
SEETHE

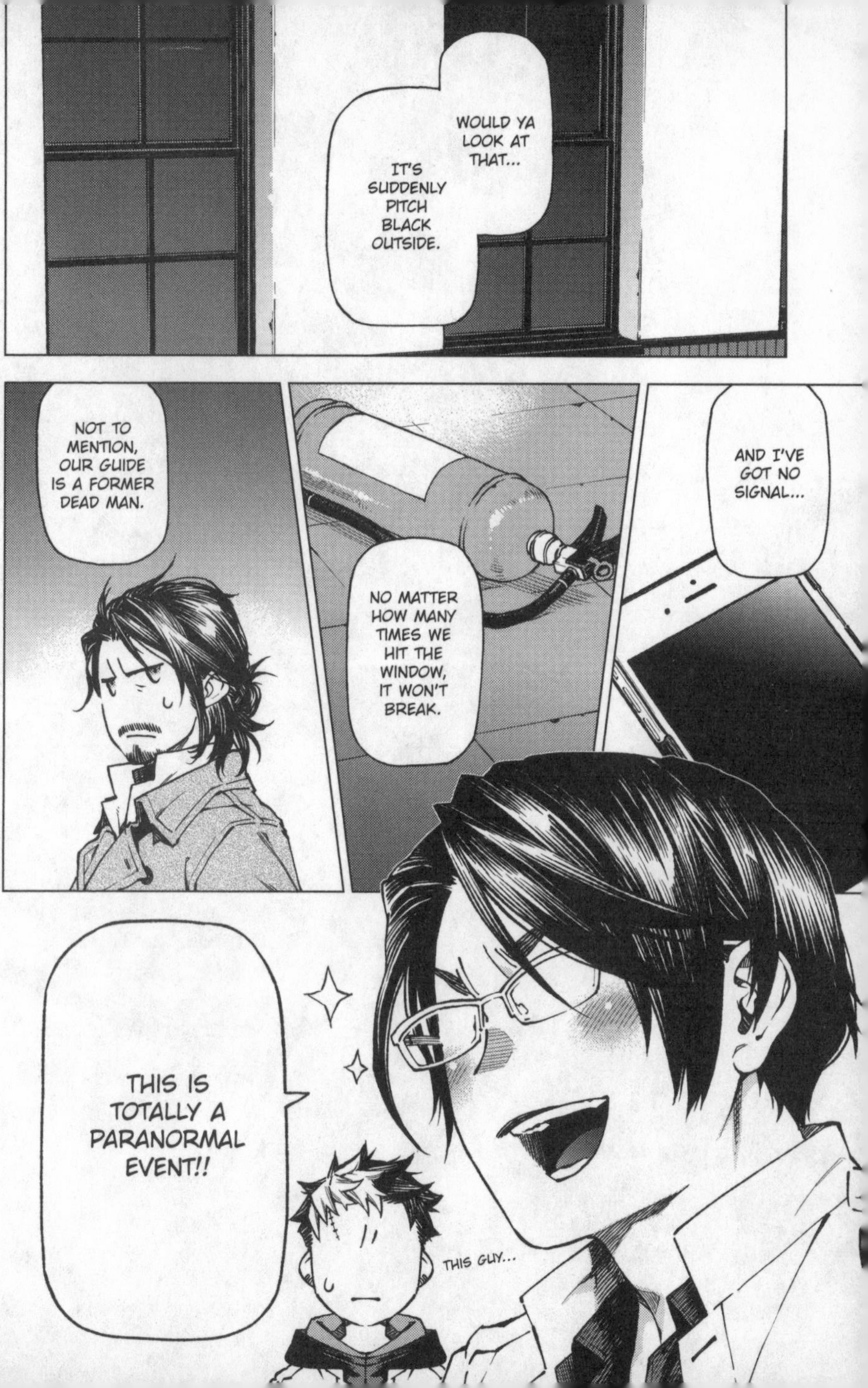
WOULD YA LOOK AT THAT...
IT'S SUDDENLY PITCH BLACK OUTSIDE.
AND I'VE GOT NO SIGNAL...
NO MATTER HOW MANY TIMES WE HIT THE WINDOW, IT WON'T BREAK.
NOT TO MENTION, OUR GUIDE IS A FORMER DEAD MAN.
THIS IS TOTALLY A PARANORMAL EVENT!!
THIS GUY...

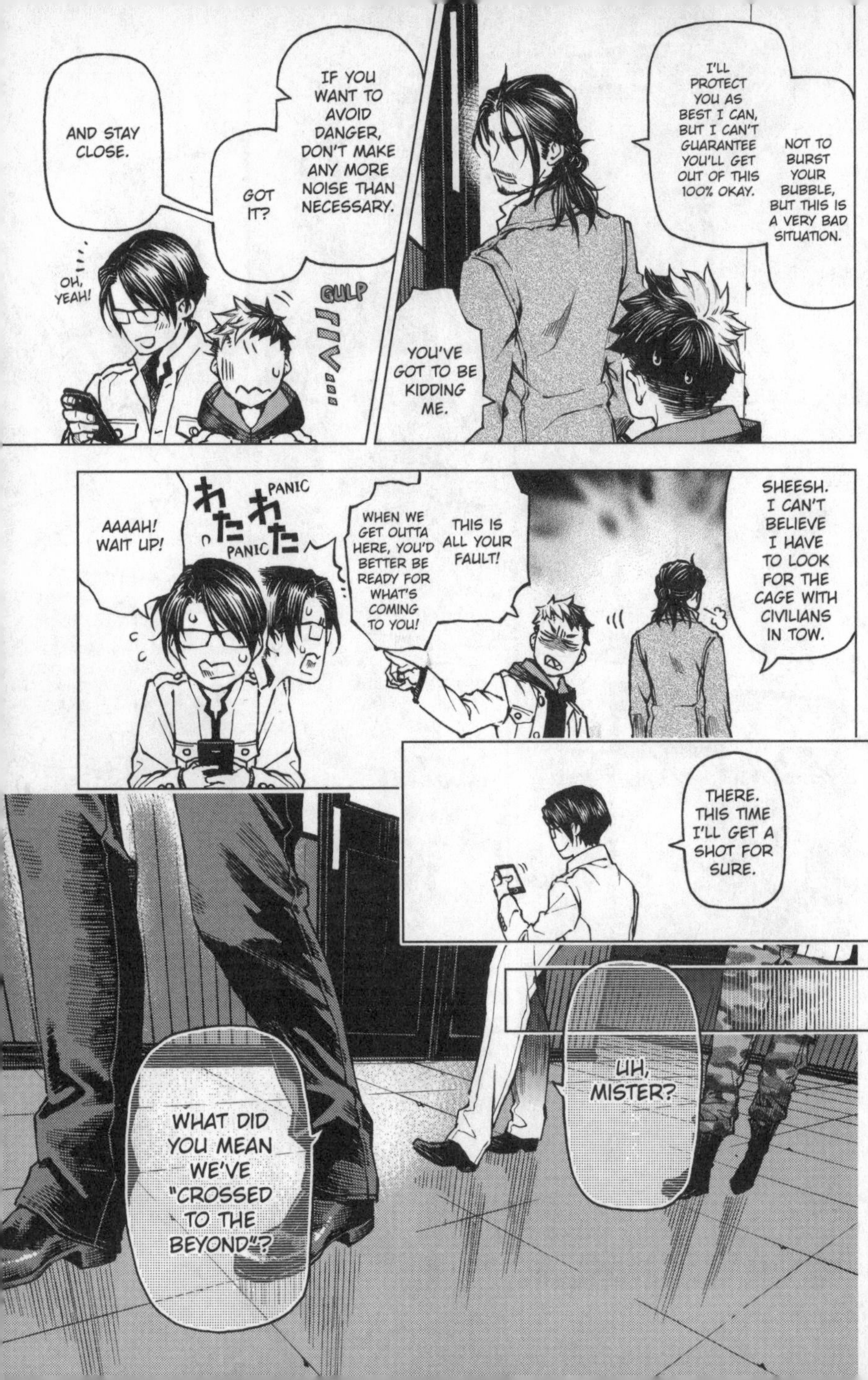
I'LL PROTECT YOU AS BEST I CAN, BUT I CAN'T GUARANTEE YOU'LL GET OUT OF THIS 100% OKAY.
NOT TO BURST YOUR BUBBLE, BUT THIS IS A VERY BAD SITUATION.
YOU'VE GOT TO BE KIDDING ME.
IF YOU WANT TO AVOID DANGER, DON'T MAKE ANY MORE NOISE THAN NECESSARY.
GOT IT?
AND STAY CLOSE.
GULP
OH, YEAH!
SHEESH. I CAN'T BELIEVE I HAVE TO LOOK FOR THE CAGE WITH CIVILIANS IN TOW.
THIS IS ALL YOUR FAULT!
WHEN WE GET OUTTA HERE, YOU'D BETTER BE READY FOR WHAT'S COMING TO YOU!
わた PANIC
わた PANIC
AAAAH! WAIT UP!
THERE. THIS TIME I'LL GET A SHOT FOR SURE.
UH, MISTER?
WHAT DID YOU MEAN WE'VE "CROSSED TO THE BEYOND"?

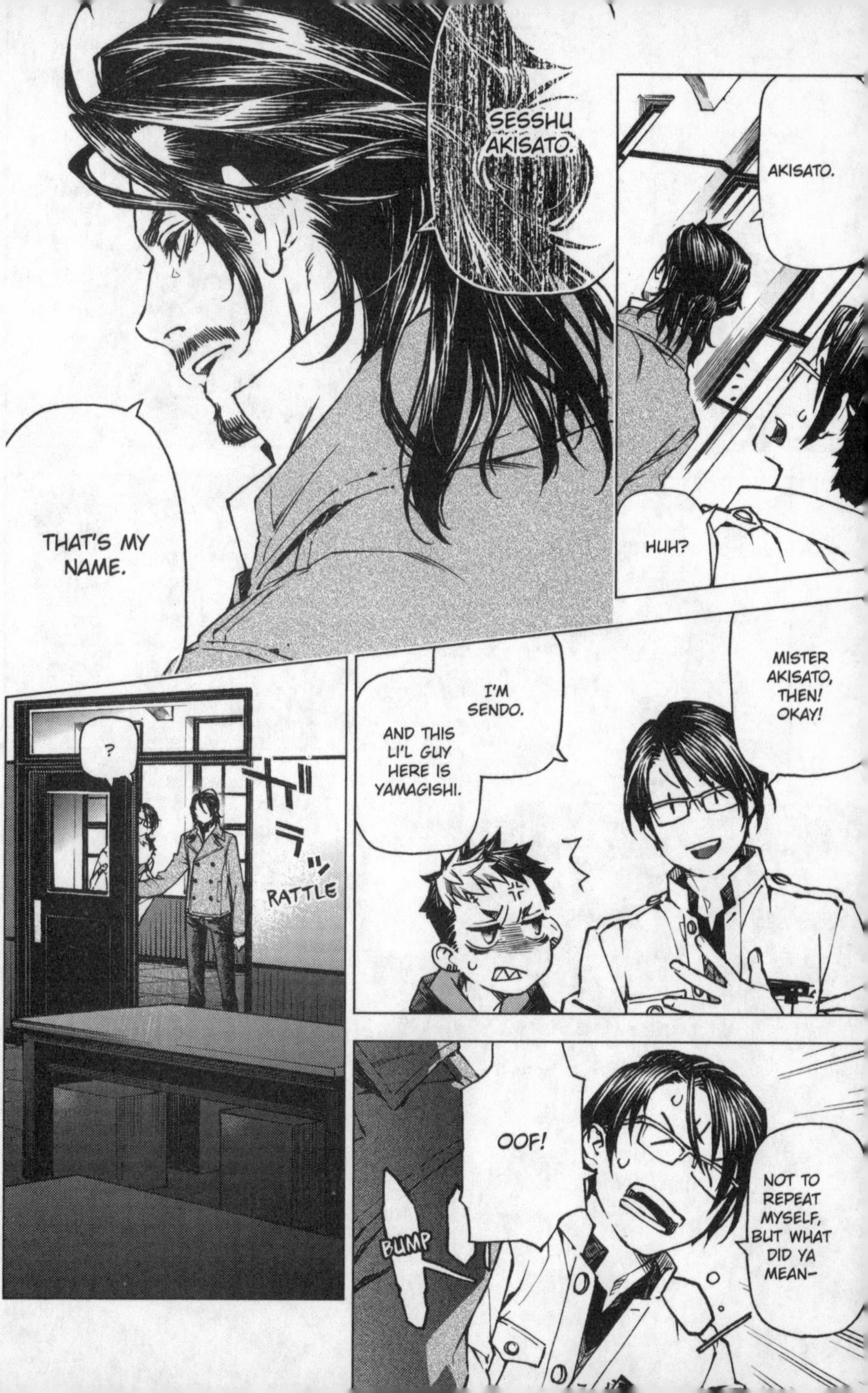
AKISATO.
HUH?
SESSHU AKISATO.
THAT'S MY NAME.
MISTER AKISATO, THEN! OKAY!
I'M SENDO.
AND THIS LI'L GUY HERE IS YAMAGISHI.
NOT TO REPEAT MYSELF, BUT WHAT DID YA MEAN—
OOF!
BUMP
?
ガラッ
RATTLE

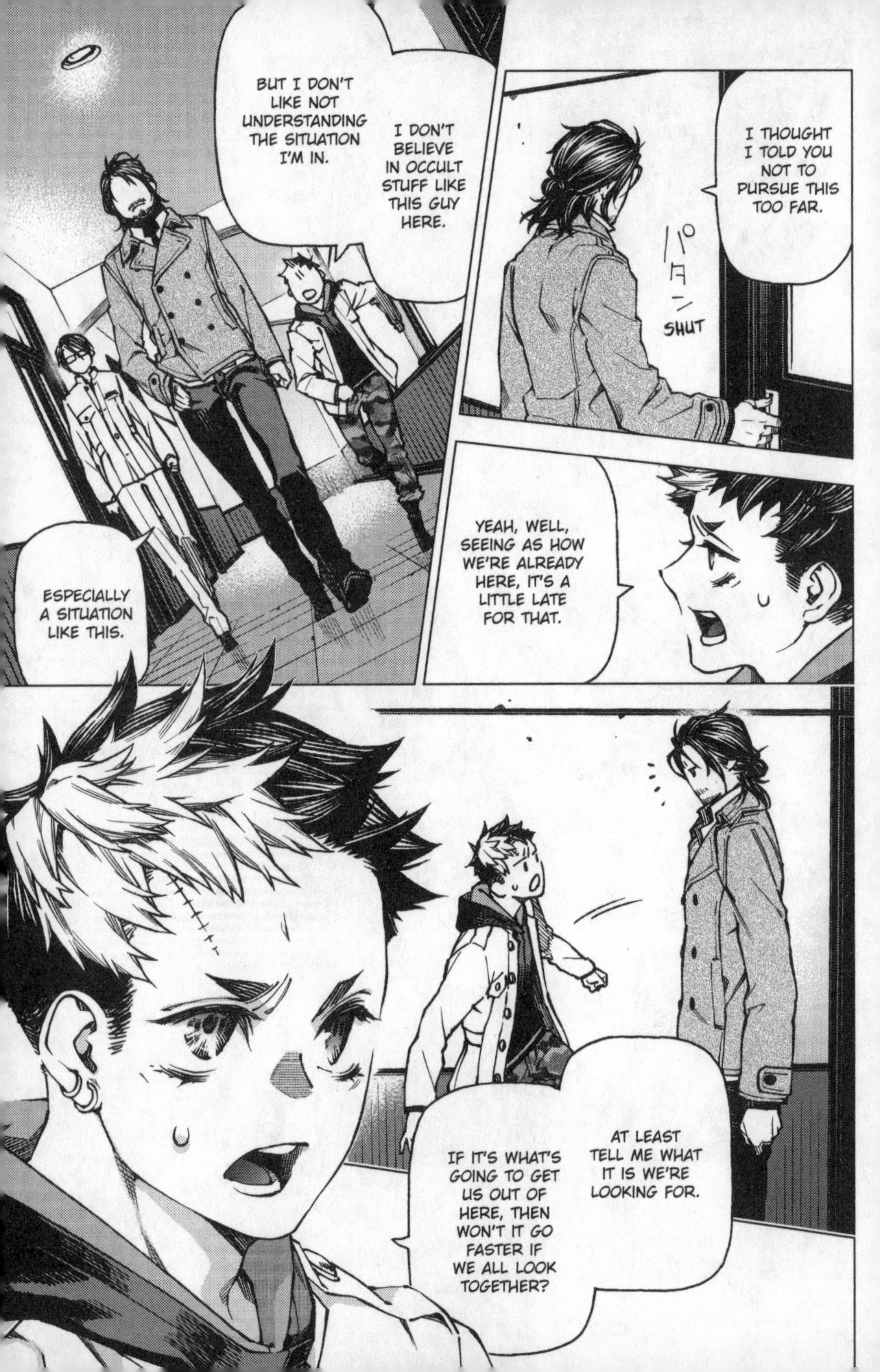
I THOUGHT I TOLD YOU NOT TO PURSUE THIS TOO FAR.
パタン
SHUT
YEAH, WELL, SEEING AS HOW WE'RE ALREADY HERE, IT'S A LITTLE LATE FOR THAT.
BUT I DON'T LIKE NOT UNDERSTANDING THE SITUATION I'M IN.
I DON'T BELIEVE IN OCCULT STUFF LIKE THIS GUY HERE.
ESPECIALLY A SITUATION LIKE THIS.
AT LEAST TELL ME WHAT IT IS WE'RE LOOKING FOR.
IF IT'S WHAT'S GOING TO GET US OUT OF HERE, THEN WON'T IT GO FASTER IF WE ALL LOOK TOGETHER?

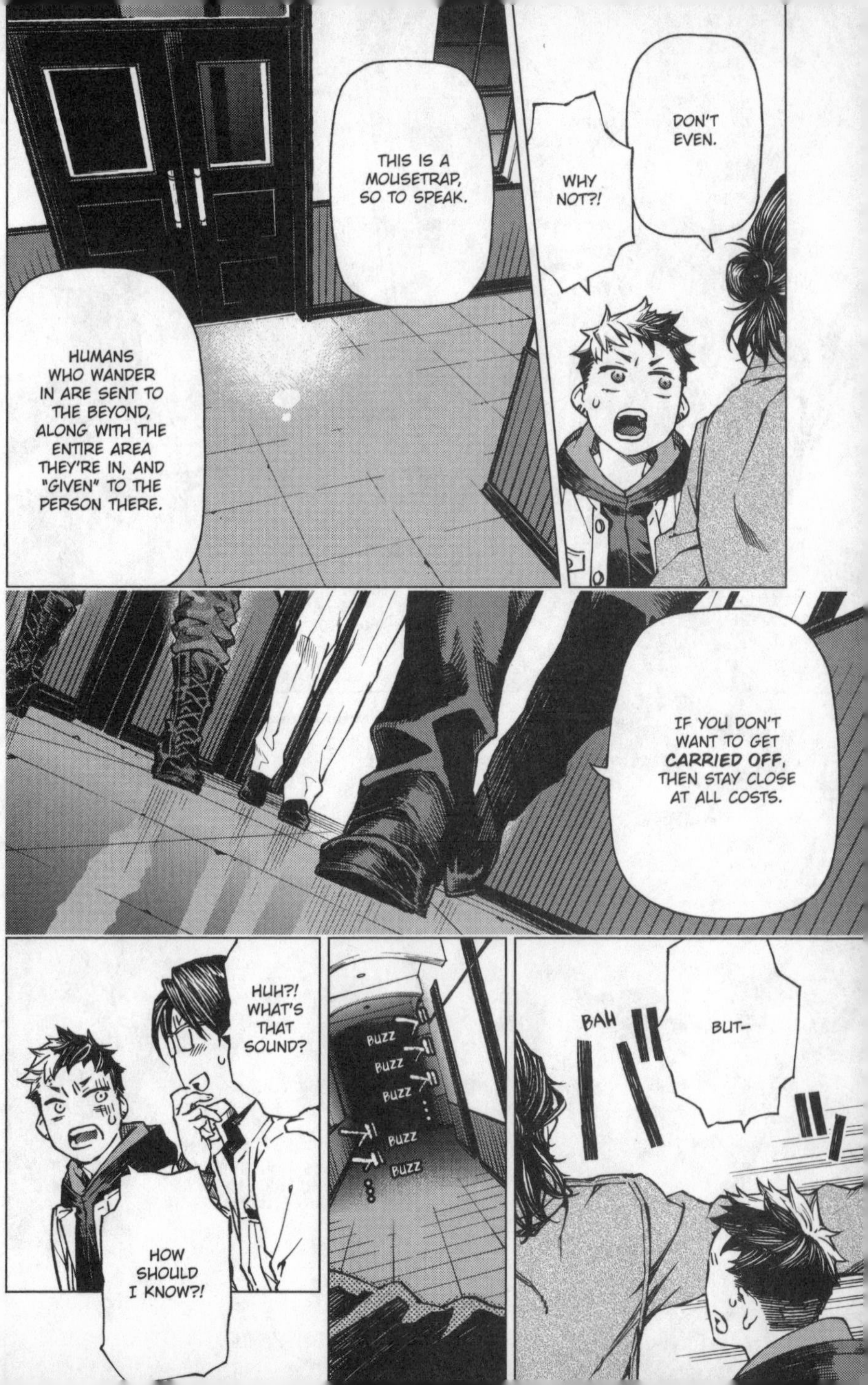
DON'T EVEN.
WHY NOT?!
THIS IS A MOUSETRAP, SO TO SPEAK.
HUMANS WHO WANDER IN ARE SENT TO THE BEYOND, ALONG WITH THE ENTIRE AREA THEY'RE IN, AND "GIVEN" TO THE PERSON THERE.
IF YOU DON'T WANT TO GET **CARRIED OFF**, THEN STAY CLOSE AT ALL COSTS.
BUT-
BAH
BUZZ
BUZZ
BUZZ
...
BUZZ
BUZZ
...
HUH?! WHAT'S THAT SOUND?
HOW SHOULD I KNOW?!

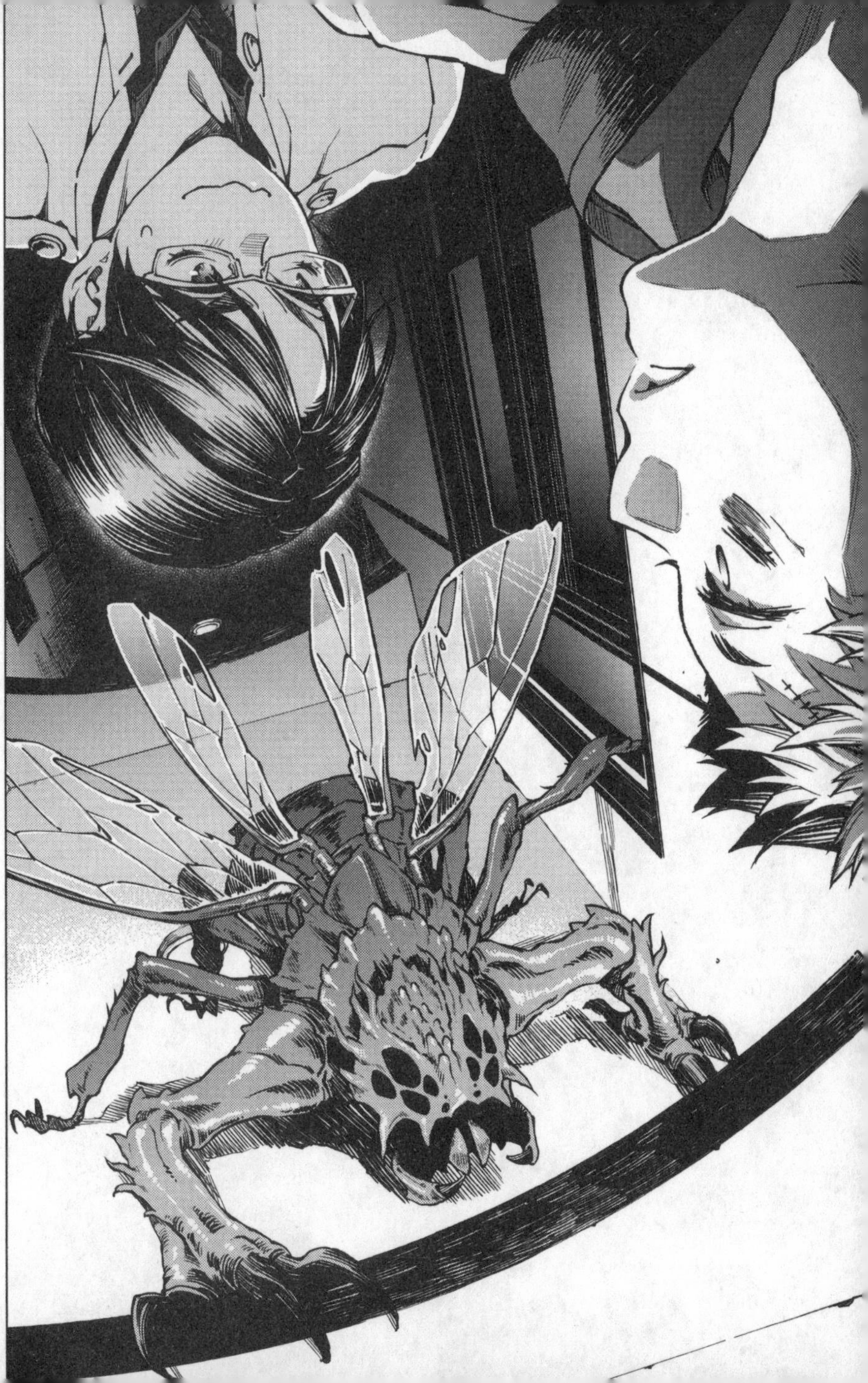

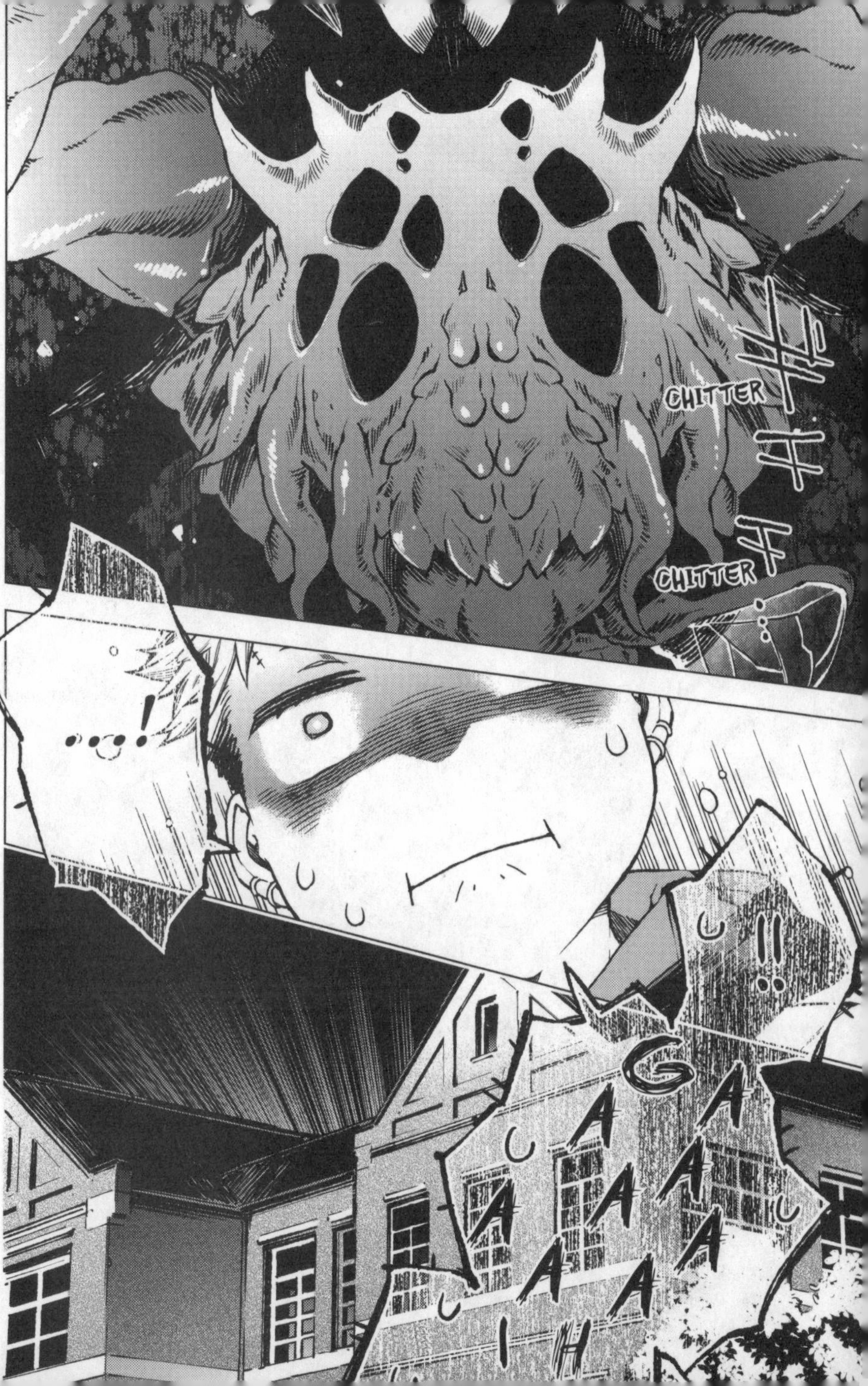
CHITTER
CHITTER
...!
!!
GAAAAAAAH

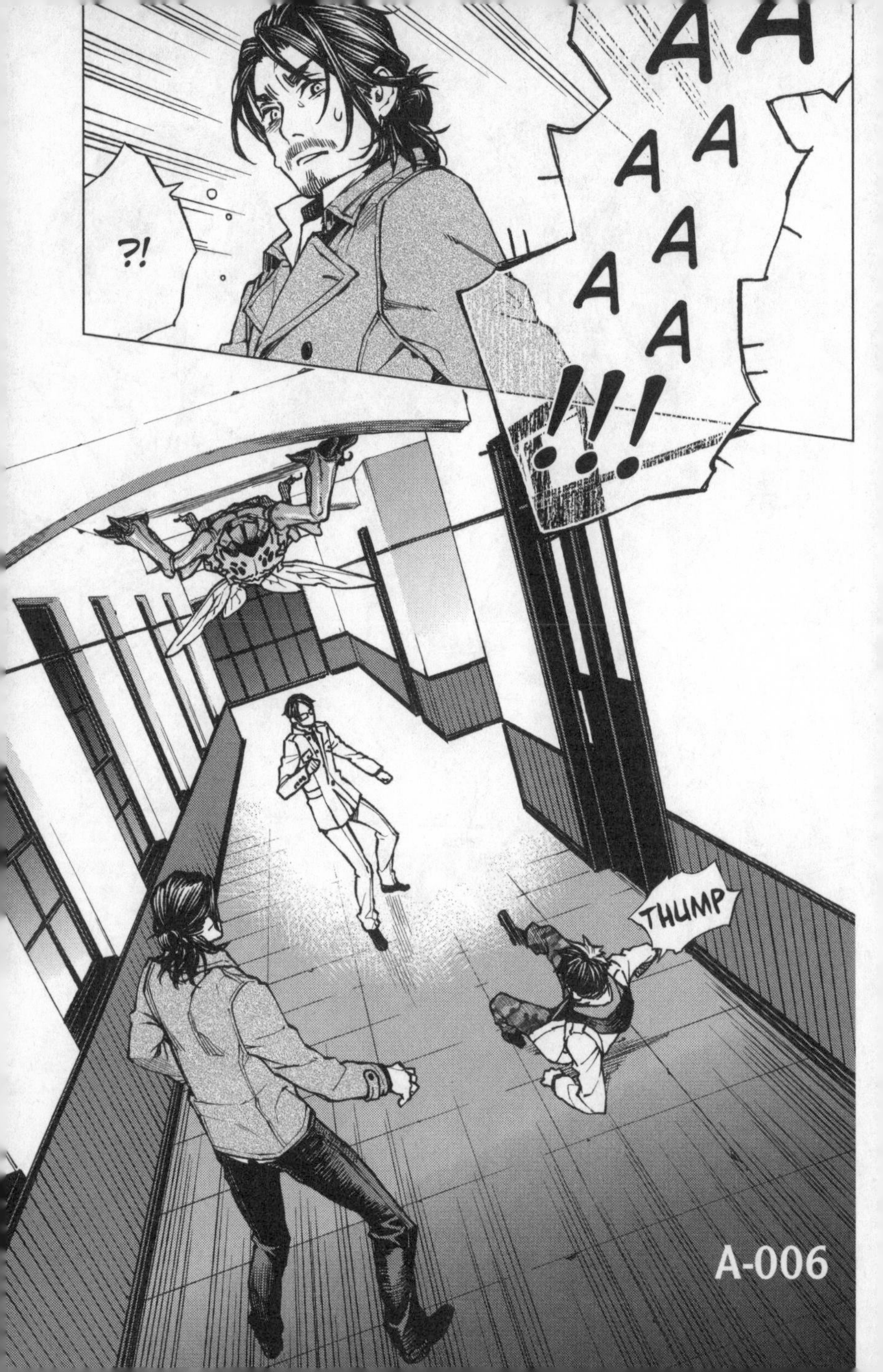
AAAAAAA!!!
?!
THUMP
A-006

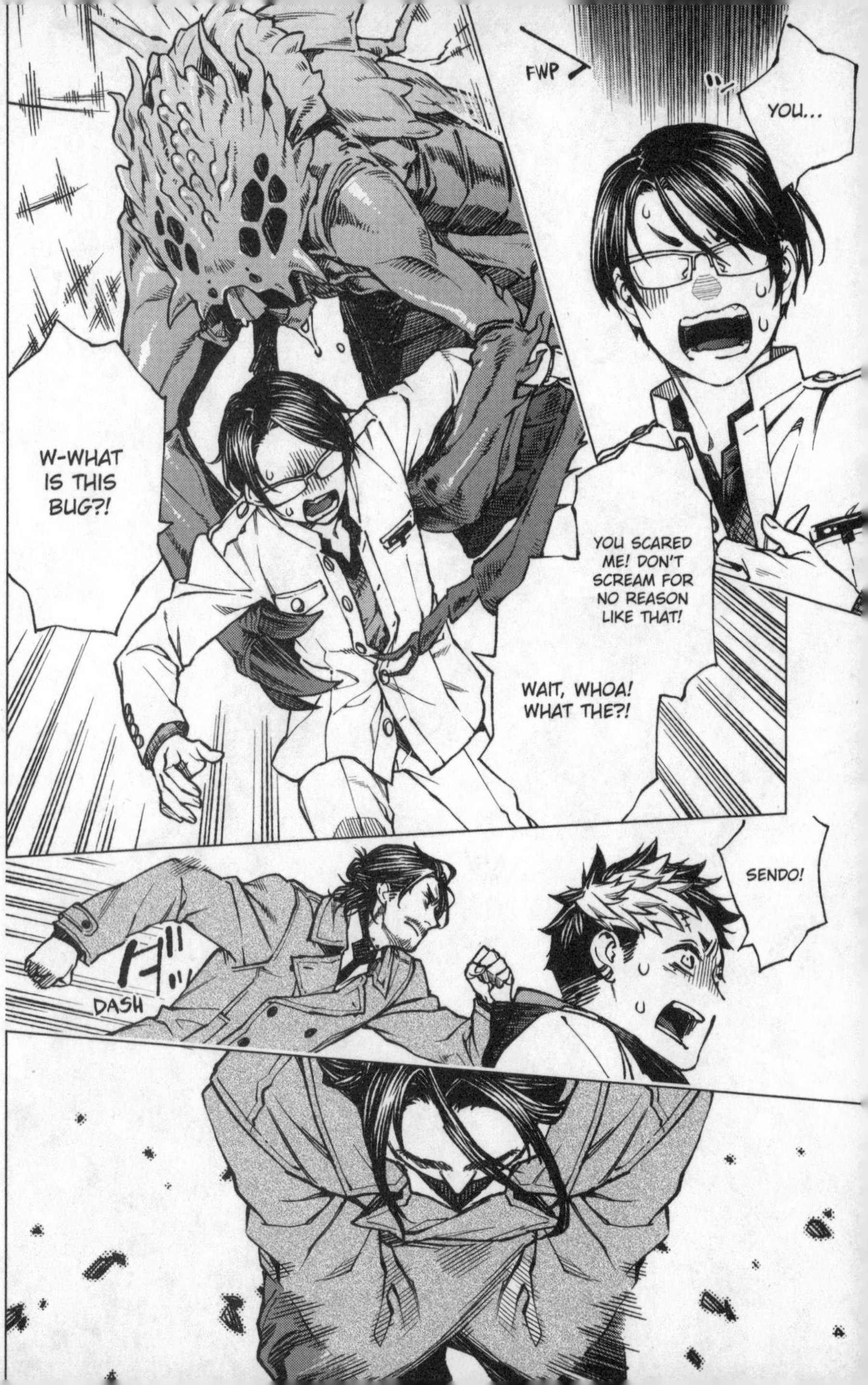
FWP
YOU...
YOU SCARED ME! DON'T SCREAM FOR NO REASON LIKE THAT!
W-WHAT IS THIS BUG?!
WAIT, WHOA! WHAT THE?!
SENDO!
DASH

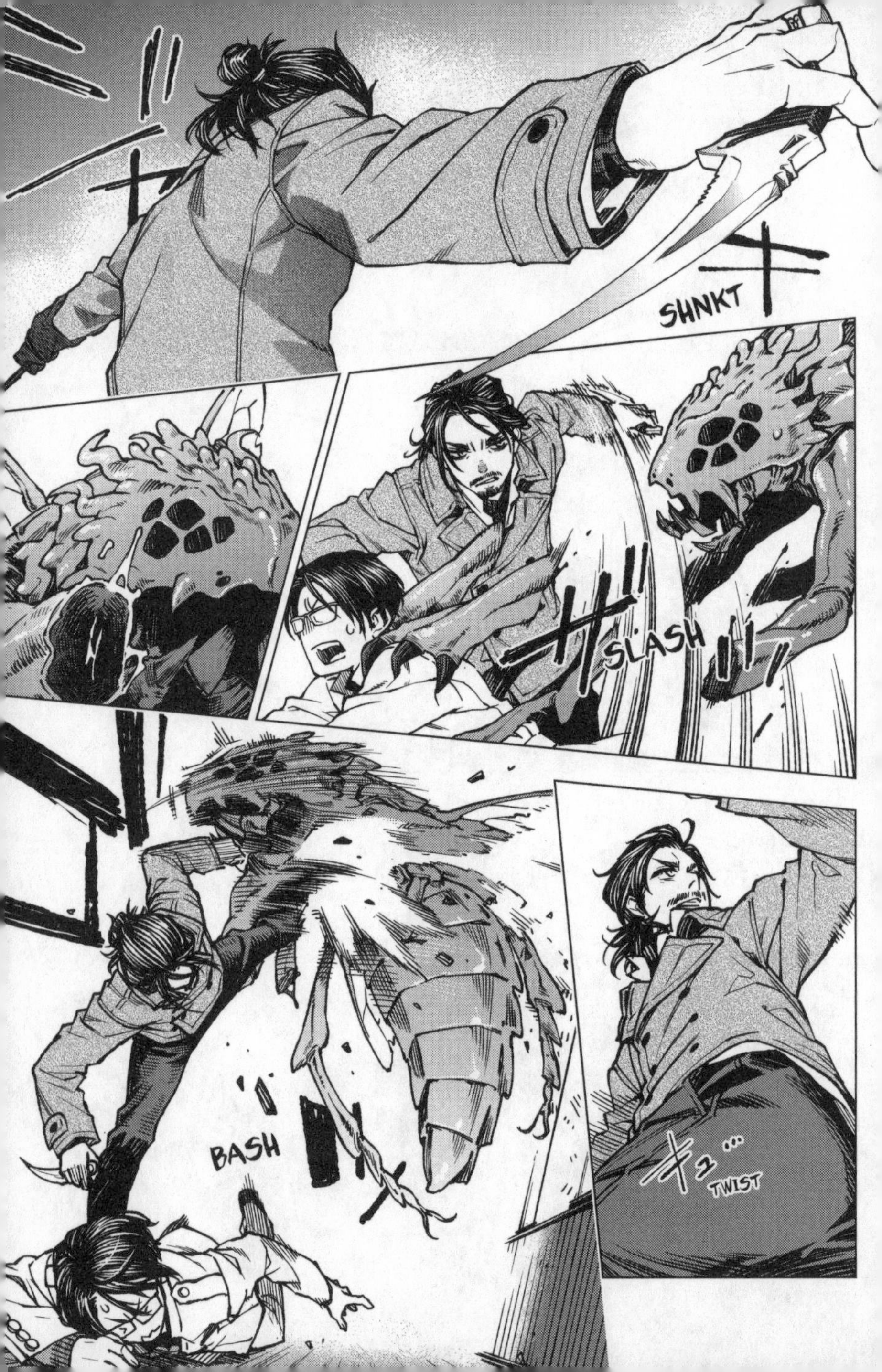
SHNKT
SLASH
...
TWIST
BASH

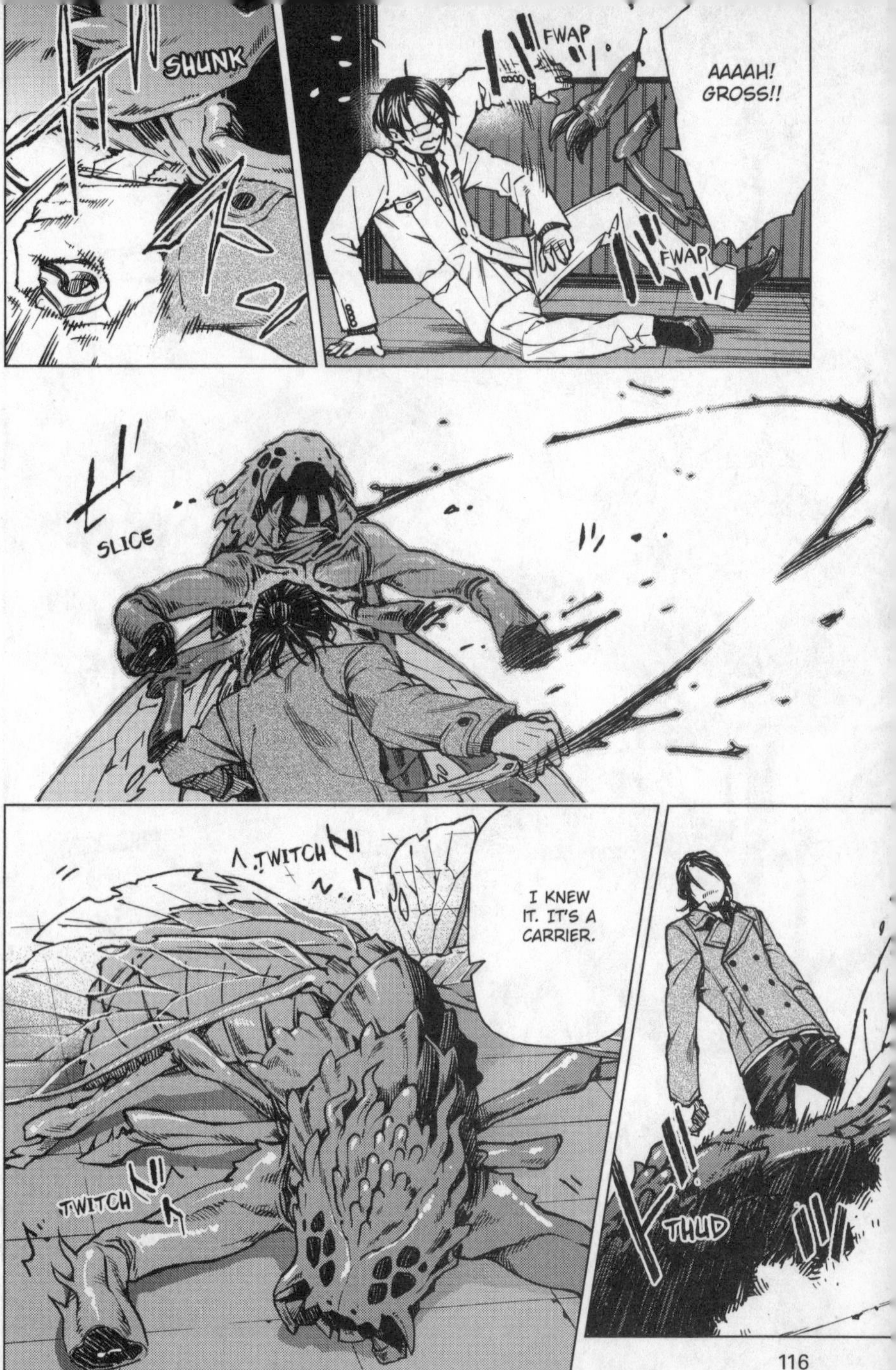
AAAAH! GROSS!!
FWAP
FWAP
SHUNK
SLICE
THUD
I KNEW IT. IT'S A CARRIER.
TWITCH
TWITCH

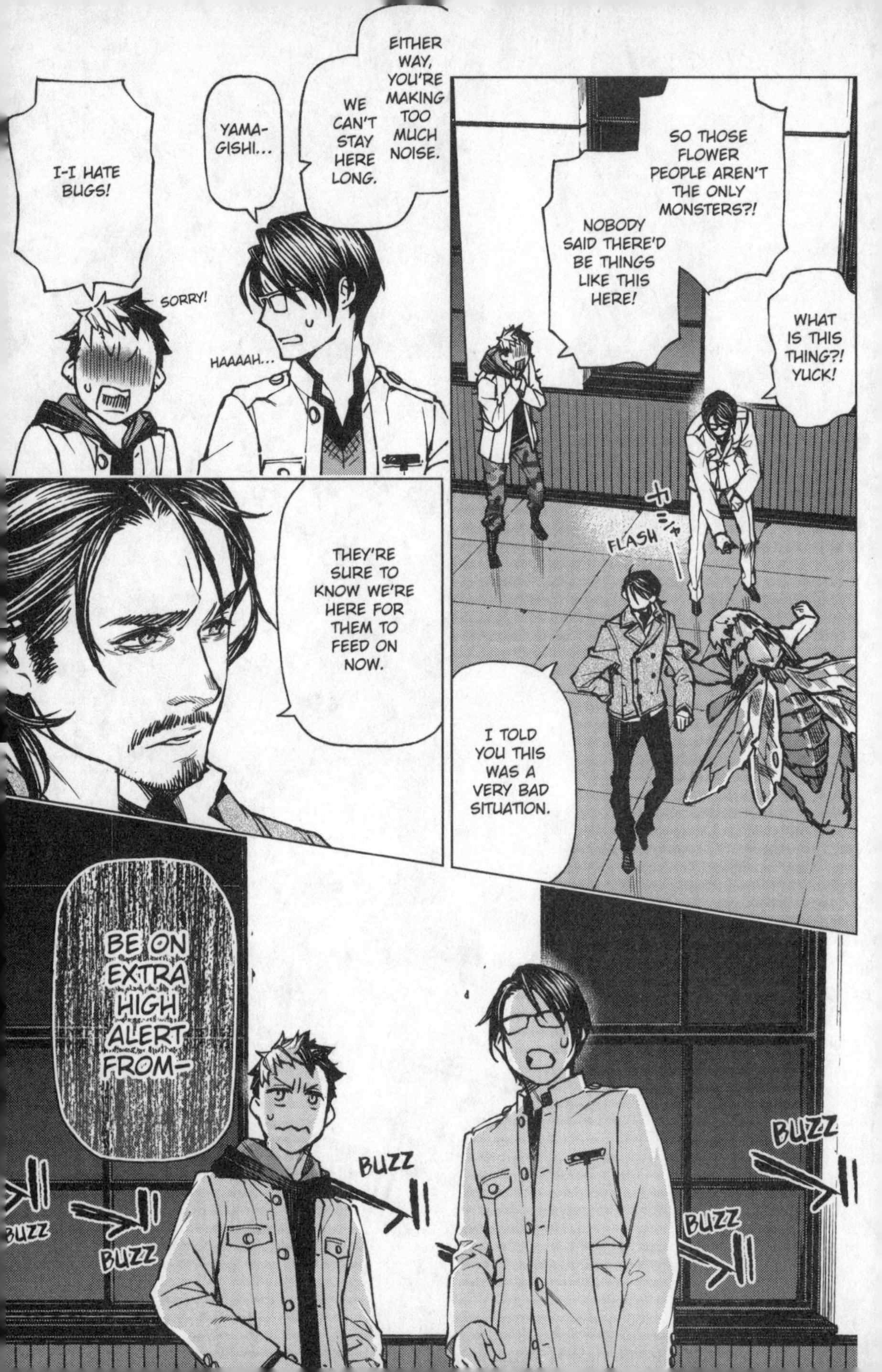
WHAT IS THIS THING?! YUCK!
SO THOSE FLOWER PEOPLE AREN'T THE ONLY MONSTERS?!
NOBODY SAID THERE'D BE THINGS LIKE THIS HERE!
FLASH
I TOLD YOU THIS WAS A VERY BAD SITUATION.
EITHER WAY, YOU'RE MAKING TOO MUCH NOISE.
WE CAN'T STAY HERE LONG.
YAMA-GISHI...
I-I HATE BUGS!
SORRY!
HAAAAH...
THEY'RE SURE TO KNOW WE'RE HERE FOR THEM TO FEED ON NOW.
BE ON EXTRA HIGH ALERT FROM-
BUZZ
BUZZ
BUZZ
BUZZ
BUZZ
BUZZ

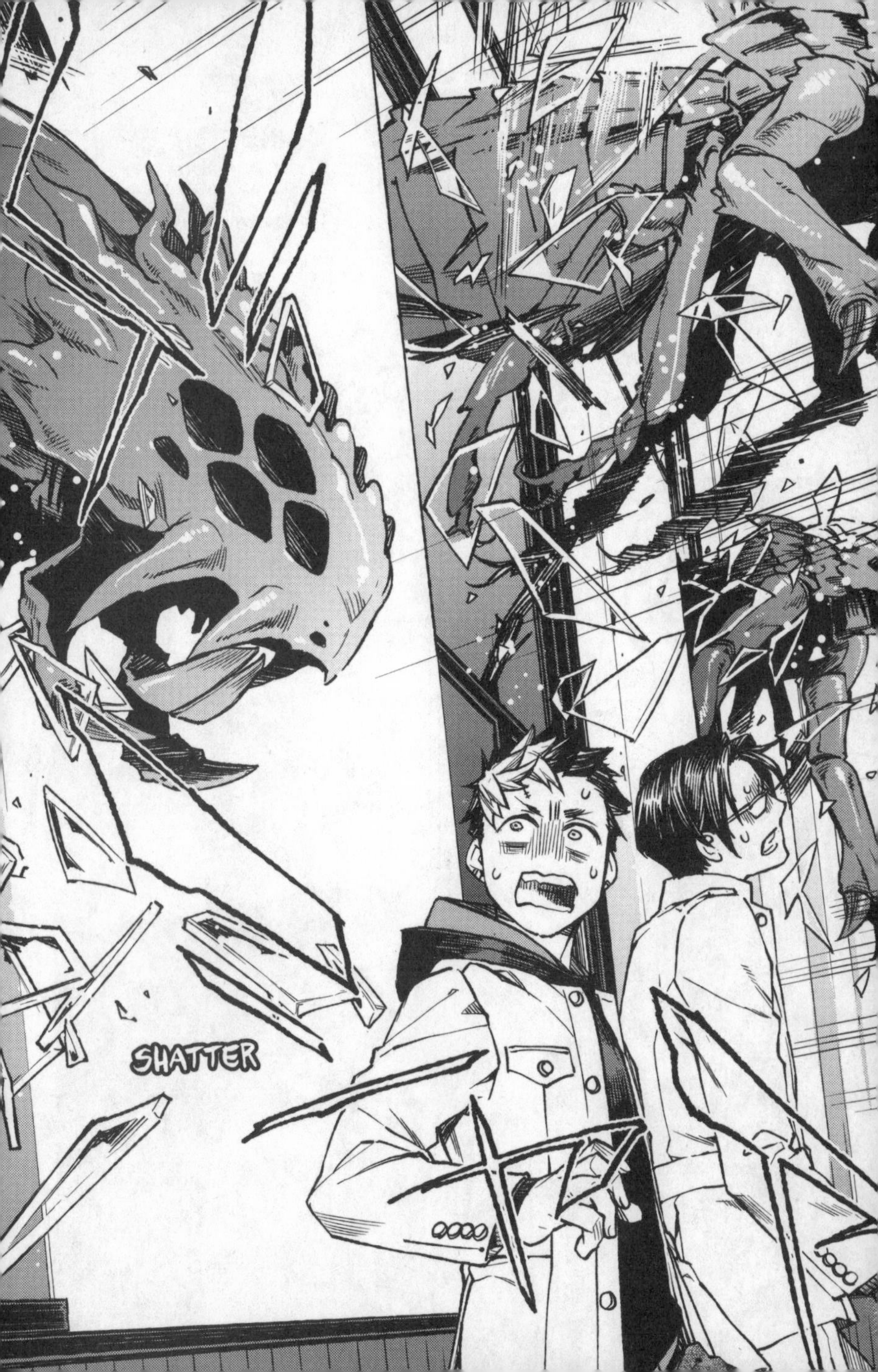
SHATTER

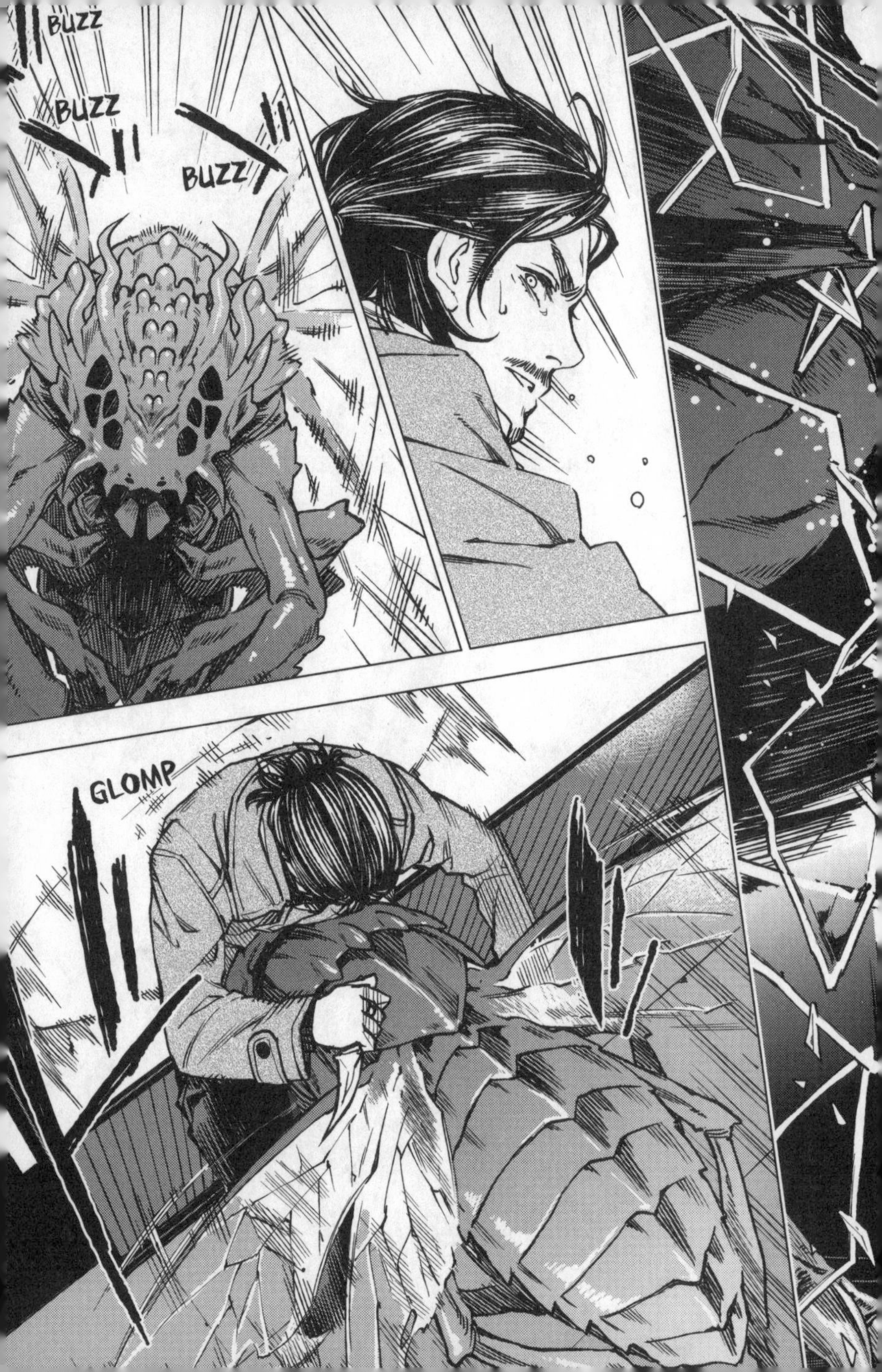
BUZZ
BUZZ
BUZZ
GLOMP

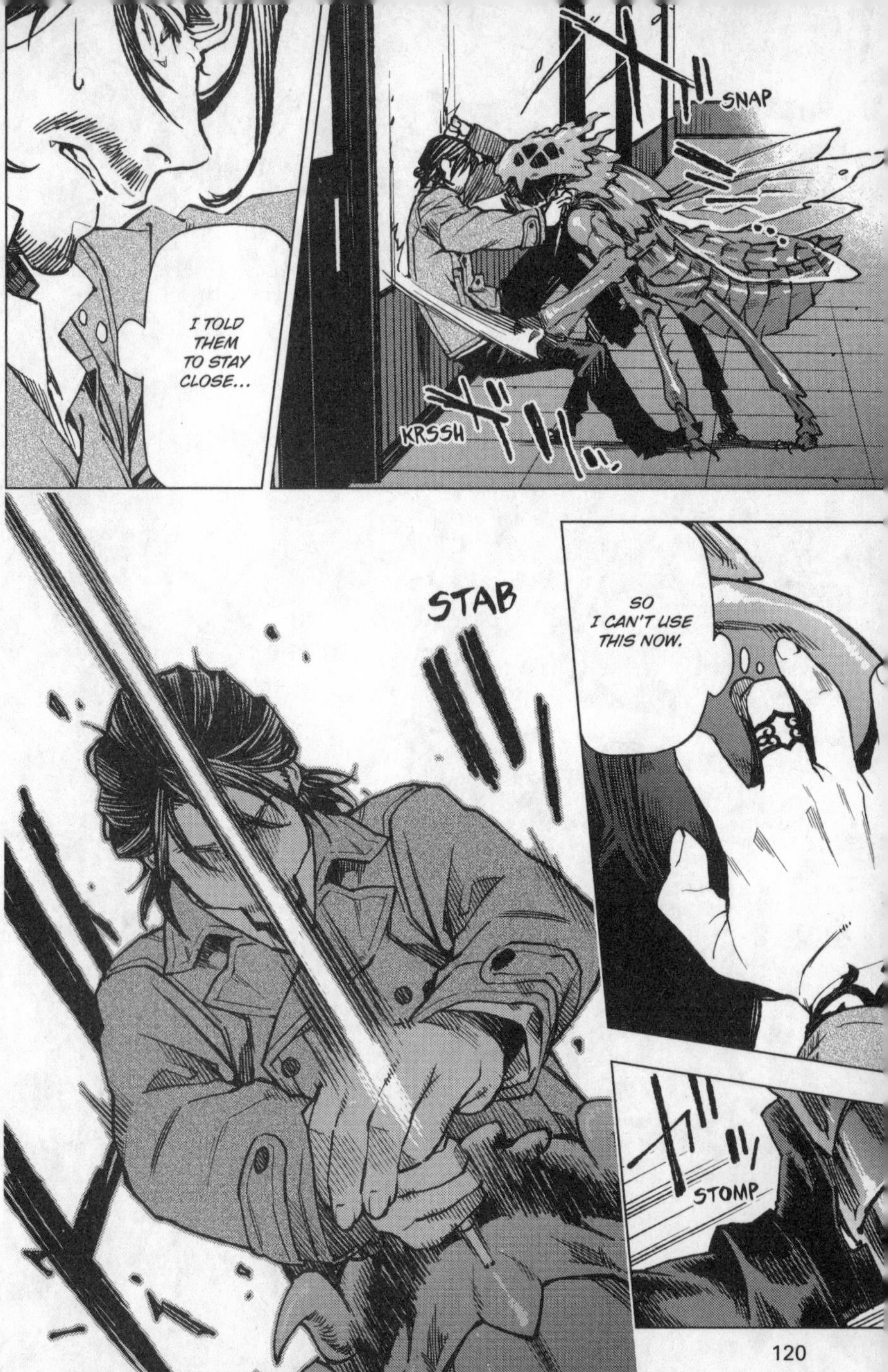
SNAP
KRSSH
I TOLD THEM TO STAY CLOSE...
SO I CAN'T USE THIS NOW.
STOMP
STAB

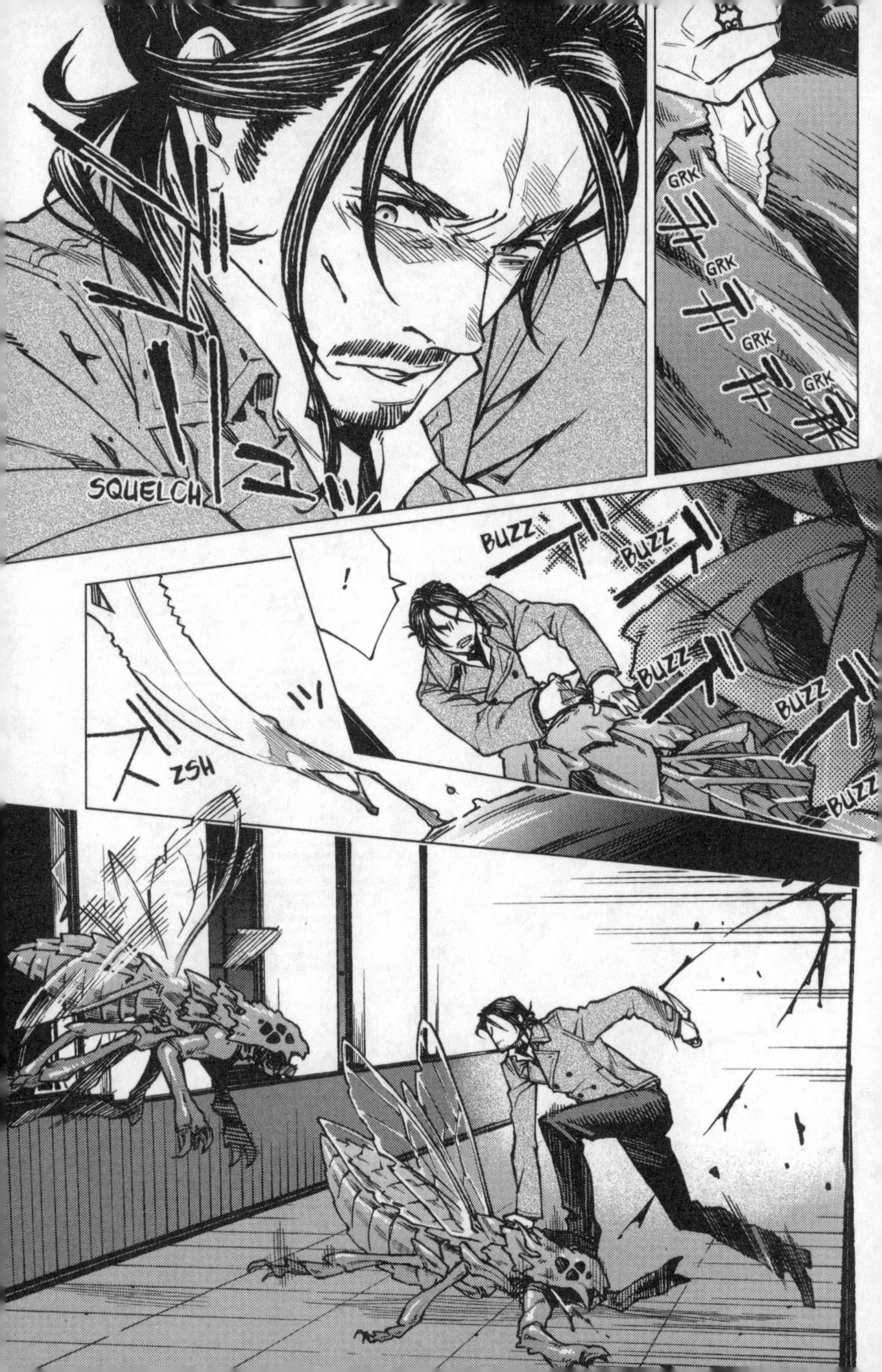
GRK
GRK
GRK
GRK
SQUELCH
BUZZ
BUZZ
BUZZ
BUZZ
BUZZ
!
ZSH

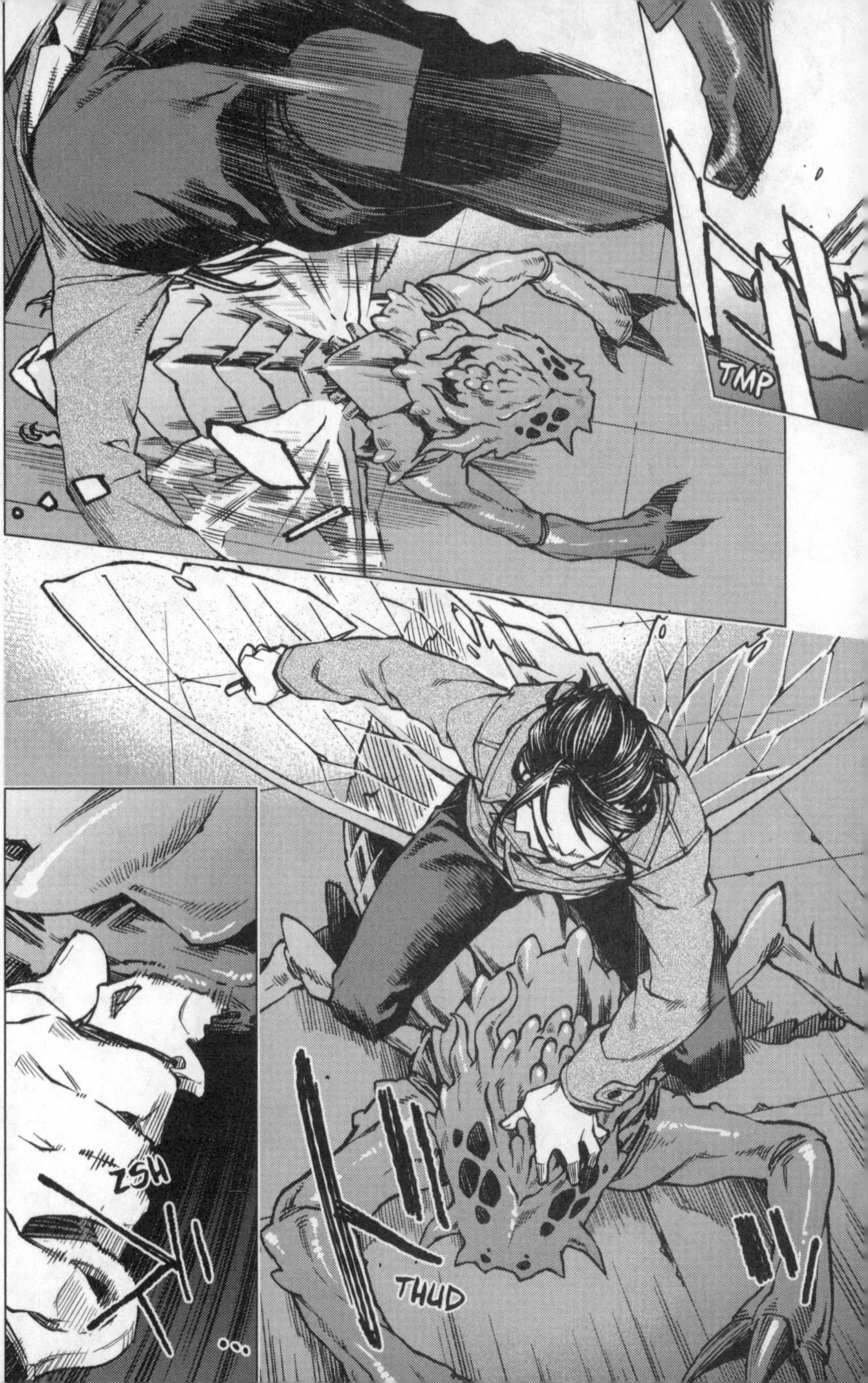
TMP
THUD
ZSH

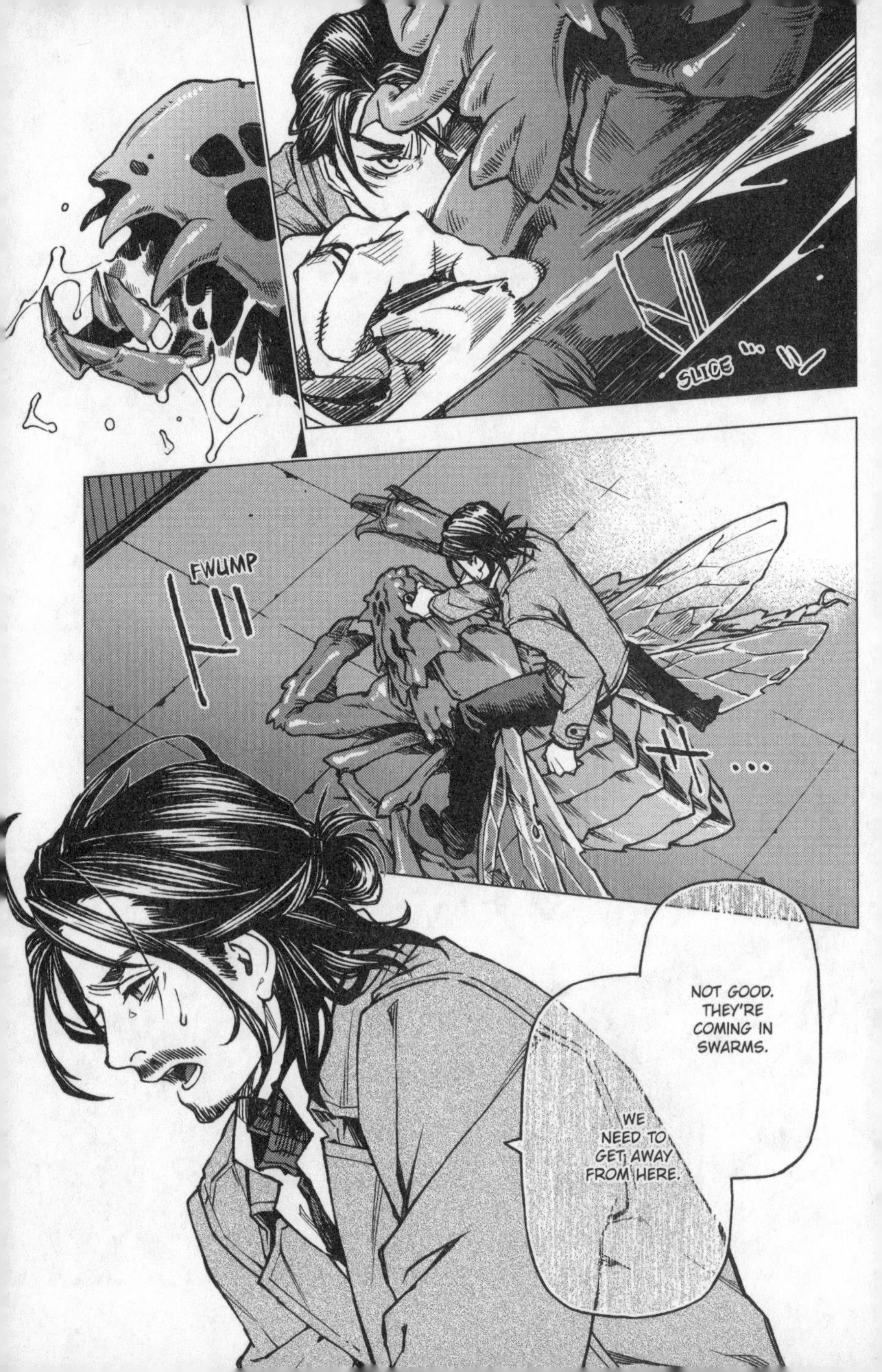
SLICE
FWUMP
...
NOT GOOD. THEY'RE COMING IN SWARMS.
WE NEED TO GET AWAY FROM HERE.

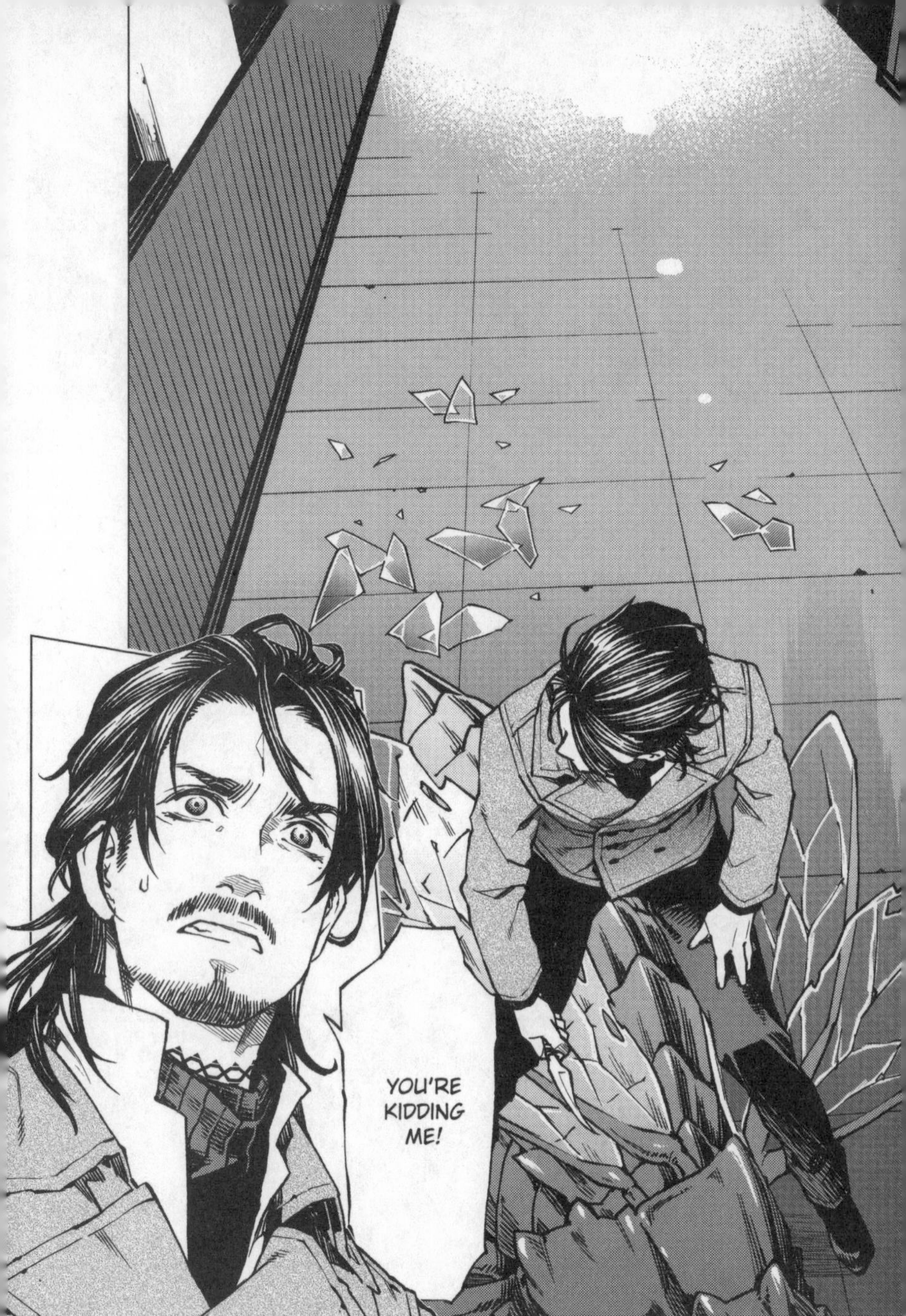
YOU'RE KIDDING ME!

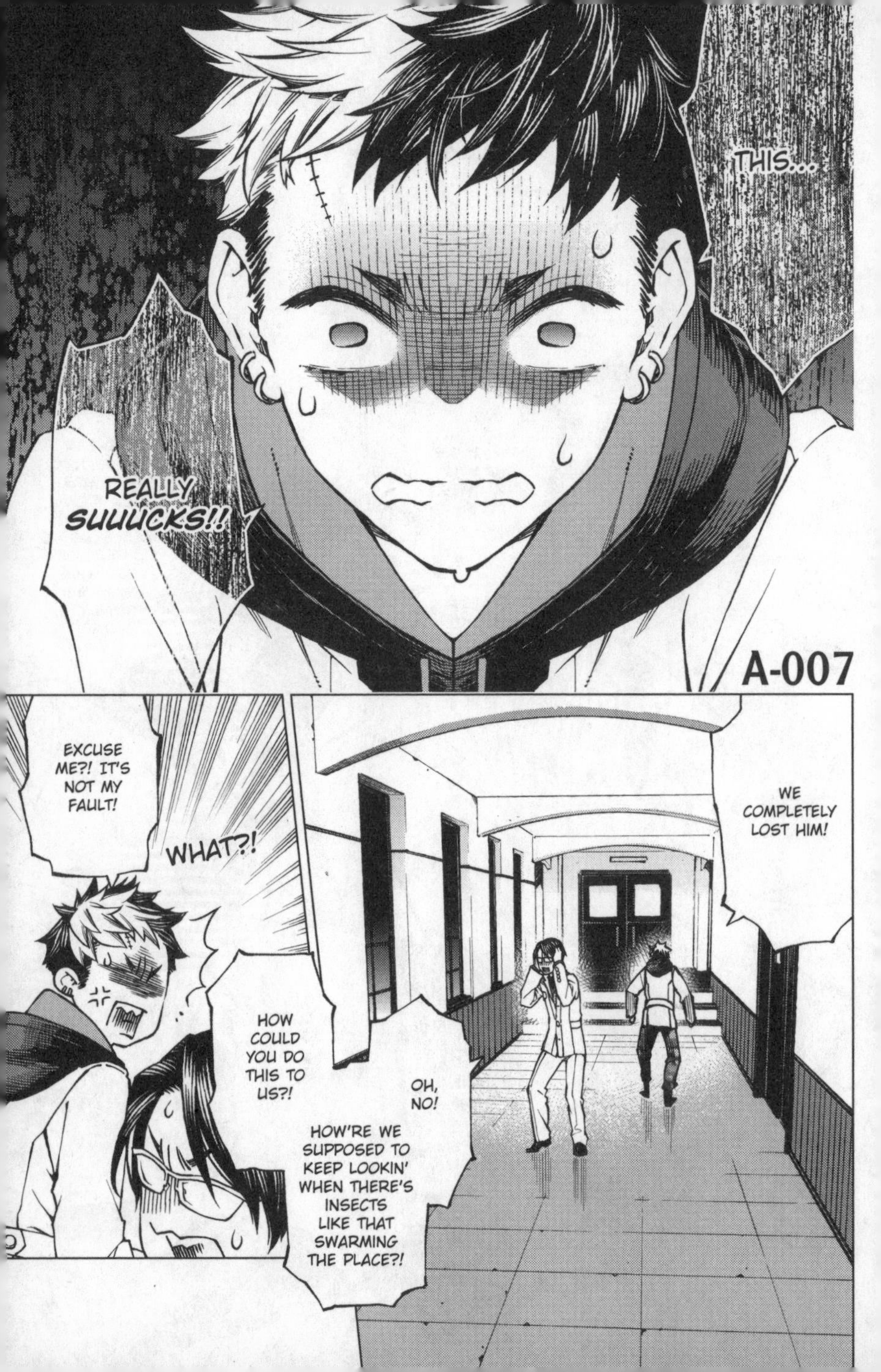
THIS...
REALLY SUUUCKS!!
A-007
WE COMPLETELY LOST HIM!
HOW'RE WE SUPPOSED TO KEEP LOOKIN' WHEN THERE'S INSECTS LIKE THAT SWARMING THE PLACE?!
OH, NO!
HOW COULD YOU DO THIS TO US?!
WHAT?!
EXCUSE ME?! IT'S NOT MY FAULT!

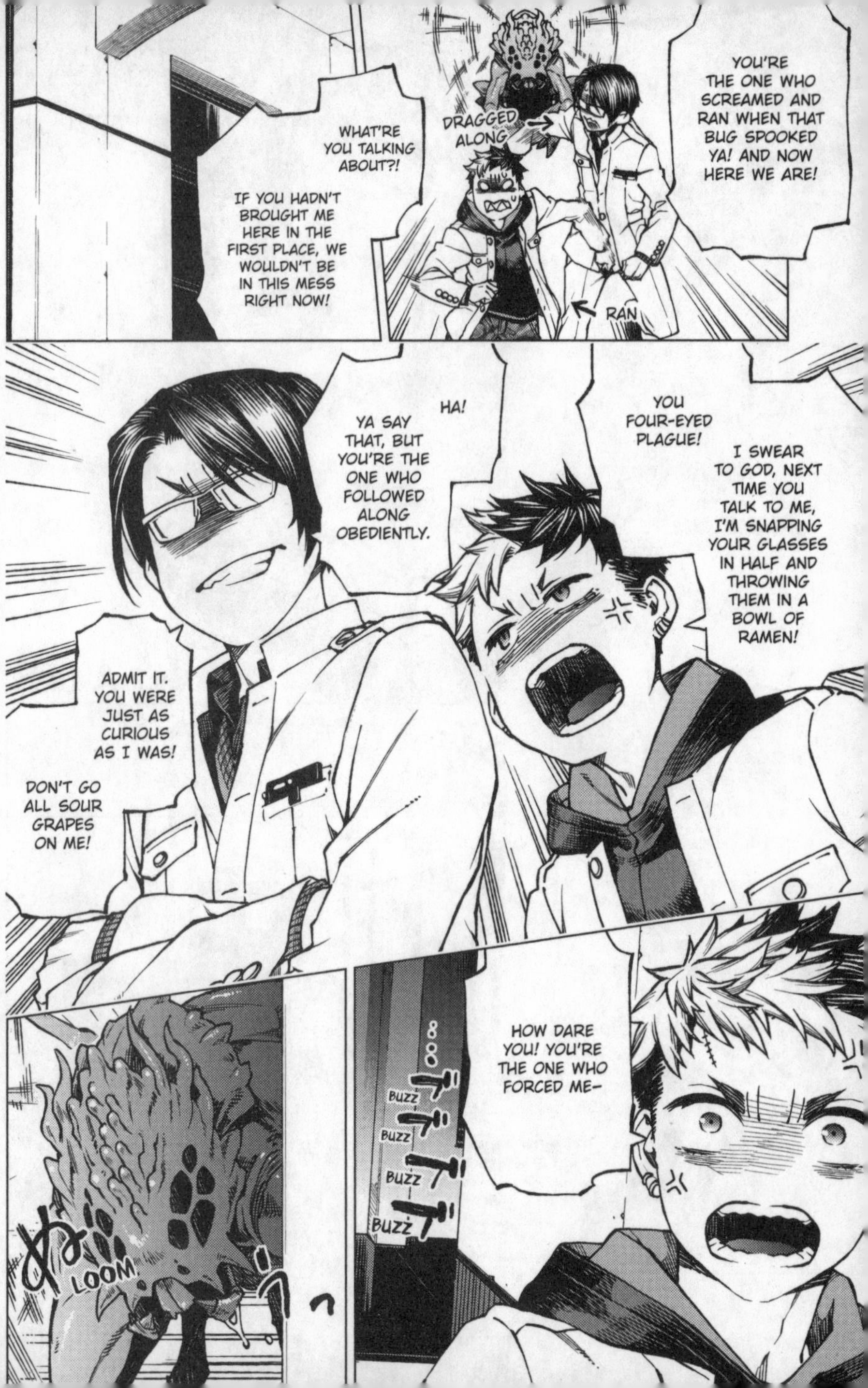
YOU'RE THE ONE WHO SCREAMED AND RAN WHEN THAT BUG SPOOKED YA! AND NOW HERE WE ARE!
DRAGGED ALONG
RAN
WHAT'RE YOU TALKING ABOUT?!
IF YOU HADN'T BROUGHT ME HERE IN THE FIRST PLACE, WE WOULDN'T BE IN THIS MESS RIGHT NOW!
YOU FOUR-EYED PLAGUE!
I SWEAR TO GOD, NEXT TIME YOU TALK TO ME, I'M SNAPPING YOUR GLASSES IN HALF AND THROWING THEM IN A BOWL OF RAMEN!
HA!
YA SAY THAT, BUT YOU'RE THE ONE WHO FOLLOWED ALONG OBEDIENTLY.
ADMIT IT. YOU WERE JUST AS CURIOUS AS I WAS!
DON'T GO ALL SOUR GRAPES ON ME!
HOW DARE YOU! YOU'RE THE ONE WHO FORCED ME-
BUZZ
BUZZ
BUZZ
BUZZ
LOOM

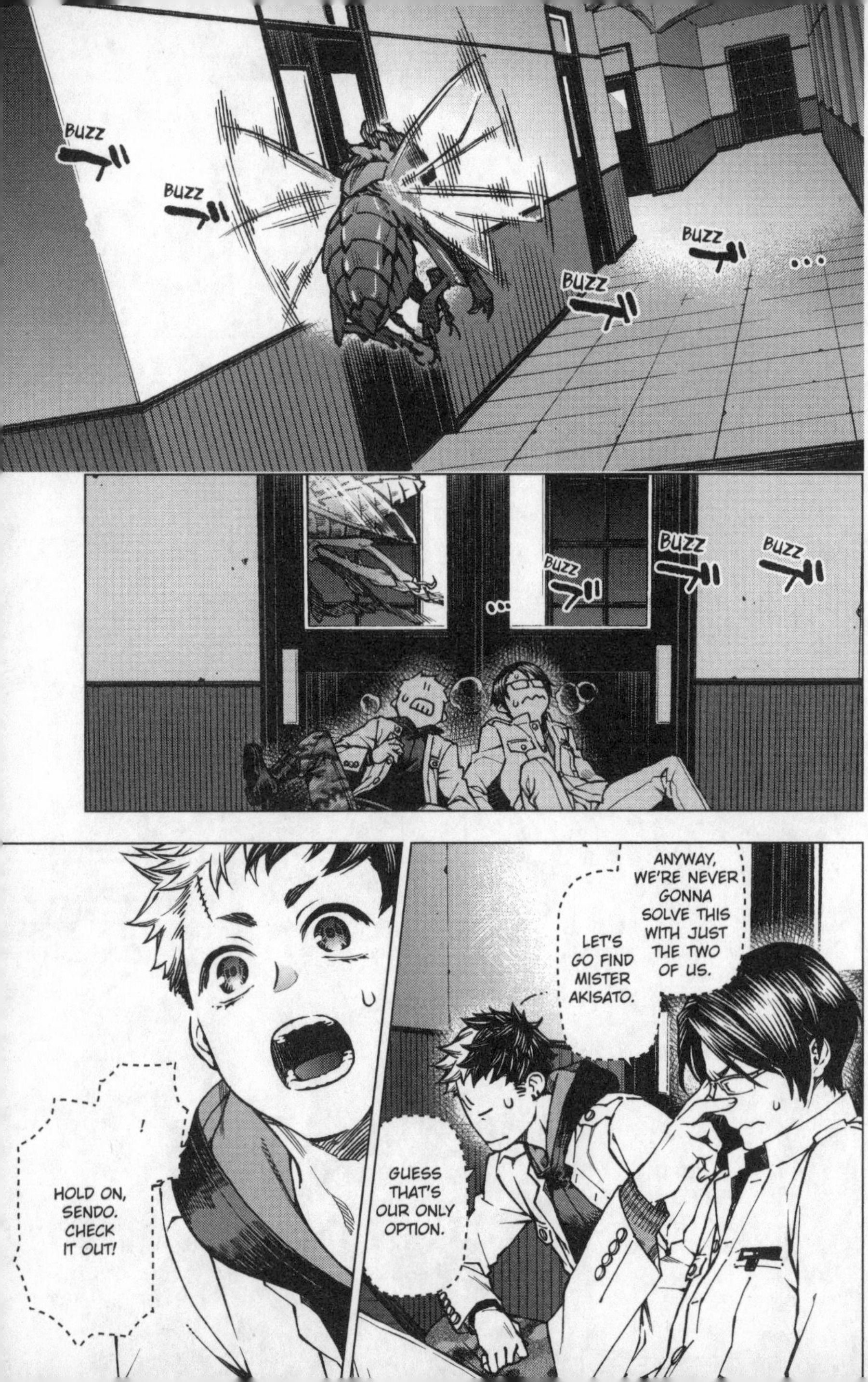
BUZZ
BUZZ
BUZZ
...
BUZZ
BUZZ
BUZZ
BUZZ
...
ANYWAY, WE'RE NEVER GONNA SOLVE THIS WITH JUST THE TWO OF US.
LET'S GO FIND MISTER AKISATO.
GUESS THAT'S OUR ONLY OPTION.
!
HOLD ON, SENDO. CHECK IT OUT!

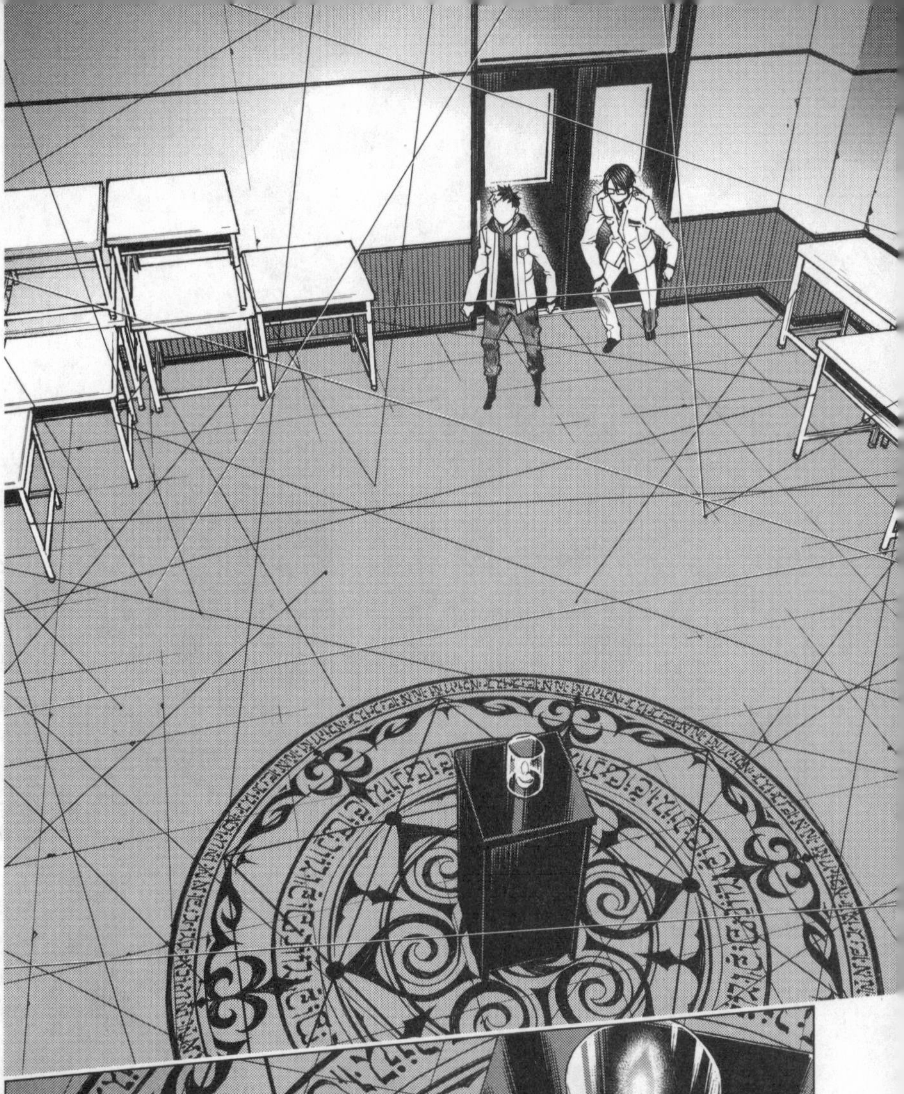
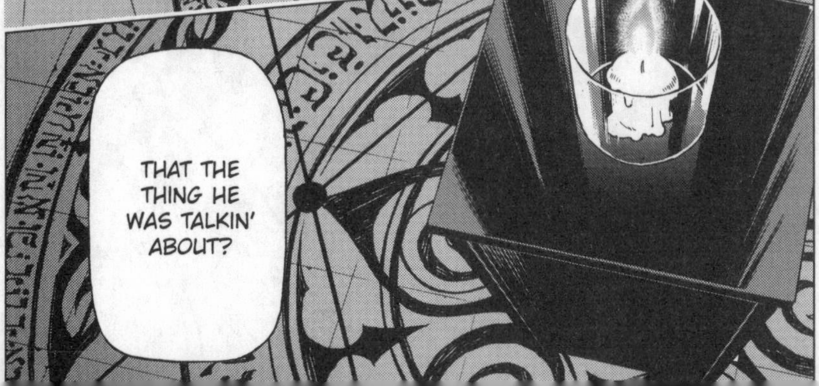
THAT THE THING HE WAS TALKIN' ABOUT?

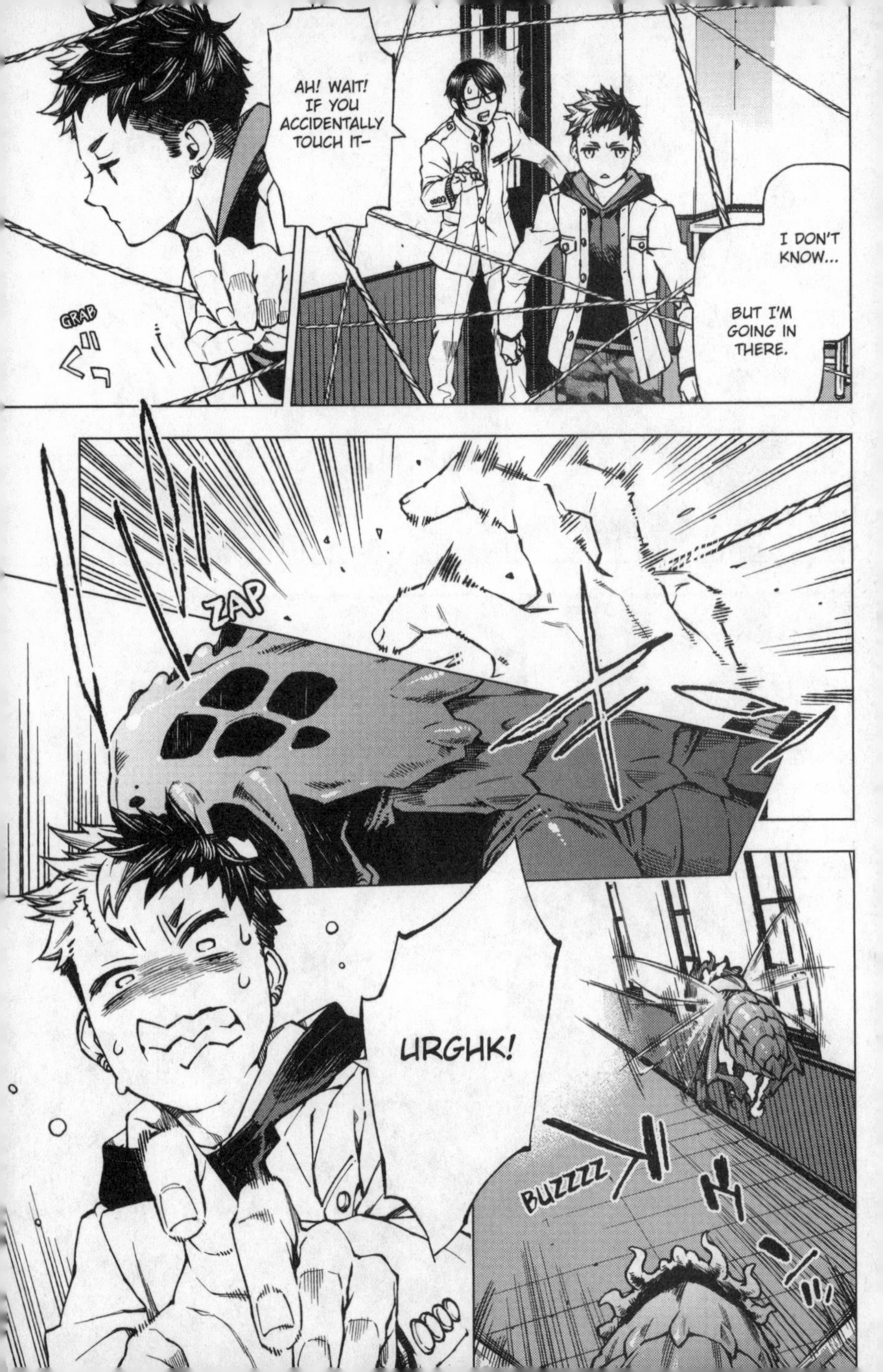
I DON'T KNOW...
BUT I'M GOING IN THERE.
AH! WAIT! IF YOU ACCIDENTALLY TOUCH IT-
GRAB
ZAP
BUZZZZ
URGHK!

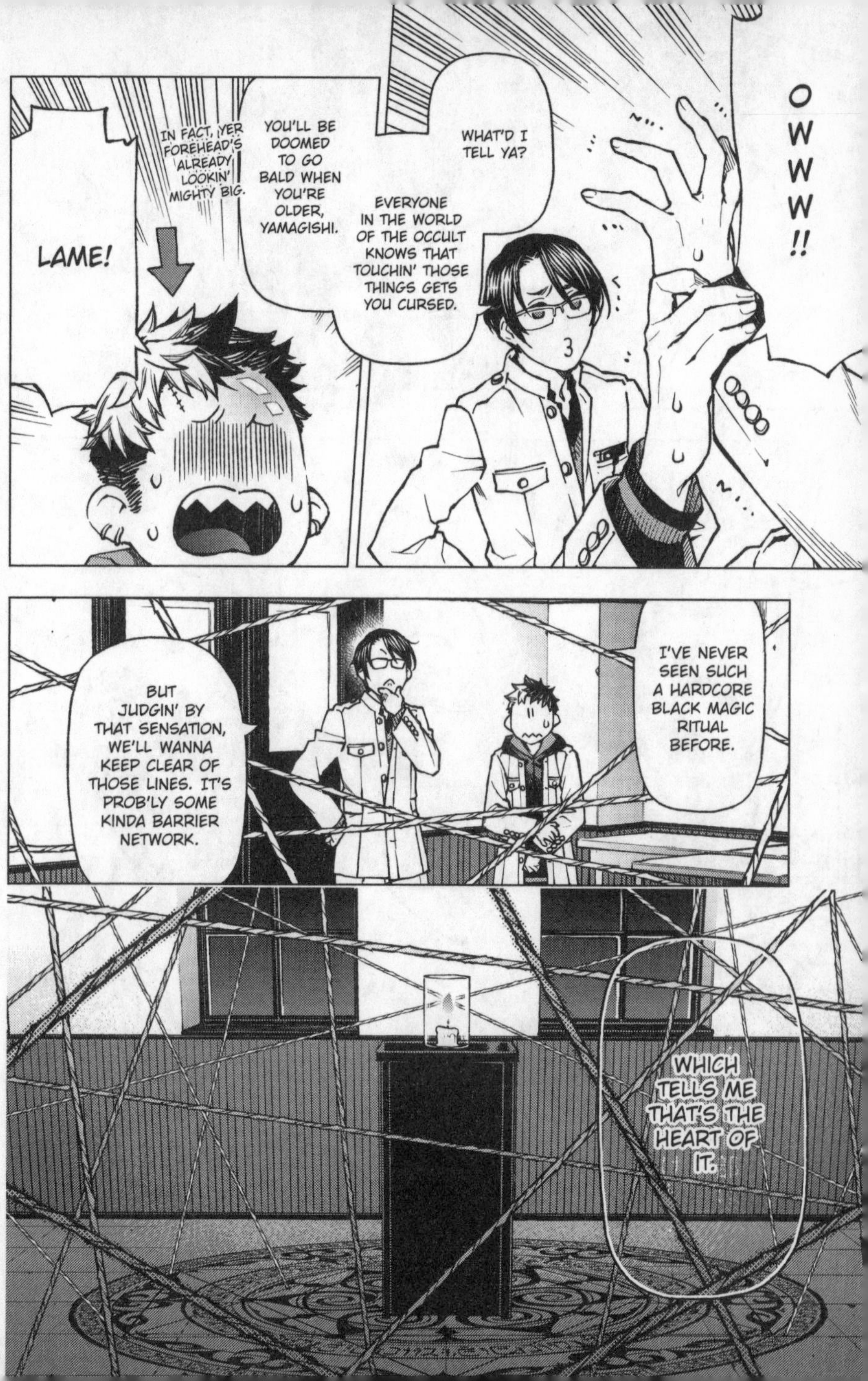
OWWW!!
~...
WHAT'D I TELL YA?
EVERYONE IN THE WORLD OF THE OCCULT KNOWS THAT TOUCHIN' THOSE THINGS GETS YOU CURSED.
YOU'LL BE DOOMED TO GO BALD WHEN YOU'RE OLDER, YAMAGISHI.
IN FACT, YER FOREHEAD'S ALREADY LOOKIN' MIGHTY BIG.
LAME!
I'VE NEVER SEEN SUCH A HARDCORE BLACK MAGIC RITUAL BEFORE.
BUT JUDGIN' BY THAT SENSATION, WE'LL WANNA KEEP CLEAR OF THOSE LINES. IT'S PROB'LY SOME KINDA BARRIER NETWORK.
WHICH TELLS ME THAT'S THE HEART OF IT.

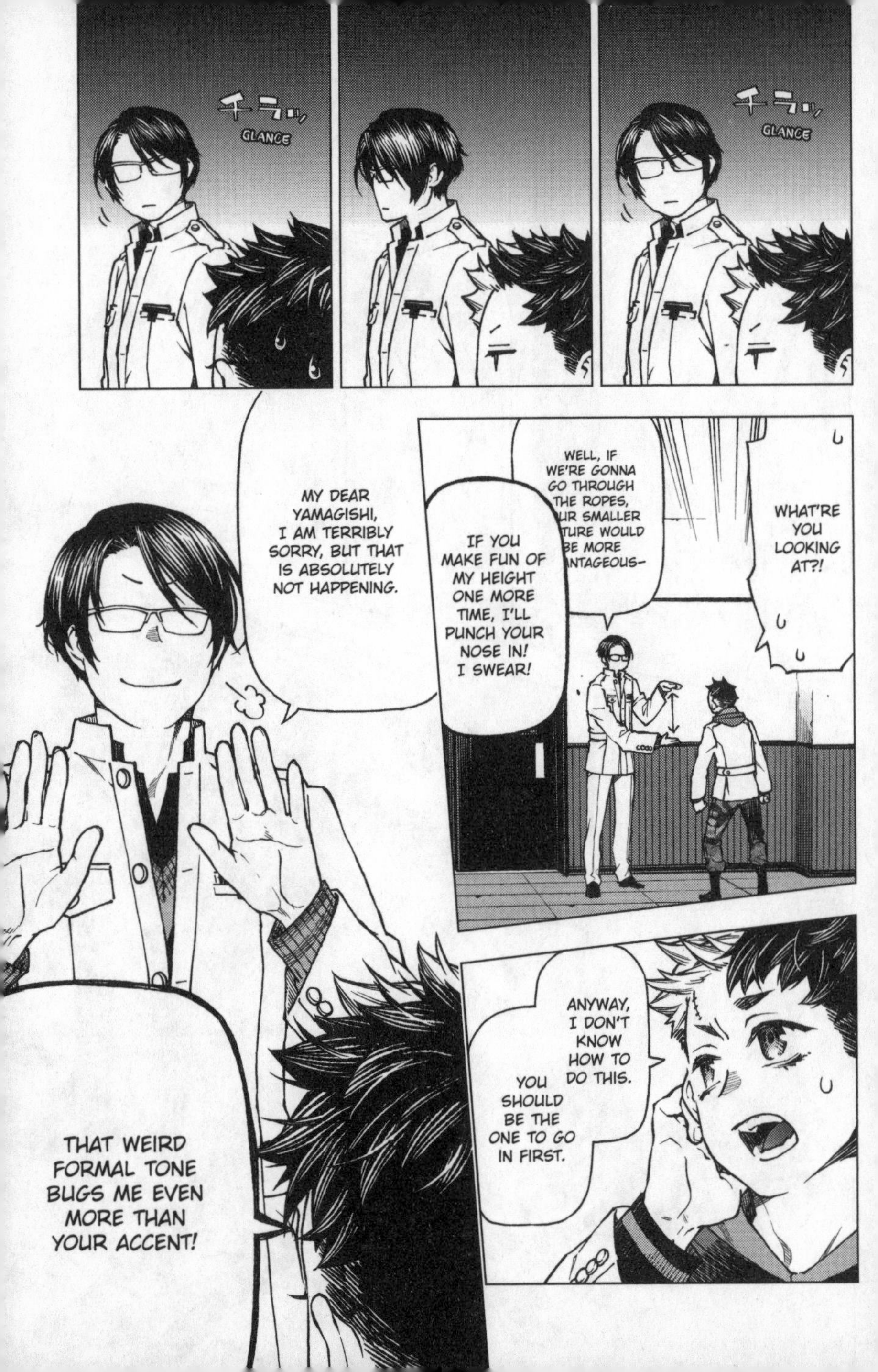
チラッ
GLANCE
チラッ
GLANCE
WHAT'RE YOU LOOKING AT?!
WELL, IF WE'RE GONNA GO THROUGH THE ROPES, UR SMALLER TURE WOULD BE MORE ANTAGEOUS–
IF YOU MAKE FUN OF MY HEIGHT ONE MORE TIME, I'LL PUNCH YOUR NOSE IN! I SWEAR!
ANYWAY, I DON'T KNOW HOW TO DO THIS.
YOU SHOULD BE THE ONE TO GO IN FIRST.
MY DEAR YAMAGISHI, I AM TERRIBLY SORRY, BUT THAT IS ABSOLUTELY NOT HAPPENING.
THAT WEIRD FORMAL TONE BUGS ME EVEN MORE THAN YOUR ACCENT!

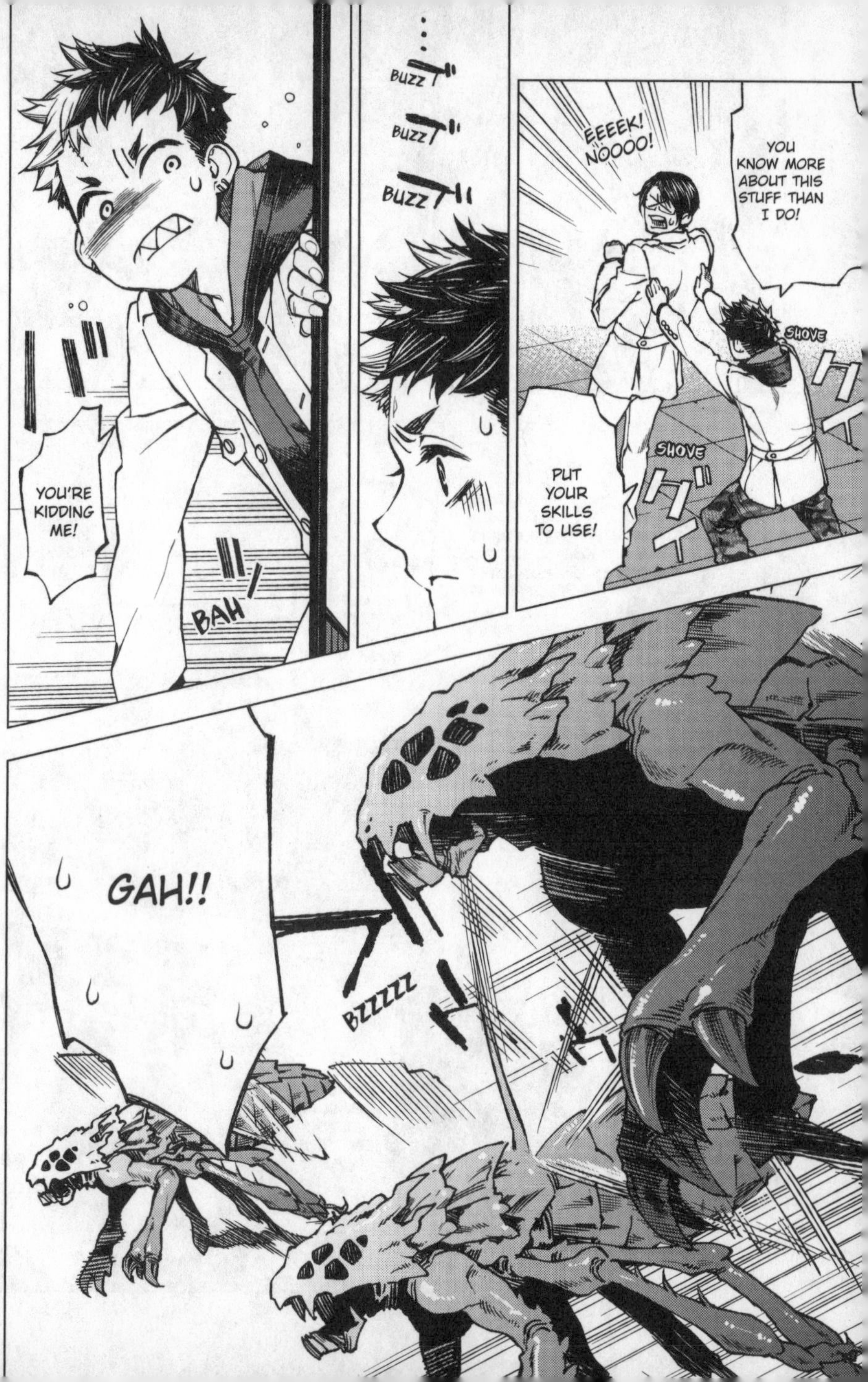
YOU KNOW MORE ABOUT THIS STUFF THAN I DO!
EEEEK! NOOOO!
SHOVE
SHOVE
PUT YOUR SKILLS TO USE!
...
BUZZ
BUZZ
BUZZ
YOU'RE KIDDING ME!
BAH
GAH!!
BZZZZZ

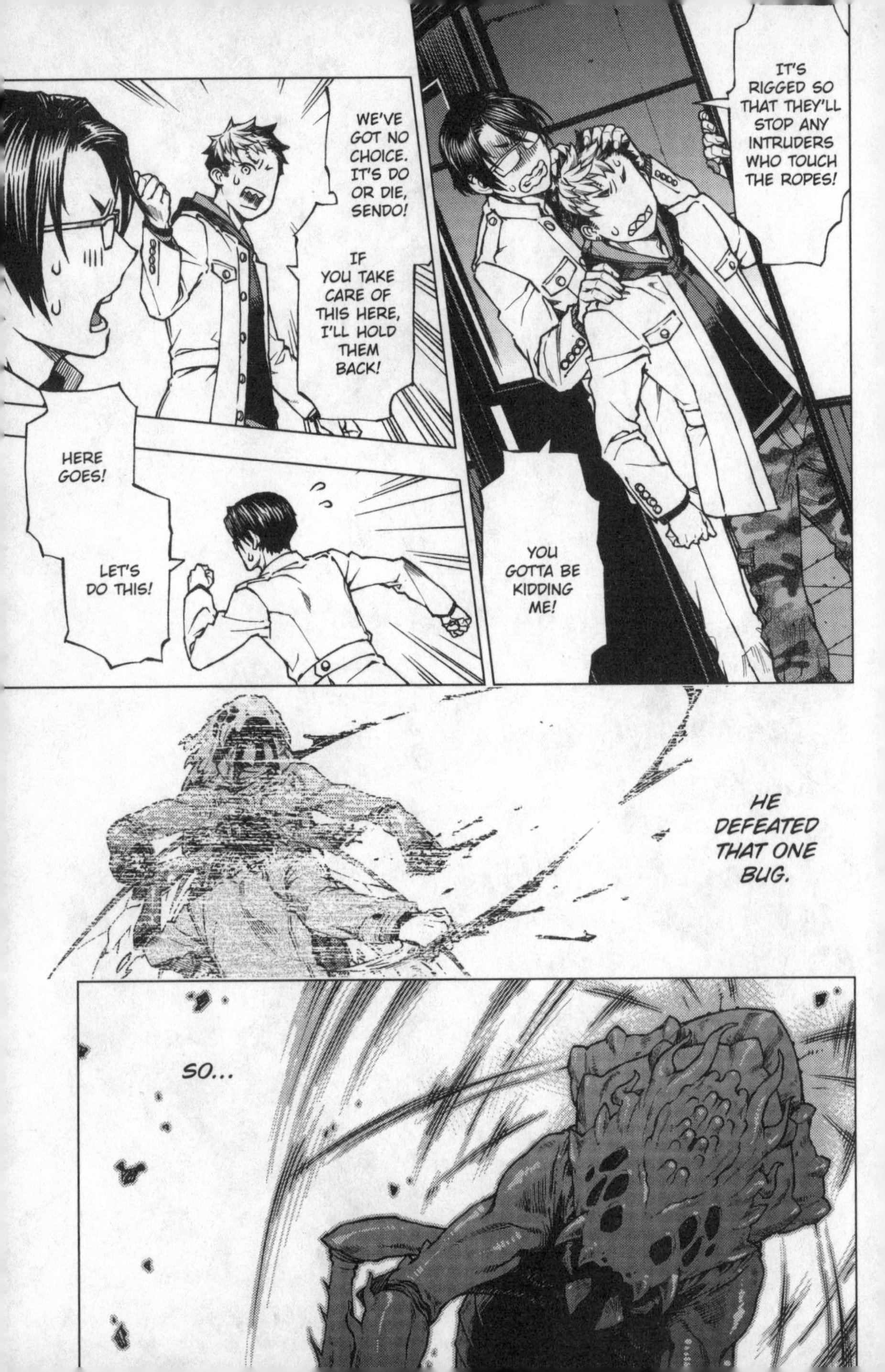
IT'S RIGGED SO THAT THEY'LL STOP ANY INTRUDERS WHO TOUCH THE ROPES!
YOU GOTTA BE KIDDING ME!
WE'VE GOT NO CHOICE. IT'S DO OR DIE, SENDO!
IF YOU TAKE CARE OF THIS HERE, I'LL HOLD THEM BACK!
HERE GOES!
LET'S DO THIS!
HE DEFEATED THAT ONE BUG.
SO...

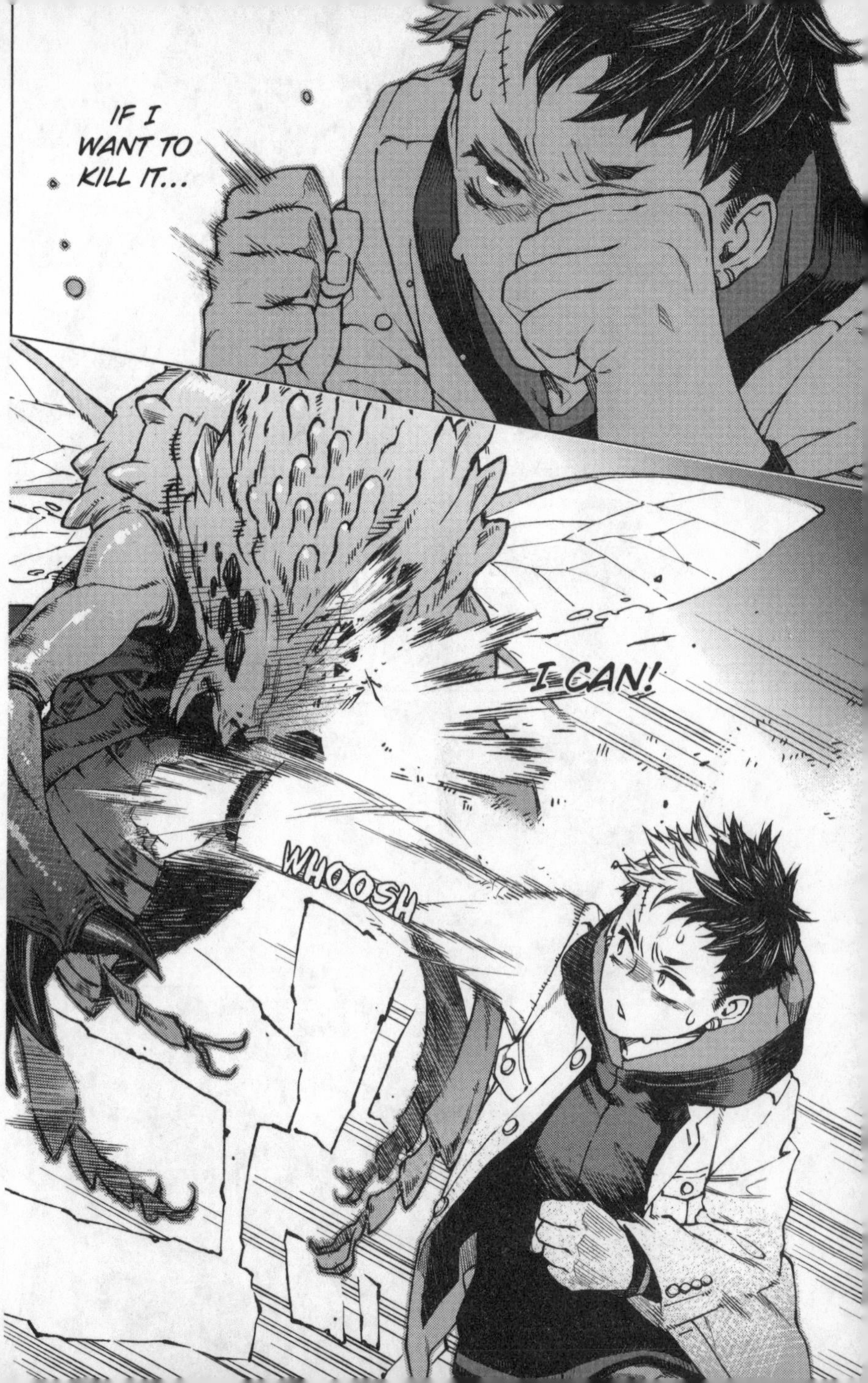
IF I WANT TO KILL IT...
I CAN!
WHOOSH

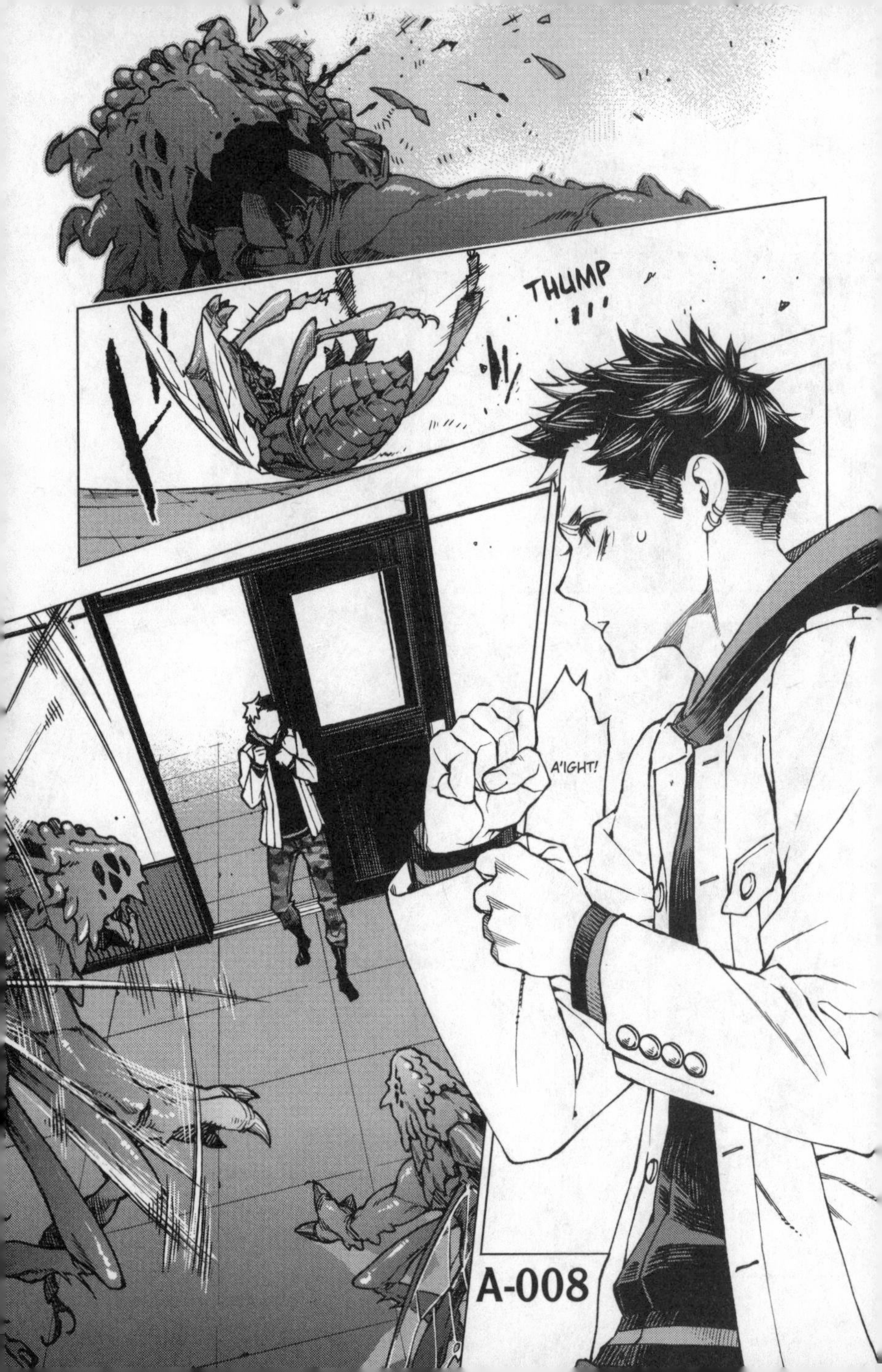
THUMP
A'IGHT!
A-008

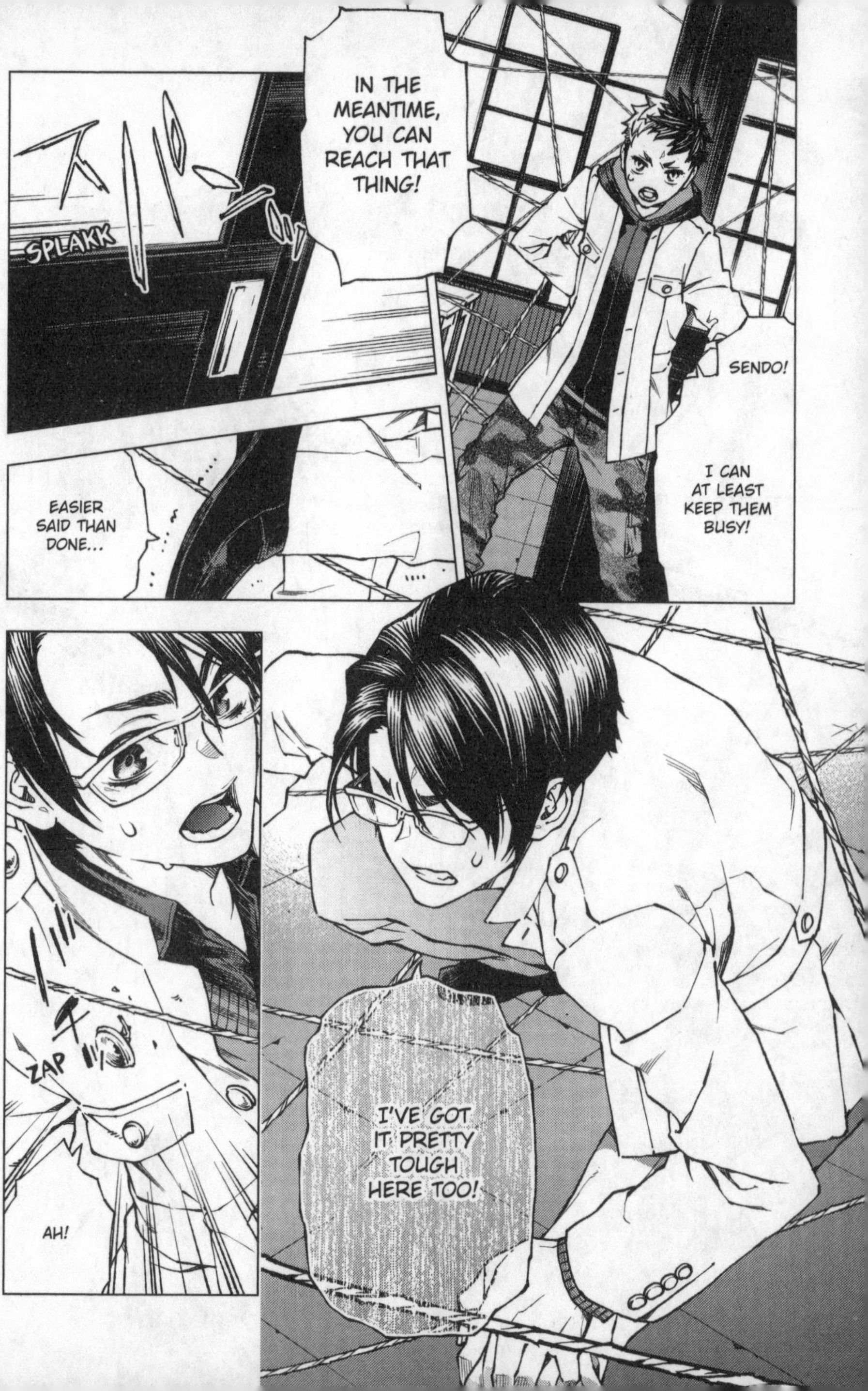
IN THE MEANTIME, YOU CAN REACH THAT THING!
SENDO!
I CAN AT LEAST KEEP THEM BUSY!
SPLAKK
EASIER SAID THAN DONE...
I'VE GOT IT PRETTY TOUGH HERE TOO!
ZAP
AH!

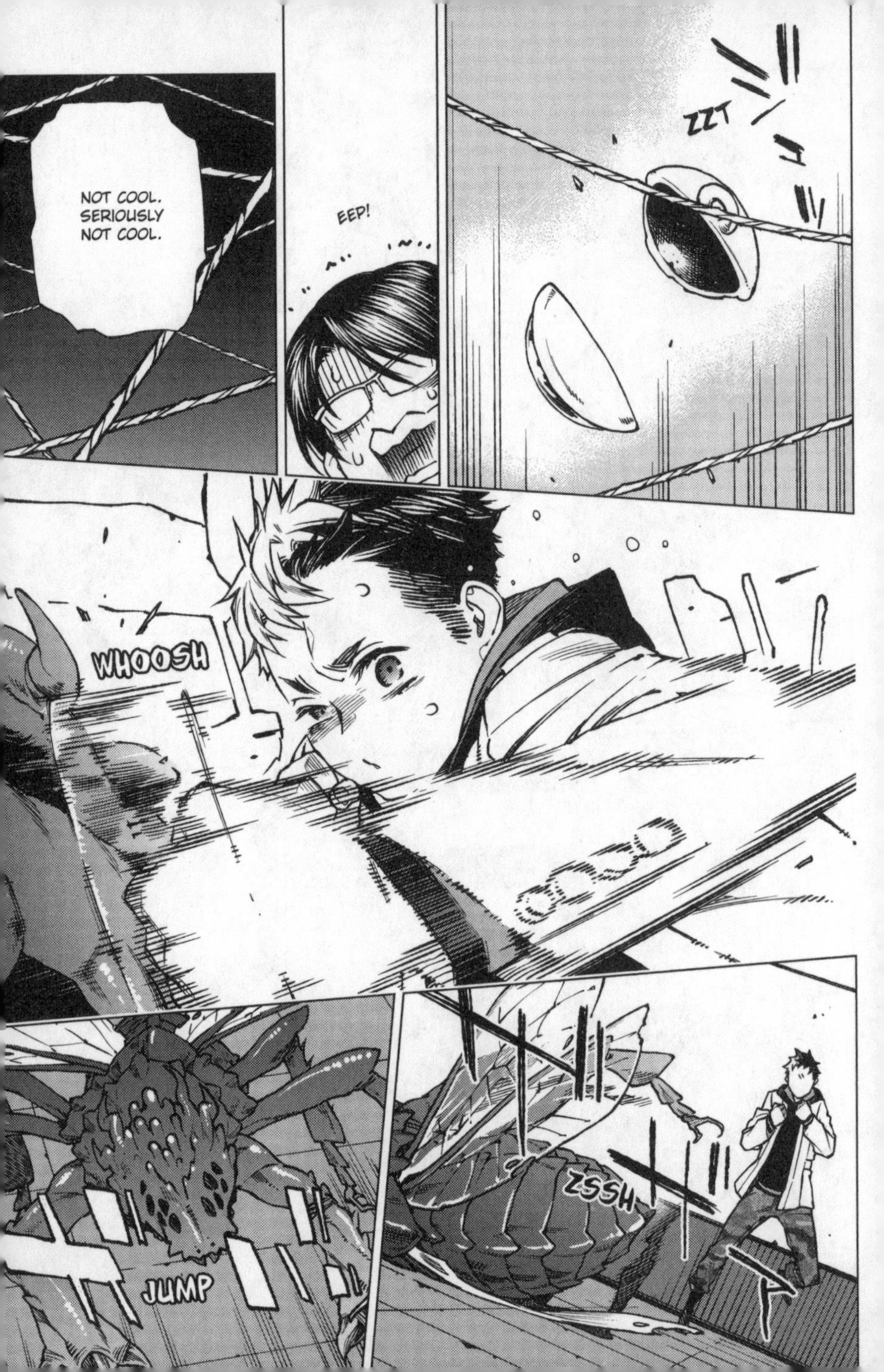
ZZT
EEP!
NOT COOL. SERIOUSLY NOT COOL.
WHOOSH
ZSSH
JUMP

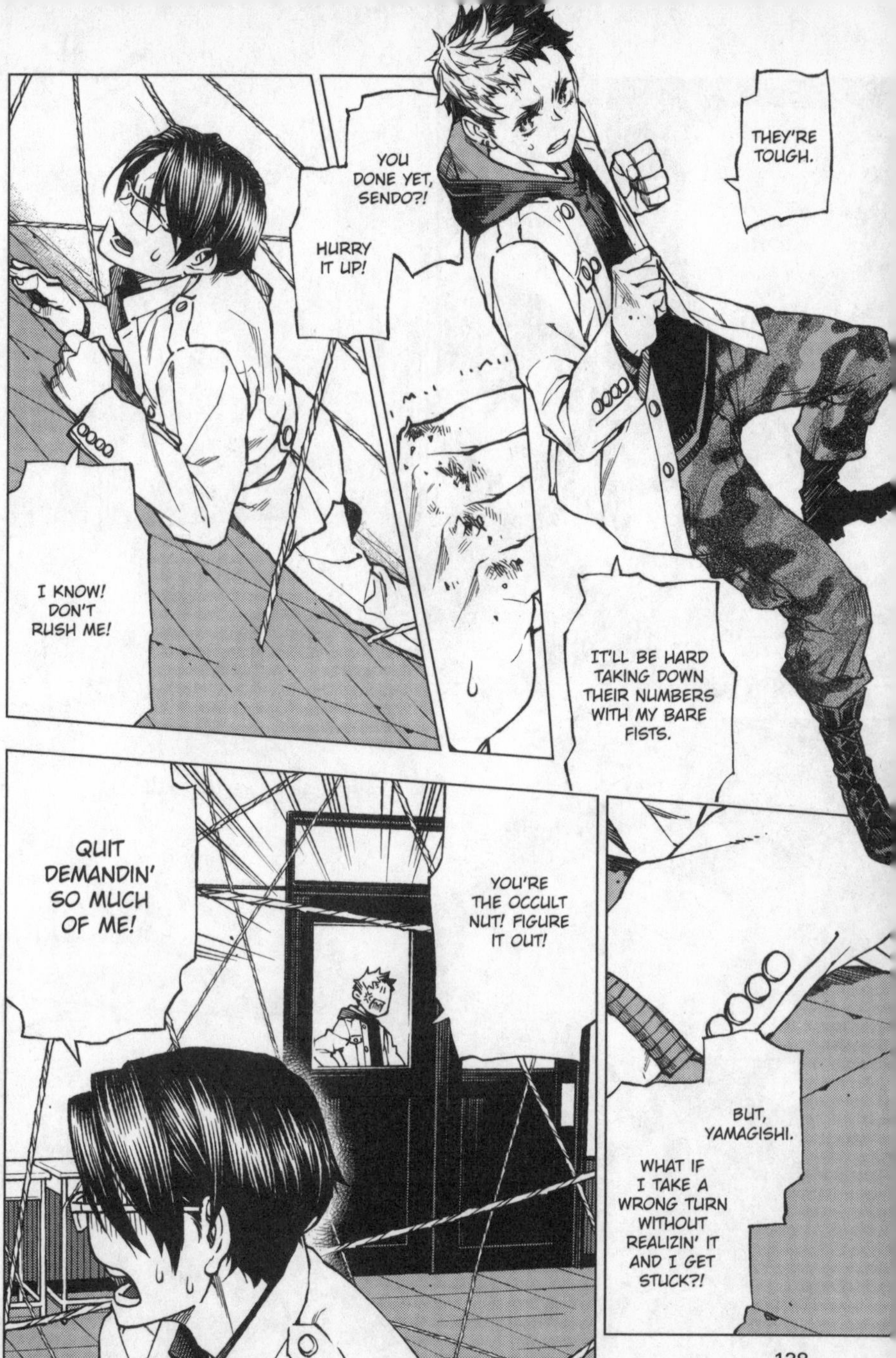
THEY'RE TOUGH.
YOU DONE YET, SENDO?!
HURRY IT UP!
...M...
IT'LL BE HARD TAKING DOWN THEIR NUMBERS WITH MY BARE FISTS.
I KNOW! DON'T RUSH ME!
BUT, YAMAGISHI.
WHAT IF I TAKE A WRONG TURN WITHOUT REALIZIN' IT AND I GET STUCK?!
YOU'RE THE OCCULT NUT! FIGURE IT OUT!
QUIT DEMANDIN' SO MUCH OF ME!

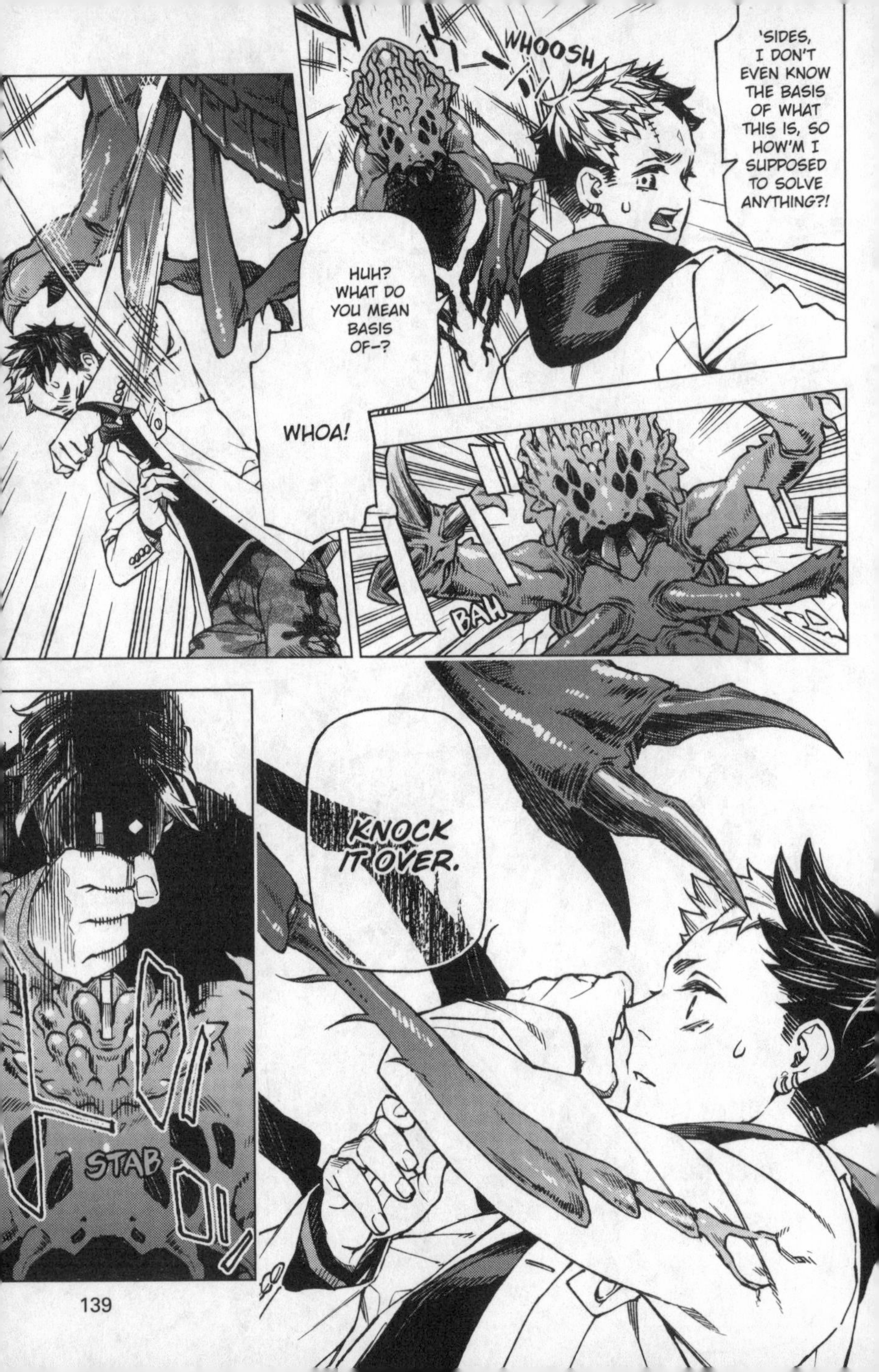
WHOOSH
'SIDES, I DON'T EVEN KNOW THE BASIS OF WHAT THIS IS, SO HOW'M I SUPPOSED TO SOLVE ANYTHING?!
HUH? WHAT DO YOU MEAN BASIS OF-?
WHOA!
BAH
KNOCK IT OVER.
STAB

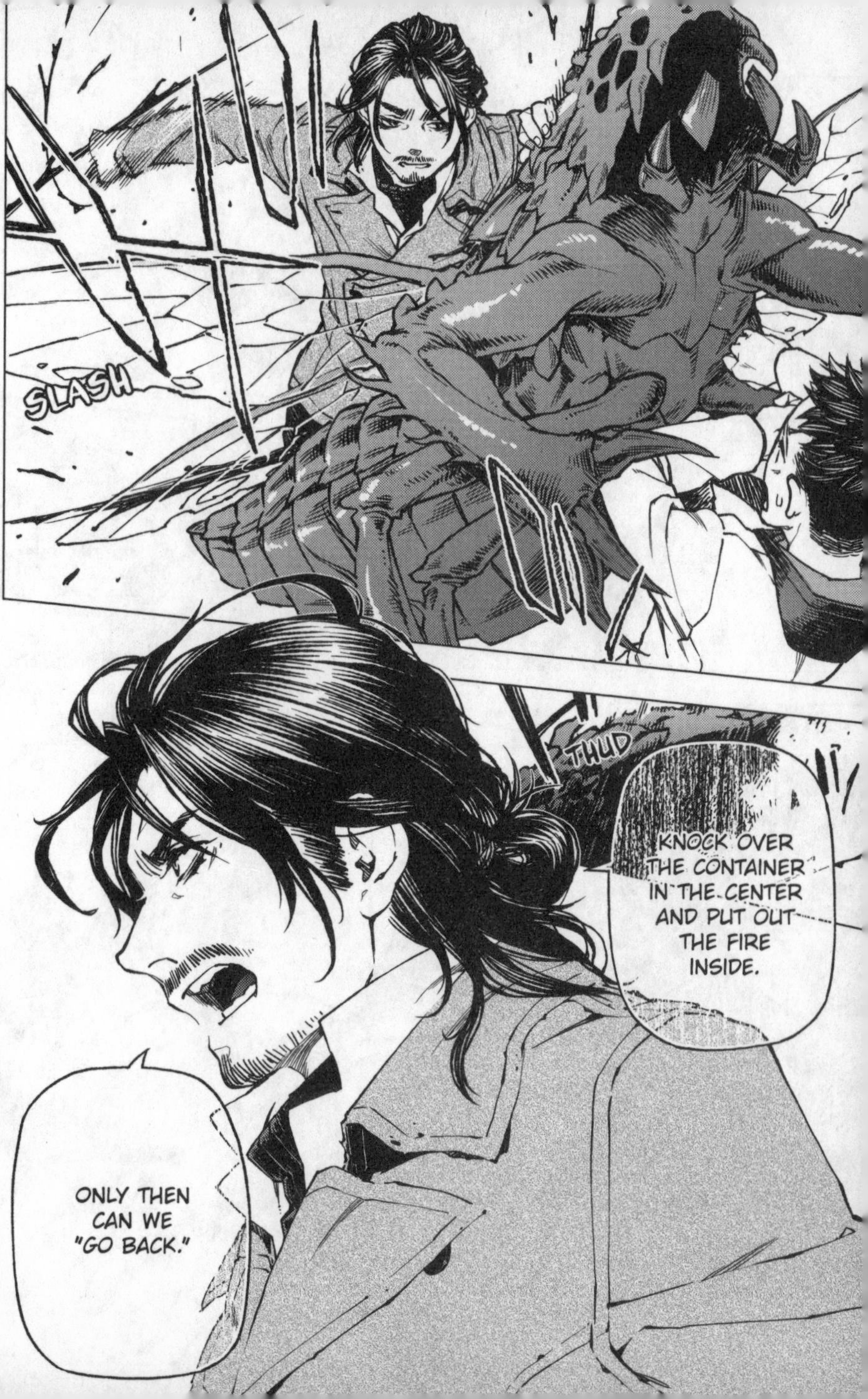
SLASH
THUD
KNOCK OVER THE CONTAINER IN THE CENTER AND PUT OUT THE FIRE INSIDE.
ONLY THEN CAN WE "GO BACK."

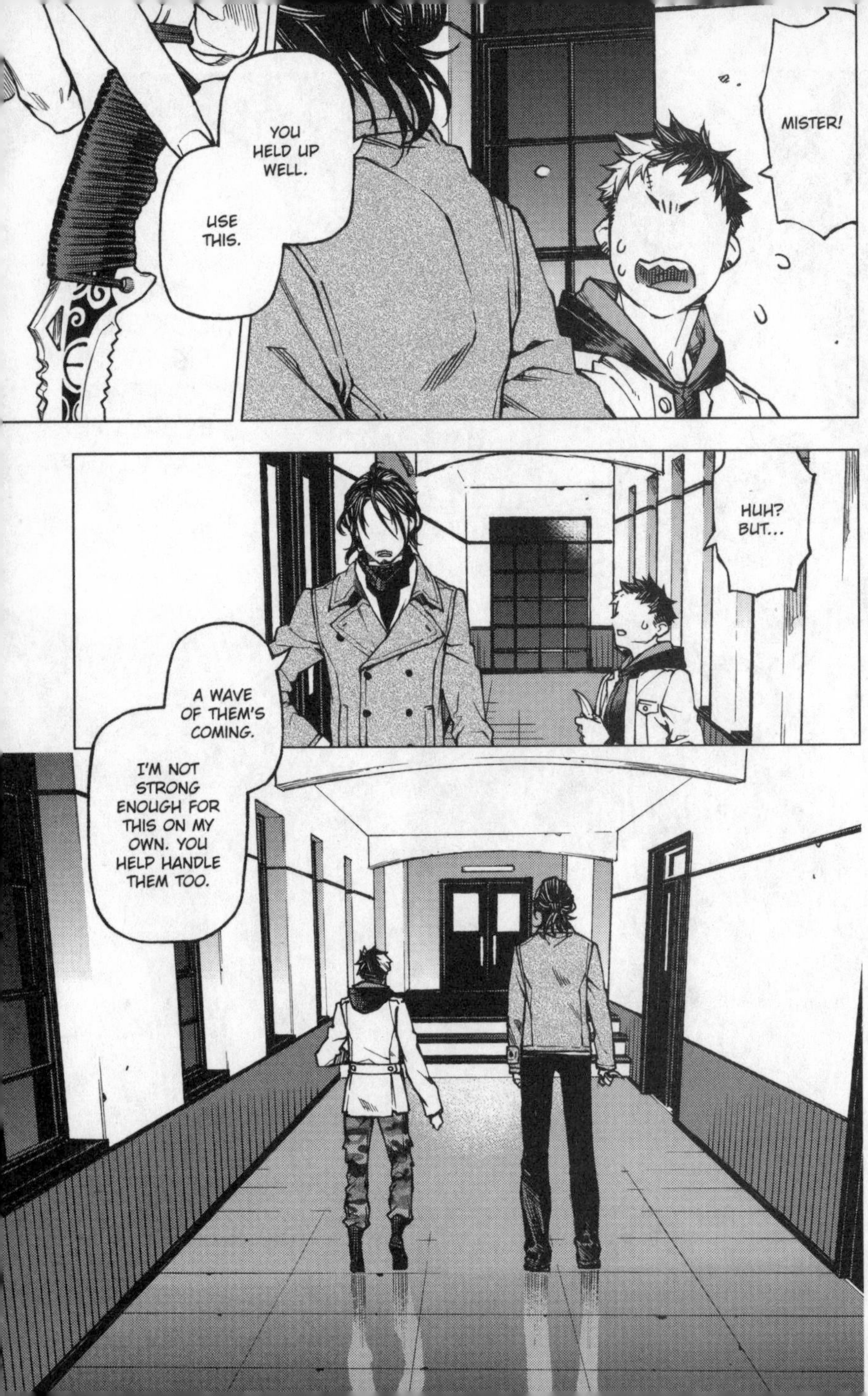
MISTER!
YOU HELD UP WELL.
USE THIS.
HUH? BUT...
A WAVE OF THEM'S COMING.
I'M NOT STRONG ENOUGH FOR THIS ON MY OWN. YOU HELP HANDLE THEM TOO.

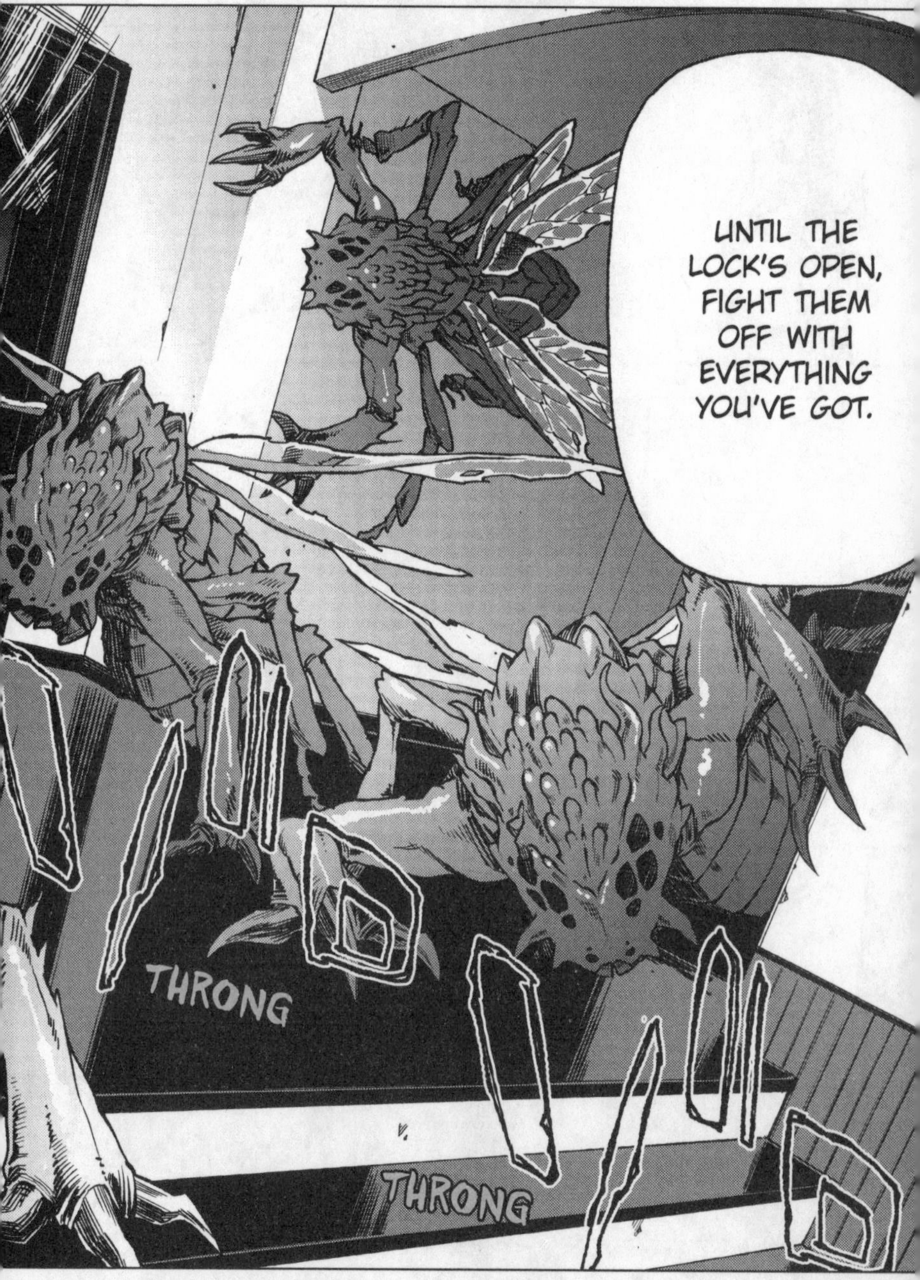
UNTIL THE LOCK'S OPEN, FIGHT THEM OFF WITH EVERYTHING YOU'VE GOT.
THRONG
THRONG

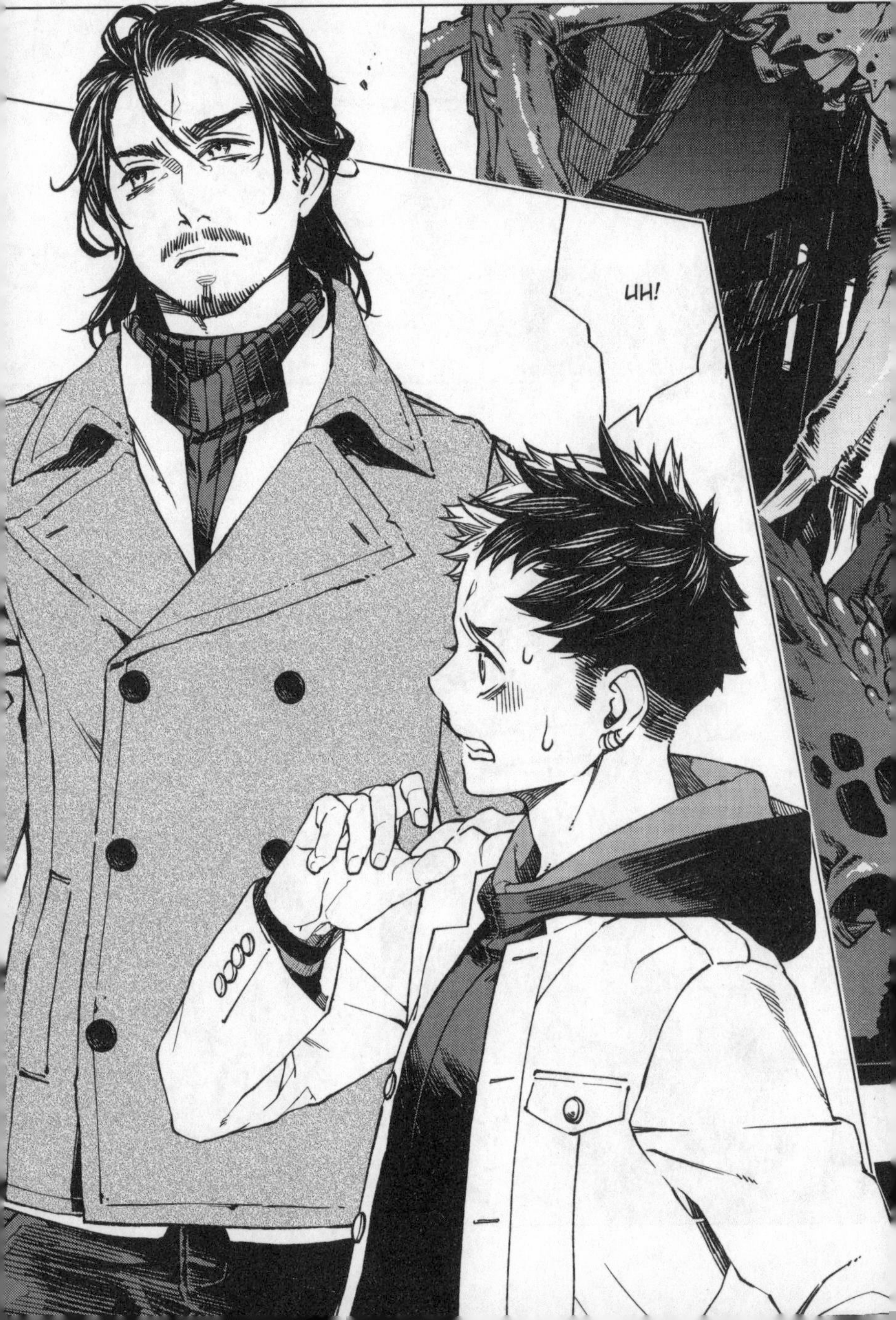
UH!

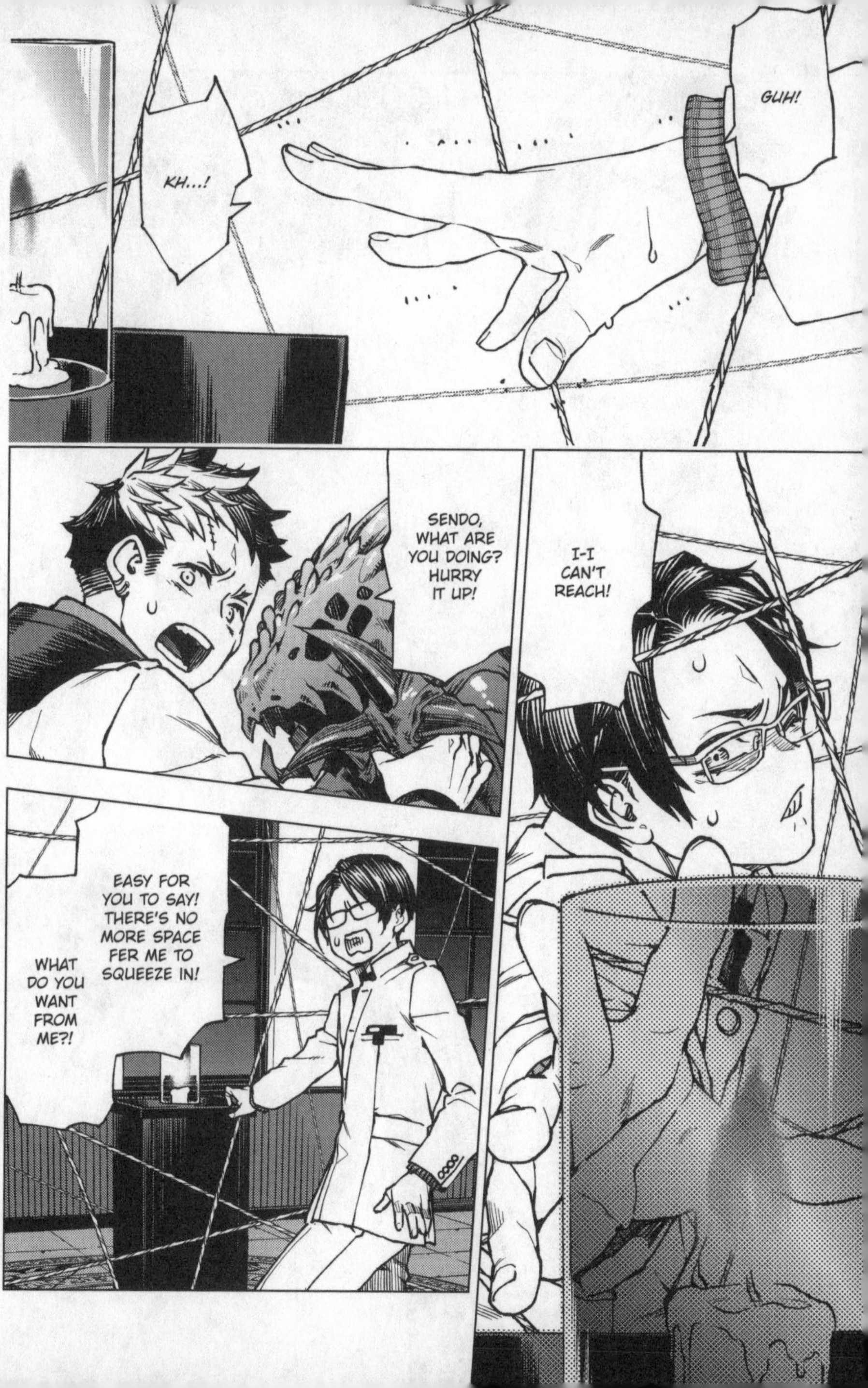
GUH!
...
...
...
...
...
...
KH...!
I-I CAN'T REACH!
SENDO, WHAT ARE YOU DOING? HURRY IT UP!
EASY FOR YOU TO SAY! THERE'S NO MORE SPACE FER ME TO SQUEEZE IN!
WHAT DO YOU WANT FROM ME?!

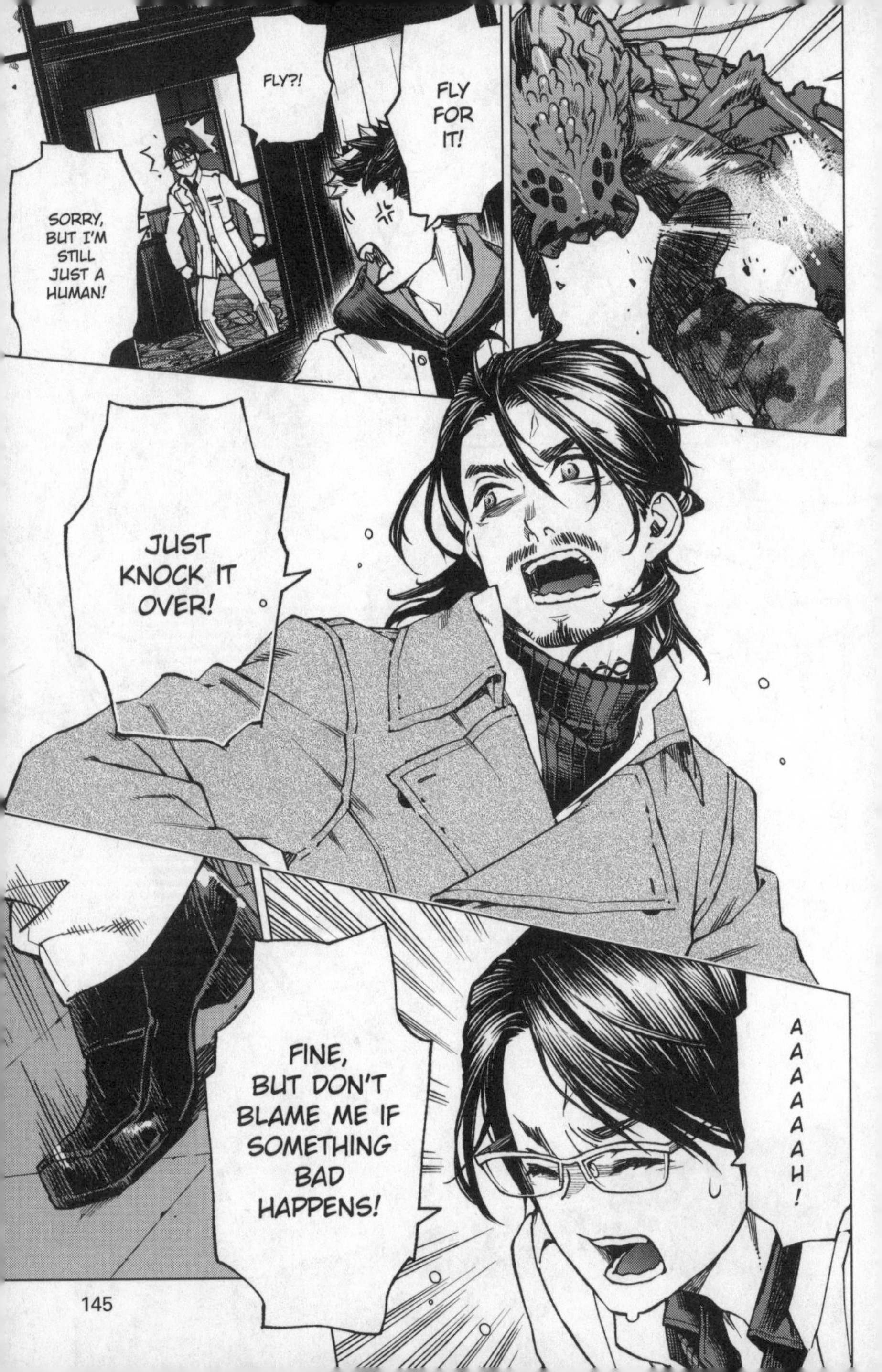
FLY FOR IT!
FLY?!
SORRY, BUT I'M STILL JUST A HUMAN!
JUST KNOCK IT OVER!
AAAAAAAAH!
FINE, BUT DON'T BLAME ME IF SOMETHING BAD HAPPENS!

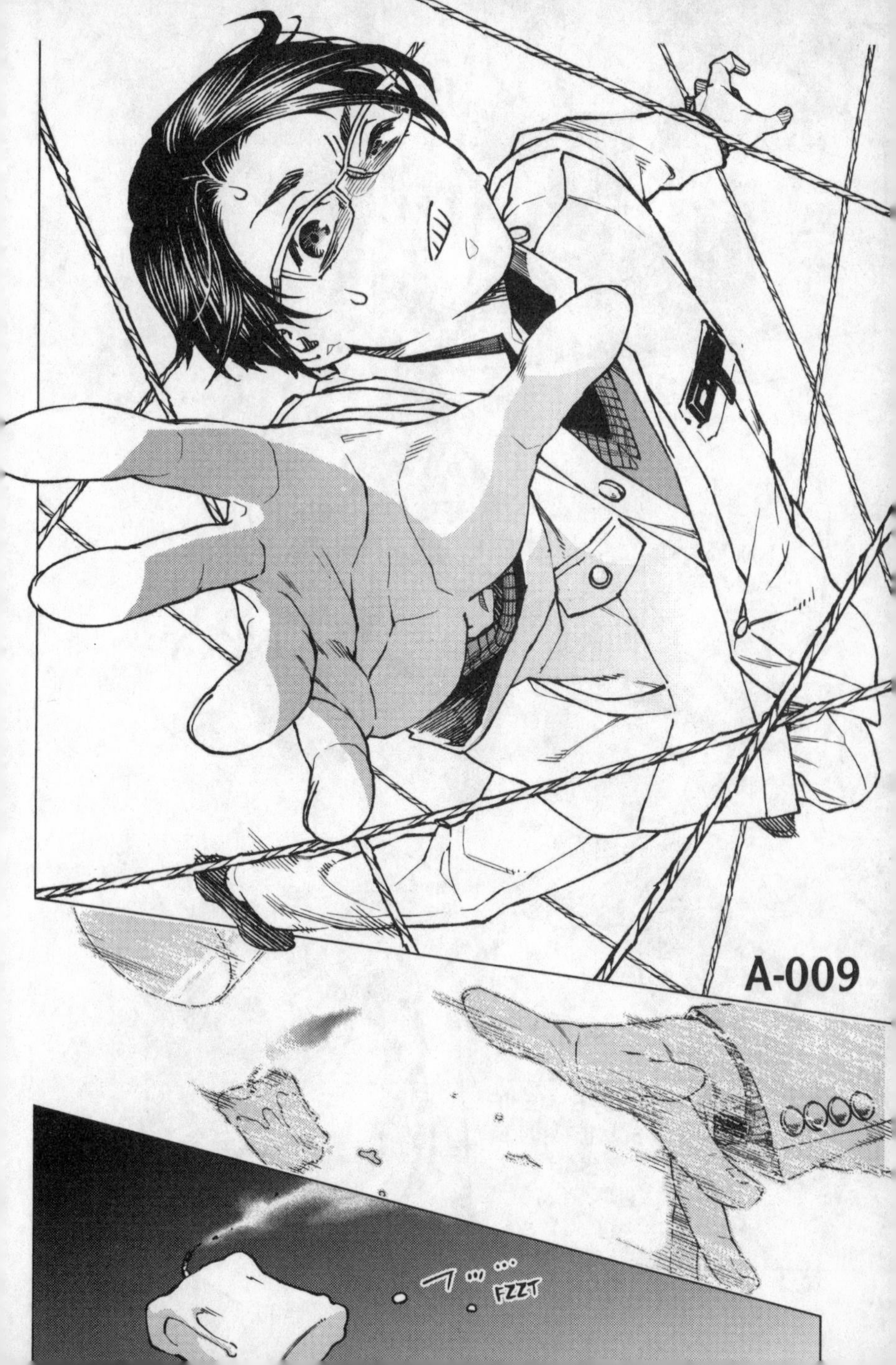
A-009
FZZT

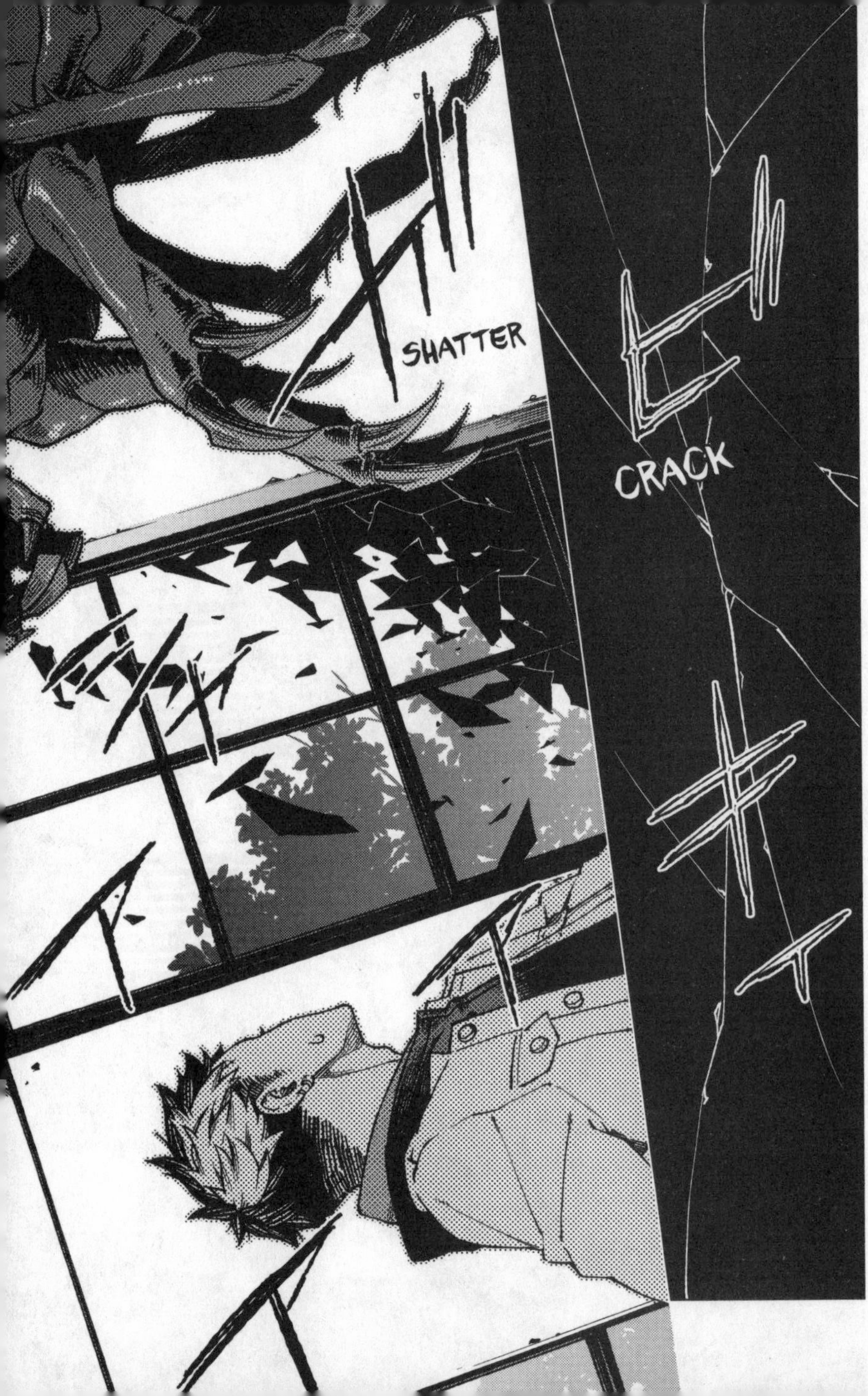
CRACK
SHATTER

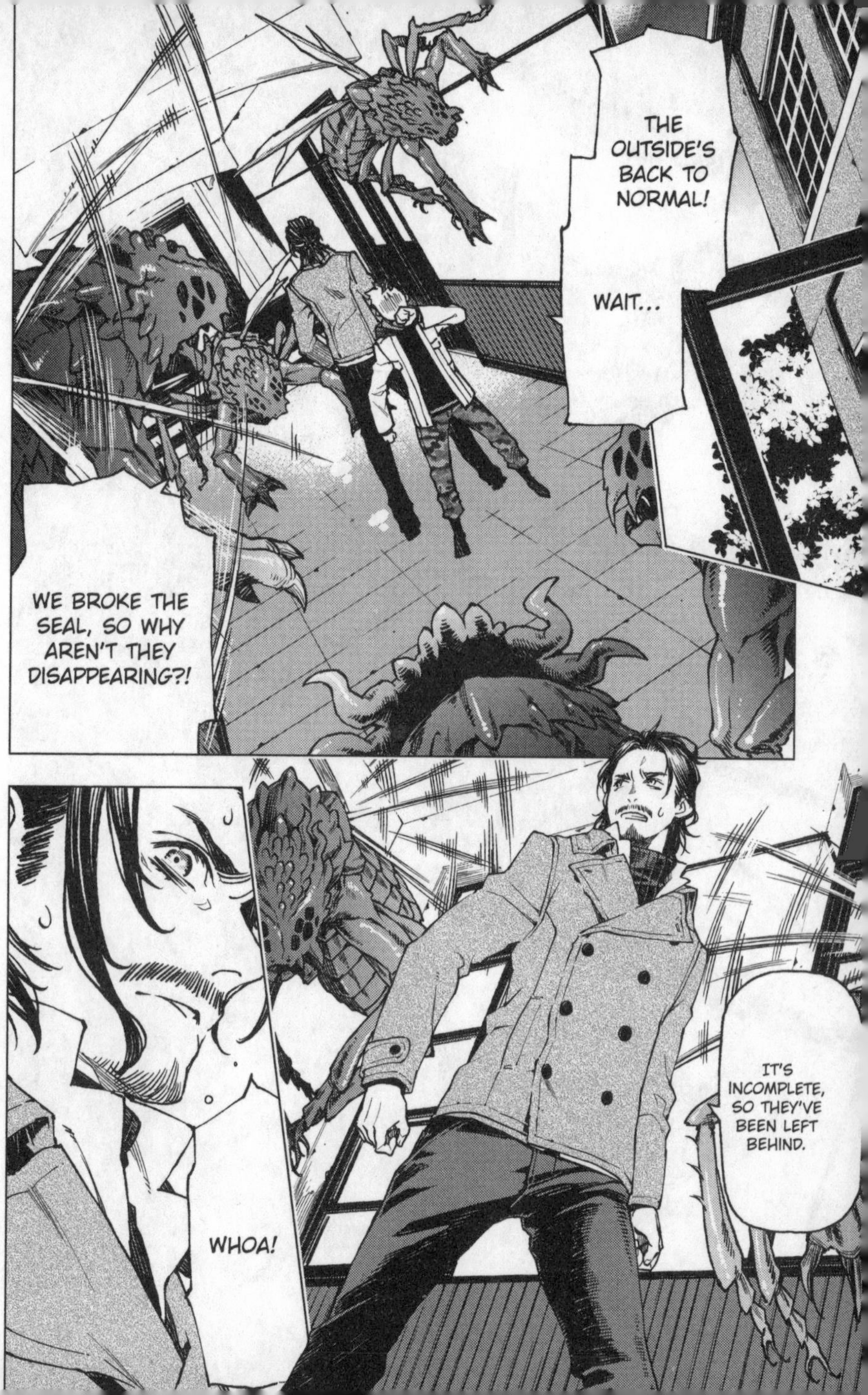
THE OUTSIDE'S BACK TO NORMAL!
WAIT...
WE BROKE THE SEAL, SO WHY AREN'T THEY DISAPPEARING?!
IT'S INCOMPLETE, SO THEY'VE BEEN LEFT BEHIND.
WHOA!

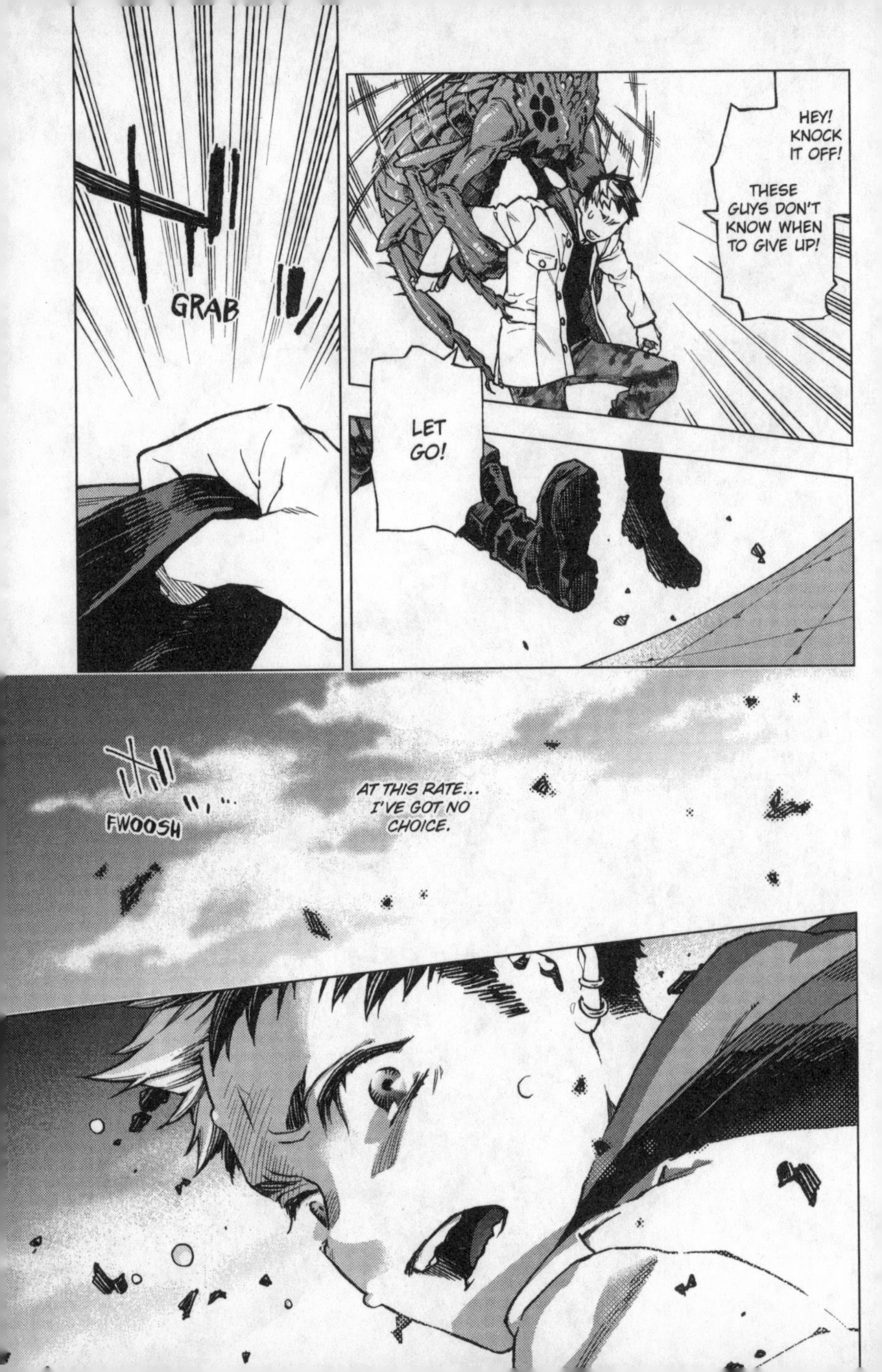
HEY! KNOCK IT OFF!
THESE GUYS DON'T KNOW WHEN TO GIVE UP!
LET GO!
GRAB
AT THIS RATE... I'VE GOT NO CHOICE.
FWOOSH

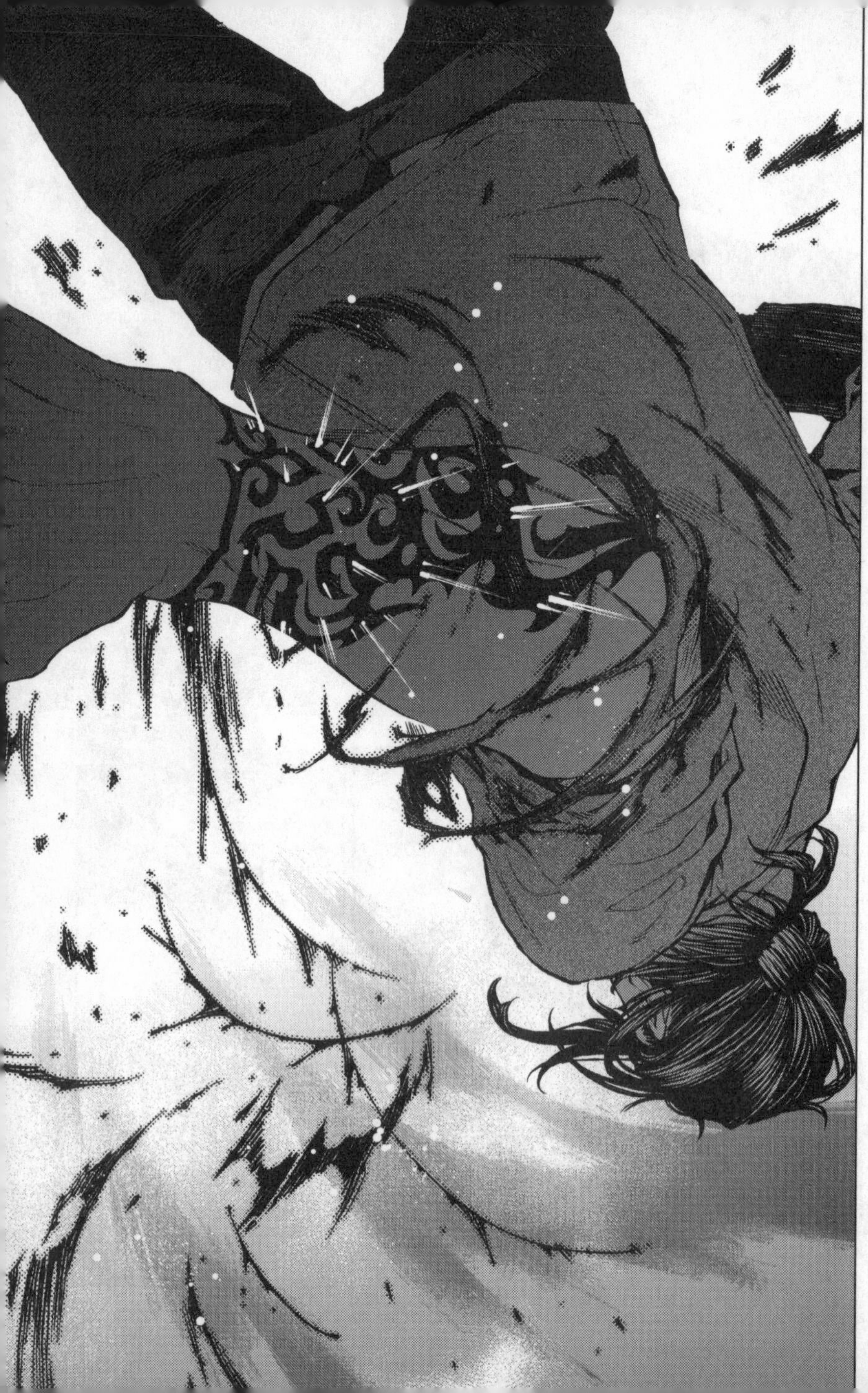

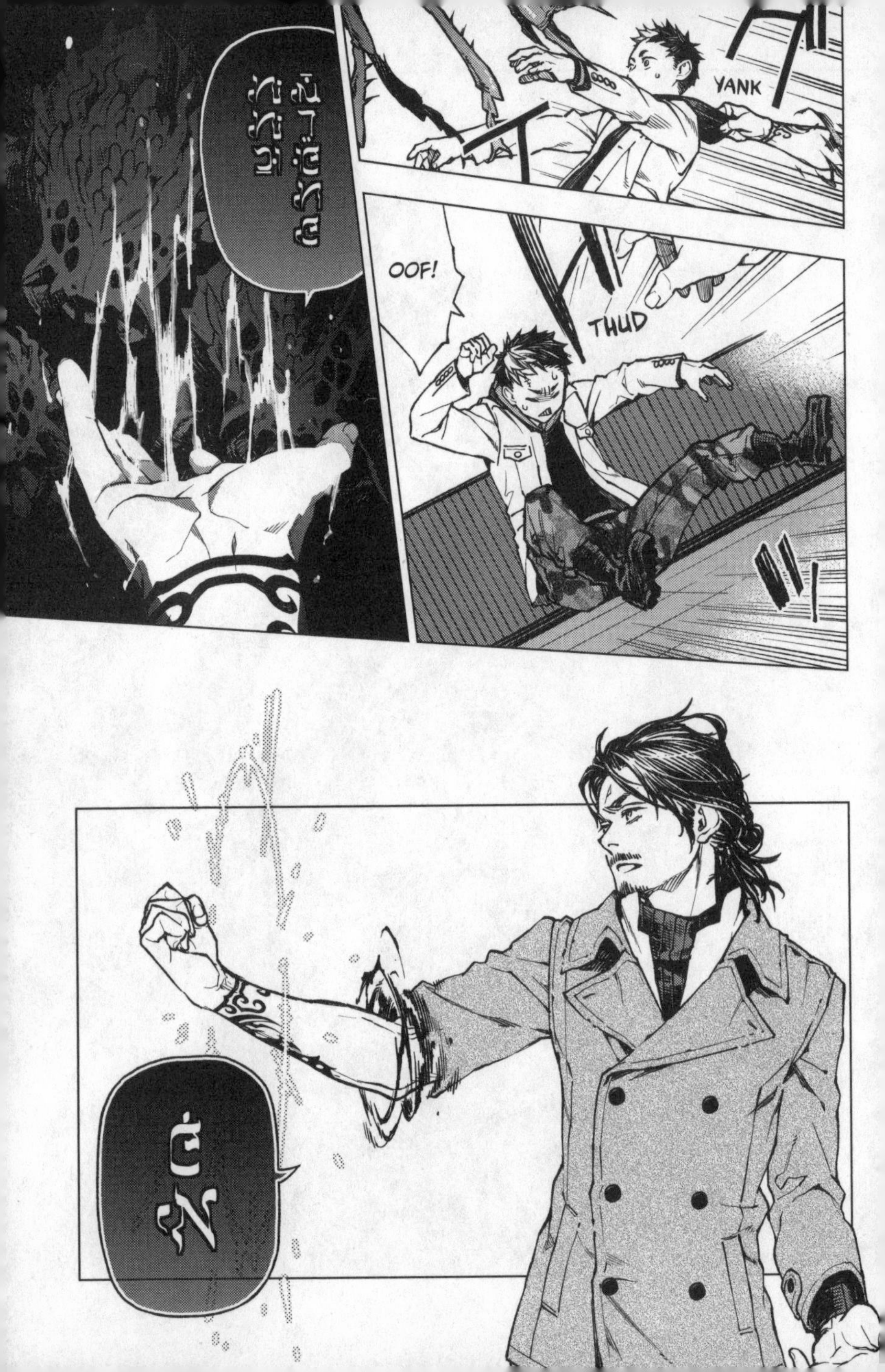
YANK
OOF!
THUD

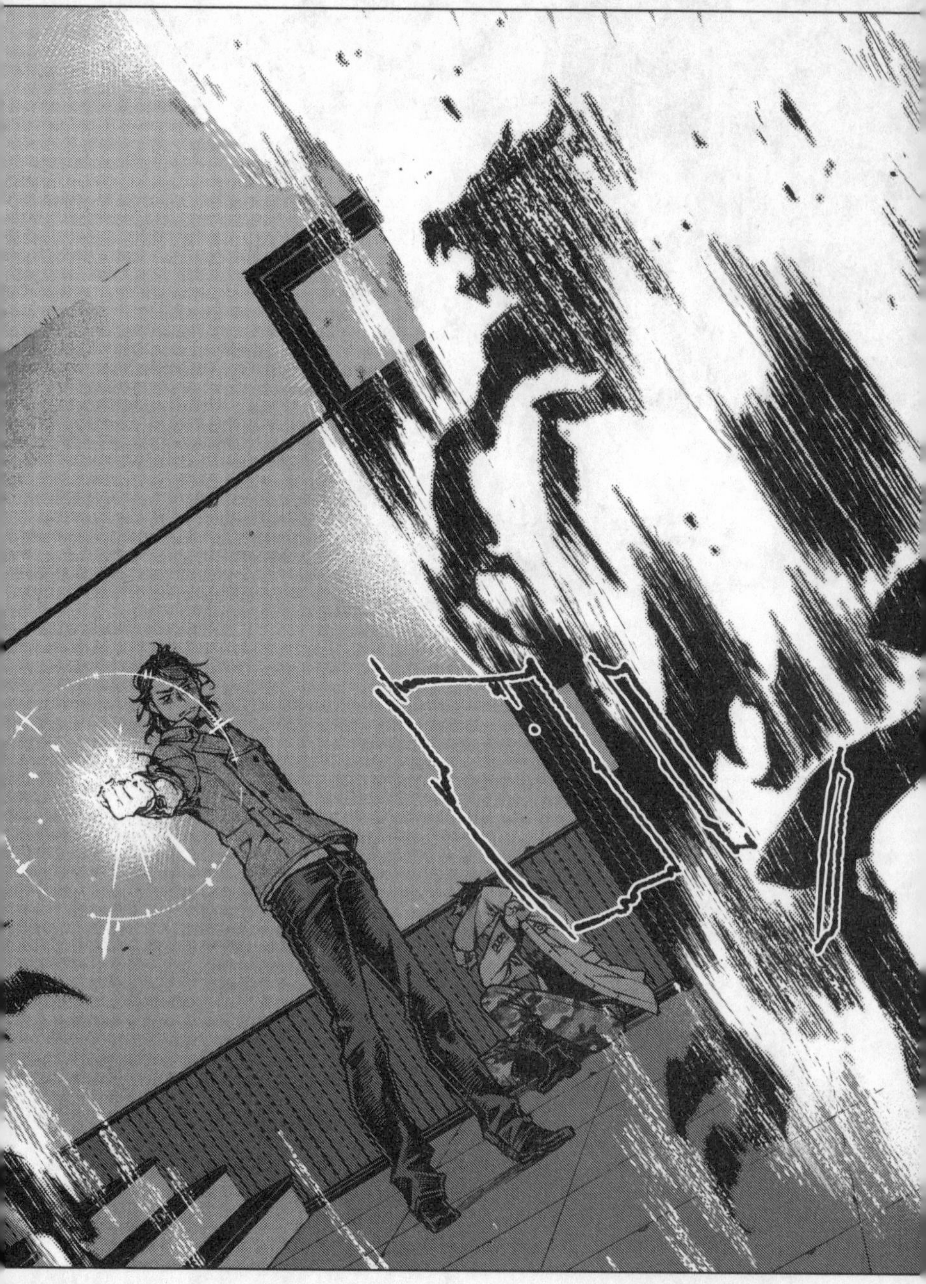

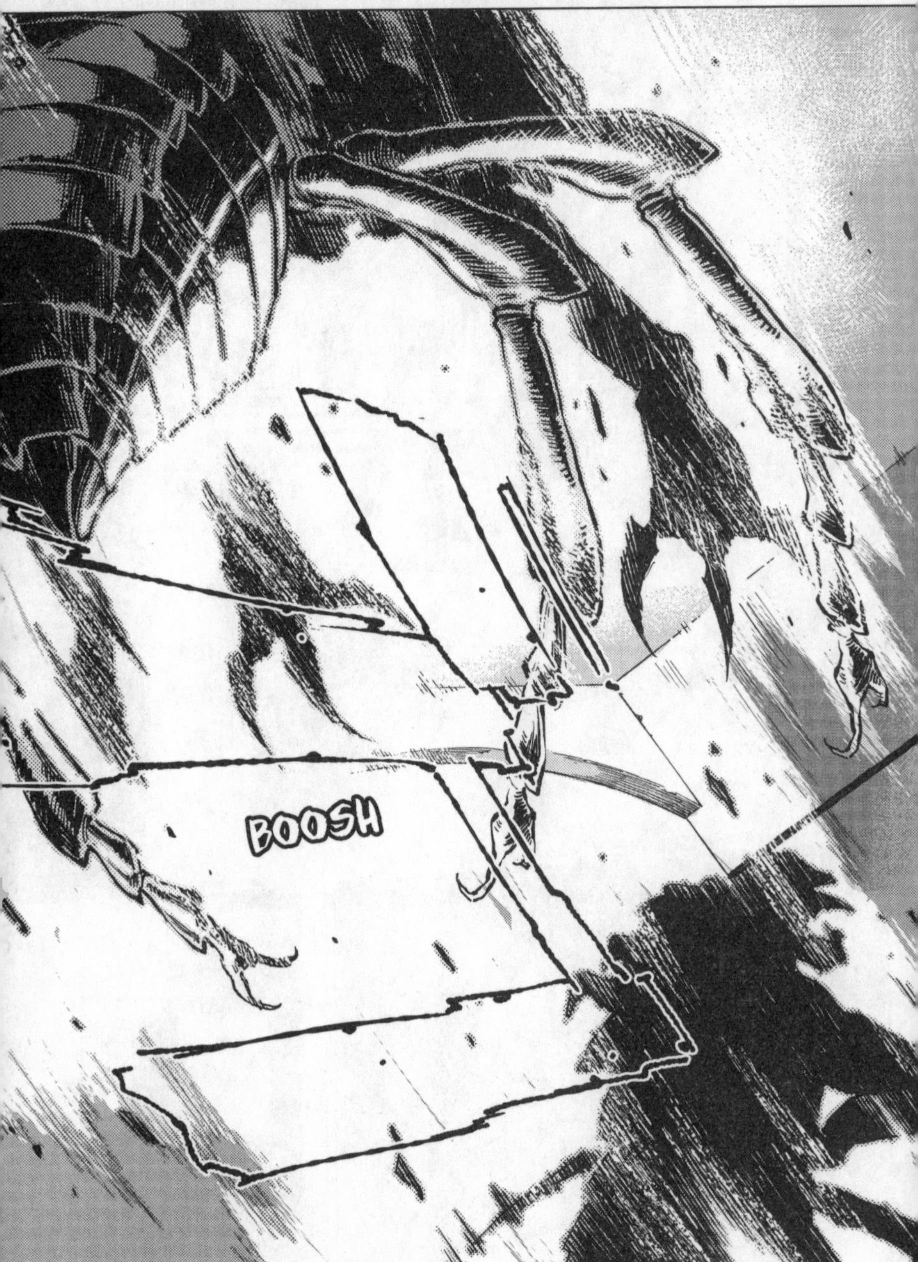
BOOSH

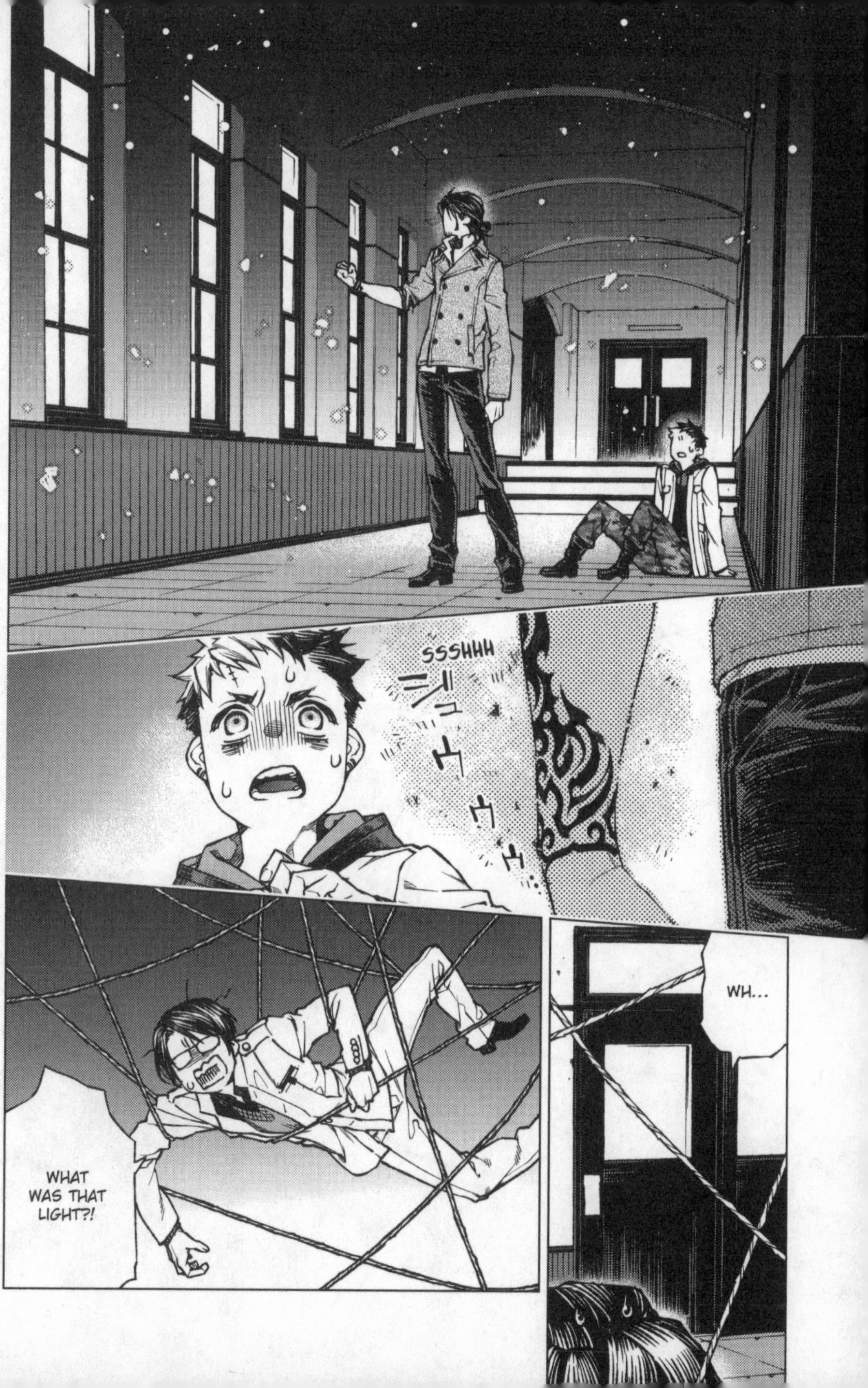
SSSHHH
WH...
WHAT WAS THAT LIGHT?!

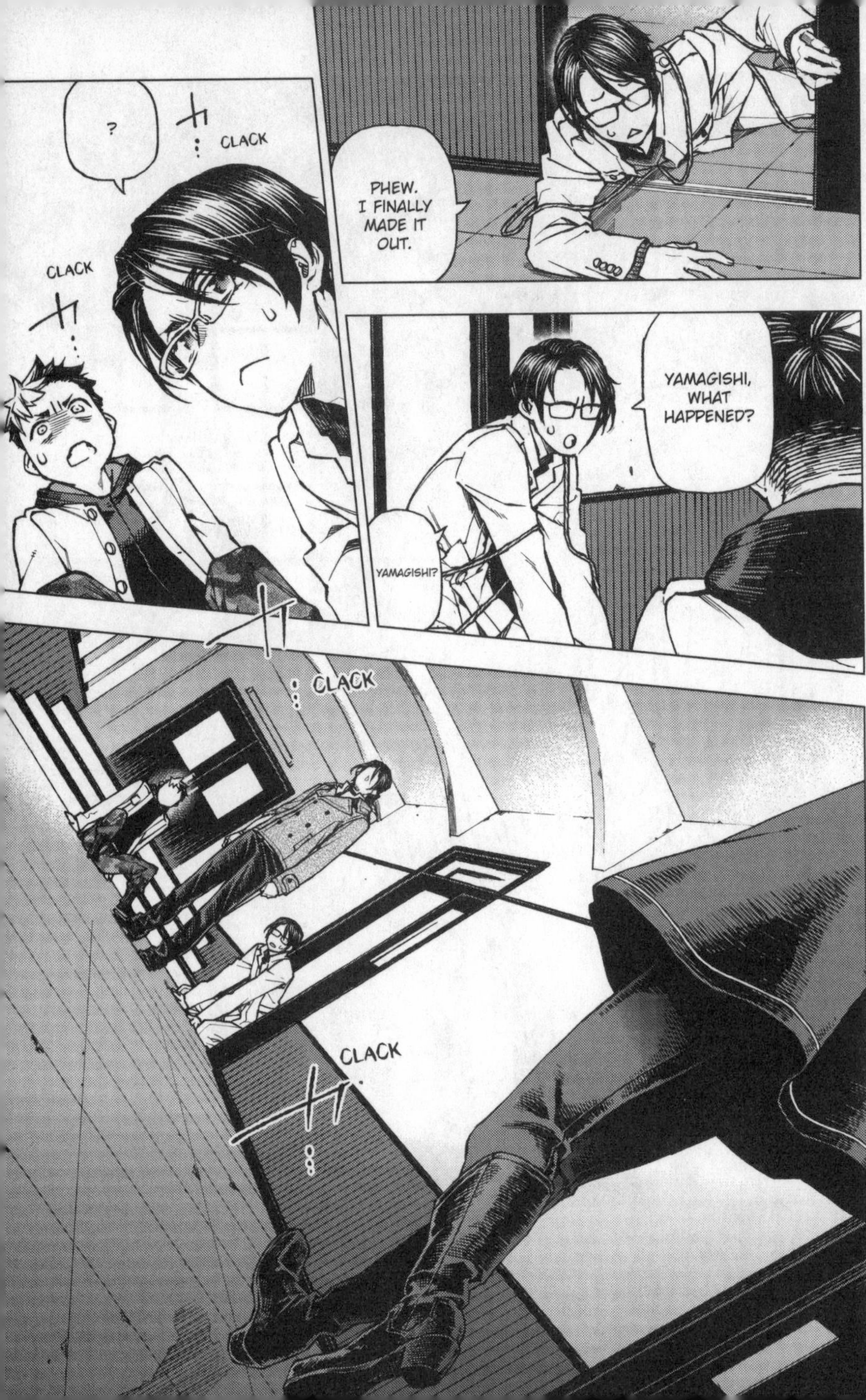
PHEW. I FINALLY MADE IT OUT.
YAMAGISHI, WHAT HAPPENED?
YAMAGISHI?
?
CLACK
CLACK
CLACK
CLACK

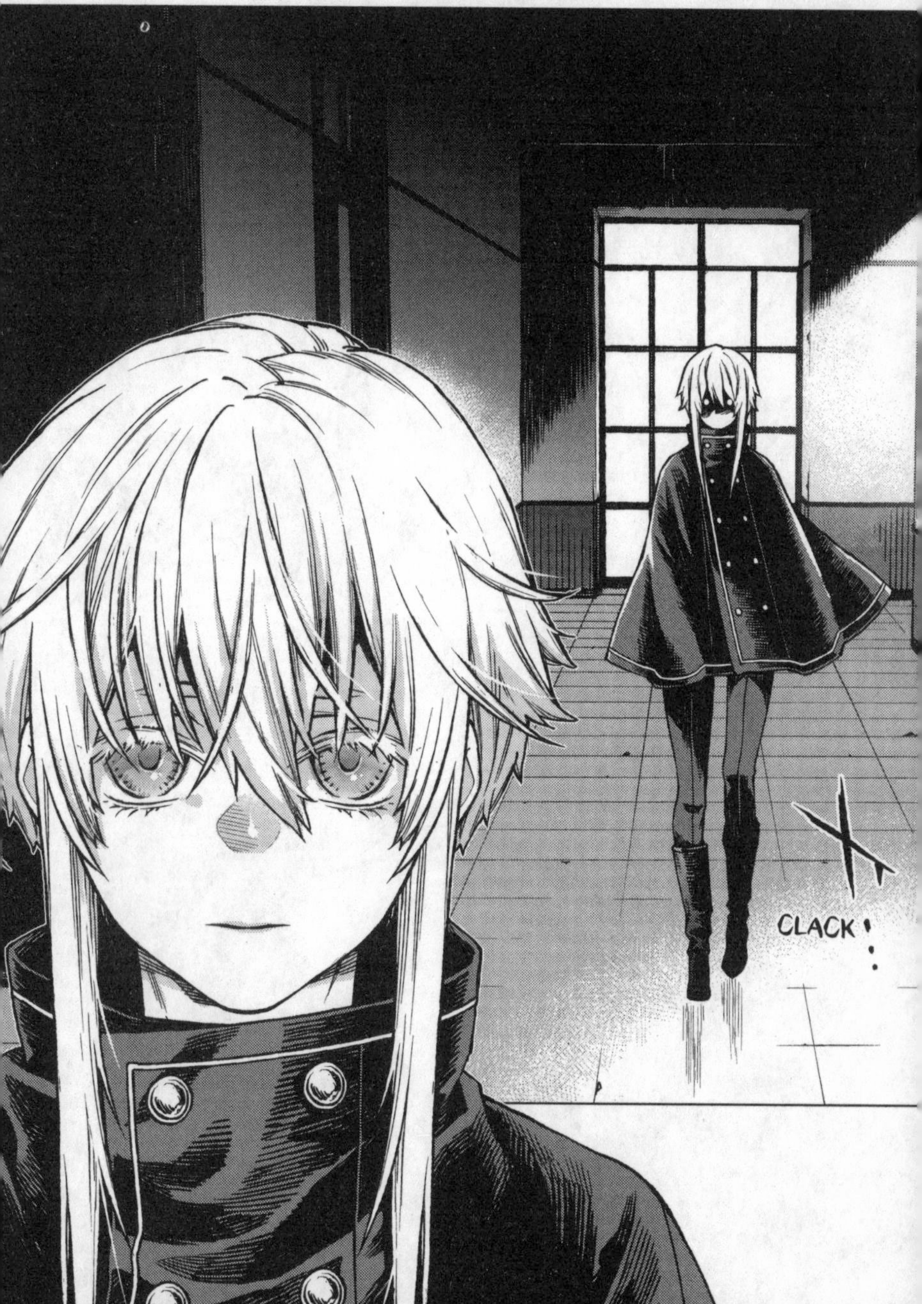
CLACK...

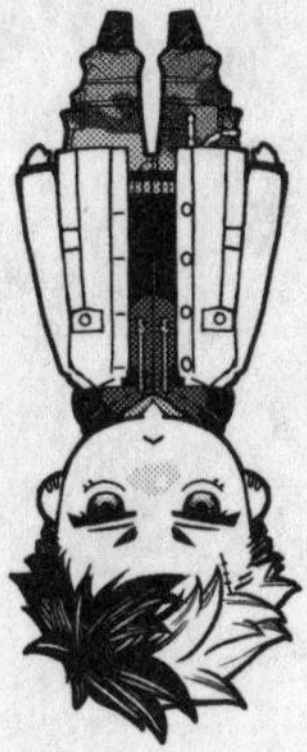

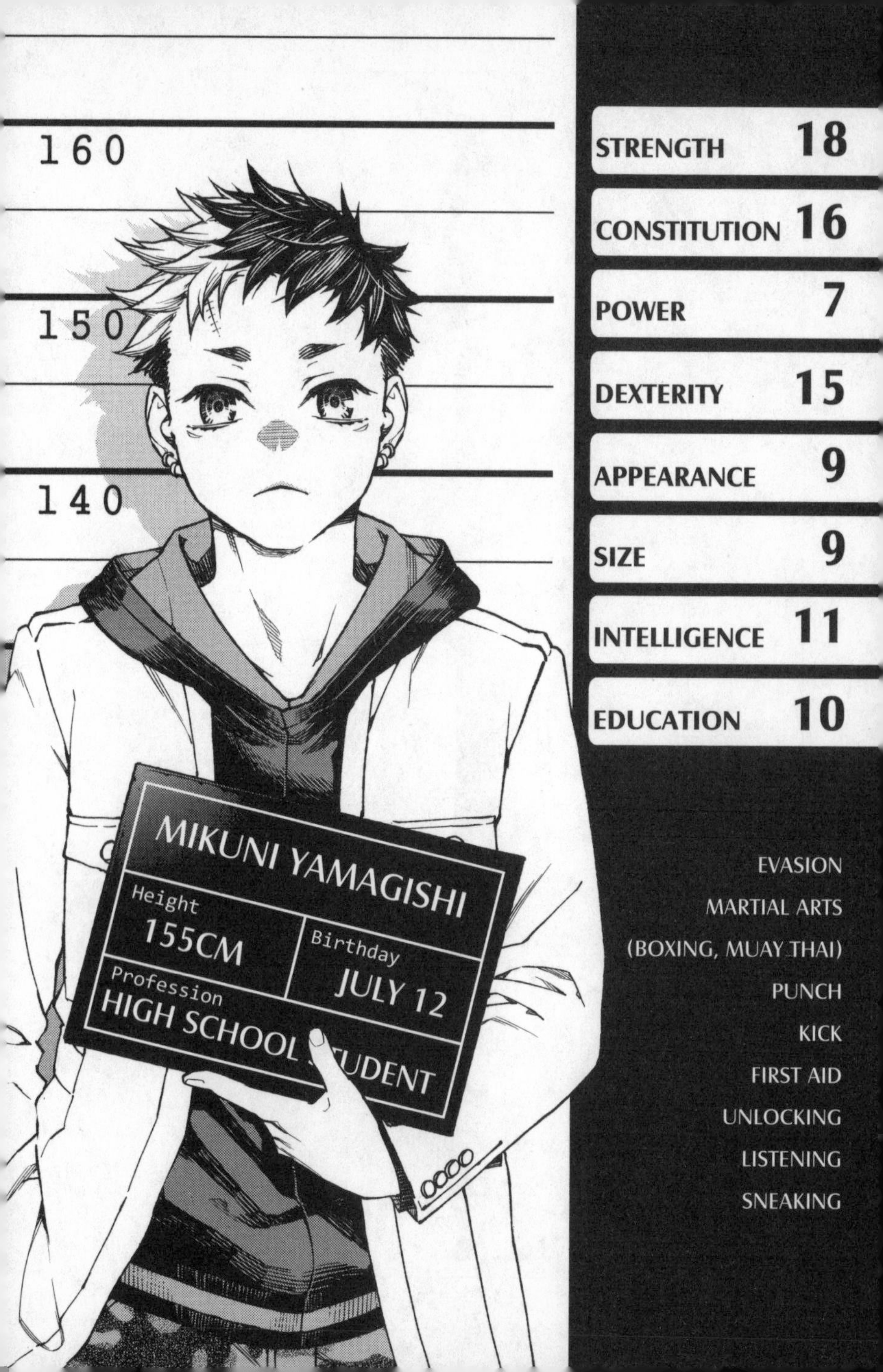
160
150
140
MIKUNI YAMAGISHI
Height
155CM
Birthday
JULY 12
Profession
HIGH SCHOOL STUDENT

STRENGTH	18
CONSTITUTION	16
POWER	7
DEXTERITY	15
APPEARANCE	9
SIZE	9
INTELLIGENCE	11
EDUCATION	10

EVASION
MARTIAL ARTS
(BOXING, MUAY THAI)
PUNCH
KICK
FIRST AID
UNLOCKING
LISTENING
SNEAKING

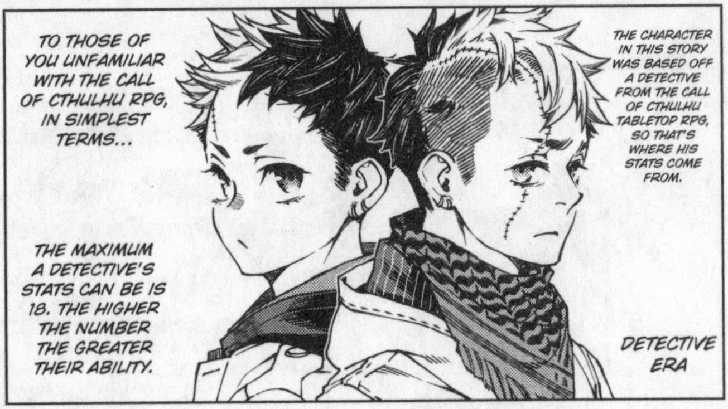
THE CHARACTER IN THIS STORY WAS BASED OFF A DETECTIVE FROM THE CALL OF CTHULHU TABLETOP RPG, SO THAT'S WHERE HIS STATS COME FROM.
TO THOSE OF YOU UNFAMILIAR WITH THE CALL OF CTHULHU RPG, IN SIMPLEST TERMS...
DETECTIVE ERA
THE MAXIMUM A DETECTIVE'S STATS CAN BE IS 18. THE HIGHER THE NUMBER THE GREATER THEIR ABILITY.

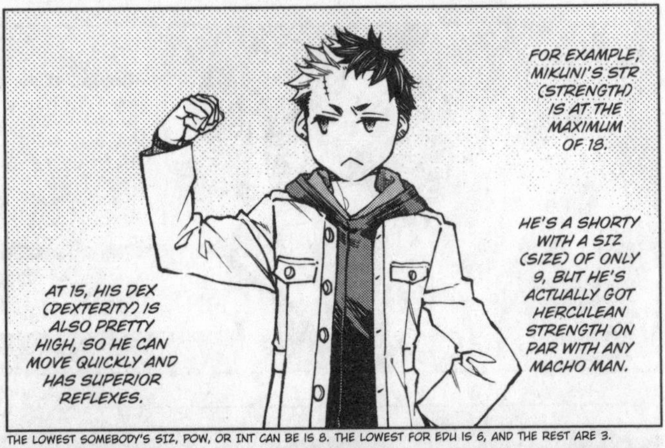
FOR EXAMPLE, MIKUNI'S STR (STRENGTH) IS AT THE MAXIMUM OF 18.
HE'S A SHORTY WITH A SIZ (SIZE) OF ONLY 9, BUT HE'S ACTUALLY GOT HERCULEAN STRENGTH ON PAR WITH ANY MACHO MAN.
AT 15, HIS DEX (DEXTERITY) IS ALSO PRETTY HIGH, SO HE CAN MOVE QUICKLY AND HAS SUPERIOR REFLEXES.

THE LOWEST SOMEBODY'S SIZ, POW, OR INT CAN BE IS 8. THE LOWEST FOR EDU IS 6, AND THE REST ARE 3.

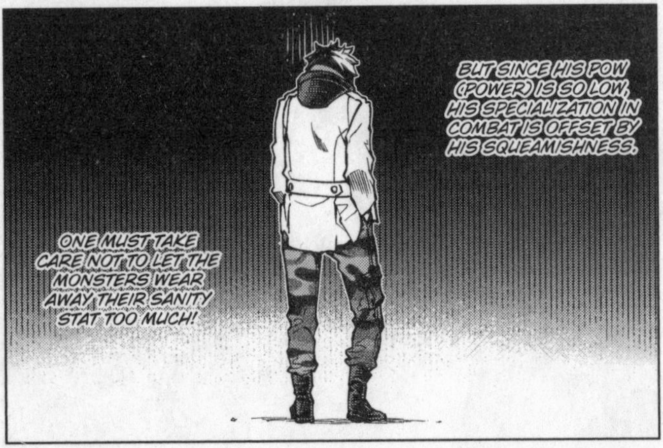
BUT SINCE HIS POW (POWER) IS SO LOW, HIS SPECIALIZATION IN COMBAT IS OFFSET BY HIS SQUEAMISHNESS.
ONE MUST TAKE CARE NOT TO LET THE MONSTERS WEAR AWAY THEIR SANITY STAT TOO MUCH!

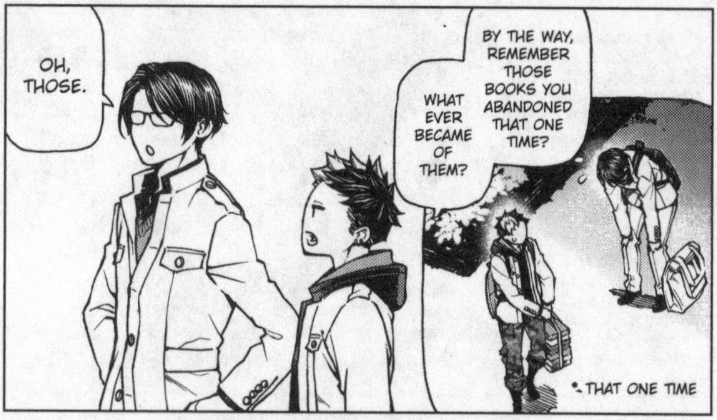
BY THE WAY, REMEMBER THOSE BOOKS YOU ABANDONED THAT ONE TIME?
WHAT EVER BECAME OF THEM?
OH, THOSE.
*THAT ONE TIME

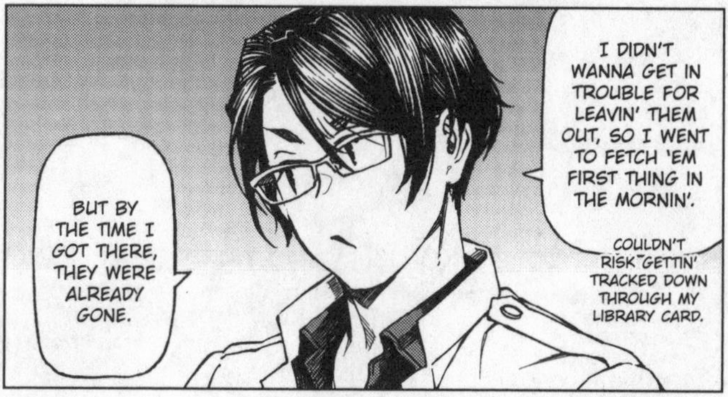
I DIDN'T WANNA GET IN TROUBLE FOR LEAVIN' THEM OUT, SO I WENT TO FETCH 'EM FIRST THING IN THE MORNIN'.
COULDN'T RISK GETTIN' TRACKED DOWN THROUGH MY LIBRARY CARD.
BUT BY THE TIME I GOT THERE, THEY WERE ALREADY GONE.

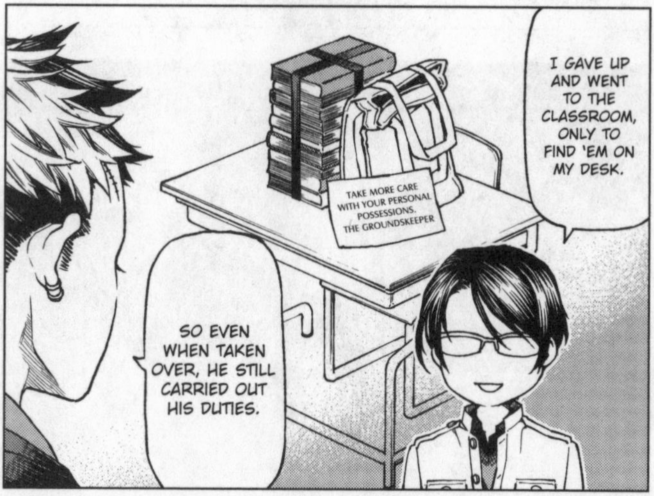
I GAVE UP AND WENT TO THE CLASSROOM, ONLY TO FIND 'EM ON MY DESK.
TAKE MORE CARE WITH YOUR PERSONAL POSSESSIONS. THE GROUNDSKEEPER
SO EVEN WHEN TAKEN OVER, HE STILL CARRIED OUT HIS DUTIES.

TO ALL THE PEOPLE I'M MEETING FOR THE FIRST TIME: HELLO! TO THOSE FOR WHOM IT'S BEEN A WHILE: LONG TIME NO SEE! IT'S ME, SORANO.

WITH THIS NEW SERIALIZATION, I'VE DECIDED TO CHALLENGE MYSELF ONCE AGAIN WITH A SCHOOLYARD STORY. I'D ORIGINALLY WANTED TO WRITE A STRAIGHT-UP CTHULHU MANGA, BUT ONE THING LED TO ANOTHER AND THIS STORY HAS MORE CTHULHU *ELEMENTS* IN IT INSTEAD. AS FAR AS ITS GENRE, IT'S LESS COSMIC HORROR AND MORE OF A CTHULHU TRPG FLAVOR, SO THE CHARACTERS HAVE STATS LIKE TYPICAL DETECTIVES FROM THAT GAME. MY PREVIOUS STORY ENDED WITH A FEELING OF INCOMPLETION, SO I'VE GOT TO WORK EXTRA HAD WITH THIS ONE!

THANK YOU FOR CHOOSING THIS BOOK AMONG THE MANY OUT THERE. I'M TURNING A NEW LEAF AND HOPING TO APPROACH THIS WITH THE ENTHUSIASM OF ANY NEW PROJECT. I'M GOING TO WORK HARD TO DELIVER A GREAT STORY!

I HOPE YOU'LL STICK AROUND TO SEE THE STORY GO THROUGH ITS COMBO OF UPS AND DOWNS!

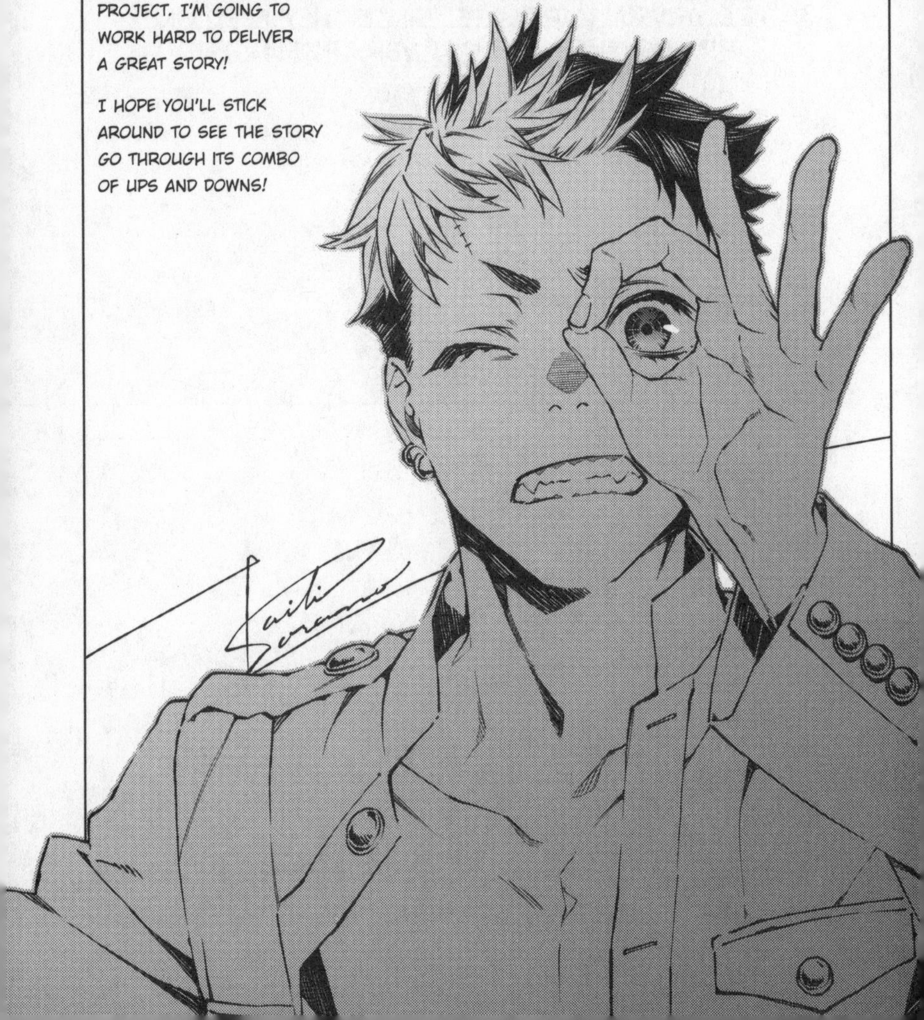

01

A SELF-SUPPORTING SPECIES THAT LIVES BY INFECTING THE BRAINS OF THEIR VICTIMS. THESE CREATURES SLIPPED OUT OF THE BEYOND AND HAVE EXPANDED THEIR HABITAT IN OUR WORLD. OTHER THAN ON NIGHTS OF THE FULL MOON WHEN THEY ARE PROPAGATING, THEY'RE RELATIVELY HARMLESS. SINCE THEY FEED ON BRAINS, THEY ARE NOT VERY INTELLIGENT.

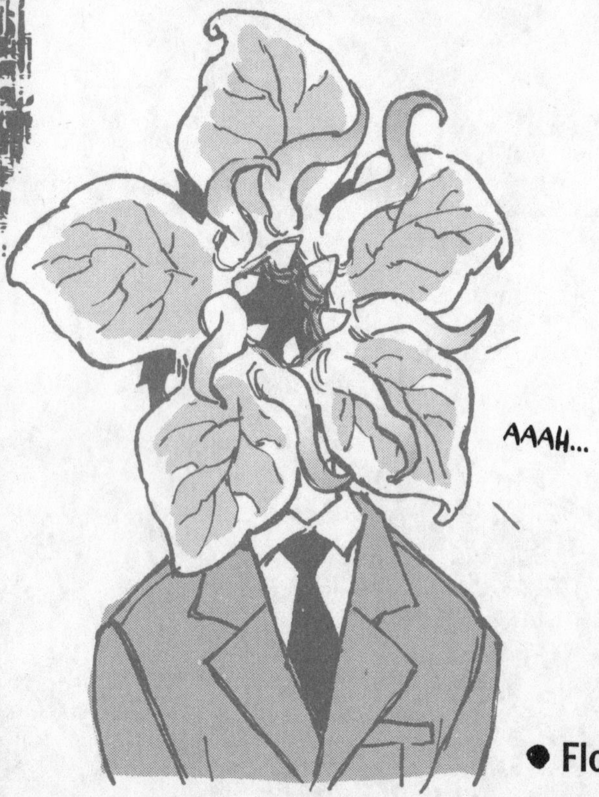
AAAH...

● Flower Person ●

U-Yatei

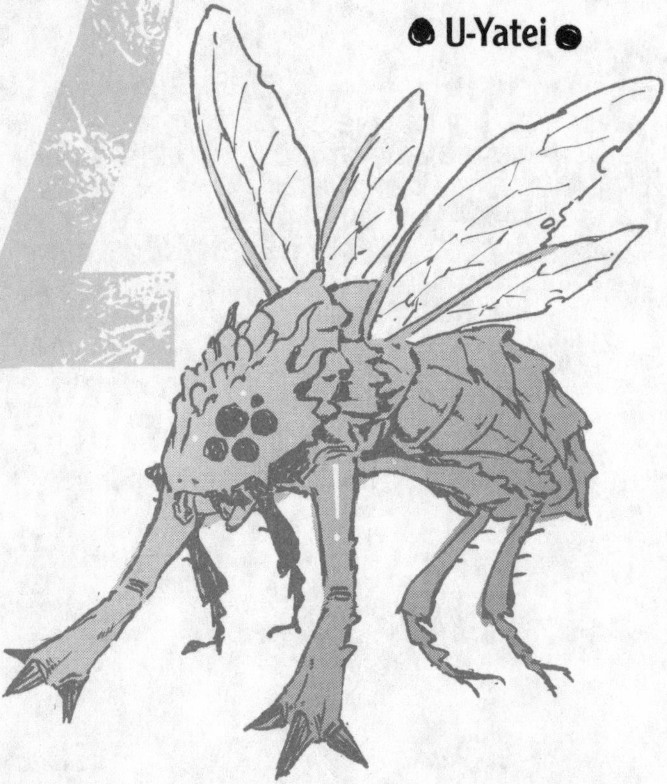

A LARGE, BEE-LIKE SERVICE SPECIES. THEY COLLECT VICTIMS INSIDE THE BEYOND. THEY GO AFTER THEIR PREY VERY OBSTINATELY BUT WILL NOT EAT THEM SO THAT THEY CAN DELIVER THE PREY TO THEIR MASTER INSTEAD.

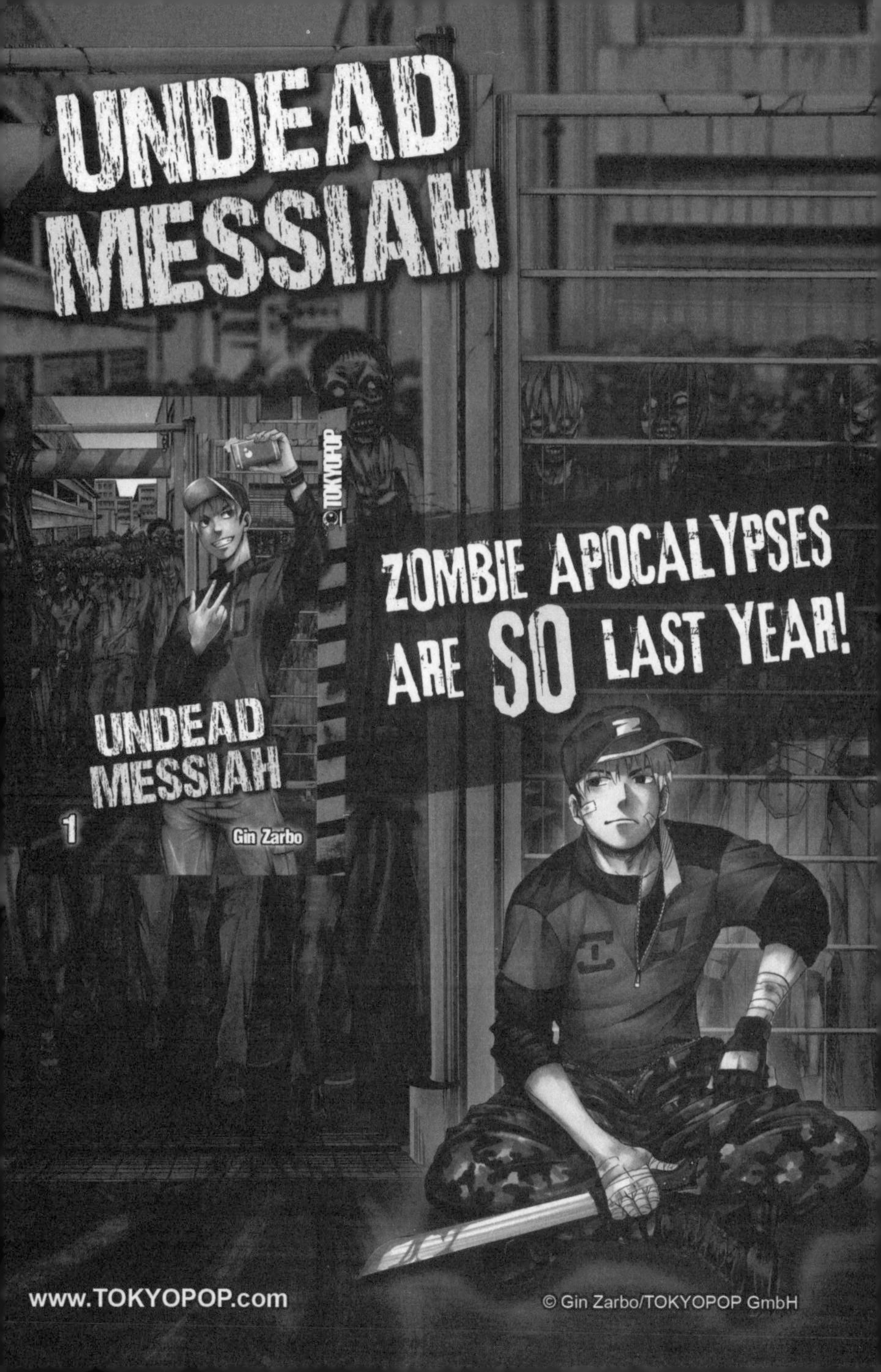
UNDEAD MESSIAH
UNDEAD MESSIAH
1
Gin Zarbo
TOKYOPOP
ZOMBIE APOCALYPSES ARE SO LAST YEAR!
www.TOKYOPOP.com
© Gin Zarbo/TOKYOPOP GmbH

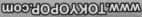

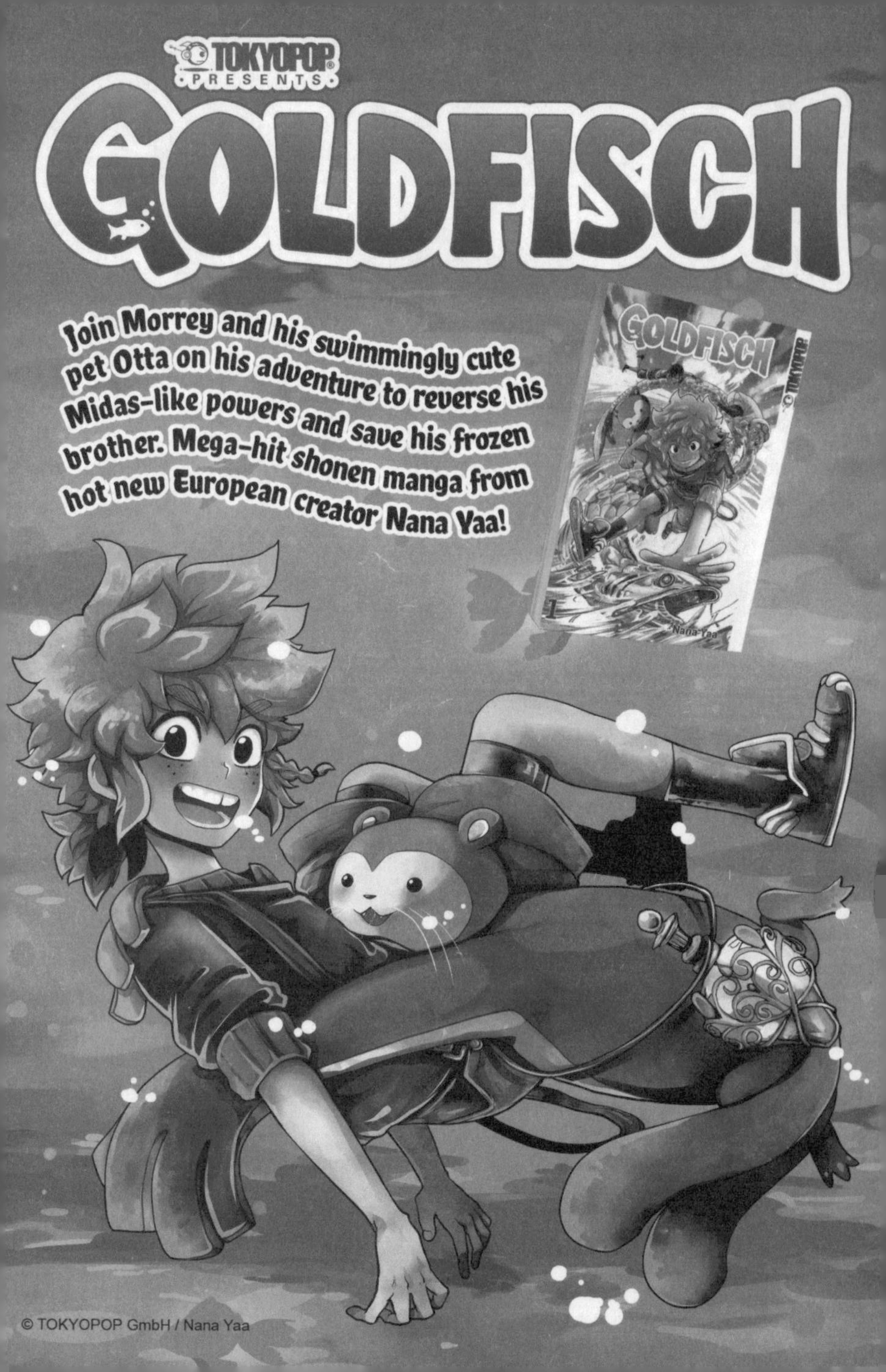
TOKYOPOP® PRESENTS
GOLDFISCH
Join Morrey and his swimmingly cute pet Otta on his adventure to reverse his Midas-like powers and save his frozen brother. Mega-hit shonen manga from hot new European creator Nana Yaa!
GOLDFISCH
TOKYOPOP
1
Nana Yaa
© TOKYOPOP GmbH / Nana Yaa

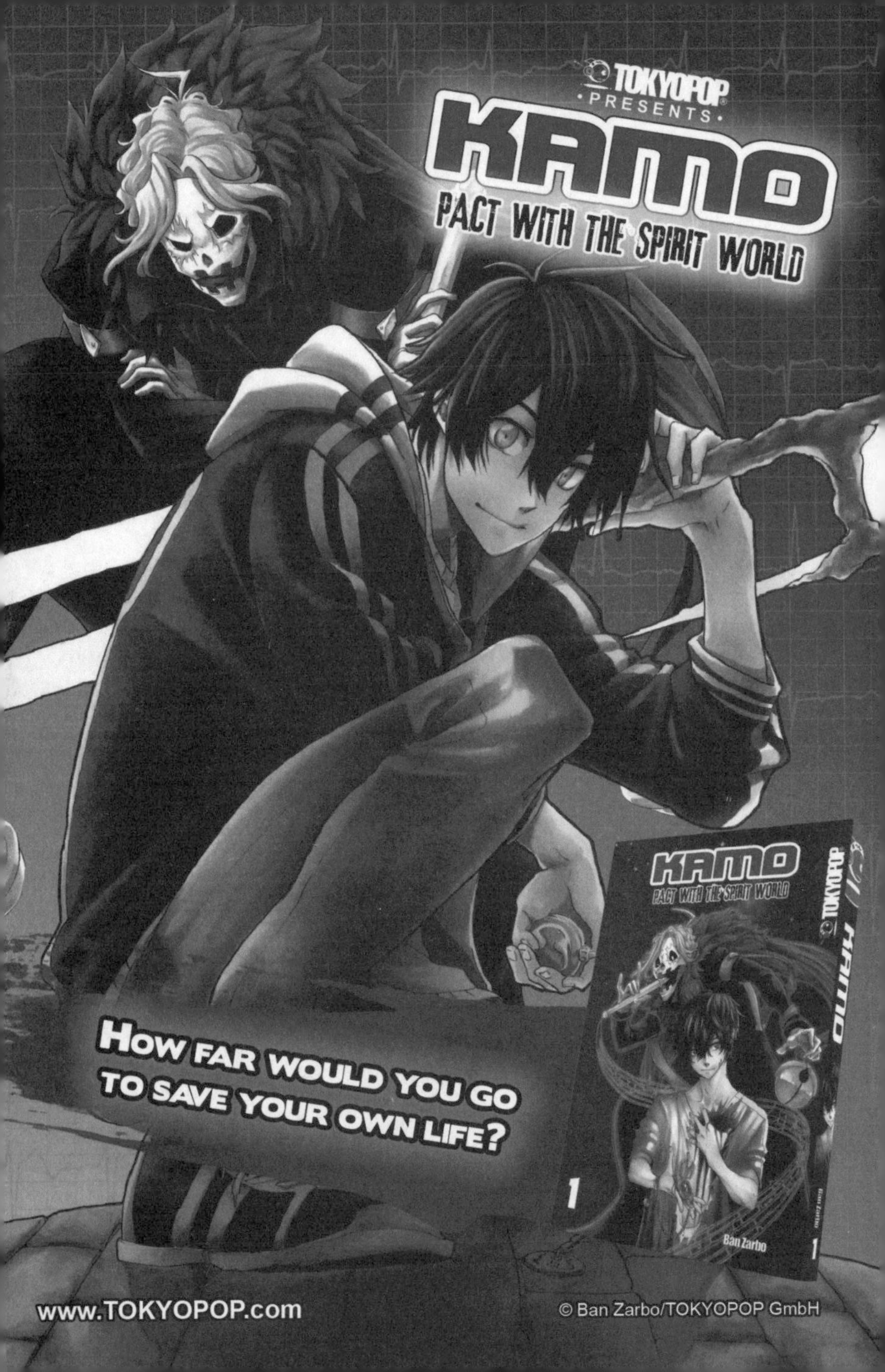
TOKYOPOP
PRESENTS
KAMO
PACT WITH THE SPIRIT WORLD
KAMO
PACT WITH THE SPIRIT WORLD
TOKYOPOP
1
Ban Zarbo
1
HOW FAR WOULD YOU GO
TO SAVE YOUR OWN LIFE?
www.TOKYOPOP.com
© Ban Zarbo/TOKYOPOP GmbH

GOLDFISCH

Sword Princess AMALTEA

Ocean of Secrets

UNDEAD MESSIAH

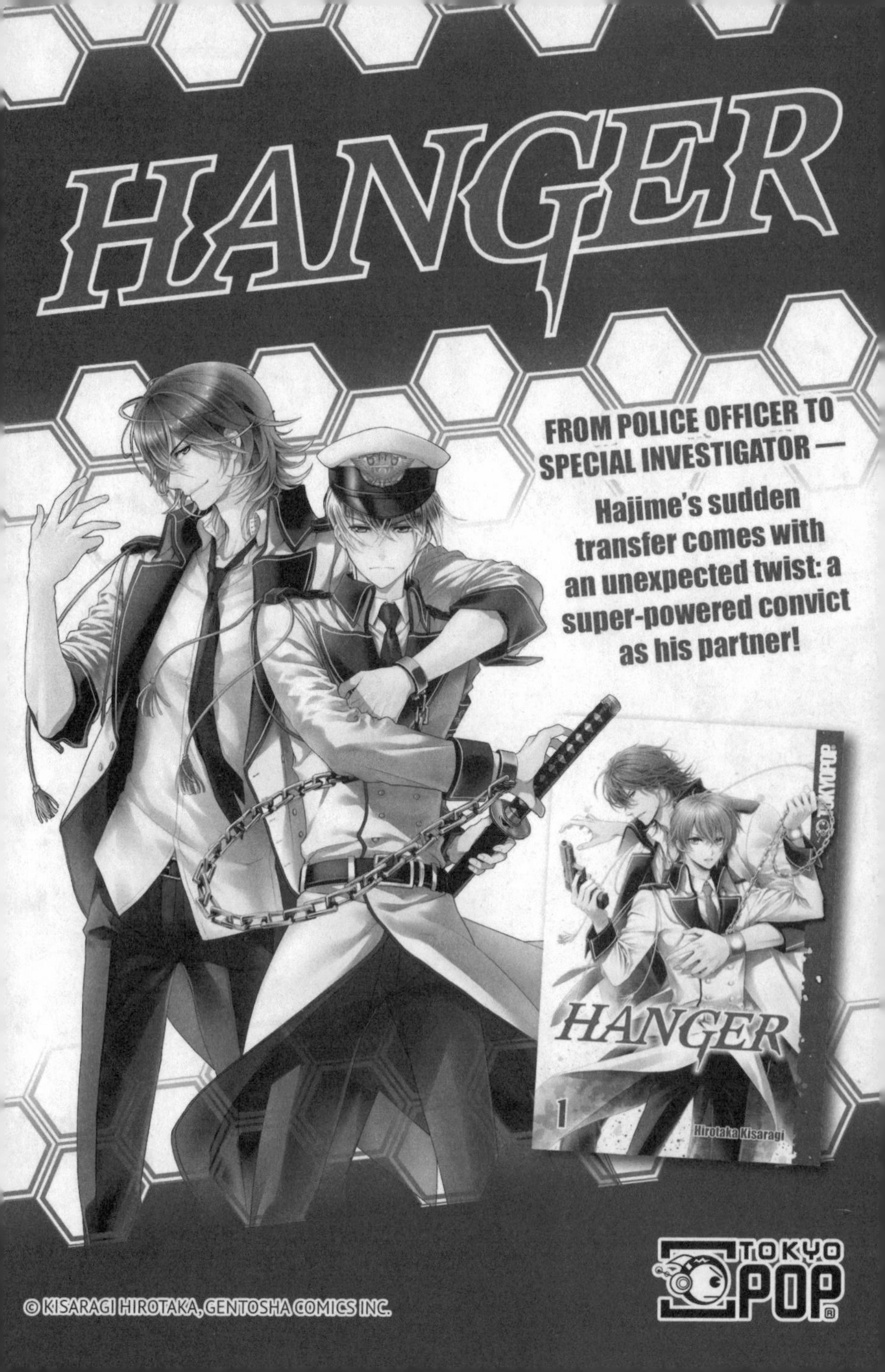
HANGER
FROM POLICE OFFICER TO SPECIAL INVESTIGATOR —
Hajime's sudden transfer comes with an unexpected twist: a super-powered convict as his partner!
HANGER
1
Hirotaka Kisaragi
TOKYOPOP
© KISARAGI HIROTAKA, GENTOSHA COMICS INC.

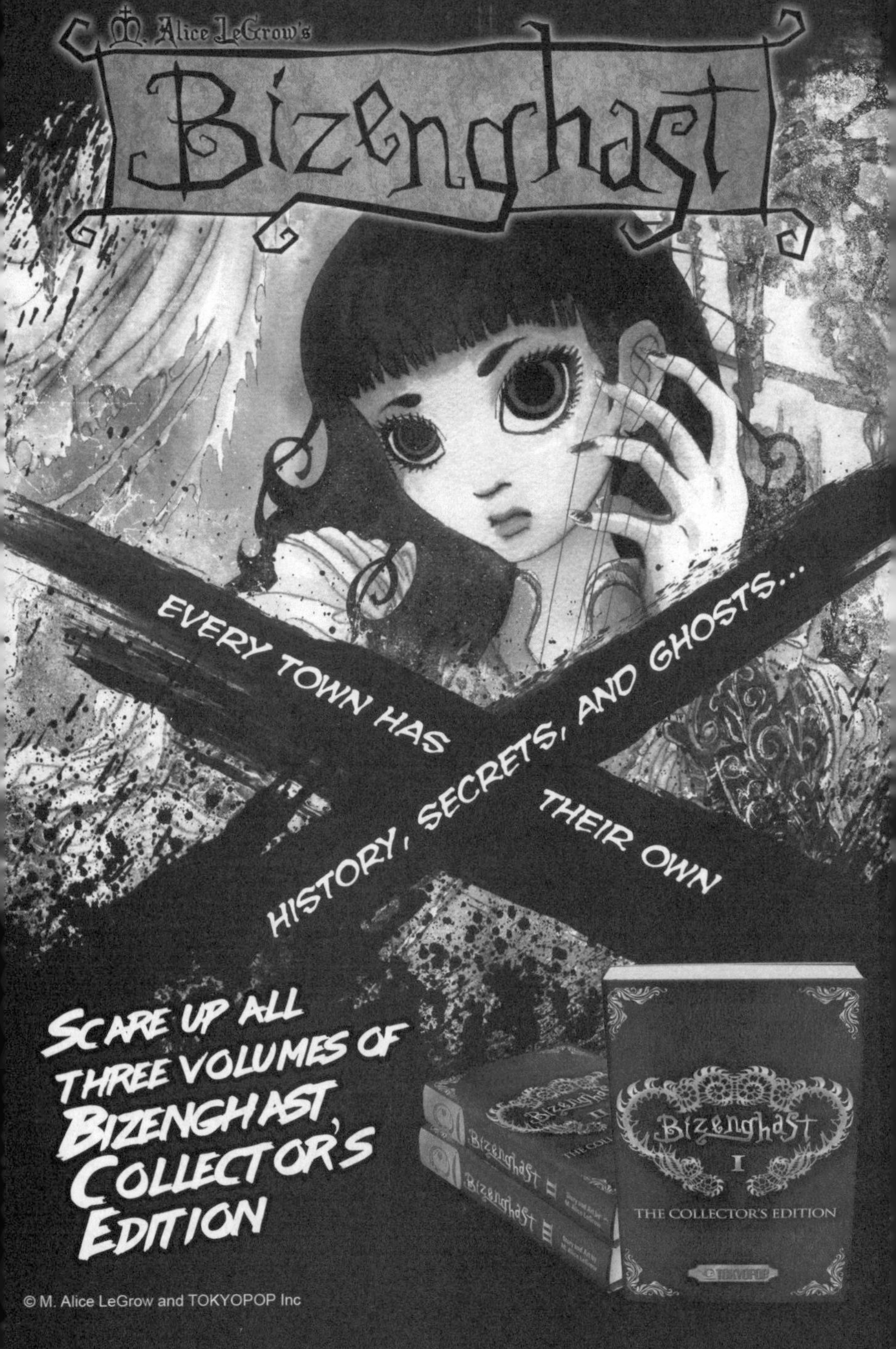
M. Alice LeGrow's
Bizenghast
EVERY TOWN HAS HISTORY, SECRETS, AND GHOSTS... THEIR OWN
SCARE UP ALL THREE VOLUMES OF BIZENGHAST, COLLECTOR'S EDITION
Bizenghast
I
THE COLLECTOR'S EDITION
TOKYOPOP

Parham Itan: Tales From Beyond, Volume 1
Manga by Kaili Sorano

Editor - Lena Atanassova
Marketing Associate - Kae Winters
Technology and Digital Media Assistant - Phillip Hong
Translator - Christine Dashiell
Graphic Designer - Phillip Hong
Retouching and Lettering - Vibrraant Publishing Studio
Licensing Specialist - Arika Yanaka
Editor-in-Chief & Publisher - Stu Levy

A **TOKYOPOP**® Manga

TOKYOPOP and are trademarks or registered trademarks of TOKYOPOP Inc.

TOKYOPOP Inc.
5200 W. Century Blvd. Suite 705
Los Angeles, 90045

E-mail: info@TOKYOPOP.com
Come visit us online at www.TOKYOPOP.com

www.facebook.com/TOKYOPOP
www.twitter.com/TOKYOPOP
www.pinterest.com/TOKYOPOP
www.instagram.com/TOKYOPOP

ISBN: 978-1-4278-6226-6
First TOKYOPOP Printing: January 2020
10 9 8 7 6 5 4 3 2 1
Printed in CANADA

STOP

THIS IS THE BACK OF THE BOOK!

How do you read manga-style? It's simple! Let's practice -- just start in the top right panel and follow the numbers below!

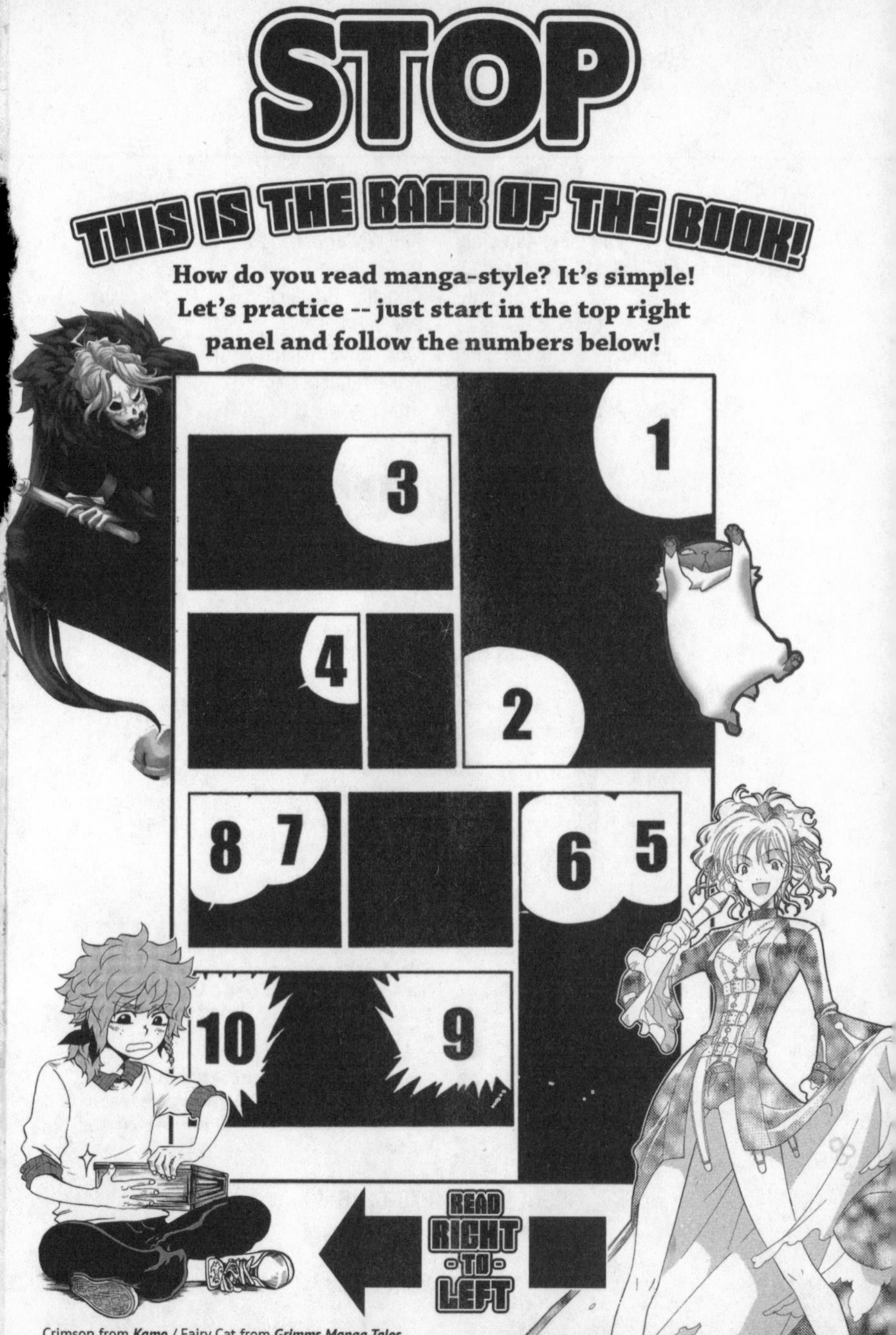

1
2
3
4
5
6
7
8
9
10
READ RIGHT -TO- LEFT

Crimson from ***Kamo*** / Fairy Cat from ***Grimms Manga Tales***
Morrey from ***Goldfisch*** / Princess Ai from ***Princess Ai***